India's National Security

Concerns and Strategies

India's
NATIONAL SECURITY

Concerns and Strategies

□ Security Policy Options for India □ External Security
□ Energy Security □ Maritime Security □ Human Security
□ Environmental Security

Edited by

Mohanan B. Pillai

Professor and Director,
UNESCO Madanjeet Singh Institute of
South Asia Regional Co-operation (UMISARC),
Pondicherry University, Puducherry

New Century Publications
New Delhi, India

NEW CENTURY PUBLICATIONS
4800/24, Bharat Ram Road,
Ansari Road, Daryaganj,
New Delhi - 110 002 (India)

Tel.: 011-2324 7798, 4358 7398, 6539 6605
Fax: 011-4101 7798
E-mail: indiatax@vsnl.com • info@newcenturypublications.com
www.newcenturypublications.com

Editorial office:
LG–7, Aakarshan Bhawan,
4754-57/23, Ansari Road, Daryaganj,
New Delhi - 110 002

Tel.: 011-4356 0919

First Published: **July 2013**

ISBN: **978-81-7708-356-9**

Published by New Century Publications and printed at Salasar Imaging Systems, New Delhi.

Designs: Patch Creative Unit, New Delhi.

PRINTED IN INDIA

FOREWORD

March 9, 2013

I have enjoyed reading the book titled, **India's National Security: Concerns and Strategies** edited by Professor Mohanan B. Pillai, Director, UNESCO Madanjeet Singh Institute of South Asia Regional Co-operation, Pondicherry University with a great deal of interest and enthusiasm and I have found that this book distinctly brings out various aspects of India's security which are widely acknowledged and delved into.

The book is useful for a cross-section of readers interested in various dimensions of India's security problems. It will, hopefully, bring academicians and practitioners of Indian diplomacy together.

Professor (Mrs.) Chandra Krishnamurthy
Vice-Chancellor
PONDICHERRY UNIVERSITY
Puducherry

About the Book

Security forms an important component of the way international relations are played out. After Independence in 1947, India followed a policy of non-alignment to protect and promote the interests of the new born nation. India's security concerns at that time revolved around the threats emanating primarily from Pakistan. China was also perceived as a threat to India's national security.

However, the age of neo-liberal globalization has added additional dimensions to the conventional threats. In the post-Cold War period, the major security concern of India emanates from cross-border terrorism. The challenges posed by international terrorism, global economic meltdown and environmental degradation including climate change are also security concerns that India has to address seriously. The crisis in the energy sector is another major security challenge. On the domestic front, India faces many challenges including poverty, illiteracy, social and economic inequalities, communalism, regional imbalances, development-based displacement etc.

This book contains 21 research papers—authored by experts in various fields—which examine various dimensions of India's security concerns and suggest appropriate policy formulations in this regard. In general, the need for out-of-the-box approach for ensuring security in its holistic dimension has been emphasized.

Editor's Profile

Mohanan B. Pillai is Professor and Director, UNESCO Madanjeet Singh Institute of South Asia Regional Co-operation (UMISARC), Pondicherry University, Puducherry. A teacher of repute for more than three decades, he is the founder editor of ISDA Journal—*Studies in Development and Administration,* Trivandrum. He is also the founder Editor of *International Journal of South Asian Studies,* Pondicherry University. Specialising in development studies, South Asian studies and political theory, he has published several books, research papers and articles in these areas. His major books include, *Politics of Regionalism in South Asia* (1991); *Globalization of Economy* (1995); *Gandhi's Legacy and a New Human Civilization* (1999); *Quest for a Just World Order* (1999); *Women and Law* (2003); *Decentralised Governance and Participatory Development* (2005) and *Foreign Policy of India: Continuity and Change* (2010). He has travelled widely in India and abroad to participate and present papers in several international and national conferences, seminars and workshops.

Contents

Part III: Energy Security

Part IV: Maritime Security

Contributors

Krishnan Srinivasan	Formerly, Foreign Secretary, Ministry of External Affairs, Government of India.
Radhavinoda Raju	First Director, National Investigation Agency (NIA), Ministry of Home Affairs, Government of India.
P.P. Rajkumar	Air Marshal (Retd.) PVSM, AVSM.
Suresh R.	Associate Professor, Sree Narayana College, Kollam, Kerala.
Himanshu Roy	Associate Professor, University of Delhi.
P.M. Kamath	Director, VPM's Centre for International Studies, Mumbai.
Josukutty C.A.	Assistant Professor, University of Kerala.
Rahul Tripathi	Assistant Professor, Department of Political Science, University of Goa, Goa.
Mukund Narvekar	Research Scholar, Department of Political Science, University of Goa, Goa.
P.V. Rao	Osmania University, Hyderabad.
A.K. Pasha	Director, Gulf Studies Program, Centre for West Asian Studies, School of International Studies, Jawaharlal Nehru University, New Delhi.
Dharitri Parija	Research Scholar, Department of Politics and International Studies, Pondicherry University, Puducherry.

Mohanan B. Pillai	Professor and Director, UNESCO Madanjeet Singh Institute of South Asia Regional Co-operation, Pondicherry University, Puducherry.
Harvir Sharma	Emeritus Professor in Defence Studies, University Grants Commission (UGC), New Delhi.
R.S. Vasan	Commodore IN (Retd.), Centre for Asia Studies, Chennai.
C. Vinodan	Assistant Professor and Chair, Centre for Strategic and Security Studies, School of International Relations and Politics, Mahatma Gandhi University, Kottayam, Kerala.
W. Lawrence S. Prabhakar	Associate Professor, Department of Political Science, Madras Christian College, Chennai.
S.Y. Surendra Kumar	Assistant Professor, Department of Political Science, University of Bangalore, Bangalore.
A. Subramanyam Raju	Associate Professor, UNESCO Madanjeet Singh Institute of South Asia Regional Co-operation, Pondicherry University, Puducherry.
Kadloor Savitri	Associate Professor, Jamia Millia Islamia, New Delhi.
R. Alagu Perumal Ramasamy	Assistant Professor, Loyola Institute of Business Administration (LIBA), Loyola College, Chennai.

Editor's Note on the Book

India has always attracted the attention of spectators from all over the world—spectators who are awed by her size, who are surprised by her numbers, who are amazed by the democratic resilience that it has shown over the years. There have been innumerable discussions about *how does India do it?* and there exist ample expert analyses of the same. However, equally large is the literature on *how India could do it better?* And this is where most inter-state dialogues and talks are stalled as the answer to this question, for most part, entails debates over security issues.

Security forms an important component of the way international relations are played out. Though it took some time for India to break out of its *enlightened national interests* cocoon, it has since focussed on its security concerns to a great extent. Internationally, India has been included in the strategic plans of several nations, including the United States of America. It has acquired an important position globally on international matters and issues directly or indirectly affecting it. In fact, it is at the regional level that India faces a number of challenges on the security front.

Being the largest nation in South Asia, India has been timelessly accused of its benevolently despotic attitude and its initiatives in the region have been taken often as attempts to outshine, rather out power the other smaller nations of the region. They feel insecure in the face of India's gigantism. Often likened to a typical South Asian joint family that has broken up, analysts draw attention to the ways in which these broken families are turning to outside help (especially China) in order to protect themselves from India. This has given rise to manifold security concerns within the region and in India in particular and of variegated textures. Terrorism, illegal immigration, trafficking, resource constraints and so on, have all gradually led India to flex its muscles outside South Asia in order to deal with them. This international dimension to

India's security policy has infused changes in relations within South Asia. India's security policy and the relation that it shares with the larger world are deeply intertwined where one impacts upon the other and vice versa.

The ascendancy of the neo-liberal global regime coupled with the demise of Soviet Communism had drastically altered the international power configuration during the closing decades of the 20th century. The bipolar power structure that ruled the roost in the post-World War governance architecture got replaced by a uni-polar (or non-polar, if we may call so) one, which has given a jostle to the sluice valves of the new security concerns like global terrorism, environmental issues, energy security, food security etc., in addition to the traditional security issues, for the entire world in general and for re-emerging countries like India in particular.

It is a fact that the security perceptions of states underwent drastic changes in the post-Cold War era. Economic security appears to be the foremost concern of all nations and thus economic cooperation has been a priority area for all the nations of the world. Though the conventional security perception has not been abandoned outright, it has lost much of its sheen. The emergence of new forms of threat from the transnational terrorist groups has added new dimensions to the security concerns of nations. The operations of these groups have demonstrated that a traditional approach to security is redundant. No nation, howsoever powerful, can single-handedly tackle the threats posed by terrorist groups. This again demands multilateralism in international relations to meet the challenges posed by transnational non-state actors.

The process of globalization—the free flow of finance capital across the world—has brought together all nations onto a common platform. If anything happens in any corner of the world, its impact is felt everywhere. Therefore, the security of a nation is interlinked with the security of every other nation. The globalization process has not only brought the nations together on the global platform but also forced nations to take a fresh look at regional cooperation efforts to ensure security and economic growth.

The emergence of non-state actors in international relations is comparatively a new phenomenon. In the changed situation, domestic and global civil societies are gaining prominence. The interaction among people as a result of information revolution has contributed substantially towards strengthening the bonds of universal brotherhood. Better understanding among the people and transcending artificial boundaries would further weaken the role of the state as a player in international relations. Presently, the strength of a nation is based not only on the possession of destructive weapons but on many other factors including the strength of its economy, democratic institutions and the security that is provided to the people.

After Independence in 1947, India followed a policy of non-alignment that got incubated in the nest of freedom movement. The experiments in diplomacy and foreign policy on a platform of non-alignment with its core value of strategic autonomy were to protect and promote the national interest of the new born nation. The autonomous space that was carved out of the non-alignment policy facilitated the growth of domestic capital in the age of *embedded liberalism*.

During the period of *embedded liberalism*—precisely during the period of Cold War—India's security concerns revolved around the threats emanating primarily from Pakistan. On a conventional analytical frame, China was also perceived as a threat to India's national security. However, the age of neo-liberal globalization has added additional dimensions to the conventional threats. In the post-Cold War period, the major security concern of India emanates from cross-border terrorism. All other traditional security concerns are overtaken by economic issues. The challenges posed by international terrorism, global economic meltdown and environmental degradation including climate change are also security concerns that India has to address seriously. The crisis in the energy sector is a major security challenge. On the domestic front, India faces many challenges including poverty, illiteracy, social and economic inequalities, communalism, regional imbalances, development-based displacement etc.

India's quest for national security—in its conventional frame of reference—needs to be dovetailed with the larger concept of human security. The other most important security theatre, that requires a distinct treatment particularly in the aftermath of the Mumbai terrorist attack, seems to be the Indian Ocean.

From a broader Indian perspective, the security of the nation is nothing but the welfare of its people. This is in fact a realization based on inputs from the non-conventional concept of human security. There appears to be a shift in focus from military security to economic and environment security. The plea for a human security approach is a post-Cold War development. The positive as well as negative impacts of the globalization process have accelerated the momentum for a human security approach. On the positive side, globalization has helped the growth of civil society organizations at the national and international levels. These organizations make the democratic system more participatory and people friendly. With regard to the negative impact of globalization process, the withdrawal of state from welfare activities has further worsened the position of the poor and marginalized sections of the society.

All the papers included in this volume take us through the new security concerns and also draw our attention to the need for out-of-the-box approach for ensuring security in its holistic dimension.

I place on record my deep appreciation and gratitude to all the contributors to this volume for their scholarly analysis of various dimensions of India's security concerns and appropriate policy formulations in this regard. I particularly remember Shri Radhavinoda Raju (IPS), the illustrious first director of National Investigation Agency (NIA) for his thought-provoking contribution. Through this volume, his words will continue to reverberate in the security and strategic studies circle, despite the fact that he left us suddenly to join the heavenly abode.

I take this opportunity to extend my heartfelt gratitude to the esteemed Vice-Chancellor of Pondicherry University, Professor (Mrs.) Chandra Krishnamurthy for taking keen interest in this work and also writing the foreword for it.

Finally, I am thankful to Mr. Sandeep Sury of New Century Publications, New Delhi for extending unstinting co-operation at various stages of the completion of this work and taking personal interest in publishing it.

Puducherry **Mohanan B. Pillai**
June 2013

PART I
Security Policy Options for India

1

India's Security Policy: Shifting Paradigms and Emerging Frontiers

Krishnan Srinivasan

Recent international developments have caused some strategic commentators to speak of a shift of wealth from the West to the East, with the emergence of new powers, new aspirations and new ambitions. South and Southeast Asia are no longer in the international backwaters, and global attention is shifting towards them. At the same time, India is at the hub of an Arc of Instability and an Arc of Prosperity; the instability running from the Levant through Syria, Iraq, Iran Afghanistan and Pakistan to Central Asia, and the prosperity—at least by GDP growth standards—from the oil-rich Arab Gulf States through India towards ASEAN, China, South Korea, Japan and Taiwan. This situation can be propitious for India provided we create the necessary conditions to benefit.

In world politics India does not punch its true weight. It is the elephant in the drawing room. India does not fit comfortably into any international groupings, whether the G-20, the G-77, the G-15, the BRICS, IBSA (India-South Africa-Brazil), ARF, the IORARC, or any other. It has to be a loner. In the Third World, India is considered out of place, and it is also an obvious misfit in the First World. Among developing countries it is developed, and in the developed world it is still developing. In the liberal world, it is considered doctrinaire, and among the few socialists that are left, it is regarded as liberal. In the free market it is viewed as state-centred, and with the controlled economies it is seen as market-oriented.

Among the Cold War relics, it is viewed as pro-West, and in the West it is viewed as unpredictable and not fully in tune with western values. It takes finances from the World Bank and IMF, but among non-oil developing counties it is probably the biggest aid donor.

There can be advantages as well as disadvantages in this neither-here-nor-there situation.

India should strive for issue-based alliances while maintaining an independent foreign policy and strategic autonomy, and steering a difficult course between the aforesaid arc of instability from the Arab peninsula to Central Asia and the arc of future prosperity from India to Taiwan.

Within these theme-based alliances there are specific issues that have to be addressed and there is room for manoeuvre. For example, India broke ranks with BRICS on Syria, Sri Lanka and Iran which caused some surprise. Have we abandoned our traditional policy of paramount respect to Article 2 of the UN Charter regarding state sovereignty, or is it only a tactical retreat?

Even in any theme-based alliance, it will be a mistake to ally anywhere, anytime, with anyone, overtly against China. The need for balancing our strategic requirement for close relations with USA, Australia, South Korea, Japan and Vietnam to cope with potential security challenges from China, with the need to avoid any action that will sound alarm bells in Beijing must continue to be our objective. We are in no position yet to change gear to move from a defensively cautious to a confidently activist mode.

In South Asia we face domestic challenges; Maoism, the centrifugal urge for mini-sovereignties, and terror both indigenous and imported from Bangladesh, Nepal and Pakistan. In addition, we confront non-conventional threats like cyber, nuclear and chemical warfare, access to raw materials, water sources and energy.

No big country is loved by its neighbours. India is a big country and we have no designs to become bigger. But we have no wish to become smaller either, just because it suits the agenda of some of our neighbours. India has on its land borders six countries, including the most populous and fastest growing big economy on earth, and another one that is correctly described as an international migraine. We also have several more neighbours on our maritime borders. With some neighbours, both our territorial and our maritime borders are yet to be mutually settled. We live in a very dangerous neighbourhood–the least integrated region in the whole world. It is stating the obvious that there is no political or economic structure that tends towards unity in South Asia. There is no machinery for meaningful security discussions or for conflict resolution. And there cannot be, while there is such a high level of trust deficit.

It has often been mentioned that India has a land border with all other SAARC countries, except Afghanistan of course, while none of the others have. India is the only country that has air connectivity to every other SAARC capital. India has to be at the heartbeat of any South Asian success. But India's very centrality can cause jealousy and resistance.

The countries of the SAARC have less than 5 percent of their total trade among themselves, due to high tariffs, the lack of a common customs union and absence of harmonized commercial processes. This low level of commerce does not help us in fostering any spirit of mutual interdependence in the sub-continent.

To reach a position of becoming a country that counts in the world, India will have to have a mutually cooperative sub-region. But India can never achieve global status unless it reaches out beyond its immediate neighbourhood to the wider world. Our former National Security Adviser Brajesh Mishra has said recently that India is diminished by being boxed into the sub-continent. But can India do otherwise with neighbours like China and Pakistan? These are the paradoxes that need to be resolved.

India's actions as a manager of security in the South Asia

region have been limited to crisis situations, and by and large it is inclined to keep a hands-off policy. This is partly because of sensitivity about its actions being misrepresented, and partly because it looks beyond South Asia. Its role in organizations like the SAARC is accordingly very low-key with only sporadic interest or involvement.

We have to rate the threat of conventional warfare as low. Pakistan can never overcome India and the most dangerous border in the world is the Afghan-Pakistan border and not the Indo-Pakistani one. The increasing Chinese presence in Gilgit-Baltistan adds to our anxiety, but in 1965 and 1971 China could have joined Pakistan to confront India but did not. While we can never rest on assumptions, there is no reason to think of a joint China and Pakistan collective against India in open conflict.

Developments in India's neighbourhood illustrate the larger point about the transformation of conflict from 'ordinary war' between organized armies to a hybrid of war, insurrection, ideological, ethnic and religious grievances, and covert operations. A serious security concern for us today is that across the world, terror groups and their sponsors terrorize innocent people and pressurize governments.

Pakistan is the main exporter of terrorism in the world and is sliding into anarchy. No one can guess where it will be one year down the line. If it goes out of control, the spill over effects on India would be considerable. A second big question is what would be the nature of Pakistan in the post-Osama years. Will Pakistan move closer to what Jinnah wanted it to be: a moderate Muslim country, or the hotbed of hard line Islamic fundamentalism that it has become?

When we think of security threat perception, there is little point in looking too far a field to hypothetical possibilities that will never prove a menace to India. It is our near abroad that will have to command our attention.

China and India relations are equable. China is India's leading trade partner—and the turnover will be US$ 100 billion by 2015. But Beijing is and will remain New Delhi's greatest rival as it seeks strategic space where Indian and Chinese peripheries meet and overlap. With China arming Pakistan with missiles and nuclear weapons and giving Islamabad diplomatic support, its intention is of keeping New Delhi bogged down in hyphenated Indo-Pakistan rivalry. China's agenda is to build its international stature, grow its economy, and modernize its military to dominate Asia and perhaps one day the world.

China lays stress on its core interests, on which China's assertive actions appear to be based. Perhaps to gauge military opinion or test public reaction, a number of serving and retired officers have been permitted to recommend an aggressive policy beyond their country's borders. A Chinese Air Force officer writes that China is surrounded by hostile nations, predicts war in 10-20 years and even identifies the enemy; 'if the US can light a fire in China's backyard, we can also light a fire in their backyard'. China's rise implies it is more self-confident and assertive, and bound to come into conflict with the strategic interests of the USA. As China's trade minister bluntly told The Washington Post, 'America is the one that needs to adjust'.

But the Chinese authorities have no desire to jeopardize ties with their key trading partner and the biggest military and economic power, the USA.

Indian analysts are divided between viewing the rising China as a dove or a dragon. Some say China is not fated to be an enemy, unless we decide to make it one. Treat China like an enemy, the belief goes, and it will become an enemy. Treat China like a friend and it will become a friend. Smarting from what it sees as a century or more of subjugation by outsiders, China may want to avoid being dictated to, but it has been dictating to others in the region. In the South China Sea, it has fired at Filipino fishermen and cut the cables of Vietnam oil vessels. It presses its claims on others. China is the first country to deploy land-based anti ship missiles which creates strategic problems for freedom of navigation. Its hostile cyber activity is rampant. It is not wise to pre-determine China as an enemy, but China still views others as enemies, or on better days, as just its rivals.

Relations between India and China, both major economic and nuclear powers with differing political and cultural traditions, are unlikely to be smooth and we must expect periods of a costly state of tension. India's main problems with China are presently threefold–the Dalai Lama, China's support to Pakistan and the common border. These will need to be acceptably contained.

Analysts have written about a 'string of pearls' by which China seeks to encircle hostile countries. The fear of being encircled lodges deep in every major country's mind, whether India, China, Russia, Israel etc.—everyone other than the United States, which, to its great good fortune, has huge oceans to the west and east, and a benign neighbourhood to its north and south.

The new US approach towards the Asia-Pacific region, like India's, is dominated by awareness of China. This holds the key to understanding the US approach to Asia and much of the world today. In Asia the greatest potential military conflict is between USA and China and not between India and China.

The USA is in the process of formulating for the first time since the Cold War a coherent Asian strategy. Its policy is an 'integrated diplomatic, military, and economic strategy that stretches from the Indian sub-continent through Northeast Asia' with the warning that 'America is going to play a leadership role in Asia for decades to come'. Lee Kuan Yew, one of the most astute observers of the Chinese, put it clearly when he spoke of 2010 marking the beginning of a "decade long tussle between the USA and China for pre-eminence in the Asia-Pacific".

There is too heavy an American dependence on the Asian region, and especially China. For the maintenance of its economic and financial stability to try and limit the Chinese into the continental landmass, they are seeking to break out of the strength of their achievements. The US needs China's cooperation on several critical problem areas, like for example, the Iranian and the North Korean nuclear proliferation.

Will an era of US-Chinese tension be dangerous for India? Or not, because of the inter-connectedness of the two countries? According to the Chinese, 'China has more resources to oppose the US ambition of dominating the region than the US has to fulfil it'.

India shares the US concern about China's economic, military and cyber-war potential, but hopes China will gradually step into the role of a 'responsible stakeholder' in world security. We must never disregard the fact that, like India, China suffers many handicaps and disabilities that are sometimes concealed by its economic rise and ignored by its admirers. In this century, China possesses almost as many reasons to fall apart as it does to hang together. It has serious problems with ethnic minorities like the Uigurs in Xinjiang and Tibetans. They also have banks riddled with bad loans, an employment difficulty in finding pensions for a massive rapidly ageing workforce and social inequality of destabilizing levels. These are among the highest in the world, with a Gini co-efficient greater than even that in the USA. There is simmering dissent among netizens and civil society with frequent flash-points. There is rampant corruption at all levels, and environmental degradation. The country has grown to an extraordinary extent over the past three decades, but it may be harder to achieve internal consensus on what comes next.

In the coming years, Myanmar may achieve a measure of plurality in political decision-making. This will present a novel and challenging environment for New Delhi. India must make contact with various national political parties and regional ethnic parties. When sanctions are lifted, the advantage of demi-exclusivity will disappear, and India will have to compete with many powerful countries to promote Indian interests. On the other hand, the opening up of Myanmar could prove a blessing, because India by itself is not in any position to stop the Chinese juggernaut from making huge in-roads into Myanmar's politico-economic space. When sanctions are eased, foreign investment pattern will be diversified and Indian companies could participate vigorously in Myanmar's economic opportunities.

To develop its Southwest, especially Yunnan, China desires access, by means of highways and a modern port, to the Bay of Bengal to bypass the Malaccan Straits. At the same time, there is the Indian 'Look East Policy'; which includes building a new Burmese seaport and reopening the Stilwell Road. For both aspiring powers, Burma is a link, and as Burma opens up, the question is whether India or China will be its primary inspiration and conduit to the wider world. Burmese nationalism is wary of China whose consumer culture and expeditionary economic expansion has created neither jobs nor socio-economic equality.

But Burma knows India cannot balance China and modern Indian influence in Burma is non-existent. Its trade is by sea and Rangoon and not overland. It does not help that Burma is next to a conflict-ridden and neglected part of India. Like Yunnan with Burma, this area sits at a possible crossroads of India and China. Both the Northeast and Yunnan are landlocked and adjoin Burma; both have populations different in character from the mainstream. But Yunnan is flourishing, the Northeast is not. This is because in India, I am sorry to say, security considerations are paramount and lead to a closing down rather than an opening up. India has to think again and reset this attitude.

The Indian 'Look East Policy' accorded with the market model already in place in South East Asia. Compared to China, India had fallen far behind in the movement for regional integration, although the political and strategic situation on India's Northeast flank affected its security, even more so after the admission of Myanmar brought ASEAN adjacent to India's land border.

In general terms, compared with the early 1990s, India is now a reasonably confident participant in the Asia-Pacific political and strategic domain.

The ASEAN Regional Forum (ARF) is the first and only multilateral security forum ever to be joined by India. It had been India's traditional approach to keep security issues out of the scope of regional groups such as SAARC and the Indian Ocean Rim Association, in both of whose formation it had played a key role. But with the ARF, the objective of 'containing' China influenced India to reverse its historic position on such groupings. Competition between India and China in the region is predictable because there are overlapping and contested perceptions of their spheres of influence and interest.

There is therefore a competitive edge in India's policy to achieve some kind of equal footing with China. But it will be necessary for India to draw China into discussions on cooperation and security in the Asia-Pacific region. An approach of 'containing' China by aligning with some individual powers whose strategic goals and military practices do not necessarily complement ours, nor share the long term vision of India's relationship with its northern neighbour, will be most unwise. India's strategic engagement with East Asia should be premised on valuable soft power assets like culture, technology, IT, trade and investment. It has to make much greater efforts towards making East Asia an important stakeholder in Indian prosperity.

It is appropriate that this paper also deals with non-conventional security threats. I would like to mention of three—cyber space, energy and human security.

1. Internet Security: Inflation is threatening India's economic growth. It may be a world-wide phenomenon, but with domestic prices rising and having a knock-on effect on wages, a higher salary bill for IT companies will have a negative impact on Indian aspirations to play a larger economic and political role on the world stage.

India's service industry accounts for 57 percent of the country's GDP, and information technology and business process outsourcing contribute 25 percent of the country's exports. Over the past two decades, exports of services regularly grew between thirty and fifty percent annually, but rising production costs now threaten to constrain this sector severely. Until a short while ago, Indian information technology professionals were paid one-sixth of the salaries drawn by their counterparts in the USA or the European Union: today they are paid about one-third and this gap is steadily dwindling, nullifying the cost advantage previously enjoyed by India in global markets. Once cost competitiveness is no longer assured, the Indian services sector will have no option but to compete on the strength of quality alone. Frankly, this may be difficult. The effects of rising costs are already ominous. Several companies are shutting down for cost reasons; the shrinking difference in salaries no longer justifies the expense of employing staff here, and China and some Latin American and Southeast Asian countries are aggressively pushing into the global market of low-cost off-shoring.

The cheapest services mean the most vulnerable as well. Low cost software services mean low cost protection, leaving India open to cyber attacks, not necessarily against India but directed to the Western customers of Indian software. We may ask: Why has India, a software giant, never developed any international virus protection software like Norton or McAfee? Cost and security are the challenges confronted by the leaders of Indian business process off shoring and information technology. If they fail, the goose that laid the golden eggs will fly away and the Indian image could revert to what it was in the pre-globalization period.

2. Energy: We can predict a contest for natural resources including water and energy. Oil and gas fossil fuels have been the ingredients of economic development in the West, but now they have to share these critical resources with Asia's expanding economies. This has ushered in a new situation where the major buyers and sellers are both located in Asia.

This new geopolitical dynamic has resulted in an increase of pressure in the race for access to energy resources reflected in an increase in energy prices as well as in the development of new methods and routes for supplies. Added to this is the pressure from increase in the price of coal and its impact on electricity prices.

Development of nuclear power in Asia has gone into a tail spin post-Fukushima, which has put more pressure on fossil fuels such as coal, oil and gas as the primary source of energy for India. There are also environmental factors for the developing world, post Kyoto and Copenhagen and their impact on the global commons.

These dilemmas are reflected in various geopolitical and economic issues straddling from the Caucasus and Central Asia to the various territorial claims regarding the Spratly Islands in the South China Sea.

3. Human Security: Our neighbourhood governments emphasize hard external threat and give minimal thought to non-military threats. To an extent this is due to the presence of nuclear weapons and a host of unsettled issues. Is South Asia unipolar, polypolar or bipolar? Only Pakistan challenges India in hard threat in South Asia and vice versa. China's nuclear potential is a component of the hard threat in South Asia, but are China's nuclear weapons contextualized for South Asia? Military budgets reduce expenditure on social sectors, and when governments focus mainly on military solutions to problems of national security, non-military tasks grow ever more difficult. Cooperative security could change the attitude of state policy makers towards neighbours who suffer the same insecurity scenario, since no single state can address the wide range of security problems.

A case can be made for a new framework of international cooperation; the setting up of epistemic communities to deal with non-conventional threats to human security comprising economic, food, health, environment, personal, community and political security, with human rights, development, democracy, rule of law, gender, and ecological dimensions. An interdependent world is facing multiple threats and the purely state-centric approach is no longer adequate. The nature of remedy through democracy is questionable, since there are nonperforming democracies, assertions of sub-national identity, and corruption, social exclusion, and inefficient civil services. Regional integration is not possible in our part of the world due to immature nationalism and economic disparities. Another factor militating against a regional multilateral cooperative approach is that all South Asian governments will strongly resist any external interference, however well-intentioned, in their sovereign spheres of influence.

I have laid out some of the challenges in evolving an Indian security policy. These are complex issues and cover a wide landscape. If taken holistically, and if India can give the world an initiative in addressing these in a meaningful way, it can move from a reactive to an active player on the world stage. It can never be a global power unless it is first a global player.

2

India's Security Policy: Emerging Frontiers of Co-operation

Radhavinoda Raju

Addressing scholars, students and opinion makers in Chennai last July, United States' Secretary of State Hillary Clinton said that it is time for India to lead, that India should not just look east, but engage and act east as well. She made these observations in the background of China's assertiveness in Asia. She said India's leadership had the potential to positively shape the future of the Asia-Pacific. Touching upon India's leadership role, Hillary Clinton said that India was taking its rightful place in meeting rooms and conference halls where the world's consequential questions are debated and decided. It is obvious that India's huge population, with an impressive youth bulge, its fast growing economy, its civilizational background and its geographic position in an area of vital interest to the world have together raised India's geopolitical profile.

According to scholars, good demographics alone will not place a country on the path of growth; there has to be good governance as well. When demographics are not so favourable, "they need excellent education, good macroeconomic management and adequate regulation of labour markets" to increase productivity and maintain growth. Else they would fall into a middle income trap. The questions these scholars ask is whether countries like India can afford to sit back and wait for the democratic dividend to just flow in? Obviously not, they say. Citing the example of Japan in the fifties and sixties when Japan was in its fast growth period, scholars say that they brought in literate and well educated workers in their factories and offices. As against this, India has a 'patchy' system of education where it "produces some excellent elite students but fails tens of millions who attend state schools that are often devoid of the basics–including teachers. Some worry that India's demographic dividend could mutate into a demographic time bomb".

According to our National Security Advisor, the chief goal of India's internal and external security policies now as well as in the foreseeable future is to transform and improve the standard of living of the nearly 400 million of our compatriots who have been living in perpetual poverty. To quote from one of his addresses, "Our quest is the transformation of India, nothing less and nothing more. If we have consistently sought to avoid external entanglements or outside restraints on our freedom of choice and action it is because we have been acutely conscious of this overriding priority and wanted nothing else to come in the way of its pursuit. This was and remains the essence of the policy of non-alignment. If we have sought the strategic autonomy that nuclear weapons bestow upon us it is to be able to pursue this goal without distraction or external entanglement. This is the touchstone against which policy should be measured both for desirability and effect".

While statistically speaking we have come a long way since gaining our independence, when literacy was 14 percent and average life span of an Indian was 26 years, we still have a long way to go to ensure our people have a satisfactory standard of living. It has been estimated that we need to grow at between 9 to 10 percent of our GDP for the next at least 15 years to achieve this objective. And we have already fallen below 7 percent last year! Coalition politics and global economic factors are responsible for this fall in growth. This means that India's overriding priority is to maintain its high economic growth, and raise the level of standard of its educational institutions and prevent students from dropping out of schools so that we have a highly educated work force in the coming years.

How do we do that in practice? Is it by turning our back on the world, in the name of autonomy? That led to poor economic growth till the eighties. No, we will have to engage strongly with the world, but stay focussed on our objectives. How do we achieve this? Firstly, we have to deal with our internal security issues. Then comes our neighbourhood. And then we will have to deal with our extended neighbourhood.

India has been subjected to jihadist attacks off and on. It started with Jammu & Kashmir, but the jihadists had threatened to attack our economic power centres, and they have kept their promise, no doubt, inspired by the ISI. Our response has been patchy, not focussed and professional. We created a National Investigation Agency in the aftermath of the Mumbai attacks of 26/11. But only one terrorist attack, that took place in the Delhi High Court last year, was given to the NIA for investigation, though there have been several terrorist attacks after the NIA was created. The various Anti-Terror Units of the States have not put up a united front while investigating jihadist attacks, losing out on a number of clues and leads.

The National Counter Terrorism Centre that has been set up is mired in controversy from the very beginning, and unless the Centre and States learn to live and work together, we will have more and more such attacks, as the adversary will exploit the chinks in our armour. It is important that the Union Government and the Governments in the States have a common stand on security issues, and agree to work together. This is essential if we are to successfully face the jihadist enemy. The local police have to be strengthened, they have to be better trained and equipped, and their numbers should match international standards. They should be trained to operate against urban and rural terrorism, and their capabilities of intelligence gathering and penetration strengthened. Finally, it will be the local police which will put down the extremists, be they the jihadists or the naxalites. Agencies like the NIA will come in only when a case has pan India or international dimensions, and when there will be need for all India or international databases on jihadists etc. The NIA has made useful contributions in tackling the Dima-Halam Daogah (DHD) group of militants of Assam and the NSCN (IM) through its professional investigations. The Government is in talks with these two groups and the ULFA.

There was peace in Kashmir last year, but there is no doubt it is fragile. Lasting peace can come only after the external dimension of the problem is tackled with Pakistan. It is still not clear whether Pakistan will give up its futile policy of using jihad as an extension of its foreign policy. But that need not stop us from tackling the internal dimension of the Kashmir problem, which is political in nature, and no amount of economic aid or jobs is going to help tackling it. The mainstream parties have been asking for autonomy or self-rule, within the Indian Constitution. We could engage them, and all others who are willing to talk within these parameters, look at the recommendations of the interlocutors and address the internal dimension of the problem.

South Asia has tremendous potential for economic growth, there is no doubting that. But a history of violence and mistrust holds it back from realising its true potential. As the biggest power in South Asia, India has a special responsibility to help its neighbours take advantage of its own growth, and help them grow too. While a climate of trust and bonhomie prevails in our relations with Bangladesh and Sri Lanka, there are irritants that need to be removed. We have openly and covertly supported Sri Lanka in its war with Prabhakaran and his LTTE, but the Tamils there feel India has let them down by not questioning Sri Lanka's conduct of the last stage of the fratricidal war, in which nearly 40,000 innocent civilians are alleged to have been killed.

The political reconciliation that President Rajapaksahad promised has also not come yet. While it is essential that we help in Sri Lanka's economic growth, we should also nudge it towards a political solution of the ethnic dimension of the

Tamil problem. India had signed a Free Trade Agreement with Sri Lanka even when the conflict between the LTTE and the Sri Lankan security forces was on and bilateral trade is already expanding. But we cannot afford to ignore the sentiments of sixty million Indian Tamils, who are angry at the Government's support to Sri Lanka over the human rights violation issue.

Bangladesh has been an excellent neighbour these last few years, with the top leadership of several militant groups having been arrested and handed over to us, including that of the ULFA. Yet, the Prime Minister of India could not achieve the objective of his visit to Bangladesh last year, with Mamta Banerjee playing spoilsport on the understanding that had been reached by the two countries on sharing the waters of the Teesta River. Our leaders seem to be lacking a minimum level of understanding on national security issues.

India's relations with Myanmar have been marked by realism rather than idealism. Our cautious engagement with the Generals in Yangon has helped in the Northeast regaining some semblance of stability. Further, our 'Look East Policy' would receive a boost with the opening up of Myanmar to India.

India has had close relations with Nepal, and they go back a long way. Nepal has been struggling to establish itself as a Republic, and draft a Constitution. Another major issue there is integrating the thousands of Maoists into the Nepalese army. India has to assist Nepal without appearing to dictate to it, and the success of our Nepal policy should reflect that.

India and China are the powers of tomorrow. We have a long un-settled border with our giant neighbour. China has built capabilities for quickly transporting its armed forces and equipment onto our borders, while our own infrastructure in the border regions has not kept pace with that of the Chinese. China has exhibited its missile capabilities as well, and can target any major city in India. On the other hand, trade between India and China is poised to reach US$ 100 billion soon, and this could be a major deterrent to war mongers in both countries. India believed that China assisted insurgents in the Northeast, and that even now, sections of ULFA get patronage there. China believes that India can, and does cause them trouble in Tibet.

It is in this background that our Prime Minister's statement, made during a visit to Beijing, that the world can accommodate both India and China, needs to be seen. Another area of concern to us with regard to China is its all-weather friendship with Pakistan, and China's role in building Pakistani capabilities in the nuclear field. While a solution of the border issues with China does not seem to be in the offing any time soon, we need to keep engaging with this powerful neighbour, without adversely affecting our preparation for a war if it is thrust on us. For this we need to strengthen our infrastructure in the border regions without any further delay.

While India's focus will be to build its economy to raise the living standard of its poor, and do this in our own unique democratic way with our emphasis on plurality in religious, social, ethnic and linguistic dimensions, there are forces that are bent on disrupting our progress and destabilising our country. Pakistan has been trying this for over a quarter of a century, with the ultimate aim of capturing Jammu & Kashmir, but has failed miserably in all its attempts. In these twenty odd years, while India has seen unprecedented economic growth and won admiration of the world for doing this in a democratic manner, Pakistan has spiralled into one after another crisis, with its economy in doldrums, depending on foreign powers and institutions to bail it out each time. Our attempts to engage with Pakistan to work out all issues that plague our relationship have not yielded the desired results so far. Pakistan has not taken any step to dismantle the terrorist infrastructure that it has been using all this time, though Pakistan itself has now become the victim of terrorist attacks on its own soil. Pakistan will continue to remain a challenge to our diplomatic and security policies in the foreseeable future.

India had signed a strategic partnership with Afghanistan. India's relations with Afghanistan go back centuries, except for a few years when the Taliban were ruling that country. Today, we have invested heavily in Afghanistan, and the projects include the Delaram-Zaranj Highway, electricity transmission lines from Uzbekistan to Kabul, the hydro-electric Salma Dam and the new Parliament building in Kabul. Recently, the Afghan Government awarded the development of 3 of the 4 Blocks of the Hajigak mines in Bamian province to Indian companies. The last one is a multi-billion dollar project, and the Indian consortium plans to build a power plant, a steel plant and transportation links to take the ore out of Hajigak. So India has a lot of investment to protect in Afghanistan, apart from ensuring that Afghanistan is not used to train Indian insurgents, which happened when the Taliban were ruling Afghanistan. We have also agreed to help train Afghan police and armed forces. India is energy deficient, and needs to explore the world's markets for oil and gas. With its abundant supply of oil and gas, Central Asia is a natural market for us, and Afghanistan its gateway.

We need to help in creating an enabling international environment, including peaceful order, freedom of the seas and open sea lanes. More than 20 percent of our GDP is now accounted for by our exports and our growth and survival depend on our imports of fertilizer, energy and capital goods. We need to have connectivity with our extended neighbourhood, including East Asia and the Middle East, which become part of our strategic goals.

With an increasingly domineering China looming in the background, it is not surprising that the United States Secretary of State invited India to engage with the East. Japan, the Asean countries and even Australia would like India to figure more prominently in the security architecture of Asia, to balance an assertive China. However, let me close by once again quoting from a speech of the National Security Advisor:

"For a considerable time to come, India will be a major

power with several poor people. We must always therefore be conscious of the difference between weight, influence and power. Power is the ability to create and sustain outcomes. Weight we have, our influence is growing, but our power remains limited and constrained and should first be used for our domestic transformation.

History is replete with examples of rising powers who prematurely thought that their time had come, who mistook their influence and weight for real power. Their rise, as that of Wilhelmine Germany or militarist Japan, was cut short prematurely.

So at the risk of disappointing those who call on India to be a 'responsible' power, (meaning that they want us to do what they wish), and at the risk of disappointing some of you who like to think of India as a superpower, I would only say, as Mrs. Indira Gandhi said: 'India will be a different power' and will continue to walk her own path in the world. That is the only responsible way for us".

3

National Security: Different Strokes

P.P. Rajkumar

Non-military Aspects of National Security

1. When we talk about National Security, there are two aspects, which we have to keep in mind. The first is–what is a nation? The second is–security from what? The very word 'Nation' comes from the Latin word 'Natio' [1] which was originally used to denote the College students, especially at the University of Paris, who spoke the same language and were willing to be ruled by their own familiar law. A country, on the other hand, denotes a defined territory. The word 'State' expresses a legitimatized administrative institution. Therefore, when we talk about a Nation, what we are talking about is people. However, a Nation-State today means a territory with a single Govt. and having a distinctive population with a common culture that gives identity to its citizens.

2. Security means "Safety, freedom from danger or anxiety". [2] So, security has to be against a threat/danger. In the present day context, threats could be–terrorist attacks, HIV/AIDS, environmental degradation etc. Therefore, National Security means security of the people, which also includes security of territory. Till some time ago, national security exclusively meant security of the territory. This has undergone a major change. In 1998, the UK carried out a Strategic Defence Review, and concluded that they did not face any significant threat to their territory. This resulted in re-orientation of their military posture to that of an expeditionary force. [3] This means that their forces are also trained to safe guard their interests outside their country rather than just at their borders.

3. Most threats to national security emerge from disparities. Disparities could be in economic, social, political, health and other spheres. The worst form of disparity is income inequality. Income inequality automatically brings about education inequality, inequality in access to health services, in access to water and many other inequalities. Many of you may recollect that extreme economic inequality led to the French Revolution and changed the course of history. Therefore, the prime concern in India is to reduce the economic inequality as much as possible. About fifty-three percent of India's income comes from the services sector, as per 2008 estimates and about twenty-nine percent comes from the industries sector. Thus, only eighteen percent of income is from the agriculture sector. [4] In India, sixty percent of our population live in villages depending solely on agriculture. Therefore, about eighty percent of India's income is shared by forty percent of the people and twenty percent of income by sixty percent of the people. This is certainly a cause for concern.

4. We used to talk about population explosion as a major threat, just a few years ago. We do not hear that word very much these days. Instead, we hear a lot about demographic dividend. India seems to be at an advantage compared to most other countries with regard to this demographic dividend. What does this dividend means? It means that if the majority of the population is between the ages 18 to 64, which are the working ages, the country has an advantage. In India, 64.9 percent or 65 percent of the population, as per 2011 estimates, are in the age group of 15 to 64. Most of this group form the potential working force. India's median age is 26.2 years as of Jan 2012. [5] This means fifty percent of the population is below this age and the other half is above this. With about sixty-five percent of the population at the working level, the work force alone is double the total population of the US. The US, incidentally, is the third most populous country in the world, after India.

5. Having a large younger population does not automatically mean that all of them would get jobs. The supply does not mean that there would be a demand. In order to create a demand, this work force needs to be properly educated and trained so that they can be employed. Therefore, education becomes an extremely important factor for future employment. As of now, we do not have the basic infrastructure in place to educate the majority of our children between the ages of 5 and 18. These are the very people who are to be gainfully employed between now and 2020. It is against this fact that one needs to see the importance of the Right to Education Act. For every low level government job, there are thousands of applicants. Therefore, education and job creation become a major task for the government, if India has to progress. Having a large number of unemployed youth is also a sure recipe for unrest.

6. We also need to factor in the threat of HIV/AIDS. The young population on which the future of India depends is also the same group that could be the target of AIDS. As per 2009 estimates, HIV/AIDS prevalence rate is 0.3 percent of the population-which places India at 84th position in the world. However, if we look at the number of people with AIDS–2.4 millions, and deaths due to AIDS–170000, we are no. 3 in the world, coming just below South Africa and Nigeria. [6] The frightening aspect of HIV/AIDS is that when the cases go past a certain low percentage, say 1 percent or so of the population, it can then go out of control and keep accelerating. Therefore, if we have to attain higher growth rate and better economy, combating AIDS would be one of the top priorities for India. AIDS will not only cause greater outlay on health services but also reduce the number of working hands in India and can lead to a double jeopardy.

7. The growing population would also increase the stress on the available water resources. We are already familiar with the inter-State friction between Tamil Nadu and Karnataka. Such frictions would increase in future and test the will of the

Central Government. A weak and unresponsive Government could lead to secessionist tendencies, as had happened in the case of erstwhile USSR. That is something that will seriously affect national security. The USSR imploded after about 74 Years of existence and the US faced a civil war after about 85 years of Independence. We have been independent only for 64 years and cannot afford to lower our guard.

8. Now, we come to the familiar territory of terrorism. Terrorism is nothing but propaganda by deed. It has now come to occupy public stage in international affairs. Terrorists think that they can bring about change, either in social or political system, by spectacular acts of violence. Unfortunately, once terrorism takes root, it takes a long time to put it down. Some of the groups may splinter but they continue with the orgy of violence. At times, even the terrorists have no idea of the kind of retaliation that they can bring about on themselves. The young Serbian student, who assassinated Archduke Ferdinand, could not have imagined that it would start the First WW. Similarly, the people who planned the 9/11 strike, could not have imagined attacks on Afghanistan, Iraq and other targets in the war on terrorism. We need to make a distinction between terrorism and insurgency, as different approaches are required to tackle each of them.

Insurgent movements have to be supported by the population, where as terrorism can be effective with just a few sympathizers and supporters. In insurgency, it is a fight for the hearts and minds of the people and the people have to be won over. With terrorism, it is the leadership who is to be targeted. Insurgency usually has rural roots while terrorism has an urban bias. The terrorists are as well trained as an army soldier and often better equipped than the army. Therefore, to pit para-military and police forces against them is an unequal equation. In India, we have been dealing with it as a law and order issue. Only after the Mumbai attack, there has been a change on how we should combat terror. Still, there are many political hurdles to cross before an effective anti-terror organisation is put in place.

9. How does terrorism end? There is no clear victory or defeat in this war. Terrorism slowly dies out after many years, when its actions fail to arouse masses. They may then move out to another phase of political struggle through other means. You may recollect that the Basque Separatists Organisation the ETA, after 30 years of struggle, asked their members to lay down arms in November 2004, as they felt that there was no future for the struggle. In some cases, external sponsors may also stop supporting, as happened in the case of Libya in 2003 when it reversed its stance and paid compensation to terror victims. Conditions may also change socially or politically, which may weaken the support base.

Genuine multi-party elections that safeguard the interests of minorities can also under-cut support for terrorism. Finally, if there is a stalemate reached, both parties try to reach a negotiated settlement with mutual concessions. Of course, in this case the Government has to accept that the terrorists had some valid cause for grievance. In combating terrorism, if the Government aims at complete elimination of terrorism, it may fail, because every act of terrorism then would be seen as a success for the terrorists. However, as it happened in the case of North Ireland, where the Government had lowered the aim and set reduction in acts of terrorism as an aim, and not complete elimination, then people would stoically accept certain acts. This may finally lead to complete elimination of terrorism.

Military Aspects

1. Now, we will look at the old-fashioned use of the military for national security. "All wars represent a failure of diplomacy". [7] Diplomacy and Defence are closely related. Both go hand in hand to–prevent a war, recover lost territories, gain fresh territories or change the behaviour of a target country. In this paper, we will only dwell on the use of military by India in wars, other situations, and the changes that we need to cope with in future.

2. Indo-Pak Conflict 1947-48: The Indian military history during post-Independence, started with recovery of territory by war. Within two months after independence, Pakistan launched an aggression to capture Jammu & Kashmir (J&K). J&K had not acceded to either India or Pakistan at that point in time. The Maharaja of J&K had worked out an agreement with both countries to permit him more time to decide. In spite of such an agreement, Pakistan decided to capture J&K by force. India did not want to interfere initially because J&K was not a part of India then.

By the time the Maharaja decided to accede to India, the intruders who were Pathan tribals guided by the Pak military, were just eight kilometres from Srinagar. The two officials who were sent to get the Maharaja's signature on the accession treaty were Mr. V.P. Menon, the Union Home Secretary (then know as Secretary of the Ministry of the States) and Colonel SHFJ Manekshaw (later Field Marshal) from the Army HQ. Within a few hours of the treaty being signed, troops were air lifted to Srinagar. The intruders were pushed back and the valley was soon cleared. The Pakistani Army had occupied many places in J&K. This war carried on for more than a year. India took up this issue with the UN. The UN sponsored a cease-fire from 01 Jan 1949. At the end of this conflict, India held 101,400 sq. km. and Pakistan held 78,000 sq. km. of Kashmir territory. [8] The Kashmir issue is the basis for two more wars and numerous terrorist actions on the part of Pakistan.

3. Liberation of Goa: In 1961, the defence forces were used to vacate the Portuguese from Goa. The Portuguese had earlier been asked to vacate this pocket and hand it over to India. They did not do it. Following an attack on a fishing boat in their territorial waters, India launched an attack. The Portuguese fled and India took over that territory. India was severely criticised by the western powers for this action. The Soviet Union supported India. The Defence Minister during this period was Shri V.K. Krishna Menon.

4. In 1962, we had a conflict with China. There were differences in view over the actual border demarcation in the North and Northeast. The Indian Government had instructed the Army to set up posts at the most forward positions on the border. India was convinced that China would never attack over this issue. The Chinese initially protested to these forward positions. When there was no response from India, they attacked. Indians had not fully factored in the likely Chinese responses to their forward deployment policy. The Indian Army was ill equipped and ill prepared to face a full Hedged Chinese assault. The Chinese overran all Indian forward positions and invaded most of what is now Arunachal Pradesh. They also captured some positions in the Ladakh region. However, they did not hold on to their positions in the East and retreated to their original positions. In the Ladakh region, they held on to the captured territories.

5. This war was a massive diplomatic and military failure for India. As generally stated, there are no permanent friends or permanent enemies in international relations. India supported China at every international forum and pressed for a permanent seat for them in the Security Council. However, it had failed to note the Chinese capabilities across the border. In international relations, it is very important to monitor the capabilities of friends and foes alike. Intentions can change overnight and friends can turn into foes. Therefore, defence plans should be based on the capabilities of countries of interest to us. In this War, India lost territory. More than territory, India lost face internationally as its policies of Panchsheel and non-alignment came under severe stress. Shri Krishna Menon, the then Defence Minister, lost his post due to this debacle.

6. Indo-Pak War 1965: In 1965, Pakistan again tried to wrest Kashmir from us, by trying a variation of their earlier military strategy in Kashmir. This time again, they sent troops disguised as locals to Kashmir. Fortunately, for us, we realised their game before it was too late and immediately reacted

militarily. Soon the Indian troops were at the gates of Lahore. The US stopped all aid to both India and Pakistan. At that time, India was receiving Food Aid from the USA, under Public Law 480 or PL 480. Already reeling under draught conditions and severe food crisis, the PM, Shri Lal Bahadur Shastri, requested the citizens to forgo one meal a week. The Green Revolution, which was just starting got a push by this threat. India was determined never again to be threatened in such a manner, especially on the food front. Shri Lal Bahadur Shastri memorably coined the slogan 'Jai Jawan Jai Kisan' at that time. We had 22 days of war before a cease-fire was announced. Though India had gained territory during the war, it was returned as part of the negotiations. During the war, Indonesia, Iran and many Arab countries gave military support to Pakistan against India. They gave the latest aircraft and other equipment for Pakistan's war effort. Indonesia, even offered to invade Andaman and Nicobar Islands as a diversionary tactics to ease the pressure on Pakistan. Fortunately, before Pakistan could reply to this offer, the war was over. We had no military resources in those islands at that time. If there had been an invasion, it would have been a cakewalk for the invaders.

7. Indo-Pak War, 1971: In 1971, again Pakistan thrust a war on India. However, Kashmir was not the focus of attention this time. Because of massive atrocities committed by West Pakistan on East Pakistan, there were millions of refugees in India. India could not support them. Western Countries only paid lip service to the unfolding tragedy. India signed a Treaty of Friendship and Co-operation with the USSR. Under General SHFJ Manekshaw, Indian Forces prepared meticulously for a war that was considered inevitable. Pakistan planned an air strike against Indian Airbases on December 3, 1971. It was hoping to repeat the success of Israelis against the Arabs in 1967. In that war the entire air power of the Arabs were destroyed on the ground by Israeli pre-emptive strikes.

However, India was ready for such a move and the rest is

history. This was both a diplomatic and a military victory for India. The Soviets vetoed all actions by the US, UK and China against India in the Security Council. Towards the end of this war, the US sent the nuclear-armed Seventh Fleet to Dacca, as a show of force to India. The UK also had their warships sailing to Dacca. However, the Soviets allowed the West to know that their nuclear submarines and other assets were also shadowing the Seventh Fleet. This did put a spoke in the plans of the west. However, before the ships could reach Dacca, the Pakistani Army surrendered. Nobody expected the war to be over so quickly. One of the reasons for such a quick end was the excellent support given by the Mukti Bahini. Though not well equipped militarily, they helped tremendously by harassing the Pakistani troops and attacking their installations. They also provided hot intelligence on all Pakistani movements. Therefore, India's victory was a multi-national effort. This point needs to be remembered.

8. This war conclusively proved India's military prowess. After this, Pakistan stopped trying to wage a war frontally. Instead, they decided to concentrate mainly on covert war. Their strategy was to make India 'bleed through a thousand cuts'. This did bring about many flash points but the maturity shown by India in diplomacy ensured that no full-fledged war broke out. We did have the Kargil Operations but it was confined to a limited area. This again was a variant of their 1947 strategy of sending soldiers disguised as locals. They hoped to cut off the Srinagar-Leh road link thereby trying to isolate Leh and Siachen.

9. Returning to the 1970s, it was a tumultuous decade for India. We had the first nuclear explosion, emergency, first non-congress govt at the centre, etc. The 1980s saw an assertive use of military power for enhancing national security. Until 1984, Siachen glacier was not considered important by India. However, when it was discovered that Pakistan was trying to use it as their territory by taking sporting expeditions and other people, it was decided to have it under our control.

Occupation of this glacier gave many strategic advantages to India, as it overlooks both Pakistan and China. Pakistan made many attempts to dislodge us from there but to no avail. Subsequently, in late 1986, China had moved certain men and material that was considered aggressive. Immediately, India carried out a massive movement of troops, guns and armour within about 72 hours to the Line of Control. This did catch the Chinese by surprise and they extended conciliatory gestures. Subsequently, there was a thaw in relations, leading to the Foreign Minister's visit in 1987. This was followed by the PM's visit in 1988. This was the return visit to Mr. Chou En Lai's visit in 1960–after a period of 28 years.

10. IPKF in Sri Lanka: In 1987, India sent the Indian Peace Keeping Force to Sri Lanka. This was the first time India had sent such a large force outside its shores for a Peace Keeping mission on its own. Almost 60,000 troops were supported in Sri Lanka from July 1987 to March 1990–the longest operation undertaken by India since Independence. It showed India's confidence in deployment of troops outside India to further our national aim. It also sent a message to all that India may not be a silent spectator if her interest is threatened close to home.

11. In 1988, India also undertook the rescue of the Maldives Govt, which was under threat by a few Sri Lankan mercenaries. This again was an operation a long distance from home. It was conducted successfully. This again showed the world that India was willing to back up its diplomacy with force if needed.

12. In the 1990s India was very active diplomatically. The Soviet Union had collapsed. Since most of our military equipments were of Soviet origin, getting spares for them became a problem. Our military might was weakened. During this period 'economic liberalisation' and 'Look East', policies were implemented. Towards the end of the 1990s we also had Pokhran II–heralding the nuclear weaponisation capabilities of India. Nuclear explosions by Pakistan followed this. India had

now to content with two adversaries who were both nuclear. Very soon thereafter, we had the Kargil Operations, which was a conflict between two nuclear weapon countries. That the conflict was not allowed to escalate speaks for the maturity of our political leadership.

13 The period of 1990s and after, was our diplomacy's finest hour. Within 15 years of the Soviet collapse, India was able to re-orient its foreign relations in such a manner that it was considered a strategic partner by the US. This is no mean feat. Sanctions imposed on India were lifted. India was given a special waiver for nuclear supply. Even when all the plans for civil nuclear plants are implemented in the next 25 years, they will cater to only about nine percent of our total power requirements. [9] It is about three percent now. [10] Therefore, even though the nuclear reactors are important, they are unlikely to make a major difference to our power requirements. What the nuclear deal has done is that it had removed sanctions imposed on India in various technological fields that were restricting our military and technological growth. Hence, we have to see beyond civil nuclear reactors for other benefits, which are enormous.

14. In the first decade of this century, we had two serious incidents that again brought India into conflict with Pakistan. The first was the Parliament attack in 2001. India undertook a massive mobilisation of the armed forces called Operation Parakaram. This was the first time that India had used a force at readiness for coercive diplomacy. The second incident was the Mumbai attack in 2008. The night of the attack, even before the information filtered in to the services HQ, Pakistan had all their military radars operating and their forces at the ready. They were prepared for Indian air strikes even before India had found out as to who were behind the attack.

15. India had slowly expanded its military capabilities over the years. It had taken part in various inter-national military exercises. Interestingly, increase in these exercises had begun soon after Pokhran II. We have had exercises with China also.

These exercises help in inter operability between the militaries. To some extent, the procedures are standardised and an understanding of each other's capabilities is brought about.

16. Changes in Defence Posture: A change in our defence policy in the recent years needs special attention. Earlier, the defence forces were expected to guard the territorial integrity of the nation. As per the recent statements of the Defence Minister, the defence forces are expected to guard our interests. Even though the changes appear minimal, the import is far reaching. India's interests are now not just territorial but also economic. We have to protect our shipping from pirates and other threats. We also have oil fields as far away as Sakhalin (Russia) and South America.

In order to protect our interests, our military cannot be confined to our borders alone. They may have to move out to other areas/continents to operate. If we have to operate so far from our home bases, we need to have re-supply facilities at places away from home. Re-supply includes fuel, armament, food, repairs, medical facilities etc. We could either store them outside our country or have agreements with other countries to permit us to buy these facilities as and when required from those countries. This means our diplomatic corps have to be fully involved in cementing friendships abroad, which would permit our forces to utilise the facilities available in those countries. This is needed especially in times of conflict. Without this kind of support, India may not be in a position to safeguard its interests.

17. Does this mean that our armed forces would become expeditionary forces like that of the US or the UK? Yes, as our economic might increases, there may not be a choice. The change expected is not difficult to achieve. The Navy and the Air Force are by nature expeditionary forces. The Army, however, will need some re-orientation in training and weapons. Nevertheless, the major support needed is in the realms of diplomacy. Indian diplomatic corps is small for the tasks to be accomplished. To safeguard our interests, it is

necessary that our diplomatic arm be strengthened, with infusion of manpower and other resources. They would have to be alive to the needs of the defence forces, as discussed. This has to be done discreetly without raising the hackles of both our friends and foes.

18. As the economy grows, so would our military capabilities. For these capabilities to be exercised, we need to cultivate fruitful relationship with other countries that could support us in times of conflict. If we fail to do this, our interest will be threatened and it could be 1962 all over again.

End Notes

1. http://en.wikipedia.org/wiki/Nation.
2. A.S. Hornby (1988), Oxford Advanced Learner's Dictionary of Current English, p. 770.
3. http://en.wikipedia.org/wiki/Military_of_the_United_Kingdom.
4. http://business.mapsofindia.com/india-gdp/sectorwise.
5. https://www.cia.gov/library/publications/the-world-factbook/geos/in.html.
6. https://www.cia.gov/library/publications/the-world-factbook/geos/in.html.
7. http://epaper.timesofindia.com/Default/Client.asp?skin=pastissues2&center=LowLevel&AW=13300926988527
8. http://www.idsa.in/resources/parliament/IndianLandoccupiedbyneighbouringcountries23.11.11 & http://en.wikipedia.org/wiki/Jammu_and_Kashmir.
9. http://en.wikipedia.org/wiki/Nuclear_power_in_India.
10. http://www.quizquestions.in/2011/03/25/nuclear-energy-in-india-and-world.

4

India's Security Policy in the Post-Cold War Period

Suresh R.

Introduction

National security is the prime concern of any nation state. The very existence of a nation state largely depends on its capacity to protect its national security. The threat to national security has two dimensions. It emanates from internal and external sources. During the Cold War, the external threat to security was largely influenced by the international power structure. Therefore, in the Cold War period, nations have followed different means to ensure their national security from external threats. This includes mainly alignments with the power blocs that dominated international politics. The bipolar system provided nation states an option to join either bloc and ensure their national security. The uncommitted or the non aligned bloc acted as an international pressure group to exert pressure on the decision making at the global level.

Since the bipolar system was based on ideological divide, every international issue was looked upon from the ideological perspective. The containment of competing ideology was the most important concern of superpowers. The developing nations were mere spectators rather than players in the superpower dominated international power game. Though India championed the cause of non alignment, the existence of unresolved regional issues provided the superpowers an opportunity to challenge the non aligned policy of India and draw it closer to the superpower game. National security purely based on military security was the dominant feature of Cold War security concerns of both developed and developing nations.

The end of Cold War with the disintegration of the Soviet Union resulted in a major change in the security perceptions of nations. The pure military security concerns gave away to economic security and other considerations. Though the military security considerations has not lost its significance altogether, the end of the superpower rivalry and competition has reduced the dominant place of pure military security in international politics. In the post-Cold War period, non-traditional security concerns have overtaken the traditional security concerns based on pure military security considerations. There are two notable developments related to security threats in the post-Cold War period. They are the threat to security of the nation state that emanates from non state actors and the threat to the security of people that emanates from within the state.

The security policy of a nation is conditioned by the interplay of internal and external factors. The accelerated pace of globalization and the prevailing international power structure has prompted nation states to redefine their security policy. In the post-Cold War period, as the options are limited before the decision makers to pursue their security interest, a common perception should evolve on all issues including security. This happens mainly because of two important factors. Firstly it is due to the fundamental changes that are taking place in the domestic and external settings. And secondly it is due to the blurred boundary between international security and national security on the one hand and national security and human security on the other hand.

A marked change in India's security policy is visible in the post-Cold War period. It appears that India's quest for economic development by incorporating the basic tenants of globalization process as well as the existence of non-traditional threat to its security and present international power structure prompted India to undertake a three pronged strategy to address its new security concerns. This paper is an attempt to examine India's security policy in the post-Cold War period.

India's Security Policy during the Cold War Period

The post-Second World War bipolar international power structure and the underdeveloped nature of India's economy and its traditions appear to have compelled the decision makers to adopt a non-aligned policy. In the Cold War period, the options before newly independent nations were limited and interactions among nations were solely based on affiliation to either of the blocs led by two divergent ideologies.

Independent India had experimented an independent foreign policy to protect and promote its national interest. Consequently, India had played a major role in the formation of the non aligned movement along with Egypt and former Yugoslavia. India had also played a crucial role along with China in the initiation of Panchsheel, five principles to govern bilateral and multilateral relations between and among nations. However, the flaws in this idealistic approach in international politics were visible when China attacked India in 1962, just one year after the first non aligned summit conference held in Belgrade. When India was confronted with a real politic situation neither the non-aligned movement nor the UN was effective to curb aggression under a collective security system.

Though India claimed its foreign policy as non-aligned, the Indo Soviet Peace and Friendship Treaty of 1971 clearly demonstrated India's 'aligned policy'. The Soviet invasion of Afghanistan in 1979 and India's meaningful silence once again showed its special relation with the Soviet Union. This pro Soviet element in India's foreign policy helped the country to face external security threat and also to gain wholehearted support from Russia in its nation building process. Thus India's 'non-aligned' policy was only a label for the active pursuance of its security policy.

In the Cold War period, nation states were deprived of wide foreign policy options. None of the developing countries were free from the impact of ideology based superpower game. Any kind of interaction with one bloc was viewed as a strategy to destabilize the other bloc and vice versa. In such a suspicious situation, neither stable peace nor prosperity was possible. The regional conflicts were viewed from the context of superpower rivalry. The end of the Cold War helped nations to come out of the shadow of superpower rivalry.

India's Security Challenges in the Post-Cold War Period

India's traditional external security concerns revolved round threats from Pakistan and China. Though there is a marked change in the internal and external setting and consequently on the security challenges, India's security concerns still focus mainly on Pakistan and China. It appears that in the post-Cold War period a major threat from Pakistan government had only a remote chance because of two major developments in the region. Pakistan's decision makers both military and civilian are well aware of the fact that if there is a war between India and Pakistan they may not get any support which they received in 1971 war from their Cold War defence ally, the US. Secondly, since Pakistan also became a nuclear weapon power, no major players at the international level or the UN would allow the outbreak of a nuclear war in South Asia. With regard to the threat from China, though there is an unresolved border problem, China may not initiate a 1962 type war with nuclear India due to nuclear deterrence. Here again, the global players and the UN would not allow a nuclear war in Asia. Thus, in the post-Cold War period, India's traditional security concerns have undergone a marked change, though the defence establishments pay least attention to these developments.

In the Cold War period, another major security concern of India was mainly the presence of external powers in the Indian Ocean region. It was this fear which prompted India to support Sri Lanka's proposal for declaring Indian Ocean as a Zone of Peace by the UN in 1971. During the Cold War period, India strongly supported the elimination of great power presence in the Indian Ocean region, especially US presence. The movement of the US Seventh Fleet into the Bay of Bengal during the India-Pakistan war of 1971 to intimidate India, posed a major threat to India's security interests. Such a threat from the US in the present global scenario is totally eliminated from India's security concerns in the context of its decision to initiate defence collaboration with the US and the joint security monitoring in the Indian Ocean region.

In the post Cold War period the major security concern of India emanate from cross border terrorism. All other traditional security concerns have been overtaken by economic issues. The challenges posed by international terrorism, global economic meltdown and environmental degradation including climate change are also security concerns before India. In the domestic front, India faces many challenges including poverty, illiteracy, social and economic inequality, communalism, regional imbalance, development based displacement, etc. Thus the human security challenges are more in number as well as grave in nature.

India's Quest for Security

India's quest for security has incorporated the traditional concept of security and the new dimension of security, human security. India placed equal importance to security of the nation as well as security of the people. In the Cold War period, there was a competition among nations to accumulate more and more weapons. However, though the competition continues in the post-Cold War period, it has lost much vigour and popular support. This appears to be the reason for the shift in focus from military security to economic and environment security. The plea for a human security approach is also a post-Cold War development. The positive as well as negative impact of the globalization process has accelerated the momentum for human security approach.

On the positive side, globalization has helped the growth of civil society organization at the national and international levels. These organizations make the democratic system more participatory and people friendly. With regard to the negative impact of globalization, the withdrawal of state from welfare activities further worsened the position of the poor and marginalized sections in the society. This development has helped to place greater emphasis on human security from governmental and non governmental agencies. In order to strengthen its economic and military power, India has taken strong policy decisions toward achieving a growth rate of 8 percent by focusing on agriculture, infrastructure development along with its quest for modernization of defence forces. India's reluctance to compromise on the nuclear weapon option, its strategic interaction with the US, and strengthening the naval forces to the level of blue water force are part of this strategy. These steps also appear to be based on a new security perception rooted in a more pragmatic approach.

The international and domestic situations are favourable to India to initiate a new security strategy. The post-Cold War international power structure, which is based on multi-polar system, and the US initiative to curb international terrorism and actions against state sponsored terrorism also suit India's security policy objectives.

The emergence of two major political fronts at the federal level accelerated competition in the Indian polity. Each front tried to formulate domestic and external policy to gain maximum popular support. This trend again prompted each front to pursue a realist foreign policy. India's decision to break the shell and declare itself as a nuclear weapon power and the signing of Indo-US Civilian Nuclear Agreement and a number of policy decisions in the domestic and external fields marked this change.

In the latest federal election, strong popular support for the ruling front to form a stable government without the conditional support from minor ideology based political parties, reflects popular support to the decision-makers.

India's Multilateral Interactions and Security

India has developed a friendly and cordial relation not only through bilateral exchange with nation states but also through interaction in regional and other multilateral organizations, such as ASEAN, EAS, SCO, BRICS, ASEM, IBSA, APTA, and IOR ARC. India is vigorously pursuing its objective to become a developed nation by 2020. This requires the Indian economy to maintain an annual average growth rate of 8 percent per annum. India has framed the 'Look East Policy' in pursuance of this objective. This is a vital part of India's foreign policy. More than an external economic policy or a political slogan, the 'Look East Policy' was a strategic shift in India's vision of the world and its place in the evolving global economy. It was also a manifestation of India's belief that developments in East Asia are of direct consequence to its security and development.

Therefore India actively engaged in creating a bond of friendship and cooperation with East Asia that has a strong economic foundation and a cooperative paradigm of positive interconnectedness of security interests. India became a member of the ARF in 1996 and considered it as an experiment in fashioning a pluralistic, cooperative security order reflective of the diversity of the Asia-Pacific region. India has also successfully clinched a free trade agreement with the ASEAN which had come into force on 1 January 2010.This agreement had further enhanced the Indo-ASEAN trade to US$ 50 billion in 2010. India is also a member of the East Asia Summit (EAS) which includes the ASEAN members and China, Japan, Republic of Korea, Australia, and New Zealand. It focused on energy, environment, climate change, and sustainable development. The 'Look East Policy' of India has included not only vigorous interaction with ASEAN but also improved relation with China. The ultimate objective was to evolve an Asian Economic Community on the lines of EU.

Another major initiative of India towards multilateral interaction is the membership in the five nation grouping called BRICS (Brazil, Russia, India, China and South Africa) to strengthen bilateral relationship that will help the nation to be more effective collectively. This five nation group has several peculiar features. It represents 40 percent of the world population, covers 25.5 percent of the total geographic area and 40 percent of the global gross domestic product (GDP). It will become bigger than the G-7, collectively by 2035. This grouping and political interaction could help to alter the shape of the international financial system and the global economy. One of the objectives of the grouping is the democratization of international financial institutions. The joint declaration at the First Summit meeting held in Russia focused on global food security. The BRICS countries supported the adoption of a wide range of mid- to long-term measures in order to provide for a solution to the issue of food security. This clearly reflects the commitment of BRICS to resolve the basic problem before the international community, i.e. food security.

India is also a member of a three nation economic group known as IBSA, (India Brazil and South Africa) which took intra IBSA trade to US$ 15 billion in 2010. Though India is not a member of the SCO (Shanghai Cooperation Organization) it has actively taken part in the Summit meeting as observer. It comprises of six nations, China, Russia, Kazakhstan, Kyrgyzstan, Tajikistan, and Uzbekistan. India's interest in participating in SCO activities is mainly in the area of energy, economic development, counter terrorism and countering drug trafficking. India is an active member of the Bay of Bengal Initiative for Multi-Sectoral Technical and Economic Cooperation (BIMSTEC), another economic group that acts as a bridge between South Asia and South East Asia. It comprises of Bangladesh, Bhutan, Myanmar, Nepal, India, Sri Lanka, and Thailand.

The IOR ARC 18 member group aims at promoting economic and technical cooperation including expansion of trade and investment. The members are Australia, Bangladesh India, Indonesia, Iran, Kenya, Mauritius, Madagascar, Malaysia, Mozambique, Oman, Singapore, South Africa, Sri Lanka, Tanzania Thailand, United Arab Emirates, and Yemen.

India is one of the five outreach countries in the G-8 along with Brazil, China, Mexico and South Africa. India is also there in the G-20 along with Argentina, Australia, Brazil, Canada, China, France, Germany, Indonesia, Italy, Japan, Mexico, Russia, Saudi Arabia, South Africa, South Korea, Turkey, UK and USA. India had also taken part in the Asia Europe Meeting (ASEM). Thus, in the post-Cold War period, India has adopted a pragmatic approach to promote its national interest and is actively involved in all regional and multilateral forums. These multilateral interactions are aimed at not only enhancing the security of a nation but also human security.

India and Human Security

The end of the Cold War marked the beginning of the concept of security being increasingly scrutinized by scholars of international relations. In the classical formulation, security is about how states use force to manage threat to their territorial integrity, their autonomy and their domestic political order, primarily from other states. Some critique of classical formulation of security have opined that the protection and welfare of the individual citizen or human being is central. The conception of security that is cantered above all on the sanctity of the individual may be called human security.

Though the idea of human security in its rudimentary form may be traced to the 1960s, it was the Independent Commission on International Development Issues in its North-South Report of 1980 that highlighted the changing thinking on development and security. The chairman of the commission Willy Brandit observed, "Our Report is based on what appears to be the simplest common interest that mankind wants to survive, and one might even add has the moral obligation to survive. This not only raises traditional questions of peace and war, but also how to overcome world hunger, mass misery and alarming disparities between the living conditions of the rich and poor."

Another notable development in the idea of human security was the Common Security Report of the Independent

Commission on Disarmament and Security Issues chaired by Olof Palme. It acknowledges that Third World security was also threatened by poverty and deprivation due to economic inequality. The report noted "common security requires that people live in dignity and peace, that they have enough to eat and are able to find work and live in a world without poverty and destitution."

With the end of superpower rivalry, the call for new thinking in security matters gained momentum. In 1991, the Stockholm Institute on Global Security and Governance issued a call for "Common Responsibility in the 1990s", which maintained a wider concept of security, which deals with threats that stem from failures in development, environmental degradation, excessive population growth and lack of progress towards democracy." Again in 1995, the Commission on Global Governance's report, *Our Global Neighbourhood*, stated that, "The concept of global security must be broadened from the traditional focus on the security of states to include the security of people and the security of the planet."

The above Commission's report may be considered as precursors to human security thinking. However, a human security perspective was developed by the UNDP (United Nations Development Programme) in the Human Development Report of 1994.This report contains a section on 'Redefining Security: The Human Dimension'. It proposes an alternative to traditional security and a necessary supplement to human development.

The Human Development Report of 1994 offers an alternative to traditional security. The report discusses in details the question of security for whom by reference to traditional notion of security. These were concerned with security of territory from external aggression, or as protection of national interest in foreign policy or as global security from the threat of nuclear holocaust. It has been related more to nation state than to people. What this conception overlooked was the "legitimate concern of ordinary people who sought security in their daily lives". Human security, on the other hand, is people cantered.

The Human Development Report maintains that human security means protecting vital freedom of the individuals. It means protecting people from critical and pervasive threats and situations, building on their strengths and aspirations. It also means creating systems that give people the building blocks of survival, dignity and livelihood. Human security connects different types of freedoms—freedom from want, freedom from fear and freedom to take action on one's own behalf. To do this, it offers two general strategies: protection and empowerment. Protection shields people from dangers. It requires concerted effort to develop norms, processes and institutions that systematically address insecurities.

Empowerment enables people to develop their potential and become full participants in decision-making. Protection and empowerment are mutually reinforcing, and both are required in most situations. Human security complements state security, furthers human development and enhances human rights. It complements state security by being people-cantered and addressing insecurities that have not been considered as state security threats. By looking at "downside risks", it broadens the human development focus beyond "growth with equity". Respecting human rights are at the core of protecting human security.

In the age of globalization, protection of the vulnerable groups in the society, who are affected by development based displacement or by loss of job and income, assumes great significance. India has taken several steps to ensure human security or the security of the people. Being the largest democratic system in the world it has a strong democratic structure to implement human security measures at the national level. Though the political foundations of India are strongly based on a parliamentary system in the economic and social fields, there are many challenges like poverty, unemployment, illiteracy, social inequality communalism, casteism, the economic disparity between haves and have-nots etc. All these factors have an effect on human security.

In a democratic system, human security assumes great significance. Since the support of the people is required for the government formation, no political party can ignore human security. The globalization process has also contributed towards the inclusion of human security in the national and international sphere. The awareness of the people regarding their own basic problems and the increased interaction among people across the world as a result of the development in information and communication technology, has also promoted human security.

At the national level, India has initiated several programmes for providing security to the people. It includes measures which are aimed at both protection and empowerment of the vulnerable section in the society. The major programmes initiated include the National Rural Employment Guarantee Programme (NREGP), Right to Education Act, Right to Food, programmes for improvement of slums, National Rural Health Mission, Right to Information Act etc.

During the Cold War period, India had taken several initiatives to ensure national security. This mainly included the initiative to establish the non aligned movement, and also through the friendship treaty with former Soviet Union. In the post-Cold War period, the globalization process and the increased multilateral interactions has provided an opportunity for India to initiate a human security approach towards world peace and security.

The existence of non-traditional threats to security further necessitated human security approach. It appears that any move to ensure human security would mould and strengthen the bonds of interaction at the regional and international level. A common strategy to address the problem related to human security would also lead to evolving a common strategy in ensuring national and international security. This happens mainly because of the interconnectedness of human, national and international security.

Conclusions

The shift in international power structure from bipolar to multi polar or 'non polar' after the disintegration of former Soviet Union has posed many challenges to the erstwhile non-aligned nations. In the Cold War period, nation states were deprived of a wider foreign policy option to promote their national interests. Thus, the end of the Cold War marked the end of strict international discipline imposed by the super power rivalry on nation states. Today there is 'de-hyphenated relations' between nations and they are free to engage or disengage with anyone. The security concerns were overtaken by economic interests. In the post-Cold War period, the balance of power appears to have been replaced by balance of interest. The globalization process and challenges posed by international terrorism, global economic slowdown, and environmental degradation including the climate change, has placed 'collective action' and multilateralism in the forefront of international relations.

The protection and promotion of national interests, namely, peace, security and prosperity, are the foremost concerns of any nation, though they adopt different means to achieve these objectives. The changes that had taken place at the international setting placed India in a new security environment and compelled the nation to adapt its security policy to the changing needs. India appears to have adopted a two pronged strategy to meet the new security concerns. Firstly, India has consolidated and projected its power. Secondly it also has initiated engagement with global powers and regional groupings hitherto considered as taboo under 'enlightened national interests'. Further, while framing its security policy, India also needs to focus more on the human security issues than on pure military security, as the issues related to human security are more in number and grave in nature.

The present global order demands a pragmatic approach from the decision-makers to protect and promote the national interests. When the options are limited before the decision makers to pursue their national interests a common perception would evolve in all areas including security policy. This happens mainly because of two important factors. Firstly, it happens due to the fundamental changes that are taking place in the domestic and external settings. And secondly, it is because of the blurred boundary between human security and national security on the one hand, and national security and international security on the other. Further, a common security policy to address the grave problems related to human security would help to evolve a common security perception on national and international security.

References

India's Foreign Policy Today, Speech delivered by External Affairs Minister, Mr. Parnab Mukherjee, at Peking University on 6th June 2008.

Suresh R., Foreign Policy and Human Rights: An Indian Perspective, Madhav Books, Gurgaon, 2009, pp. 42-49.

Suresh R., Human Security: A Canadian Perspective, Holistic Thought, Vol. V, No.1 and 2, January-December 2006, pp. 103-113.

The Commission on Global Governance, Our Global Neighbourhood, Oxford University Press, New York, 1995, p. 306.

UNDP Report 1994, Oxford University Press, New York, 1994.

5

South Asian Market: Security Requiem and Regional Development

Himanshu Roy

The civilization across the south of the Hindukush and the north of the Indian Ocean constitutes a distinct part of the humanity which is, at present, divided into eight politically independent states of South Asia. Its distinctiveness constitutes unhomogenized diversities of population which is predominated by commonality of history, social structure and similarities of problems existing in similar kinds of polity and economy with an apparent conjoined future. The region is dominated by India in terms of the size of the territory, population, economy and state. Or in development and underdevelopment parameters, it imprints the developments in the other countries of the region. Even the conflict is India-centric. The fear of India's dominance overshadows everything else, both in the bilateral and multilateral relations. The formation of the South Asian Association for Regional Cooperation (SAARC) was the outcome of it. Of late, however, the integrative process of globalization has speeded up the formation of the South Asian market through South Asian Free Trade Agreement (SAFTA) that reflects readiness for transcendental borders, both for business and citizens.

South Asian Market

After the collapse of Soviet Union, global capitalism under the aegis of the World Trade Organization's conditionalities has catapulted the integration of the South Asian market which was, earlier, slow despite South Asian Preferential Trade Agreement (SAPTA) and India's improved bilateral trade relations with other countries of the SAARC except for Pakistan. Pakistan's fear of being swamped by Indian products and capital held her in check, for long years, from free trade relations. This fear of dominance had, earlier, led the Muslim Chambers of Commerce and Industries to facilitate the creation of Pakistan in 1947. Of late, however, Pakistan has overcome its inner business contradiction to grant India the most favoured Nations status. The removal of old legalities and the co-optation of different stake holders in the new policy are positive indications. The intended opening of new trade routes in Sindh corresponding to Munnabao sector of Rajasthan reflects its seriousness. Already, the cross-border trade and the visa-free regime for residents in the entire old Jammu and Kashmir province are operational for years despite terror acts and territorial intrusions of Pakistan.

Bangladesh, too, has progressed in this process with an enhanced integration of trade at new multiple border posts and removal of legal barriers in the exchange of commonalities and investment of capital. The more recent political developments —the exchange of village conclaves at the border and the detention and transfer of United Liberation Front of Assam (ULFA) cadres and leaders to India—are further indications of growing relations of the two countries. Similarly, Sri Lanka has initiated the procedural work to begin ferry services for Indian tourists travelling in their own cars to Sri Lanka. Its operation is expected to actuate paradigm shift in the bilateral relation. Bhutan and Nepal have already border transits of goods and citizens with India; and Afghanistan, in post-Taliban phase has developed good business-friendly relation.

The enhanced integration of South Asian market, which had earlier a limited role, will expedite the movements of the citizens across the nations at a larger scale which till now has been barricaded by the governments of each country under multifarious regulations. The two aspects—the trade and the people's movements—once get speeded up will transcend the boundaries of the nations in course of time. It is of course argued by the political economists that capitalism has inbuilt tendencies for global integration and universalization of its processes. The local inner contradictions may slow down the process momentarily but in due course, it leads towards integration, inevitably. It aptly fits into South Asia as it is reflected in the recent decisions taken by the Indian government to remove the barriers for the Pakistani, Bangladeshi, Sri Lankan businesses to invest in India which was earlier restricted. The integrated South Asian market, thus, will be a better requisite for India's security as the objective of threat will loose its *locus standi* since the others get integrated with India voluntarily for their own development. The development of each becomes the premise for the collective development South Asia.

Civil Society and Citizenship

With the integration of the South Asian market, the civil society and the citizenship across the countries will inevitably get integrated with each other as the market creates the premise for their integration. In other words, the three are intrinsically linked with each other; the development of the latter two is premised on the emergence and expansion of the first. It is only after the triumph of the bourgeois society (which still faces strong economic and cultural resistance from the primordial social forces) in South Asia that the modern idea of human security will become an actuality.

In the past two decades, the quest for enlargement of security cantered around regulation of market, the modern Leviathan, expansion of civil society and establishment of global citizenship. The three issues encapsulated the search for freedom of mobility of capital, commodity and labour, the development of larger individual freedom in public sphere and codification of one global citizenship for every person. The commonality in all the three issues is their common origin from modern capitalism and their desire to enlarge civil freedom at global scale transcending all boundaries of identities. The expansion of civil society and codification of citizenship have been correspondingly dependent on the success of the market in the annihilation of traditional societies. In the process of its operation and expansion, the market breaks the traditional moorings, corrodes the traditional social relations and transforms them into the mirror image of the capitalistic social structure.

It creates the condition for social mobility and larger individual freedom. The market, thus, becomes the premise for the development of civil society and citizenship; and it is inevitably global. Or globality is in-built in its existence. In order to survive, it must expand; it must explore new areas to extend its consumer base. It must satisfy old and new product requirements and it must innovate the quality of the products. It must reduce the production cost and expand the volume of production. In the process of this development, it creates standardized attributes of products at global scale and brings uniformity in production mechanism which in turn leads to global integration of diverse market and creation of standardized living condition of people. The market thus inevitably becomes global, integrates the societies and creates uniform condition for the development of civil society and citizenship at global scale.

It is the precursor for the development of the other two. This stage has arrived for contemporary South Asia which must strive for larger civil society and global citizenship, as these are the bulwarks to build a larger democratic social structure. The onset of market society in South Asia under colonialism and subsequently under post-colonialism, set rolling a process that galvanized the people with expanding participatory base of society to seek larger development and security. In recent years, the process of its expansion has been speeded up under the aegis of globalization that has subdued every other social relations under its weight.

The expanding market—industrialization, labour mobility, commodification—has created a mass society that has subsumed the traditionalities of the past as well as has acted as a bulwark against the state coercion. The market has provided space to the citizens to pursue their own agenda and also liberalized the hierarchical relations within the state structure. The more it expands in intensity and the more it permeates into the hinterland, the more rapidly does it transform the traditional social relations into wage relations and facilitates the emergence of civil society. In fact, the mergence of civil society is intrinsically linked with the emergence of new wage relations; and more the wage relations matures in its civic functioning over the generations, more will be the freedom the individual enjoys within the social relations. This process has been speeded up in South Asia by globalizations in the past two decades by rapidly breaking up the primordialities in India and in other countries of the region thereby creating a space for the further development of civil society across the region and their probable integration as one homogenized mass.

Such developments put the existence of national identity at stake. Or in other words, its existence is the result of unfinished agenda of capitalism. The more the capitalism develops in its intensity and expands spatially, the more it integrates the people and the regions into the vortex of market with an universal cosmopolitan production relation transcending the nation and the particularistic cultural features of different localities. Or it fuses the diversities through common material culture and wage relation. In the process, the multi-culturality of the nations and their identities are transformed into a homogenized culture.

The emerging homogenized components of modern culture in South Asia reflect this trend which in course of time will facilitate national relations. In the past two decades, globalization has also provided impetus to the growth of citizenship rights and the demand for multi-national citizenship, both in terms of qualitative and quantitative expansion The mobility of the business and labour has impelled this demand which was earlier restricted to a narrow base. In other words, it means growth of trans-border rights/ visa free regimes and political civic rights for every citizen across the nation which essentially translates into growth of equal rights for citizens of every nation or the creation of equal condition for them across the borders. In South Asia, the visa free regimes are already in operation among few countries and procedures are being worked out to expand it to liberalize it throughout SAARC. Its operation will bring in paradigm shift in the relationship of SAARC countries.

To sum up, the contemporary market society has yet to transcend the realm of nation in South Asia. It has, however, propelled them to come closer to each other. An integrated South Asian market will further facilitate their proximity. It will be the best requiem of security and development.

PART II
External Security

6

Pakistan, Cross-border Terrorism and Policy Options for India

P.M. Kamath

Since its birth Pakistan has survived and continues to survive on a policy of hatred of India that had often degenerated into anti-India as the main reference point to protect and promote its national security policies. This anti-India stance was sustained and kept alive with history of partition and cross-border migration in the late 1940s. However, it was believed that younger generations born in independent Pakistan would not carry the baggage of hatred. But now Pakistan continues to instil in younger generations anti-Indian feeling as a policy creed. [1]

This is because there is nothing common binding its citizens into a national bond and to keep divergent provinces of Pakistan together as a nation. Pakistan was created as a safe haven for Muslims in British India and to escape from a permanent status as a religious minority in a Hindu dominated India after the British left. However, the common religion of Islam was not enough to keep the nation bound together is demonstrated by the linguistic nationalism that led East Pakistan to emerge as an independent nation in December 1971 with the birth of Bangladesh. [2] The founding father of Pakistan, Mohammad Ali Jinnah had not envisaged Bengal or a partitioned Bengal as a part of Pakistan. That would have made Bengali-Pakistanis living in East Pakistan, as the dominant community in the entire state. Even with a divided Bengal being the part of Pakistan had made Bengalis 56 percent of the undivided Pakistan. [3]

New Pakistan and Old Policy

Once Pakistan was divided by the separation of East Pakistan, hatred of India was compounded by the intense craving for revenge by the army against India for its humiliating defeat at the hands of Indian army. This becomes clear from the utterances of the most recent military dictator of that country–General Pervez Musharraf. He mentions in his memoirs how his best friend Bilal was killed in the December 1971 war in Bangladesh. When the cease-fire was announced and Pakistani troops had to surrender, he writes that "brave soldiers cried with me. It remains saddest and most painful day of my life." [4]

However, war as an option to settle the score was not available for important reasons like: (i) internally it took two decades for Pakistan to recover from the aftermath of impact of the Bangladesh war, (ii) there was a sense of binding nature of Shimla agreement which provided for peaceful resolution of all disputes between India and Pakistan, and (iii) by 1987 Pakistan had become a covert nuclear weapons state and it had a sense of nuclear balance with India. India conducted its Peaceful Nuclear Explosion in 1974. Emergence of the US as the sole Super Power after the disintegration of the then Soviet Union in 1991, made Pakistan as an irrelevant pawn in the geopolitical strategic balance of power, regionally and globally. After the end of the Cold War, for the US geo-economics became a vital interest with India embracing economic liberalisation, privatisation and globalisation.

Cross-border Terrorism

Thus, with the end of the Cold War in 1991 and the breakdown of Pentagonal Balance of Power that had operated in the South Asian region since 1971 and consequent effect of the US moving away from blind support to Pakistan in its conflicts with India, it was evident that in an open war-like-conflict with India, the US was unlikely to support it. Hence, it embraced promotion of terrorism as an instrument of low intensity conflict (LIC) with India as a multi-purpose instrument against it. But hatred of India and urge for revenge continues to be the dominant purposes. It is a fascinating story by itself to narrate how covertly it used terrorism, first in Punjab—to gain strategic depth as well; then in Jammu & Kashmir—to complete historic process of partition on religious basis; and later made whole of India ás an experimental theatre for its use of terrorism as a permanent instrument against India—to harm its economy in addition to all goals mentioned earlier. [5]

Policy Options for India

In the light of this unfolding story of cross-border terrorism against India, let me discuss currently available options in the backdrop of missed options, like nipping Islamic Terrorism in bud with decisive use of power. Terrorism began in J&K in 1987 and in 1989 it became more violent and widespread. If the domestic causes were addressed and those who refused to heed were brought under decisive action, Indian leadership would have won international accolades. [6]

Earlier, the Americans had set the precedent in their handling of the Black Panther Movement in the US that had begun in the late 1960s. It was viewed as a national security threat by Richard Nixon and by 1974 it became a historic event. When it was a widespread phenomenon in the 1970s, the Black Panthers were indulging in arson, bombing public buildings, looting banks, kidnapping and assassinations. The US government suspected that the Black Panthers got material and moral support from Arab and North African Countries, particularly Algeria in addition to Marxists regimes in the Caribbean and elsewhere.

Considering the Black Panther movement as a national security threat, the government empowered the FBI to infiltrate into the movement. Many people were arrested, several were shot dead in encounters, and several suspected leaders disappeared, without any trace. Those who were left out fought among themselves helping the government to eliminate themselves without government help! The rationale was described by Nixon himself in his memoirs: "When the issue juxtaposes the lives of innocent citizens, however, and the possible curtailment of personal liberties we all cherish, the answers are never easy." [7] However, Indian governments considered terrorists as "our misguided youths" as described by the then Governor of Jammu & Kashmir, General Krishna Rao and generally extended them humane treatment often at the cost of national security. [8]

There is a saying that you reap, as you sow! Since Musharraf's time and more particularly after the return of semi-democratic regime in Islamabad, whenever India has highlighted terrorist attacks promoted by Pakistan, directly or indirectly from its territory, Pakistan has also moaned the fact that they too are a victim of terrorism! Pakistan probably is not aware or glossing it over or refusing to acknowledge the fundamental difference between their being a victim of terrorism [9] and unacceptable terrorists' attacks imposed on Indian society by the Pakistan based terrorist groups! The difference is: Pakistan's terrorism is home-grown because of direct training, financing sheltering and diplomatic support. But India is victim of Pakistan promoted terrorism as an instrument of state policy.

But India has been too nice and resisted the temptation to tell them that it is not the India-based and India-promoted terrorist-groups which have caused terrorist upheavals in Pakistan, despite their trying to blame India initially, as it was done in the case of an attack on Sri Lankan team! [10] But all their sufferings from the terrorists are indigenous to Pakistani state. It is time for India to politely tell the harsh truth to Pakistani policy makers and Pakistani citizens! A Pakistani scholar recently in Calcutta said Pakistan has lost 20,000 lives so far. But all that is because of internal terrorism and not external terrorism. [11] Yet, the government of India, by its policy compulsions is forced to keep silent or not respond!

Co-operation

It's a cliché "You can choose your friends but cannot choose your neighbours." Every Indian Prime Minister has said this so many times that everyone who follows India-Pakistan relations knows it. India and Pakistan are neighbours but not friends. The question is: can two nations, at least could establish a working relationship based on mutual trust? Thus, the US as a fair weather friend of Pakistan has taken upon itself to help two nations to reduce their hostilities if not to promote friendly relations between the two. Having lost the opportunities to take decisive steps against Pakistan's promotion of cross border terrorism, before it became an overt Nuclear Weapons State, India has also been left only with one option of pleading with the US to use its leverage to restrain Pakistan!

However, all American-promoted Pakistani assurance of cooperation, Pakistan always try to make it from the date of reaching that understanding, throwing all previous assurances, agreements, understandings and treaties into dustbin of history. Thus, Musharraf agreed with A.B. Vajpayee in January 2004 to see that Pakistani territory, including territories controlled by it are not used to carry out terrorist attacks against Indian interests. But before that he just got rid of the Shimla agreement of 1972, and even the Lahore agreement between Nawaz Sharif and Vajpayee of 1999 on resolving the Kashmir problem. With Musharraf gone, all responsibilities for all previous terrorist attacks against India also vanished. But now the elected government is only concerned with 26/11—Mumbai attacks of 2008. Who knows? If Kayani or some other general assumes power, even 26/11 might go into the dust bin of history forcing India to begin to search for friendly relations with Pakistan from a clean slate!

Yet, there is a thin ray of hope for a changed approach on the part of elected Pakistani government adopting a different approach, after Americans succeeded in eliminating Osama Bin Laden who was sheltered by the Pakistani Army close to the Army's Abbottabad Training Institute. The Army has been weakened by the American action, giving a greater freedom of action to the elected government. These are a few straws in the wind.

Economic Area: Despite their being important members of SAARC, Pakistan did not extend India most favoured nation (MFN) treatment in spite of the fact that India unilaterally extended the same to Pakistan in 1996. Pakistan had linked it to India first resolving Kashmir issue. But Prime Minister Gilani, just a week before SAARC Summit meeting in Maldives, extended the MFN status to India on 2nd November 2011. After fully extending MFN status, bilateral trade is likely to cross the current level of US$ 2.6 billion since trade now going through the devious route of Dubai for over 20,000 items, can go directly with normal duties.

Newspapers have hailed it as a peace dividend! No doubt it is an important step as there is a theoretical construct which argues that improved trade and commercial relations would eventually pave the way for generally improving of bilateral political relations. But it should not be an isolated instance. There is also an instance of Pakistan being supported by India in its bid for a non-permanent seat in the UN Security Council (SC). This was acknowledged by Pakistan's envoy in the UN when he said that "India supported us in becoming a non-permanent member" of the UNSC. Indian vote was crucial in as much as only that made it minimum required number of 129.

To survive as neighbours and also to prosper, nations, like friends, need to have mutual trust. As of today whatever India may do, there is a trust deficit in the relations of these two nations. Having conferred MFN, the very next day Pakistan at the highest level of then PM, Gillani said: it was only a note prepared for the consideration of the cabinet. Hard line anti-India, *Jamaat-ud-Dawa* (JUD) leader Ameer Hamza told a massive rally in Islamabad: Gillani had called Saeed, notorious leader of the organization to inform him that Pakistan might confer MFN on India. In response, he had told him that "India can never be a most favoured nation for Pakistan." Another leader of JUD, Abdul Rehman Makki said, "If this decision is not reversed, then those who are responsible for this decision will have to get reversed." [12]

Prime Minister Manmohan Singh's characterisation of Gilani as a man of peace [13] at Maldives SAARC Summit is premature. India needs to be extremely cautious despite PM, Manmohan Singh's one point programme to go down in the history as the man who settled India-Pakistan dispute. We need to examine whether Pakistan's apparent efforts to extend cooperation is because of their current problems with the US, or is it a qualitatively different approach; a change in age old policy of Pakistan.

Need is for resolving the most crucial issue of terrorism. Terrorists, terrorist supporters and Pakistan have to realise that normal ties with India are a prerequisite for Pakistan to become a normal nation by its conscious efforts to overcome the tag of a 'failed state'. For Pakistan it is a win-win situation. What it needs to do is to affirm its resolve to wipe of its title as the epicentre of global terrorism by not pursuing selective duality: move to stop promoting Islamic terrorism in Afghanistan to prove their being an honest partner of the US in its war against terrorism, while promoting it in India. Not only that it will improve relations with India and Afghanistan but will also considerably improve its relations with the US.

As of now there is no indication that Pakistani government has been able to divest its intelligence agency, ISI to give up responsibilities of conducting terrorist attacks against India because it continues to support *Laskhar-e-Taiba, Jaish-e-Mohammad* and *Hizbul Mujahedeen*. This was confirmed by Minister of State for Home, [14] Jitendra Singh in November last year in Lok Sabha. On the other hand, terrorism has been elevated, by former Pakistani dictator, General Parvez Musharraf to the status as the first line of defence.

Conclusions

Today, Pakistan faces severe problem of internal terrorism; but it continues to promote terrorism against India. On the face it, the question is: Will Pakistan survive as one nation? There is a Global Futures Assessment Report prepared jointly by the CIA and National Intelligence Council (NIC) in 2005 which forecasts "Yugoslavia like fate" for Pakistan" by 2015. It is not that all forecasts of American intelligence agencies come true. But in case it comes true, unlike in the past I would not say that it is in the interest of Indian security that Pakistan remains one united country. Hence, in case Pakistan refuses to change its behaviour, and continues to carry out directly or through proxies a terrorist war against India, India might do well to support the disintegration of Pakistan. In a worst case scenario, it must keep the option of welcoming the disintegration of Pakistan.

What are the gains and losses of such a scenario? India has a common border with West Punjab and Sindh. Sindh was very much a part of India during pre-independence times. But as an independent state after the break up of Pakistan with a natural harbour, it can prosper even faster. If Sindh becomes independent, other provinces will be required to seek the cooperation of Sindh for their maritime trade and commerce. Baluchistan and North West Frontier Province (NWFP) do not have common borders with India. Historically, NWFP and Baluchistan had cordial relations with India during pre-independence days, as we had good relations with Afghanistan then as now. These two are likely to continue to maintain good relations with India. Baluchistan and NWFP, as a matter of fact, never wanted to be independent of India. Even now Pakistan faces internal revolt in Baluchistan, which demands for independence. It is only Punjab that has been the epicentre of all problems, including terrorism. The Army is dominated by Punjabis. At least a weakened Punjab would have limited capabilities to harm Indian interests.

In the light of our experiences with this neighbour, if

fragmented, West Punjab as Pakistan cannot do more harm or cause more problems than it is causing now.

For a long time Indian political thinkers as well as Americans have held a view that a united Pakistan is in the larger interests of India. Stephen Cohen, an expert on Pakistan, for instance believes in it. He said in Mumbai that, "a stable government in Pakistan is in India's best interests. You can't rejoice when your neighbour's house is on fire." [15] I also held a similar view. But this can be considered only if he neighbour is a well-wisher and a friend. But if he has been a constant trouble-maker, I will have no regrets if my neighbour's house is burnt fully.

End Notes

1. Pakistani students visiting Mumbai reportedly said, "We were trained to hate India", *Hindustan Times* (Mumbai) 24th November 2011.
2. In first ever truly democratic elections for National Assembly held in December 1970, the Awami League of East Pakistan won 167 seats out of 169 claiming to emancipate Bengali people while the Pakistan's People's Party captured a majority of 88 seats out of 144 in West Pakistan. Despite a common religion, PPP refused to permit Awami League to rule undivided Pakistan. See Aditi Juvekar, *Partners in Conflict–Perceptions and Realities of Indo-US Relations* (Mumbai: Himalaya Publishing House, 1997), pp. 58-61.
3. Bruce Riedel, *Deadly Embrace: Pakistan, America and the Future of the Global Jihad* (Washington, DC: Brookings Institution's Press, 2011), p. 6.
4. See Pervez Musharraf, *In the line of Fire: A memoir* (New York: Free Press, 2006), p. 545.
5. Satyabrata Pal "Engaging Pakistan," India Quarterly: A Journal of International Affairs Vol. 4 (October/December 2009, http://iqq.sagepub.com/content/65/4/361.abstract.
6. P.M. Kamath, "India is not fighting a war in Kashmir," *The Sunday Times Review,* 5 February 1995. Drawing a parallel between insurgency in Kashmir and the Black Panther movement in America, I had suggested decisive steps to nip the problem in bud at the early stage since terrorists "surrender their

rights the moment they take recourse to violence against civil society and the state".

7. *R.N.:Memoirs of Richard Nixon* (London: Sidgwick and Jackson, 1978), p. 476.
8. Kamath, "India is not fighting a war in Kashmir".
9. Latest Pakistani to express this view on Indian soil is Pakistani Foreign Secretary , Jalil Abbas Jilani during Secretary level talks in New Delhi When he described terrorism as a common enemy, neither side would benefit by pointing a finger at the other. See *The Times of India* (Mumbai) 6th July 2012.
10. http://uk.reuters.com/article/2009/03/03/pakistan-srilanka-shooting-blame-idUKISL6347320090303.
11. At an International Seminar organized by Malulana Abul Kalam Azad Institute of Asian Studies on March 2012.
12. *The Indian Express* (Mumbai) 25th November 2011.
13. *The Times of India* (Mumbai).
14. *Times of India* (Mumbai) 24th November 2011.
15. Hindustan Times (Mumbai) 9th October 2010.

7

Af-Pak Policy: Implications for India

Josukutty C.A.

Af-Pak is a precarious region with unpredictable and threatening portents for the entire world. It has been a theatre of internal turmoil caused mostly by external interventions. The Af-Pak policy is President Osama's signature policy initiative born out of the predicament in which the United States finds itself in Afghanistan. The key features of the policy such as centrality of Pakistan in fighting terrorism and integration of and reconciliation with Taliban undermines the geo-political and historical undercurrents of the region. Negotiations with Taliban had accorded to it the much needed legitimacy to be the heir apparent to the current regime. In fact, the policy is an exit strategy for the US out of the complex quagmire. In the process, it gives a silent burial to all the lofty principles of democracy and nation-building and let loose the forces of ethnic conflicts and religious fanaticism in Afghanistan. This places India in a precarious position with serious security implications particularly in the context of Afghanistan as a factor in its hostile relationship with Pakistan.

Introduction

Afghanistan evolved out of the crucible of internal turmoil caused by external intervention and continues to be so. Strategically located at the transit corridor of Central Asia, South Asia and Middle East, Afghanistan has been exposed to big power politics and rivalries. In modern times, the Anglo-Afghan wars in the late 19th and early 20th centuries left an indelible mark in the internal and external politics of Afghanistan. Since then it has been divided on ethnic lines with unsettled borders. [1] The fratricidal division of the Indian sub-continent into India and Pakistan in 1947 added a new and dangerous geo-political dimension to the politics of the region. It became a contentious terrain in the historically rooted, ideologically justified and strategically sustained animosity between India and Pakistan.

The power struggle and competition between the two rekindled ethnic rivalries and Islamic radicalism. It was further refuelled by the Soviet intervention of 1979 and the resistance to it under the leadership of the US, assisted by Pakistan and Saudi Arabia. The present state of affairs is a direct result of that historicity and the subsequent developments that took place in the country. The Soviet involvement ended with the near total devastation of the country–politically, economically, and administratively. The withdrawal of the USSR and the US [2] in the 1980s plunged the country into unprecedented ethnic hostilities and civil wars among militia commanders, war lords, ethnic chieftains, Islamic fundamentalists and drug barons. In the midst of the ambiguity and anarchy that persisted, Taliban assumed power in 1996 with the strong backing of the Pakistan military and the ISI.

Under Taliban, the conflict-ridden trajectory of Afghanistan continued with massive human rights violations and practices of radical political Islam. Afghanistan came under the spell of Pakistan which began to use it as strategic asset against India especially by evoking Islam. Kashmir in India became a common target for the Islamic terrorists from across the border. Afghanistan became the epicentre of international terrorism of the Islamic variety, which culminated in the 9/11 attack on the World Trade Center. The 2001 US intervention in Afghanistan was widely acclaimed as an effort to put things right. But killings and bloodshed continued unabated. The United States has been under increasing pressure from different quarters, domestic as well as international, to find a way out of the quagmire and the answer was the Af-Pak policy announced in March 2009.

The policy has grave security implications for India. Afghanistan's geo-political and strategic location, the presence of an ideology antithetical to democracy and secularism and, the all-weather hostility between India and Pakistan make the context all the more complex. The Af-Pak policy and the scheduled withdrawal of US forces in 2014 raises number of pertinent questions for India and the region.

What are the implications of the policy for India? What does it hold for the future of the region? How would Afghanistan factor in the regional power rivalries between India and Pakistan? The paper attempts to answer these questions in the backdrop of the geo-politics of the region and in the process examines the features and implications of the Af-Pak policy for India and the region.

India and Af-Pak: A Geo-political Backdrop

India and Afghanistan share time-tested historical, cultural and political connections marked by myriad complexities. It has-been a relationship characterised by political conflicts, cultural and civilisation linkages and security anxieties. Significant to the context, from the dawn of the history of India, the Afghan plateau has been a spring board to the conquest and attack of India by invaders and raiders starting from the Indo-Aryan tribes in 1500 BC, to the Mughals in the modern period to the Mujahideen in contemporary times. (Walport, 2010:54) In all those predatory endeavours from the West of India, Islam was a major factor in terms of the motivation and identity of the conqueror and the subjugation and sufferings of the conquered who went through the trauma of conversion of faith and practice. This paved the way for future societal divisions on religious lines between the Hindus and Muslims.

The entry of Britain into the geo-politics of the region in the 18th century as the dominant player further sharpened the existing rivalries and added new dimensions to cultural interactions among divergent civilisational ethos. (Khosla,

2003:118) This schism gradually grew into the 'master cleavage' [3] not only in India's societal realm but also in its relationship with Pakistan. In the first half of the 20th century, both India and Afghanistan, as victims of colonial rule, had common grievances against the continuation of British reign in the sub-continent. After the departure of the Britishers, India's decision not to support the Afghan demand for revision of the Durand line-the border between Pakistan and Afghanistan-rendered bleak the prospects of close proximity between India and Afghanistan.

However, there was a functional and incident free relationship between the two during the days of Cold War. Not only that, the relationship between India and Afghanistan was better in many respects than it was between Pakistan and Afghanistan. Unlike Pakistan, Afghanistan did not join any of the security treaties like SEATO and CENTO sponsored by the US, but followed a policy of non-alignment, more in agreement with the Indian line of thinking, much to the chagrin of its immediate neighbour Pakistan.

In 1979, India was the first non-communist country to recognise the Soviet sponsored government in Afghanistan. It was a decision influenced more by India's relationship with Soviet Union than by neighbourhood strategic and security considerations. Thereafter, India had good relations with successive governments in Afghanistan till 1992. The capture of power in Afghanistan by Taliban in 1996 marked a fundamental turn in the relationship. The Taliban takeover enabled Pakistan to consolidate and tighten its hold over the military and political establishment in Afghanistan to the disadvantage of India. The Taliban dominated period from 1996 to 2001 is considered as Pakistan's best time in Afghanistan against India.

Gradually, political and cultural contradictions crept into the relationship. Democratic and secular values, cultural and civilizational ethos, and diametrically opposed political and security considerations became factors in the contours of the relationship. Afghanistan became more than a willing collaborator in all the anti-India activities spearheaded by Pakistan. Taliban became an instrument of terrorism against India. Afghan trained religious radicals became holy warriors to liberate Kashmir from the so called Indian yoke. This was, in a way, the result of the transformation of Kabul from a 'buffer state' of 18th and 19th centuries to the terrorists `safe haven' of the 21st century.

Afghan Factor in Indo-Pak Relationship

India's relationship with Pakistan since 1947 has been characterised by distrust, animosities reminiscent of predatory raiders of the past, ideological differences in terms of secularism and nation building, frequent border clashes and wars, terror strikes and anti-national activities against each other, blame games at all available forums and, above all, the dispute over Kashmir. This inherent hostility permeated into the realms of their relationship with adjoining countries. It was more so with Afghanistan for its strategic location and religious identity with Pakistan which prompted Robert D. Kaplanto remark, "Afghanistan has been a prize that Pakistan and India have fought over directly and indirectly for decades". (Kaplan, 2009) Good relationship between India and Afghanistan has been a matter of worry to Pakistan and vice-versa. Pakistan always wanted Afghanistan to be a vassal state in its strategic planning against India. A major goal of its policy has been to minimise India's role and presence in Afghanistan and to use Afghanistan as an asset in providing strategic depth in the event of wider conflict with India. (Weinbaum, 2008:26) It was reflective of the contradictions and conflicting-strategic interest both the countries wanted to promote in Afghanistan.

India and Pakistan never had good relationship with Afghanistan simultaneously. It was either under Indian or Pakistani influence to the embarrassment and strategic disadvantage of the other. From 1947 to the early 1990s, when

India had good relationship with Afghanistan, Pak-Afghan relationship was characterised by hostility over the Durand line and Pashtun nationalism. During the Taliban dominated period (since the 1990s), New Delhi had provided assistance to the anti-Taliban resistance-the Northern Alliance, comprising mostly of Tajik and other non-Pashtun ethnic groups. Pakistan supported the anti-Soviet Mujahideen and then the Taliban to ensure that in the event of conflict with India, Afghanistan would provide Pakistan with support and use of its land and air space if needed. (Bajoria, 2009) [4] Successive rulers in Pakistan, despite the conciliatory attitude adopted by the rulers of Afghan, had engaged in proxy operations to get a lasting stake in the affairs of its western neighbour. Big power involvement and civil war in Afghanistan provided the perfect setting for the continuation of the proxy war.

Pakistan took advantage of the civil war and disorder that prevailed in Afghanistan in two ways. One, it created the impression that it was working for a stable and prosperous Afghan, and two, it deliberately cultivated a jihadist culture. That is at the official level it strived to promote stability in Afghanistan. But at a clandestine level, it followed a policy that undermined the official policy by promoting Islamic insurgency and ethnic conflicts. Marvin and Jonathan call it Pakistan's two-track foreign policy towards Afghanistan. (Weinbaum, 2008:26) Gradually not only Afghanistan, but Pakistan too became a fertile breeding ground for thousands of terrorists of myriad varieties. They were trained militarily and indoctrinated in perverted Islamic ideology to fight India in Kashmir and elsewhere. Pakistan considers clandestine support for the Taliban and Haqqani Network—an independent group moving between Pakistan and Afghanistan with close Taliban ties—as a means of securing an Afghanistan that is ultimately friendlier to Pakistan. (Taylor, 2011)

The final outcome was the consolidation of Taliban and Al-Qaidain the political landscape of the Af-Pak region. The Taliban were fashioned as a military and political force by

Pakistan for the purpose of ensuring a client government in Afghanistan to serve its strategic interest vis-à-vis India. (Ayoob, 2002:5) It was a "hedging strategy" used by Pakistan to gain "strategic depth" in the region, because Indian influence particularly, is a "neuralgic issue" for Pakistan in Afghanistan. (Ayoob) Of particular significance was the use of Islam as a strategic weapon against India through the Taliban to foment and accelerate jihad terrorist activities in the Indian side of Kashmir. The Taliban was more than happy to send its warriors to Kashmir to fight Pak's proxy war against India. Two objectives are served by this policy—one, deny India military and political influence in Afghanistan and, two, ensure that the government in Kabul would not incite Pakistani Pashtuns to secede. Pakistan considers Taliban rule as a bulwark against foreign influence in Afghanistan. These foreign influences include Iran, Russia and Central Asian nations, who all supported the Northern Alliance in the late 1990s. But it primarily means that India, according to Pakistan is trying to encircle it.

It is also argued that Pakistan supports the Taliban and other jihadist groups as a method to channel its own domestic cocktail of frustration, anger and extremism, all fed by grinding poverty, poor education, a dysfunctional political system and an army of radical preachers that have filled the country's yawning social void. This is outlined in a U.S. intelligence assessment revealed by Wiki Leaksas follows: "Urging militant groups to be outwardly focused is perceived by Pakistani officials as a method to safeguard internal security". (Smith, 2011) By fostering the sense of an impending threat from foreign infidels, it manages its internal contradiction of development and welfare of people. This was truer in its relationship with India than with any other country.

Post-Taliban Phase

The 9/11 attack on the World Trade Center and the subsequent US intervention in Afghanistan further complicated the Indo-Pak power game in Afghanistan. Pakistan joined the US in the fight against terrorism under duress. It had to disown the Taliban hitherto patronised by the ISI and the Army. Pakistan was confronted with a classic case of dilemma in delicately balancing its strategic interests in the region and the compulsions of international commitments to fight terrorism.

The heart of Pak dilemma in Afghanistan is the India factor. The primary condition that Pakistan raised before joining the global fight against terrorism in Afghanistan was the threat factor in its Eastern border with India. Time and again Pakistan reiterated that India is its threat number one and not Taliban or Al-Qaeda. The President of Pakistan in his address to the nation on September 20, 2001 anxiously remarked, "Pakistan is facing an extremely delicate situation; and in my opinion, it is the most delicate phase since 1971. [5] At this moment our decisions may have far reaching and wide repercussions...Our critical concerns may be harmed...I mean that our nuclear strength and our Kashmir cause may be harmed". (Patnaik, 2007:152) He was making this statement keeping in mind the security challenges and the possible loss of a strategic asset in Taliban against India.

To avoid losing the strategic advantage, Pakistan devised a new two-track policy in fighting terrorism keeping in mind the India factor. On the one hand, they have been fighting terrorism along with the international community and on the other hand, supporting and promoting the same terrorists whom they have been fighting. It played the two-track policy so effectively that most of the Taliban and Al-Qaeda leadership was given refuge in Pakistan when Kabul was occupied by the US. As part of the policy, on a number of occasions, Pakistan, did not share critical information with the US regarding the activities of the Taliban and Al-Qaeda. The Americans could not do much on this as they had limited options and were trying to negotiate directly with Taliban by excluding Pakistan. (Jacob, 2009:143-44)

The two track policy is central to Pakistan's strategic

calculus in Afghanistan for two reasons. One, it would ensure an Afghanistan dominated by Taliban devoid of US influence in future. Two, it would make Pakistan a permanent strategic ally of the US infighting terrorists in the Af-Pak region. This has two obvious advantages for Pakistan: one, continued military and financial assistance from the US and two, the perennial strategic significance of Pakistan in the eyes of the US. Incidents such as the killing of Osama Bin Laden in Pakistan's military vicinity, the clandestine relationship between Haqanni network and the Isotope attempts by Pakistan to destabilise the dialogue process in Afghanistan, unilateral and arbitrary military actions such as drone attacks by the US and the killing of Pakistan soldiers in the border check point by the ISAF, have not reduced the strategic significance of Pakistan.

There are two main reasons for this strategic alliance. One, traditional clandestine links between Pakistan and the Taliban-linked Haqqani network, one of the deadliest factions in Afghanistan. (Nauman, 2012) Two, the need for Pakistani land routes to transit supplies into Afghanistan, which prior to their closure, accounted for almost a third of all NATO cargo to Afghanistan. The strategic limitations of the US in fighting terrorism in the region and its excessive dependence on Pakistan has given it the temerity to play double games.

In the post-Taliban Afghanistan, Indian has been gaining its lost ground through a number of steps. The Government in Afghanistan has tremendous amount of good will for India. It has been playing an active role in the economic, political and military reconstruction of Afghanistan. Since 2001, India has offered US$ 1.2 billion for Afghanistan's reconstruction, making it the largest regional donor to the country. In May 2011, India made a fresh commitment of US$ 500 million for Afghanistan's development.

There are frequent high level official visits to both the countries. Afghan President Hamid Karzai has made four official visits to India since 2001. A Preferential Trade

Agreement was signed between the two countries in March 2003 to boost bilateral trade. India is a major player in infrastructure development and in administrative and humanitarian training and institution building. In January 2009, India completed construction of the Zaranj-Delaram highway in southwest Afghanistan near the Iranian border; it is building Afghanistan's new parliament building, it is constructing the Salma Dam power project in Herat Province; it has trained Afghan police officers, diplomats and civil servants; and it has provided support in the areas of health, education, transportation, power, and telecommunications. India has opened consulates offices in Herat, Mazar-e-Sharif, Jalalabad, and Kandahar, cities close to Afghan border and provides military equipment and personnel training. India has built an air base in Farkhor, Tajikistan, to deal with increasing incidents of kidnappings and attacks. India's mountain-trained paramilitary forces are stationed in Afghanistan to guard its workers in various cities. A cumulative effective of all these developments is that Pakistan feels encircled by India.

The death of Osama bin Laden has generated renewed interest in India's trajectory in Afghanistan. New Delhi and Kabul have decided on a new "strategic partnership" in October 2011 that entail cooperation in security, law enforcement and justice, including an enhanced focus on co-operation in the fight against international terrorism, organized crime, illegal narcotics, trafficking and money laundering. This is the result of growing fundamental convergence between India and the US, both of whom now view Pakistan as the source of insecurity in the region. There is a genuine recognition that the borderlands between Pakistan and Afghanistan constitute the greatest threat to regional peace and security, that Islamabad is part of the problem rather than the solution, that India has a greater role to manage the Afghanistan-Pakistan region and that the US has made significant departures from its traditional posture toward South Asia. (Pant, 2011)

India's engagement with Afghanistan is driven not only by the determination to minimise Pakistan's influence in Afghanistan and ensure that Afghanistan does not become a source of terrorism against India but also long-term geo-economic interests including peace and security in the region. India's growing proximity with Afghanistan is cited by Pakistan as reason for increase in extremist's movement and instability in the province of Baluchistan. (Zeb, 2006:69-74) Pakistan considers that the best way to counter India's influence in Afghanistan is to support Taliban and scuttle all peace initiates there including the ones under the Af-Pak policy. There are evidences galore that Pakistan's military intelligence agency, the ISI, is responsible for attacks on Indian personnel and assets in Afghanistan. Pakistan does not want an Afghan National Security Force trained by India and dominated by the Northern Alliance. What it wants is a chaotic and anarchic Afghan where it can take charge of its security minus any role for India.

Af-Pak Policy: Features and Implications

The Af-Pak policy is Obama's signature foreign policy initiative to cope up with new ground realities in the terror battle fields of Afghanistan. (Cooper, 2009) [6] The US President Barack Obama categorically stated in his Af-Pak policy speech in March 2009, "I want the American people to understand that we have a clear and focused goal to disrupt, dismantle and defeat Al Qaeda in Pakistan and Afghanistan, and to prevent their return to either country in the future. That's the goal that must be achieved". (Luiza, 2009) President Obama further stated that the U.S. mission in Afghanistan is about 'making sure that Al-Qaeda cannot attack the U.S. homeland and US interests and our allies' or 'project violence against' American citizens. (Mueller, 2009) In an internal meeting in March 2009, all of President Obama's advisers agreed that the primary goal in the region should be narrow—taking aim at Al-Qaeda, as opposed to the vast attempt at nation-building the Bush administration had sought in Iraq. (Cooper) On October 22, 2009, the National Security Council produced what one official called a "consensus memo," concluding that the United States should focus on diminishing the Taliban insurgency but not destroying it; building up certain critical ministries; and transferring authority to Afghan security forces. (Baker, 2009)

The decision to create and train an Afghan National Army and police and hand over the primary responsibility to carry out counterinsurgency operations to them, the additional US troops send as a part of the new policy, which has been focusing more and more on training and non-combatant operations with limited role in direct combat operations and the economic and military aid to Pakistan have been part of this strategy aimed at an early withdrawal and reduction in US causalities. In fact, the Af-Pak policy is comprehensive security strategy for an early exit of US forces from Afghanistan.

This exit strategy worries India at two levels: One, the centrality of Pakistan in the entire scheme of things; Two, the plan for reconciliation and integration with 'moderate Taliban' and the reliance on local militia in the stabilization process in Afghanistan. There is no role for India in the plan and least attention is paid to democracy and institution building in Afghanistan. The centrality of Pakistan in finding a solution to the Afghan imbroglio is tantamount to validating the Pak argument that there is a link between Afghanistan and the unsettled relationship between India and Pakistan over Kashmir. This would enable Pakistan to use Taliban and Afghanistan as a 'strategic asset' against India. The dependence on local militia and reconciliation with the Taliban will trigger ethnic violence and undermine democracy and nation building in Afghanistan. The Af-Pak policy would facilitate the easy transformation of Afghanistan as the source and centre of anti-India activities.

Centrality of Pakistan

The Af-Pak policy emphasises the centrality of Pakistan infighting terrorism in the region. The very nomenclature 'Af-Pak' points to the fact that Af-Pak region remains the epicentre of violent extremism and the US sees it as 'as a common, interrelated problem'. (Ghosh, 2009) The comprehensive aid package under which the US promised US$ 1.5 billion in 2009 indirect support to Pakistan every year over the next five years is borne out of the realisation that Pakistan is the focal point of terrorism and it is the key to fighting terrorism in Afghanistan. The US strongly believes that without support from Pakistan it is impossible to clear out the safe havens of Al-Qaeda and other terror groups in Waziristan and Baluchistan. The US policy in Afghanistan, to be effective, must work in concert with and not in opposition to Pakistan's interests. Instead of seeking to marginalize or even eliminate the Taliban in Afghanistan, the United States and NATO should adopt a political strategy that ensures that the Taliban—and in turn Pakistan have a political voice in Afghanistan's future.

Pakistan as the key player in fighting terrorism in the region has serious implications for India. Its policy towards Taliban is steered by its antagonistic relationship with India. The Af-Pak policy recognizes the link between Afghanistan and the unsettled relationship between India and Pakistan on Kashmir. (Varadarajan, 2009) A state of permanent tension in the LOC between India and Pakistanis projected by the latter as the major hurdle for constructive action against the terrorists in the Af-Pak border region. The problem is that Pakistan worries more about its threat from India than from extremists from within and around its borders. That obsession has been driving Pakistan to support the Taliban to control Afghanistan as part of its strategic compulsions vis-à-vis India. Pakistan fights the Taliban who attack it, but nurtures the Taliban who want to control Afghanistan and fight India.

As per the Af-Pak policy, India's increasing influence in Afghanistan will have an adverse impact on the fight against terrorism. General McChrystal in his Commanders' Initial Assessment Report in 2008 said that India's rising influence in Afghan is likely to 'exacerbate regional tensions' and Pakistan is likely to take countermeasures. (McChrystal, 2009:19) That is why Indian embassy, workers, engineers etc. have been the targets of frequent terror strikes. Pakistan considers India not an immediate neighbour of Afghanistan and therefore, should have only a limited role in that country. This has been the Pak strategy vis-à-vis India even before the launch of Af-Pak policy. This is in conformity with the Pak line of promoting fundamentalists groups within Pakistan as a security shield vis-à-vis- India. Pakistani military's well established link between terrorists within and beyond its border, particular in Afghanistan is of particular security significance to India. Pakistan has been using its extended religious identity with Afghanistan to sharpen the ideological battle against India. The Af-Pak policy provides a perfect setting for Pakistan to play its two-track policy.

The large quantum of financial and military aid to Pakistan from the US to fight terrorism, as part of the Af-Pak policy, would fall into the hands of terrorists headquartered in Pakistan fighting against India in Kashmir. In future this would be the most serious issue for the region to deal with. There can be no end to terrorism in the region without clearing all terrorist safe havens in Pakistan whether they are directed against India or Afghanistan or Pakistan. The Af-Pak policy undermines this very possibility.

Pakistan has consistently followed a policy of sharpening the divisions within the Afghan society, in an attempt to weaken Afghan nationalism through socio-political fragmentation. (Khosla, 2008) It always wanted a weak, divided and troubled Afghanistan on religious and tribal lines. A weak and divided Afghanistan would be unfriendly and disconnected to India. This not only gives strategic depth to Pakistan against India but also keeps buried, the issues of Durand line and Pashtun nationalism—the two major irritants in the relationship between Afghanistan and Pakistan since long. An unsettled Afghanistan would always make available a large pool of battle-tested terrorists for 'holy war' in Jammu and Kashmir as also elsewhere in India. Therefore, Pakistan would make every effort to scuttle the prospects of a stable Afghanistan. The Af-Pak policy gives sufficient room for Pakistan to manoeuvre its plan for keeping India away from Afghanistan.

The centrality of Pakistan has facilitated a fundamental disconnect between US and Indian interests in Afghanistan. America's side lining of Indian interests and its intent on exiting Afghanistan and a quick solution has signalled to India's adversaries that they can shape the post-American landscape to serve their own ends. (Pant, 2011) While actively discouraging India from assuming a higher profile in Afghanistan for fear of offending Pakistan, the US has failed to persuade Pakistan to take Indian concerns more seriously. Pakistan wants to make Afghanistan the kind of proprietary hinterland for Pakistan, free of Indian and other outside influence, that it was from 1992-2001.

Reconciliation with Taliban

The Af-Pak policy envisages reconciliation with moderate Taliban. The US hopes to drive a wedge between what President Obama describes as 'uncompromising' Taliban and Al-Qaeda leaders on the one hand, and less implacable insurgents who may be more inclined, for the right price, to make a deal with Western forces or the Afghan government on the other hand. (Ghosh) It is a plan to reintegrate the rank and file Taliban fighters in to the political mainstream of Afghanistan.

The accommodation plan is a two-track programme. One is reintegration of fighters to entice the Taliban's rank-and-file fighters to lay down their weapons and re-join Afghan society. The core of this policy is a vast jobs programme (induction into local police force), security guarantee, and amnesty for the

Taliban fighters. (Rod, 2010) The argument is that there are lots of low-ranking Taliban foot soldiers within Afghanistan who are fighting essentially for the money and who really don't care about the ideologies. If better incentives are offered, there is no reason why they are going to be committed unto death against the Taliban, per se. (Biddle, 2009)

The other track is reconciliation, a far more diplomatically charged and complex endeavour. Its goal is to bring Taliban leaders, most of them now in Pakistan, back to Afghanistan and allow them to play a political role. In exchange, both rank-and-file Taliban fighters and leaders would have to pledge to renounce violence, separate completely and permanently from Al-Qaeda and accept the Afghan constitution. (Rubin, 2010) The Plan also includes turning some of the tribes as potentially their best hope for success against the resurgent Taliban. And, by so doing, Afghan tribal society can be reinvigorated. In January 2010, the leaders of the Shinwari tribe in Eastern Afghanistan agreed to work with the government and forbid co-operation with the Taliban. The pact was announced as a major first step for the American effort to win over the tribes. (Khapalwak, 2010)

The policy of integration of and reconciliation with the Taliban is fraught with dangers, especially for India. First of all, it is against the consensus built by the international community to focus on institution building, demobilization of existing militia, and the recreation of a stable and democratic Afghanistan. (Chellaney, 2009) Another basic promise was to free its people from despotic Islamic rule. Both these promises remain unfulfilled and the US is spearheading an effort to make peace with the Islamists. (Swami, 2012) Obama, before becoming the US President, was an ardent advocate of the need for building a just, secure and democratic Afghanistan. (Obama, 2007)

The Af-Pak policy has given a silent burial to these concerns. Any role for the radicals in the running of the country will undermine democracy and nation building in the long run. Secondly, there is no difference between moderate Taliban and extreme Taliban. Distinction between moderate and extreme would fan ethnic polarization in Afghanistan. Any attempt by the moderate Taliban to genuinely collaborate in the stabilization of Afghanistan is likely to be sabotaged by the hardliners. The assassinations of former Afghan President Barhanuddin Rabbani and Maulvi Arsala Rahmani of Afghanistan's High Peace Council are indicative of the dim future that lies ahead. [7] The British and Soviet experience shave proved that no strategy that relied on tribal or religious groups have succeeded in establishing peace and stability in Afghanistan. This is a clear departure from the 2010 National Security Strategy, of the US, which emphasized in no uncertain terms the need to deny Al-Qaeda a safe haven, deny the Taliban the ability to overthrow the government, in Afghanistan. (President of the United States, 2010) The same Taliban is all set to form the government in Afghanistan in 2014.

Setting up more militias in the name of Afghan Public Protection Force in a country already swarming with militiamen will undermine the existing Afghan army and will trigger more violence. (Chellaney, 2009) The local militias and tribal chiefs are notorious for their shifting loyalties and reluctance to any central national authority. It would be a repeat of the creation and funding of 'mujahideen' in the 1980s and would pave the way for the comeback of religious radicals. Moreover, Taliban continues to be conservative and obscurantist. They are opposed to democracy and modernity. They are driven by political Islam and nurse the ambition to convert Afghanistan and the neighbouring region into a Modern Caliphate.

The integration and reconciliation policy is a double disadvantage for India. One, it will reinstate the religious radicals to the seat of power in Afghanistan. [8] Two, in such a scenario Pakistan would have a definite say in the affairs of Afghanistan to the detriment of India. It will provide leverage to separatism in Jammu and Kashmir. The Taliban and Al-Qaeda combine have close links with terrorist groups like Maulana Abdul Wahid Kashmiri's Lashkar-e-Taiba, and Masood Azhar's Jaish-e-Mohammed that have been particularly active in India and whose main aim is to integrate Jammu and Kashmir with Pakistan. (Lambah, 2009)

Af-Pak Policy: A Mid-way Balance Sheet

A mid-way evaluation of the Af-Pak policy shows that it has not achieved any of its declared objectives and the future looks uncertain and complex. Pakistan as the key player in the fight against terrorism has turned out to be an utter failure. Pakistan's double standards in fighting terrorism is a result of both its domestic compulsions and its nefarious designs to derive maximum political and strategic mileage from the current imbroglio. From a strategic partner and reliable ally of the US Pakistan is proving to be the biggest stumbling block for a solution in Afghanistan. The fact that the current and former military figures in Pakistan maintained close ties with the Taliban undoubtedly were true and that it had no hope of meaningfully dividing the Taliban (Friedman, 2012) speaks about a basic misjudgement of the Af-Pak policy. Still Pakistan continues to be the key factor in the fight against terrorism in the region. Any negotiations with Taliban, without Pakistani involvement are meaningless. The establishment of a two-tier joint commission, in April 2011, that gave the Pakistani military a formal role in reconciliation talks between Kabul and Pakistan-based insurgents proves beyond doubt the continuing relevance of Pakistan in the Af-Pak scheme. (Pant, 2011)

The efforts towards integration of and reconciliation with the Taliban have reached nowhere. The very decision to negotiate with the Taliban has given them the much needed legitimacy. The plan to differentiate between moderate and extremists Taliban, split them politically and conduct factional negotiations has not succeeded. The US is unilaterally negotiating with all kinds of Taliban which includes both good and bad Taliban. The emergence of Yusuf al-Qaradawi, a Doha based Islamist scholar, as a key negotiator proves India's fears that jihadi groups like Lashkar-e-Taiba and Jaish-e-Mohammad would find new sanctuaries in a future Afghan regime that includes the Taliban. (Swami, 2011) [9]

The practical exclusion of Afghan government from negotiations, under pressure from the Taliban, is to secure a dominant position for them once the US leaves. In fact, the so called reconciliation remains limited to a negotiation between two hostile militaries, the Taliban and the US with Karzai seeking a parallel negotiation to secure his own position. The process fails to offer the framework for a sustainable peace that addresses the deep-rooted political and social grievances under girding the conflict. (Qazi, 2012) This challenges the establishment of a plural society in Afghanistan as negotiations exclude other ethnic groups. Also the US is forced to agree to more concessions to the Taliban in the background of the US Marines urinating on Taliban corpses, the Quran burning, and various violent episodes in which a large number of Afghan civilians were killed.

According to Peter Bergen, CNN's national security analyst, negotiations with Taliban may not be fruitful as Mullah Omar, the Taliban leader, is a rigid and fanatic leader who stands for a hard line Islamic government. (Bergen, 2011) Another difficulty is that there are many Talibans from the Quetta Shura in southern Afghanistan, to the Haqqani Network in the east, as well as smaller insurgent groups, such as Gulbuddin Hekmatyar's Hezb-e-Islami in the North-East, Making peace and settlement with all of them is just impossible. Pakistan's inclination for a veto in any kind of negotiation is another problem. Other key players such as the former leaders of the largely Tajik and Uzbek Northern Alliance who are not going to make any undue concession to the Taliban in terms of power or territory, have made negotiation further complicated. All these obstacles to negotiation are the result of Taliban's intransigence for its dominant role in any future arrangement in Afghanistan.

Another interesting argument is that the reconciliation is accommodation of 'anti-modern' and non 'anti-Western' Islamist forces. This is a reiteration of the US tried and tested policy in the Middle-East with Saudi Arabia and others, being enacted in Afghanistan—this time with the religious authoritarian regime for stability in the volatile Af-Pak region. (Swami, 2011) The new strategic partnership agreement between the US and Afghanistan in May 2012, which provides for long-term American military presence in Afghanistan, is a step in this direction. At its core, there conciliation is for a power sharing agreement in the days ahead. The US is making its position safe irrespective of the fact that, in the process, it is giving a silent burial to democracy, and nation building in Afghanistan.

The Afghan National Army and its role as per the Af-Pak policy have serious limitations. The national army is regarded as an army of Tajiks, Uzbeks and Hazaras the old Northern Alliance that battled the Pashtuns throughout the 1990s. The Afghan national government does not have the support of a large segment of its population, the Pashtuns. There is every chance that the forces will be effectively infiltrated by the Taliban and in course would be made ineffective as Taliban would not agree to a situation where they have only a secondary role in the ensuing administration. And, above all, Afghanistan's economy cannot support a large national government with a huge army. (Zakaria, 2011) [10] The conflicting loyalties within the army itself will become a major source of tension and strife in the region.

The real factor that strengthens the Taliban is the fact that the US is ambivalent about the war. According to Stephen Biddle, Senior Fellow for Defense Policy at the Council of Foreign Relations, President Obama believes that the United States has a real but limited interest and stake in Afghanistan and so wants to leave Afghan according to the calendar rather than the situation on the ground. What is certain is that there will be war in Afghan for the different forces to wage once the US leaves. The negotiations are only a steppingstone to that war which is writ large in the body politic of Afghanistan.

The only thing that is moving ahead as per the policy is the troop's drawdown by 2014-end. All other objectives are conveniently ignored mainly because there is a growing belief in the U.S. that the mission in Afghanistan has reached the point of diminishing returns. (Amin, 2012) Added to this is the complex and difficult nature of the problem. As the final moment of drawdown approaches, neither Washington nor Kabul is paying enough attention to long-term development. General distrust, suspicion and hate are the order of the day in Afghanistan. The future of Afghanistan looks exactly as that of the past—into massacres, civil wars and bomb explosion with serious repercussions for India.

Conclusion

The Af-Pak policy contradicts the geo-political realities and history of the region. There can be no peace in the region without addressing the genuine concerns of both India and Pakistan. The Af-Pak policy has been a Pak centric scheme which ignored India's concerns. It failed to take into account the geo-political undercurrents of Afghanistan as a factor in the adversarial relationship between India and Pakistan. The key concern for the US is to ensure a safe exit for its forces. Reconciliation with the Taliban would reinstate a theocratic authoritarian regime in Afghanistan under the US patronage. It would give a new impetus to terrorism, religious fanaticism and, ethnic rivalries in the region. This would have serious security implications for India given the unique nature of religious fundamentalism and terrorism in Jammu and Kashmir and in the rest of the country.

Afghan seems increasingly uncertain about their country's fate and a civil war based distrust and hate would be the order of the day once the Americans withdraw. After the US withdrawal, on account of increasing Indian influence, India would be one of the major hurdles for the Taliban to spread its wings in Afghanistan. This would invite more Pakistan and Taliban sponsored attacks against the Indians and Indian projects in Afghanistan and give a boost to terrorism in Jammu and Kashmir. If terrorism is mainly an external threat to the US, for India, it is both external and internal. The US is capable of handling terrorism with drone attacks, military operations from the proposed military bases in Afghanistan and its diplomatic might in international politics. But India would not be able to deal with terrorism emanating from the safe havens given the geo-political compulsions and unique nature of terror threats to it. Only a democratic, decentralized and neutral Afghanistan could bring lasting peace in the region. The Af-Pak policy is devoid of any such concerns and this keeps India and the region in a precarious position.

End Notes

1. Durand line, the border between Afghanistan and Pakistan cuts through tribal Pashtun residential areas and remains a serious source of contention. Since the Soviet invasion 1978 it has been overshadowed by a plethora of developments which still dominate politics in Afghanistan. See Weinbaumand Harder, (2008) Pakistan's Afghan Policies and their Consequences, *Contemporary South Asia*, Vol. 16, No. 1, March.
2. The Soviet Union withdrew as it was on the verge of defeat at the hands of the radical Islamists assisted by Pakistan, the US and Saudi Arabia. The US stopped showing interest in the region once the Soviet threat evaporated from the region.
3. Hindu-Muslim divide is widely considered as the 'master cleavage' in India due to the adversarial relationship between the two communities and the resultant communal riots and killings. See Varshney, Ashutosh (2003) *Ethnic Conflict and Civic Life: Hindus and Muslims in India*, Yale University Press, and New Haven.
4. Pakistan is geographically narrow and strategically vulnerable against India. Islamabad is just 50 miles from Indian-controlled Kashmir, and the industrial and cultural heartland of Pakistan,

Punjab, stretches along the Indian border. There is military value in having a desolate, mountainous space on the country's Western flank to which Pakistani forces can retreat from a potential Indian invasion and from where they can subsequently counterattack.

Another fear among Pakistanis is that Afghanistan, linked by road to the Iranian port of Chabahar, could challenge Islamabad's attempts to become an energy corridor linking Central Asia to the Arabian Sea. Also a strong Afghanistan has been a strategic disadvantage as it would revive the border dispute and Pashtun nationalism. Bajoria, Jayashree (2009): IndiaAfghanistanRelations", available at, http:www.cfr.org/experts/world/jayashree/b13611.

5. In the 1971 War with India, Pakistan was divided and the Eastern wing of Pakistan i.e. Bangladesh became an independent country. The creation of Bangladesh was achieved with India assistance. It is stated that Pakistan has never forgiven India for this act and continues with its agenda of bleeding India through whatever means possible. Pakistan sponsored terror strikes and insurgency in Jammu and Kashmir has to be seen in this backdrop.
6. US President Obama was greatly influenced by an observation made by Mr. Biden, after the trip he took to Afghanistan and Pakistan just before the inauguration in January. He observed to Mr. Obama that if you asked 10 people on the ground what US objectives were, he would get 10 different answers. That observation, aides said, carried weight with Mr. Obama and helped to lead to his decision to narrow the US goal in Afghanistan and to have a focused policy. Cooper and Schmitt, (2009), "Plan would narrow goals in Afghan", iht.com/articles/2009/03/28/america/policy.
7. Afghanistan High Peace Council is facilitating negotiations between the US and Taliban. These high profile assassinations of the members of the Council are a pointer to the fact that reconciliation with Taliban alone will not bring peace in that country.
8. The US policy to integrate and reconcile with Taliban was partially a result lobbying by Pakistan and Saudi Arabia. For Pakistan it would give leverage against India and for Saudi Arabia against Iran.

9. Yusuf al-Qaradawi always justified and supported jihad in Kashmir for the establishment of an Islamic State. He is widely regarded as the ideological polestar of the Muslim bother hood and he is committed to, "the spread of Islam until it conquers the entire world".
10. The budget (US$ 12 billion) for Afghan security forces is eight times the amount of the government's annual revenue.

References

Amin, Matiullah (2012), "Leaving Afghan Development in the Wrong Hands, Why Relying on Locals Isn't the Answer", http://www.foreignaffairs.com/articles/137183/matiullah-amin/leaving-afghan-development-in-the-wrong-hands., accessed on 16-02-2012.

Ayoob, Mohammed (2002), "South-West Asia after the Taliban", *Survival*, Vol. 44, No.1, Spring.

Bajoria, Jayashree (2009), "IndiaAfghanistanRelations", available at, http:www.cfr.org/experts/world/jayashree/b13611.,accessed on 26-10-2010.

Baker, Peter (2009), "How Obama Came to Plan for 'Surge' in Afghanistan", available at, http://www.nytimes.com/2009/12/06/world/asia/06reconstruct.html?pagewanted=1&_r=1&ref=global-home., accessed on 6-12-2009.

Bergen, Peter (2011), "Don't count on a peace deal with Taliban" May 26, available at, http://articles.cnn.com/2011-05-24/opinion/bergen.taliban.talks_1_taliban-leader-taliban-foreign-ministry-islamic-emirate?_s=PM:OPINION., accessed on 14-1-2012

Biddle, Stephen (2012), "Ending the Afghan War", Interview by Bernard Gwertzman, Consulting Editor, CFR.org March 16, 2012, available at, http://www.cfr.org/afghanistan/ending-afghan-war/p27668?cid=rss-analysisbriefbackgroundersexp-ending_the_afghan_war-031612., accessed on 21-03-2012.

Biddle and Gwertzman (2009), "Obama's Afghanistan-Pakistan Strategy: 'A Reasonable First Step' ", available at, http://www.cfr.org/publication/18982/obamas_afghanistanpakistan_strategy.html, accessed on 6-4-2009.

Chellaney, Brahma (2009), "Why U.S. Policy risks repeating history?", *The Hindu*, 3rd March.

Cooper and Schmitt (2009), "Plan would narrow goals in Afghan", iht.com/articles/2009/03/28/america/policy, March 28, accessed on 15-4-2010.

Friedman, Thomas (2012), "Afghanistan: Moving toward a Distant Endgame", February 7, Geopolitical weekly, available at, http://www.stratfor.com/weekly/afghanistan-moving-toward-distant-endgame, accessed on 14-02-2012.

Ghosh, Bobby (2009), "Obama Afghanistan Plan Breaks Old Ground", available at, http://www.foreignaffairs.com/articles/64932/john-mueller/how-dangerous-are-the-taliban?, accessed on 3-6-2009.

Jacob, Happymon (2009), "Afghanistan, Taliban and the Southern Asian Geopolitics", *IJPAIR*, Kottayam, Vol. 2, No. 1, January-June.

Kaplan, Robert D. (2009), "Pakistan's Fatal Shore", Atlantic Monthly, available at, http://www.theatlantic.com/doc,2008084/Kaplan–Pakistan, accessed on 31-12-2011.

khapalwak and Rohde, (2010), "A Look at America's New Hope: The Afghan Tribes", available at, http://www.nytimes.com/2010/01/31/weekinreview/13rohde.html?ref=global-home , accessed on 1-9-2010.

Khosla, I.P. (2003), "Indo-Afghan Relations Looking into the Future", in Sreedhar (ed.) *Afghanistan in Transition*, Indian Council of World Affairs, New Delhi.

Khosla, I.P. (2008), "Lost opportunities in Afghanistan", http://www.india-seminar.com/cd8899/cd_frame8899.html., accessed on 7-3-2009.

Lambah, S.K. (2009), "International Conference on Afghanistan: A Comprehensive Strategy in a Regional Context"; Statement made as Special Envoy of the Prime Minister of India at The Hague, 31st March. Annual Report2009-10, Ministry of External Affairs, Government of India, available at, http://www.mea.gov.in/mystart.php?id=500415660., accessed on 14-03-2012.

Luiza, Ch. (2009), "Full text of Obama's Af-Pak speech", December 1, available at, http://www2.macleans.ca/2009/12/01/full-text-of-obamas-afpakspeech/, accessed on 02-2-2011.

Machrystal, Stanley (2009), "Commander's Initial Assessment", International Security Assistance Force, Afghanistan August 30, http://articles.cnn.com/2011-05-4/opinion/bergen.taliban.talks_1_taliban-leader-taliban-foreign-ministry-islamic-emirate?_s=PM:OPINION., accessed on 24-12-2011.

Mueller, John, (2009), "How Dangerous is the Taliban? Why Afghanistan is the Wrong War", April 15, available at, http://www.foreignaffairs.com/articles/64932/john-mueller/how-dangerous-are-the-taliban?, accessed on 3-6-2009.

Nauman and Conway (2012), "Pakistan parliament committee demands end to U.S. drone strikes", available at, http://news.yahoo.com/pakistan-parliament-committee-demands-end-u-drone-strikes-073821827.html,Reuters, accessed on 21-03-2012.

Obama, Barack (2007), "Renewing American Leadership", Foreign Affairs, July-August, available at, http://www.foreignaffairs.org/20070701faessay86401-p60/barack-obama/renewing-american-leadership.html, accessed on 22-2-2009.

Pant, Harsh V. (2011), "New Opening for India in Afghanistan", 16th May, worldpoliticsreview.com, accessed on 14-6-2011.

Pant. Harsh V. (2011), "New Opening for India in Afghanistan", Afghanistan Special Report, October, available at, http://www.worldpoliticsreview.com., accessed on 16-12-2011.

Patnaik, Smruti S. (2007), "Musharaf Rallies Pakistani Nation", in Warikoo, (ed.), *Afghanistan the Challenge, Persuit of Strategic Depth: The Changing Dynamics of Pakistan Afghan Policy,* Pentagon Press, New Delhi.

President of the United States, "National Security Strategy", (2010), May, White House, Washington, available at, http://www.whitehouse.gov/sites/default/files/rss_viewer/national_security_strategy.pdf, accessed on 15-4-2011.

Qazi, Shehzad H. (2012), "Toward a Sustainable Peace in Afghanistan: Part I", May 22, worldpoliticsreview.com, accessed on 23-05-2012.

Rod and Alissa (2010), "Karzai Closing in on Taliban Reconciliation Plan", available at, http://www.nytimes.com/2010/01/18/world/asia/18afghan.html?

ref=asia, accessed on 18-1-2010.

Rubin, Alissa J. (2010), "Afghanistan Set to Push a New Reconciliation Plan", available at, http://www.nytimes.com/2010/01/28/world/asia/28afghan.html?ref=global-home, accessed on 28-1-2010.

Smith, Jeff M. (2011), "Friends like These: the US-Pakistan Strategic Partnership", WPR Special Report, worldpoliticsreview.com., accessed on 15-6-2011.

Swami, Praveen (2011), "Mediator in Taliban-US talks backed Kashmir Jihad", *The Hindu*, December 28.

Swami, Praveen (2012), "West's Romancing of the Taliban", *The Hindu*, 18th January.

Taylor, Guy (2011), "US-Pakistan Alliance under Increasing Strain", 26 April, worldpoliticsreview.com, accessed on 30-4-2011.

Varadarajan, Siddarth (2009), "From de-hyphenation to dual hyphenation", *The Hindu*, 30th March.

Varshney, Ashutosh (2003), *Ethnic Conflict and Civic Life: Hindus and Muslims in India*, Yale University Press.

Walport, Stanley (2010), *India and Pakistan*, University of California Press, London.

Weinbaum and Harder (2008), "Pakistan's Afghan Policies and their Consequences", *Contemporary South Asia*, Vol. 16, No. 1.

Zakaria, Fareed (2011), "Fantasy and reality in Afghanistan", The budget (US$ 12 billion) for Afghan security forces is eight times the amount of the government's annual revenue, available at, http://www.washingtonpost.com/opinions/fantasy-and-reality-in-afghanistan/2012/02/29/gIQA3ABBjR_story.html, accessed on 1-03-2012.

Zeb, Rizwan (2006), "Cross-border Terrorism; Issues Plaguing Pakistan-Afghanistan Relations", *China and Eurasia Forum Quarterly*, Uppsala, Vol. 4, No. 2.

8

Securing the Neighbourhood: A Sub-regional Approach to India's Security

Rahul Tripathi and Mukund Narvekar

Contemporary Indian security dilemma presents the policy makers and the academics with a twofold dilemma. First, given India's aspiration for a growing role in global affairs, how exactly can it get out of the vortex of the region and define security parameters for itself which are global in scope. It is often the South Asian security situation which poses greater challenges and constraints before Indian policy-making than the global one. Second, even if it recognizes regional concerns as an inseparable component of its global posturing, how does it approach the question of regional security without antagonizing the immediate neighbourhood which often sees itself as not so benevolent, regional power? The present paper tries to address the above two concerns by looking at the global vs. regional security dilemma for India and thereby attempts an alternative sub-regional approach to security guided by human security considerations which may provide the necessary clue to making India secure–both with reference to its land and maritime borders.

Introduction

South Asia as a region finds itself at a very critical location in the emerging human security discourse in the developing societies. With a population of around 1.4 billion people amounting to one fifth of global population and considered to be home to half of the world's poor, the region appears to be the ideal test case for a comprehensive human development analysis. The region continues to be plagued with the problems of endemic poverty, illiteracy, unemployment and inadequate health. The successful interventions in these areas are often few and localized. At the same time, the region also appears to be poised for a period of gradual yet sustained economic growth, given the initiation of economic reforms in most of the countries and the promise of the burgeoning middle class. In essence, the region faces a set of unique challenges and opportunities as it locates itself in the unfolding global economic and political environment.

A very critical determinant of how South Asia will be able to meet the challenges and live up to its promises will be the manner in which it would handle the question of security of its people- both economic and political. South Asia is yet to reach a stage where the economic logic takes precedence over the political and this has been manifested both within and outside the national domain. Security by itself has been a political construct around which countries of the region have shaped their national and regional policies. As a result there has often been a traditional divergence of security perception as far as India and her neighbours are concerned. While India has been inclined to take the view of 'geo-strategic unity' perspective, implying its own security and that of its neighbours being intrinsically linked, our neighbours have had a rather independent perception of their own security. The idea of a comprehensive security framework for India and her neighbourhood poses fundamental challenges.

Recent propositions on regional security focusing on economic interdependence have been a significant departure, but do not address the issue of human security adequately and consider it to be part of the larger diagnosis. There is, therefore, a need to look at the human security problematique, first as a departure from the conventional approaches to regional security in South Asia and then get on to the specifics of Human Security as they relate to the contemporary South

Asian realities. It is the proposition of the authors that a human-centric approach to regional security with its focus on sub-regional land and maritime borders may offer the basis for much needed comprehensive security paradigm for securing India in its neighbourhood.

Human Security: A Shifting Paradigm

The concept of human security marks a significant shift from the traditional notions of security both in terms of the units of analysis and the nature of security that is perceived. Rather than taking states as the units of analysis, it gives primacy to 'human beings and their complex social, political and economic relations' It differs from the competitive, possessive notions of security of the individual conceived in the contemporary neo-liberal sense. In essence, it describes a condition of existence in which basic material needs are met and in which human dignity, including meaningful participation in the life of the community, can be met. [1] Thus, it is the larger social economic and political environment and the way it impacts on the individual's well being that becomes the starting point of the debate on human security.

While the debate has reached a certain level of maturity in the west, South Asia and South Asians have had their own unique contribution, both as objects of the study as well as principal articulators of the concept. The late Dr. Mahbub-ul-Haq was among the pioneers of the concept of Human Security as articulated in the United Nations Development Programme (UNDP) *Human Development Reports*. In the 1994 Report, the emphasis on human security was clearly articulated as follows: "For too long, the concept of security has been shaped by the potential for conflict between states.

For too long, security has been equated with threats to a country's borders. For too long, nations have sought arms to protect their security. For most people today, a feeling of insecurity arises more from worries about daily life than from the dread of cataclysmic world event. Job security, income security, health security, environmental security, security from crime, these are the emerging concerns of human security all over the world." [2]

The UNDP thus played a critical role in setting the agenda for Human Security, which found a clearer articulation in the South Asian context with the initiation of South Asia Human Development Reports since 1997. [3]

The, concept was subsequently further refined in terms of the larger meaning of human security and how it coexists with the security of the state. The Report of the Commission on Human Security, 2003 saw human security as protecting the vital core of all human lives in ways that enhance human freedoms and human fulfilment. According to the Report:

"Human Security means protecting fundamental freedoms-freedoms that are essence of life. It means protecting people from critical (severe) and pervasive (widespread) threats and situations. It means using processes that build on people's strengths and aspirations. It means creating political, social, environmental, economic, military and cultural systems that together give people the building blocks of survival, livelihood and dignity." [4]

Significantly, the Report emphasized on the complementarity between state security and human security and saw the latter as being instrumental in forging a global alliance to strengthen the institutional policies that link the individuals and the state with the global world. Human security thus brings together the elements of security, rights, and development. [5]

In a significant addition to the ongoing debate on human security, the need for an appropriate methodological framework to measure the same was also emphasized. It was suggested that a human security audit can be operationalised both quantitatively and qualitatively. The quantitative measure could be constructed annually on lines of the Human Development Index (HDI) and the Human Governance Index (HGI) thereby leading to a Human Security Index (HSI). The factors not amenable for measurement may be assessed qualitatively and focus more on capabilities rather than threats. [6] In the more recent times, a Human Security Index has been finally formulated by incorporating economic, environmental and social parameters in order to provide greater comprehensiveness and coverage to the idea of Human Security. [7]

The index not only covers the national as well as regional contexts but also sub-national and community level scales. Thus, the human security debate has been strengthened in terms of both the conceptual framework in which it could be analysed and the methodological construction which will provide a greater empirical rigour. In this light an area which could pose significant analytical challenge would be the extension of this debate in any regional framework. The contours of the debate get widened—first in terms of the contestation between people vs. state security at the national level, and then is the national consensus compatible or congruent with the regional security interests. A case study of India and her neighbourhood therefore becomes a very pertinent one.

India and the South Asian Region: Divergent Security Perceptions

South Asian region is marked by a unique commonality of history, culture and socio-economic development, which binds it together in sharing some of the key aspirations and challenges in nation building. The commonalities have however been interspersed with divergent perceptions of both internal and external security, which these countries have imbibed on their respective paths to post independence national consolidation. Almost all countries in South Asia, including India, Pakistan, Bangladesh, Sri Lanka, Nepal and Bhutan have faced security threats which have had an internal dimension in terms of the genesis and an external dimension in terms of the spill over effects that have got created. India, being the only country which shares common borders with all the other South Asian countries has at times by design but more often by compulsions has become a common denominator in several of these conflict situations. Logically then, India has become a critical component of the domestic political-security discourse of its neighbours and has continued to grapple with the image of being a 'big brother' in the region and its 'hegemonic' policies are a perpetual threat to the security of some of the neighbouring countries. [8]

This view has gained ground primarily on account the Indian perception of the 'geo-strategic unity' of the subcontinent which makes the security of the entire subcontinent from external forces intrinsic to its own security. It has often appeared to be a localized though ineffective manifestation of a 'Monroe Doctrine' as pointed out in some of recent studies in India's foreign policy. [9] India's perpetual state of confrontation with Pakistan and its role during Bangladesh liberation and the Sri Lankan ethnic crisis are often seen as reminders of its inability to settle regional/bilateral problems in a peaceful manner. Though this has never really prevented the external players from playing a role within the region, yet India is always considered to be the critical player in determining the broad contours of the external engagement in the region. [10]

India's centrality to the security discourse in South Asia has been further compounded by the persisting internal conflicts that have plagued the countries within and their potential to have cross border manifestation. The Maoists insurgents in Nepal at the peak of their movement derived ideological and material support from their counterparts in India. The presence of extremist groups in Bangladesh often enabled the Indian insurgents in the North-east to maintain their supply lines. Similar links have been evident though to a lesser degree in parts of Southern India where the Tamil groups fighting in Sri Lanka used to get consistent support in the past.

With Pakistan, the security problems reflect multiple shades and colours with ideology, history and geopolitics remaining permanent markers in the relationship between the two countries. What makes the situation even more complex is the fact that the regional security paradigm in South Asia remains complicated despite the apparent positive developments that have taken place with regard to internal security structures n most of the countries particularly Sri Lanka, with end of the war against LTTE and Nepal with the mainstreaming of the Maoist movement. India remains in a rather complicated maze when it comes to locating itself in the contemporary regional security framework. Quite unlike in the past when it was more vocal and visible, it has recently preferred to play a silent role in facilitating matters when questions of security in the neighbourhood have emerged and often reconciling once things have gone beyond its reach. [11]

Thus, the divergence between the perceptions on external variables to the regional security and the inability to grapple with the internal dynamics of the security problem has left the South Asian countries with almost a non-existent framework to discuss security as a collective concern. While the South Asian countries, during the last decade or so have tried to arrive at a consensus through cooperation on some social, economic and political issues, in the specific domain of security, such an understanding has been completely lacking. While the South Asian Association for Regional Cooperation (SAARC) has discussed some key issues such as terrorism and drug trafficking, an express commitment to implement the same has been lacking. Besides regional efforts and bilateral efforts at discussing some of the key security issues have not found the much needed convergence at times. In essence, security in south Asia is considered to be a zero sum game.

Given the near impossibility of achieving the notion of collective security by arriving at a certain minimum consensus there have been some recent formulations on 'cooperative security' in South Asia. The idea is premised on the reality of profound interdependence among South Asian nations in both security and economic realms. [12] It calls for a sustained effort towards a shared prosperity in the region by depoliticizing the issues of economic cooperation and building the habits of cooperative security. It demands 'walking on both legs–expanding economic cooperation wherever possible and making sustained efforts to resolve political disputes.' [13] In essence, the proposition is that the logic of globalisation will necessitate a certain regional integration, which will automatically pave the way for greater accommodation within the security sphere.

In all such formulations on security in South Asia, state has been the definite and decisive factor in shaping the broad contours of the debate. It has been the central actor, which has to act on the basis of either reciprocity or unilateralism in defining its security parameters.

These parameters in turn are expected to make the people secure and thereby pave the way for human security. State security and human security therefore are not seen as exclusive but it is the former, which in a way is seen as providing the basis for the latter. The challenge therefore is to see the two as being interlinked and mutually reinforcing each other–something, which indeed happens when we discuss human security in the regional context.

Human Security and the Region

Recent years have seen a considerable attention being given to the issues of both human development and human security in the South Asian region. The South Asian human development reports have very comprehensively documented the challenges and opportunities, which the region faces in meeting the expectations of the 1.4 billion people of the region. The central argument was that economic growth was a necessary but not a sufficient condition for human progress. The governments need to actively focus on human development goals, and direct and use their resources efficiently, so that economic growth leads to empowerment of people. Thus people's needs and their aspirations have to be at the centre of all development efforts. [14]

Though South Asia did show considerable progress in maintaining some economic development parameters, it continues to be plagued with colossal human deprivation. The region is home to nearly one-fifth of the global population but forty percent (515 million) of the world's poor subsisting on less than US$ 1 a day. The GDP per capita of the region is US$ 2000, much less compared to other developing regions of the world. Compounding the problem is the existence of very high rates of illiteracy (54 percent) in the region. In terms of basic human development indicators, south Asia ranks only above sub-Saharan Africa, but below Latin America the Caribbean and South East Asia. The Human development Index for the countries varies considerably between different South Asian countries. While Bangladesh and Nepal were at the bottom, for Sri Lanka the HDI values were far in excess of the regional average. [15]

The low levels of human development in South Asia pose a challenge not only in terms of policy formulation but also have significant implications for order and stability in the region. Most of the current conflicts in the region have their genesis in a certain economic and political deprivation, which has led to the demands of secession and autonomy. The inability of the states to address some of these core issues has led to the greater marginalisation of a section of people who have been easily lured countervailing political beliefs. Economic reforms and globalisation have done little to address this question of the increasing gap between the promise and the reality of economic development.

At a more fundamental level, the problems relating to lack of human development and the concomitant challenge of providing human security are of a universal concern and necessitate an approach, which cuts across the limits of 'national terrains'. With human beings as the focus of analysis, the very idea of human security places a great deal of emphasis on collaborative efforts which address the issues from a regional perspective, particularly when the nature of the problem and its associated impact has a regional context. Such a perspective automatically takes care of the 'national' context of the problem, thereby thinning the apparent divide between the security of the state and that of the people.

Unfortunately, the existing mechanism of regional cooperation provided by the South Asian Association for Regional Cooperation (SAARC) does not provide an appropriate framework to address the questions of human security, though the institution is very much mandated to do that. [16] Political differences within the region and the bureaucratic pace with which the SAARC machinery performs have together made the organization incapable of having a visionary approach to collective human security. The real efforts in to addressing the challenges to human security therefore have to be initiated at different levels where commonality of interests and the stakes for enhanced cooperation are much deeper. The mechanism of sub-regional cooperation rather than regional cooperation appears to be one such principle, which may hold a better promise. Such a sub regional approach could have the following components.

Land Borders as Hub of Human Security: Borders have conventionally been source of much tensions and discord in South Asia. They have conventionally been perceived as dividing lines between countries often ignoring that borders are also human settlements where ties of history, culture and economy necessitate a greater easing of movement and interaction rather than creating greater barriers. While the national security perspective demands that borders must be protected and preserved, the human security dimension calls for easing of borders to make best use of local resources, connectivities and aspirations.

Development of contiguous border areas as hub of cross border economic, social and cultural connectivity could help in checking those factors that are inimical to national security and create pressures in interstate relations. Hence, there could be a clear linkage between the national security objectives and the sub-regional human security actions that could make prosperous borderlands as intrinsic components of national security. There have been some limited initiatives already in this direction, but not enough to bring the convergence between the two security paradigms.

The project of a South Asian Sub-regional Cooperation supported by Asian Development Bank's South Asia Regional Cooperation Strategy and Program set out five key operational objectives: to improve connectivity, to facilitate trade and investment, to develop regional tourism, to facilitate co-operation in energy, and to promote private sector co-operation. One such program included creating a South Asia sub regional information highway network across and within rural border communities which could help in governance, education and health by providing access to information and facilities. [17]

Besides, India too momentarily shedding its inhibition towards SAARC has in the past emphasised on enhancing regional connectivity as key to developing greater linkages within South Asia. The SAARC Summit held in New Delhi in 2007 gave regional connectivity a serious consideration with the Indian Prime Minister himself giving a call to make border as connecting points for people, ideas and commerce. While the movement on regional connectivity projects remained limited, India's desire to pursue them has sustained. A more recent example is the unprecedented visit of the Indian Prime Minister to Dhaka last year along with four Chief Ministers of the Northern Eastern states. The North Eastern part of India requires easy transit facilities across Bangladesh to ease its own economic constraints, and Bangladesh could do well by sourcing its power requirements from the North eastern states which have huge untapped hydro power potential. Sub-regional co-operation pursued in right earnest in this 'human insecure' region can indeed lead to a win win situation for both, reducing the pressures on illegal migration and conflicts across borders. [18]

Maritime Human Security Concerns: In addition to the land frontiers as discussed above, maritime security is one of the other vital areas which have a very important human security dimension. Marine trade and resources across the sea line of communication and coastal routes offers an access to energy resources and merchant traffic, which in fact amount to 80 percent of all global economic interaction. Therefore, there is an urgent need for a comprehensive approach to the economic, political, environmental and nutritional aspects of human security as it pertains to sea and ocean. The immediate players which contribute to above aspect are the fisherman. This community continues to explore challenges and threats in the sea. At times they have got arrested for fishing in wrong waters and some time got highjacked for ransom and yet they have to pay the cost for contribution to economy. The root cause of their appearance are stemming from the lack of human security, ineffective social security and bad governance in their home land.

Unfortunately in South Asia, concerns relating to maritime security have totally ignored the essential human concerns when it comes to the predominant national security concerns. Maritime zones contiguous to two countries often create problems to the communities like fishermen, who get caught between the competing claims which the two nations may have over maritime borders.

Hence there is a need to understand human security from the coastal and marine point of view, keeping is and the environment of human beings directly or indirectly through sea. According to the 1982 United Nations Convention on the Law of the Seas (UNCLOS), which makes provisions for innocent passage, the captured crews should be repatriated as soon as they are arrested on account of border violation, but, in reality, the fishermen are kept for long periods in prison and their release often depends on the overall political climate between the two neighbours.

Fishermen and Human Security

India and Sri Lanka: The narrow Palk Straits separating India and Sri Lanka have served as traditional fishing grounds for both countries. A long-standing dispute over the ownership of a 3.75 square kilometre island, Kacchativu, 12 nautical miles off the Indian coast and 10.5 nautical miles off the Sri Lankan coast, was resolved in 1976 by a bilateral agreement awarding the island to Sri Lanka. Two maritime agreements of 1974 and 1976 define the maritime boundaries between the two countries. Since then, there has been several incidents involving fisherman from both the side poaching over both sides. During the Sri Lankan ethnic conflict, in order to put a check on the increasing activities of the LTTE, the Sri Lankan navy intensified its surveillance in this area. According to them, they have to be strict because of security reasons and due to this innocent Indian fisherman often became victims. Article 73 of the UN Law of the Sea prohibits shooting of straying fisherman but Sri Lankan navy has been quite trigger-happy.

The fishermen issue has affected the history, economic and culture of the coastal region of both India and Sri Lanka. For the fishermen of both the sides it has been a question of livelihoods which appears to be coming in the way of national security concerns of the two countries. What is even more distressing is the fact that even in the post LTTE scenario, the instance of shooting at innocent fishermen has continued. Perhaps there is a strong case for declaring the Palk state area as a Maritime human security zone, where rights of traditional fishermen to secure their means of livelihood should be jointly recognized with security assurances and guarantees given by both the Navies.

India and Pakistan

The 60 kilometre long Sir Creek lies on the boundary

between Pakistan and India in the marshes of the Rann of Kutch and flows into the Arabian Sea. It was not included in the 1968 Tribunal Award on the Indo-Pakistan Western Boundary because both sides had agreed to exclude the area from the deliberations of the tribunal.

The area adjoining the creeks is rich in fish, is a breeding ground for prawns, and may also be rich in hydrocarbon deposits. Any change in the land boundary will greatly affect the Extended Economic Zone (EEZ) of either country. Though Sir Creek involves a disputed area of only about 4-5 kilometres of marshy swamp, resulting changes with respect to the ocean and ocean bed could be significant.

The dispute is over the interpretation of the boundary line dividing the creek. The Pakistani view is that a mid-channel boundary (Thalweg Doctrine) is not applicable as the creek is not navigable. Therefore the boundary should run along the eastern bank of the creek, giving it full possession of the creek. The Indian view is that the creek is navigable at high tide and is in fact being used by fishing boats.

Therefore the mid-channel principle should apply. The two countries' proposals for resolution are not mutually acceptable. As per the UN Convention on the Law of the Seas, India and Pakistan must demarcate the Continental Shelf by 2004 or they will be subject to third-party arbitration. In the meantime, fishermen of both counties are being regularly apprehended and jailed by both sides in the creek area, leaving their families without breadwinners and the release often being delayed due to prolonged security and bureaucratic procedures. While one cannot envisage a common maritime zone between India and Pakistan because of a host of extraneous issues involved, certainly there could be a mechanism for greater sensitivity to the cases of transgression on a mutually acceptable basis as the ultimate sufferers are the poor fishermen again.

Blueprint for Comprehensive Maritime Human Security

1. The need for horizontal and vertical interaction, trust and

an accepted rule of law to allow for increased information exchange incorporating all stakeholders.

2. Strategies for catching fish in traditional fishing grounds and reducing conflict and risk by integrated socio-economic assessments from both the side.
3. Need for Integrated Coastal Management (ICM):

- Addressing multiple sustainable coastal development issues.
- Resolving multiple use conflicts.
- Resolving trans-boundary issues.
- Providing integrated planning and management frameworks for rural and urban coastal cities.
- Providing a "soft approach" to coastal management.
- Being applicable in different local conditions.

4. Ocean and sea governance to create awareness and implementation of various studies for welfare of the fishing community.
5. Need for a *change in perception* regarding what constitutes maritime human security; moving from an overarching focus on state-based defence to a maritime approach to understand multi-disciplinary approach that incorporates the ideals of human security including coastal community, fisherman, and sailor who in fact are the pulses of growing economy of a country, as well as which define the environmental, and maritime security `network in the sea.

End Notes

1. Caroline Thomas, *Global Governance, Development and Human Security: The Challenge of Poverty and Inequality*, (London: Pluto, 2000) p. xi.
2. Ibid., p. 7.
3. Till now there have been fourteen such reports with there being a focus on a singular human development theme every year.
4. Cited from the Asian Dialogue Society Concept Paper on *Building a Better Asia, Dialogue on Culture and Human Security*, held at the International Centre, Goa, 14-17th February 2005.
5. Ibid.

6. Kanti Bajpai, 'The Idea of Human Security', *International Studies*, Vol. 40, No. 3, p. 227.
7. See www.humasecurityindex.org accessed on 20th March, 2012.
8. Ayesha Siddiqa Agha, 'Pakistan's Security: Problems of Linearity', *South Asian Journal*, January-March 2004, p. 39.
9. C. Raja Mohan, *Crossing The Rubicon: The Shaping of India's New Foreign Policy,* (New Delhi: Viking, 2003), p. 238.
10. For instance, though India abstained from playing an active role in Sri Lankan ethnic crisis since the 1990s, Norway, the facilitator of the peace process regularly informed India of the ongoing initiatives.
11. Some recent examples corroborate this point. India's role was conspicuous by its absence in the recent coup against the Maldivian President. It also kept a hands off policy in the final stages of the war against LTTE and prefers Nepal to work its own way towards consensus and consolidation for the new constitution.
12. C. Raja Mohan, 'Cooperative Security in South Asia', *South Asian Journal*, October-December 2004, p. 39.
13. Ibid., p. 40.
14. Human Development in South Asia 2002, (Karachi: Oxford, 2003), p. 8.
15. In the year 2007, HDI values for South Asian Countries were India: 0.612, Pakistan: 0.572, Bangladesh: 0.543, Nepal: 0.553 and Sri Lanka: 0.779. Cited from Human Development in South Asia 2009, p. 171.
16. The SAARC Charter places considerable importance to social and economic well-being of people of South Asia, and has an explicit social agenda. There has also been a SAARC Independent Commission for Poverty Alleviation which has outlined the plan of action to tackle poverty.
17. http://pid.adb.org/pid/LoanView.htm?projNo=40054&seqNo=01 &typeCd=3 accessed on 20th March 2012.
18. Swadesh Roy, Sub regional Cooperation: Northeast India and Bangladesh, Times of Assam, February, 2012, http://www.timesofassam.com/headlines/sub-regional-economic-cooperation-north-east-india-and-bangladesh/ accessed on 21 March, 2012.

PART III
Energy Security

9

Energy Security: India's Global Search

P.V. Rao

Energy security has gained universal acceptability in India's public domain as a critical raw material for the country's progress. Consequent upon the introduction of market reforms, India's dependence on oil resources has increased manifold. No doubt the country had been traditionally importing about seventy percent of total domestic energy need from abroad, mainly from the gulf region. But the growth-led economic policies have necessitated larger inputs of oil and gas to lubricate accelerated production agenda. In fact from a global perspective, ever since the advent of globalization process and the adoption of liberal economic policies by many developing countries, energy, the scarce but indispensable requirement of industrial growth has become the major source of global competition.

Various governmental authorities have acknowledged the critical need of oil to the nation's progress and hence formulated relevant policies to ensure its regular supplies and conservation. The Planning Commission of India defines energy security as follows, "We are energy secure when we can supply lifeline energy to all our citizens irrespective of their ability to pay for it as well as meet their effective demand for safe and convenient energy to satisfy their various needs at competitive prices, at all times and with a prescribed confidence level considering shocks and disruptions that can be reasonably expected" While this is a rather ideational statement on the state's responsibility to ensure regular energy availability at levels of the society, the precise and concrete policy framework to meet the above objective was pronounced in the *Hydrocarbon Vision 2025*. The *Vision* is by far the most comprehensive policy document that draws a practical roadmap of acquiring, promoting, conserving and distributing different types of energy to the growing needs of Indian society. Key components of the *Vision 2025* are highlighted below:

1. Focus on oil security through intensification of exploration efforts and achievement of 100 percent coverage of unexplored basins in a time bound manner to enhance domestic availability of oil and gas;
2. Secure acreages in identified countries having high attractiveness for ensuring sustainable long-term supplies;
3. Maintain adequate levels of self-sufficiency in refining (90 percent of consumption of middle distillates);
4. Establish adequate strategic storage of crude and petroleum products in different locations;
5. Open up the hydrocarbon market so that there is free and fair competition between public sector enterprises, private companies and other international players.

Recognising the very limited capacity of India's indigenous energy production which is just about thirty percent of the country's total requirement, the document lays down important guidelines for pursuing foreign energy sources. In other words, the need for active energy diplomacy to ensure regular supplies from abroad is implicit in this policy framework. Such guidelines are as follows.

1. Acquisition of assets abroad, which are of two types:
   - Equity participation in producing fields.
   - Exploration and production (E&P) contracts in different parts of the world, both on-shore and off-shore.
2. Participation in downstream projects (refineries and petrochemicals) in producer and consumer countries on the basis of crisis-cross investments;
3. Finalization of long-term LNG contracts;
4. Setting up transnational gas pipelines;

The rapid rise of Asian economies registering higher

growth levels has been another key factor in making heavier demands on the global energy supplies. Developing countries like China, India, Vietnam, in sharp departure from their past protected economies to growth-sponsored economies along with Japan and the ASEAN (Association of Southeast Asian Nations) group of countries are the major Asian competitors of the global hydrocarbon resources. In fact, the late twentieth century phenomenon of the global economic power centre moving away the Euro-Atlantic dominant centre towards the rapidly growing Asia-Pacific region, aptly coined as the 'Asian Century' is directly held as the leading cause of pressure on global energy sources.

The all too evident fact that three of the four largest global economies, China, the second largest, followed by Japan in the third position, and India ranked at fourth, are located in the Asian continent alone bespeaks of their rapid appetite for hydrocarbons to fuel their rapidly growing economies. Oil is the lifeline of growth economies and the growth trajectories of all these countries are therefore competitively exploring the possibilities of increased oil supplies from the traditionally known as well as the newly emerging energy domains in such areas as Africa, Central Asia and even South America.

Table 9.1 gives a bare view of the Asian demand for oil in the coming decades. It can also be noticed from the figures below that India would be the second largest oil demanding country surpassing Japan by 2030.

Table 9.1: Asian Crude Oil Demand *(percentage share)*

Country	2000	2030
China	12.4	29.1
India	10.2	15.6
Japan	38.7	14.4
Korea	15.3	10.0
Others	23.4	30.9

Source: Results from Supply Demand Forecast for World, Asia and Asian Countries,' IEEJ, http://eneken.ieej.or.jp/en/data/pdf/364.pdf.

Energy supplies were conventionally understood as the import of fossil fuels—crude oil and natural gas—from the regular and rich Arab sources. However, for a variety of reasons—competitive pressure, rising prices, political fluidity, climate change mandates, etc. consuming countries are steadily moving toward alternative energy sources. This does not mean a complete shift away from the hydrocarbons, but an evident tendency to prefer non-conventional fuels like nuclear, solar, tidal, wind and bio-diesel. Hence, today the noticeable trend is that the energy importing countries are simultaneously trying to explore the globally available sources of nuclear material and technologies as also the technologies in solar, tidal and bio-fuels. What needs to be understood therefore is that energy security is no more the craving for conventional supplies, but also the demand for unexplored non-fossil energy minerals and technologies.

What follows is a region-wise analysis of India's quest for global energy supplies. The four major global regions in which India is actively engaged in pursuit of her oil demands are examined. In the ensuing analysis, the nature of problems unique to each region and their impact on Indian energy participation are discussed. The argument is that energy security can not be seen as an independent activity, but is an interdependent phenomenon conditioned by a multitude of variables such as the diplomatic clout, relationship with supplier country, negotiating skills, global competition, price mechanisms, regime character and political climate of the outsourced country, international security environment, maritime order and the safety of sea lanes of communication (SLOC).

Sourcing from the Traditional Oil Supplier: West Asia

'Energy security' and all its conceptual variables have full relevance to India's sourcing of oil from West Asia, the traditional supplier. While the region continues to account for about 65 percent of the country's total global oil imports, it is not just the import of energy supplies *per se* that matters any more. The recurring political vagaries in the region including the current Arab spring movements, west-led political and military interference in the regional politics, the impact of jihadi militant outfits on the ruling regimes, threats to the crucial SLOCs (Persian Gulf, Gulf of Hormuz, Gulf of Aden, Red Sea and Suez Canal) from state but more from non-state violent actors like pirates to the smooth sailing of oil vessels are among the several other recurring developments that condition the Indian energy imports from the Arab world and the Gulf. Moreover for India, the Gulf region is not only a mere supplier of oil but it also serves as the crucial transit route to gain access to the neighbouring Central Asia and the Caspian Sea which too are major energy destinations.

Iran is the critical transit country for India to reach out into the Central Asian region which is now a constituent of India's extended neighbourhood. This strategically powerful Persian Gulf country, always involved in geo-political power struggles with the regional (Iraq, Israel, Saudi Arabia) and global (US) powers is the second largest exporter of crude oil to India, at 18 million tons a year. Indian Oil Corporation (IOC) and Hindustan Petroleum (HP) receive 3 million tons of crude oil each annually. OVL has huge investment stakes in the Iranian gas fields of Farsi and South Paras.

Iran's importance to India has to be measured not only in terms of her oil supplies, but also her strategic location in the Persian Gulf which is key to Indian access to the neighbouring oil producing Central Asian countries. Iran has already offered several transit routes to India through her territory to reach Turkmenistan via Afghanistan as well as to the Caspian Sea. But the severe sanctions imposed by the US-led western powers against Iran for the latter's refusal to comply with the non-proliferation regime has been seriously affecting the Indian oil supplies from Iran. Compulsions of Indo-US civil nuclear cooperation agreement (2005), which committed India to support the US global non-proliferation policies, forced

New Delhi to vote against Iran thrice at the IAEA, favouring the US inspired resolution.

As the UN sanctions bar countries from transacting with the Iranian banks and also ban oil payments through the Asian Clearing Union (ACU), India is facing the acute problem of paying the US$ 11 billion annual payments to Iran. As a media source put it, "In a move that is being seen worldwide as an example of India succumbing to American pressure, the Reserve Bank of India has barred (Indian) companies from using the Asian Clearing House (ACU)—a process that directly hits at Indian energy imports from Iran". To circumvent the problem, India is in search of alternative channels, for instance Turkey. India hence is engaged in a diplomatic trapeze exercise to balance between the US enforced ban on dealing with Tehran and the indispensability of ensuring uninterrupted flow of oil and hydrocarbons from her second largest source, Iran.

Eurasia

As the pressures on conventional and non-conventional energy sources is growing, new areas of oil competition are engaging the nations today. Energy demands are redrawing the global energy map, rather global geo-politics. Oil importing countries have been eagerly rushing toward those hitherto less known or less explored oil regions to meet their rapid domestic oil demands. The Central Asian Republics (CAR) have attracted serious international competition to gain control over their rich energy deposits following their secession from the Soviet Union. In a historical perspective, the classical nineteenth century imperial power struggles in Eurasia, the so-called 'great game' between the British and Czarist Russian empires, is being replayed. Today, a century later, "only the players are different and the 'game' far more complicated. All the major global players, including the United States, have a presence in the region, and energy has emerged as an additional important factor in the strategic equations."

The energy inspired 'new great game' in Central Asia is therefore a bizarre competitive arena between the global strategic and energy players. India's oil imperatives have obviously promoted Central Asia to the country's vital foreign policy priorities in the aftermath of the Soviet disintegration. It is not surprising therefore that the region became a natural addition to the 'extended neighbourhood' concept of India's redefined foreign policy domains. But treading into this fairly unexplored region, despite its deep historical footprints on the Indian subcontinent left behind by generations of northern horsemen (Mongols, Uzbeks, Turks, Persians, etc.) was not an easy job for the Indian diplomacy in the late twentieth century. Thus "unlike the Great Game of the past in which Calcutta (British India) played the key role, New Delhi had to work extremely hard to be counted in the region amidst wider and more complicated rivalries involving the Soviet Union, the United States, China, Pakistan, Iran, Saudi Arabia and Turkey. Nevertheless, there was considerable progress in India's engagement of the region which went through many twists and turns."

Apart from the difficulties posed by the competitive powers, the landlocked Central Asian region carries additional difficulties for India to gain access to the region. One singular historical development of the partitioned Indian subcontinent had drawn a deep wedge between New Delhi and the Islamic republics of Central Asia which under the imperial British rule neighboured the north-western fringes of the Curzon Doctrine. Given this geo-political barrier of reaching into the oil-rich region, India had to find a few new channels of physical connectivity to the CAR republics through the Arabian Sea and the turbulent Persian Gulf. Hence, a number of road-rail and land-sea transport linkages to connect the hinterland CAR destinations were initiated.

A tripartite India-Iran-Turkmenistan rail-road agreement was signed in the nineties. Another such projected connectivity is the India-Iran-Afghanistan linking India through the Iranian port of Chabahar to Afghanistan for gaining access to Turkmenistan and beyond. Unlike other planned but unexecuted projects, this project is a successful venture, though the Afghan political crisis inhibits its use for the purpose intended. TAPI (Turkmenistan-Afghanistan-Pakistan-India) is another transnational Asian gas pipeline project which as per the latest reports is under the consideration of the four countries. It is a diplomatic effort to reactivate an abandoned pipeline project being built by the American oil giant UNCOL way back in the nineties.

The rise of Taliban in Afghanistan and its subsequent rule had forced the closure of this gigantic trans-Asian gas project. In recent years, presumably goaded by the Americans, the four neighbouring countries have shown resolve to engage themselves to reconsider the viability of the unfinished undertaking. At the ministerial level, the four countries have met more than once to reaffirm concrete plans to execute the TAPI. The United States is interested in pushing the four countries toward the TAPI in lieu of the Iran-Pakistan-India (IPI) gas pipeline as Washington is firmly against the involvement of India and Pakistan–a sure example of the US overshadow over Asian regional energy cooperation plans.

At an individual level, India has been venturing though rather modestly into the Central Asian oil fields. With almost all the CAR republics India has inked multi-sectoral agreements in such fields of mutual interest as agriculture, trade and investment, information technology, human resources and, energy. Kazakhstan, the largest and economically more powerful of the Central Asian republics, is equally far ahead of its regional neighbours in oil, natural gas and uranium resources. It has about 25 percent oil stake in the Caspian Sea basin. India having well recognized the Kazakh importance has entered into some concrete deals to ensure access to the country's different energy opportunities. Apart from signing few oil and gas E&P (exploration and production) deals with Kazakhstan, bilateral agreement on civil nuclear cooperation was also signed at the prime ministerial level when the Indian Prime Minister visited this uranium rich country in the year 2011.

In return for the Kazakh uranium supplies, India undertook to exchange her nuclear reactors, the first such country to be promised Indian nuclear reactors. Kazakhstan extended her support to the Indian case at the Nuclear Supplier Group (NSG) for the waiver of nuclear export restrictions, as India is not a signatory to the Nuclear Non-proliferation Treaty (NPT). The NSG in fact waived such restrictions on India paving thus the way for supplying the much needed nuclear material to India's nuclear energy production by all NSG countries, including Kazakhstan. India also honoured the Kazakh President as the chief guest at her Republic Day ceremony in 2009, symbolising the highest political importance that New Delhi accords to the oil-rich Central Asian republic. It should however be noted that India encounters serious energy competitors in building close relations with Kazakhstan. China of course is a major strategic competitor which has predominant Chinese ethnic presence as well as strategic and political influence there. China has planned an 1800 mile long pipeline to carry the oil supplies from the neighbouring Kazakhstan. Once this three phase Sino-Kazakh joint project is completed, part of which is already built, it may be "connected with the pipeline grids of Russia and Iran, creating the 'pan-Asian Global Energy Bridge."

In examining the Indian energy engagement with the Central Asian countries, one can not obviously ignore the vital significance of Russia, the giant Eurasian power with powerful stakes and influence on the regional oil producers. Notwithstanding the traditional Indo-Russian Cold War friendship, both vitally recognize their mutual strategic stakes in the contemporary Asian balance of power, a fact pre-eminently conveyed by the Russian President when he declared India as the 'special and privileged partner' of his country during his Delhi visit in December 2009.

In energy terms, Russia, the energy super power of the world, with her abundant oil, gas and uranium endowments carries unmitigated opportunities for India, the global energy hunter. OVL has an established presence in the Russian oil and gas fields, in particular the world's gas rich Sakhalin. Its major project Sakhalin-I, has been completed and natural gas has been supplied to India. Successive projects under similar code names are in the pipeline. Not only in the traditional energy sectors, but in the nuclear sector too, Indo-Russian cooperation has been very close and visible. As is well known, Russia has been a major supplier of nuclear material, reactors, fuel and ENR (enrichment and reprocessing) technology to India, including the Kudankulam supplies, in recent years. It should be recognised that the Indo-Russian civil nuclear cooperation is mired in some public controversies as being currently witnessed at Kundankulam in Tamil Nadu. At the strategic level, American pressure to withhold Russian nuclear supplies to India is well known. Reportedly at one time, Russia was prepared to offer four nuclear reactors, but India backtracked at the last minute from inking the deal obviously under US pressure. Nevertheless, Russian readiness to continue to meet Indian nuclear supplies is too evident a fact to be ignored.

South and Southeast Asia

As part of her search for diversified energy sources, India has been staking her interests in some of the neighbouring countries and the countries further to the east in Southeast Asia. In her immediate neighbourhood in Sri Lanka, IOC's subsidiary, IOC Lanka, is actively involved in the oil retail market so much so that more than one hundred local petrol outlets are operated by this Indian subsidiary. IOC was also leased the Trincomalee oil tank of World War II for repair and use. More recently in 2009, an MoU was signed between the Powergrid Corporation of India Limited (PGCIL) and the Ceylon Electricity Board for establishing a power transmission link that would enable future electricity transfer between India and the island republic. Myanmar, the Bay of Bengal littoral has become the hub of energy exploration in the Bay of Bengal region. This strategically located state has been inviting several foreign oil ventures in the Rakhine coast along the Bay of Bengal. Mynamarese offshore jurisdiction in this gas rich region is divided into about twenty five blocks. India's OVL is an active stakeholder in some of these blocks with 20 percent, and the GAIL with 10 percent investment.

A trilateral India-Myanmar Gas Pipeline agreement was signed in 2005 under which Myanmarese natural gas will be transported from her Sittwe gas fields by pipeline across the Bay of Bengal through the territory of Bangladesh to eastern India. This much hailed regional energy cooperation agreement involving the littorals of the region however could not take off as Bangladesh backed out of the projected pipeline for her neighbourly differences over other unrelated issues with India. The issue was well summed up Talmiz Ahmad, a senior Indian diplomat intimately connected with Indian energy diplomacy, "Bangladesh, by insisting on references to bilateral India-Bangladesh issues in the agreement pertaining to the Myanmar-Bangladesh-India pipeline project ensured that the project would be a non-starter". This derailed trilateral deal however did not prevent bilateral India-Bangladesh energy cooperation, though modest, as evidenced by a recent Indian offer to supply 250 mw power to her eastern neighbour by 2013. There are reports of the Indian private oil company, Tata Power showing keen interest in investing in Bangladesh's energy sector.

Indian energy diplomacy is busily venturing into the Southeast Asian region to strike oil deals with some of the countries with which New Delhi otherwise has cultivated close relations through its well known 'look east' policy. In fact, energy cooperation is a prominently identified area of mutual cooperation in the India-ASEAN Partnership Agreement, 2004, (*Vision 2020*). Under this Agreement, five broad strategies of mutual energy cooperation are devised, viz. joint exploration in the region; joint ventures for exploration in third countries; ASEAN-India Gas grid; ASEAN-India association of gas and oil companies, and; exchange of experiences in non-conventional energy sources. Apart from this formal multilateral agreement, India is bilaterally involved in the ASEAN countries.

Indonesia, the largest of the regional states with energy endowments in her vast archipelagic maritime domain offers enough potential for Indian companies. In July 2000, IOC signed an MOU with Pertamina, an Indonesian oil company to explore offshore oil. Similarly, Bharat Petro Resources ltd., subsidiary of BPCL entered into a joint venture agreement with the Indonesian Nunukan PSC for a 12.5 percent participating interest in an offshore oil farm, in 2009. Malaysia is another important regional energy source catering to Indian needs. IOC signed a contract in 2007 with Petronas, the Malaysian oil giant to buy 1.5 million crude oil.

Indian oil diplomacy is venturing beyond Southeast Asia into the Pacific region. ONGC is already present in oil drilling operations off the Vietnamese coast in the South China Sea. South China Sea is a quagmire of conflicting maritime jurisdictional claims between several regional states. There was a military confrontation in the eighties between China and Vietnam over the oil rich Spratly islands and it continues to be a tense domain. ONGC is thus risking its operations by involving in the South China and as late as 2011 a Chinese warship had sent warning signals to the Indian naval warship, *Arihant* which apparently is deployed in the troubled South China Sea to protect India's energy objectives. Outsourcing India's oil requirements is no less a function of regional strategic equations.

The South Pacific region is the latest area of India's energy interest. Australia and India have been showing greater strategic interest in each other which includes energy cooperation too. In fact a new geo-political phrase, 'Pacific India' is a recent entry into the lexicon of international relation. India and Australia figure as the prominent actors in this geo-political framework. In such mutually complementing environment, both the democracies have begun serious search for concrete areas of engaging each other's energy agencies in cooperative ventures. An India-Australia Joint Working Group on Energy and Minerals (JWG) was formed in 2000 which devised a practical agenda of action plans in coal, power, mining, petroleum, renewable and clean energies. Mine rich Australia with its coal, gas and uranium endowments offers attractive participatory opportunities to energy hungry India. According to Pankaj Jha, India's first long-term LNG contract was signed in 2009. ONGC inked an MoU with Australian Arrow Energy for a cooperative venture in the coal sector.

Australian oil giant BHP Billiton has recently succeeded in bidding for a production-sharing deal in the deepwater offshore block on the western coast in the Mumbai basin. BHP won this jointly with the British BG Group under India's New Exploration Licensing Policy (NLEP) IX issue. NLEP is Indian government's periodic policy of inviting global tenders for participation in the country's onshore and offshore hydrocarbon fields, a policy regime aimed at attracting international oil capital and technology for exploring and sharing the national energy resources. In its latest IX issue of NLEP, 2010, the government called for E&P bids in thirty four oil and gas areas.

India is equally interested in obtaining uranium from Australia, the third largest exporter of uranium. Canberra's stringent NPT policy had denied India any such prospects till recently. In fact Australia had been a virulent critic of India's 1998 nuclear explosions, and rather in a fit of temper withdrew her military attaché from New Delhi, only to return not much later of course. NSG's recent waiver on India appears to be melting the Australian rigidities on nuclear cooperation with India going by the Australian ruling Labour Party's latest decision to lift the four year old ban on uranium exports to India. Prime Minster Julia Gillard defunding the government's policy shift on economic grounds as civil nuclear cooperation with India would create more jobs for the Australians wrote in Australia's leading daily, *Sydney Morning* in November 2011, as follows, "We must, of course, expect of India the same standards we do of all countries for uranium export—strong adherence to International Atomic Energy Agency arrangements". She further reasoned that the change in Labour Party's position on nuclear supplies to India was "due to a change in diplomatic circumstances around the world," obviously referring to the NSG's waiver and the decision by some NSG members like France, Kazhakstan and South Africa.

Africa's Oil and India's Stakes

India's cold war perspectives of Africa have come to be replaced by the current imperatives of energy drive. Though as the leader of the NAM and third world liberation struggles, Nehru's India had inspired and led the African anti-colonial struggles, there had been some setback to the relationship when in the immediate aftermath of the cold war New Delhi was accused of neglecting its traditional African friends. India however soon initiated fresh and innovative diplomatic measures to lay a new roadmap for rebuilding close relations with the African nations, at bilateral and multilateral levels. The underlying objectives were more to ensure Indian access to the continent's energy domains as its northern and western regions began attracting the global oil players, both European and Asian, especially China. In short, India has joined the global 'scramble for African oil,' a euphemism for the intense competition for the more recently discovered oil and gas reserves in most parts of Africa.

OVL has entered into E&P partnership agreements with several major African oil producing countries including Angola, Egypt, Gabon, Ivory Coast, Libya, Nigeria and Sudan. In the North African country of Sudan, OVL invested about US$ 1 billion on the oil sector, obtained E&P stakes in the

Sudanese Greater Nile Oil Project (GNOP). The effectiveness and the efficient discharge of its commitments had won much official Sudanese appreciation for the Indian OVL. In Libya, another North African country, OVL acquired about 100 percent participatory rights in the country's oil assets.

It is in Nigeria, the West African oil rich state which is the largest producer of oil in Africa, that the OVL has been exhibiting greater role. Such is the political importance attached to Nigeria that two of the Indian prime ministers had visited it recently and signed several energy related as well other concerned with trade, investment and information technology cooperation. Angola is another West African country attracting OVL for oil exploration. It should however be noted that in many of the African states in which the Indian oil companies are involved, they have to operate under precarious conditions of local civil strife and wars as in Egypt, Libya, Sudan and Tunisia; popular protest movements against the profit-making and exploitative policies of the oil giants as in Nigeria which has been a scene of most violent civil society challenges to the oil operations.

It is not in the oil and gas sectors alone that India is engaged in the African continent. Coal and uranium, and other energy sources have also attracted Indian interest. South Africa, for instance, is a major country with which New Delhi has been cultivating very close relations at every level-political, strategic, economic, energy and of course cultural, given the large Indian diasporic presence and the Gandhian background. In the energy sector, both the countries have been exploring opportunities of mutual cooperation. A global mining leader in coal, uranium, gold and diamonds that South Africa is traditionally known for, Indo-South African relations had undergone a paradigmatic shift in the post-Nelson Mandela era. It is the South African uranium material that India is vitally interested as the latter has been emphasizing atomic energy production in the country in recent years.

Following the NSG waiver on India in 2008, India has

been actively seeking civil nuclear cooperation with South Africa. South Africa also has advanced technology of coal gasification which is an eco-friendly means of producing thermal power. Indian coal mining companies have exhibited interest in this technology and reportedly their personnel were deputed for exchanging cooperation in such technology. Coal India has invested considerably in the neighbouring Mozambique as also have other Indian oil companies in the east African countries of Kenya, Tanzania and Uganda, though rather in a modest degree.

Energy Security and the Role of Naval Forces

Considering the fact that global energy transportation across the seas is severely threatened by violent non-state actions like pirates and maritime terrorists, it is imperative that the naval forces of the concerned countries should offer maritime security to their oil vessels and gas tankers. The Horn of Africa is the endangered maritime zone as oil takers are frequently attacked by the pirates and mercenaries for ransom. Growing energy traffic across the Indian Ocean can witness higher incidence of such organized assaults on the passing tankers. Since India has declared her maritime interests spanning from the Red Sea to Malacca Straits, by implications the Indian Navy is the custodian of SLOCs along this route. Thus energy security and SLOCs have become the sin qua non of maritime security. *Indian Maritime Doctrine* (2009) in recognition of such threats says that "overall naval development must be directly related to the support of our national interests and not just perceived threat. This includes India's seaborne trade, the safeguarding of our EEZ, the growing offshore oil production"

The need for synergizing energy security with maritime security is officially recognised. In the Annual Report (2001-02) of Ministry of Defence (MoD), energy security finds mention in the section on 'maritime dimensions in Indian Ocean.' But it is the Group of Ministers (GoM, 2001) Report, the important official policy document on national security, that places 'energy security' under 'maritime security'. The relevant GoM section says, "India has a vital interest in the security and stability of the Sea-lanes of Communications (SLOC) in the Indian Ocean; our energy security is closely linked to maritime security." Naval officials have been frequently endorsing publicly this view and one such statement attributed to the Indian Navy Chief Admiral Sureesh Mehta is, "Our area of operation is not just restricted to the Indian Ocean; we are also engaged in securing energy lines and sea lines of communications."

In conclusion, what needs to be emphasized is that India's growing dependence on global energy sources and ensuring their safety and smooth transportation to the country is not a singular responsibility of any particular governmental agency. It is an integrated activity in which several concerned agencies such as the policy-making ministries, implementing agencies, Indian diplomatic missions abroad, public and private stakeholders and maritime security forces which include the Indian Navy as well as the Indian Coast Guard.

References

C. Raja Mohan, *Crossing the Rubicon, the Shaping of India's new Foreign Policy*, Viking, New Delhi, 2003, p. 17.

Ministry of Defence, Integrated Defence Headquarters, *Indian Maritime Doctrine*, 2009 see, P.V. Rao, "Energy Security-Role of the Indian Navy", *Journal of Indian Ocean Studies*, Vol. 15, No. 2, August 2007.

Mushtaq A. Kaw, Aijaj A. Banday (ed.), *Central Asia: Introspection* Centre for Central Asian Studies, University of Kashmir, Srinagar, 2006, p. 218.

P.V. Rao (ed.), *India-ASEAN, Partners at Summit,* Knowledge World, New Delhi, 2008, p. 12.

Rajiv Sikri, *Challenge and Strategy, Rethinking India's Foreign Policy,* Sage, New Delhi, 2009, p. 170.

Sudhir T. Devare (ed.), *A New Energy Frontier, the Bay of Bengal Region,* Institute of Southeast Asian Studies, Singapore, 2008, p. 52.

Vrushal T. Ghoble, *"India's policy of acquiring overseas energy assets: A study of ONGC Videshi Limited in select West Asian and African countries."* Unpublished Ph.D. thesis, Jawaharlal Nehru University, New Delhi, 2010.

Y. Yagama Reddy, (ed.) *India-Australia, Towards Sustainable Partnership in 21st Century,* Akansha Publishing House, New Delhi, 2012, p. 54.

10

Turmoil in West Asia and India's Quest for Energy Security

A.K. Pasha

The Gulf region has about 63 percent of oil and 39 percent of gas reserves globally. 45 percent of OECD oil is from the Gulf and bulk of US oil imports come from the Gulf. Oil production/reserves outside Gulf are declining. At current rates of production, Gulf oil is likely to last at least for the next 50 years. Besides the Gulf region, the entire West Asia and North Africa also has substantial oil and gas resources. Due to this, the region has become the focus of attention especially of the USA, China and India as well. Oil was an important reason for the US invasion of Iraq, and NATO's military intervention in Libya, not to mention the mounting threats from Al-Qaeda in Saudi Arabia. This has led to growth of religious groups which are opposing regimes allied to West especially in the GCC, using violence to sabotage/destroy oil/gas facilities.

The unresolved Arab-Israeli conflict and continued Palestinian sufferings has further aggravated this issue. Foreign support to corrupt dictators, escalating US-Israeli threats to Iran, disintegration of Somalia, uncertainty in Yemen, etc, has led to growing maritime security threats. Thus, lack of democracy and related instability, rise of religious groups and religious extremism, terrorism, sectarianism, border disputes, human rights violations, quest to acquire WMD's, besides the above reasons are the emerging threats. India imports over 70 percent of its oil needs and bulk of it comes from the Gulf region.

There are over six million Indians gainfully employed in the GCC States and sending over US$ 40 billion as remittances, Indo-GCC trade is of the order over US$ 100 billion and from investment point of view GCC is also very important. At the same time, India has been affected by the oil shocks—at least six times in the last 35 years. Now due to US-Iran conflictual relations India is being pressured not to import oil from Iran? The paper apart from highlighting the above issues will also discuss what measures need to be adopted to ensure India's energy security given continued instability and turmoil in West Asia and North Africa but especially in sensitive the Gulf region.

India and US Strategy towards the Gulf Oil

The Congress party under Nehru supported freedom movements in West Asia and North Africa since the end of First World War. India's support to the Palestine cause was in line with this policy. Nehru-Nasser friendship and their role in NAM were crucial to restrict the Baghdad Pact and later the CENTO. India's support to Egypt in the 1956 Suez Crisis led Nasser's to support India to liberate Goa in 1961. The Indo-Egyptian friendship also contained Pakistan's effort to raise the Kashmir issue as well as other issues. The defeat of Egypt and other Arab states in the 1967 war with Israel and the subsequent policies of Sadat of Egypt [after the 1973 Arab-Israeli war when the Arabs used oil as a political weapon] to accept US mediation to secure occupied Arab lands in return for peace led to US domination of the region.

Until 1973, India's policy towards West Asia was mostly Cairo-centric and it was premised on support to Arab nationalism, Palestinian cause, and support to Arab secular regimes, need to contain Pakistan's attempt to isolate India in the region as also Western attempts to enlist Arab states in a western sponsored military alliance. Since the 1979 Iranian revolution, India became cautious about Islamic fundamentalism, fallout from Afghanistan and also the growing Saudi-Pakistani cooperation. The prolonged Iran-Iraq war [1980-88], accumulation of sophisticated weapons and rise in oil prices were areas of concern in the 1980s.

The 1990 Kuwait crisis and growing US military, especially naval presence in the Gulf region led to Pax-Americana in the entire West Asian region and this became a matter of concern for India. India, after the disintegration of the USSR, lost a strategic partner and slowly began to establish closer political, military and strategic ties with the US. The US took advantage of India's financial predicament and insurgency in Kashmir and conflictual ties with Pakistan to put pressure on India. The emergence of the US as the pre-eminent power after the end of cold war and disintegration of USSR and India's own domestic economic and political problems in the period 1990-1991 made India vulnerable to US pressure.

The world was seen as unipolar in the 1990's. But at the same time India always aspired for an autonomous foreign policy and the 1998 nuclear tests have to be seen from this perspective. 9/11 pushed the US to pursue unilateral policies like the invasion of Afghanistan and Iraq under the garb of containing terror and threat from WMD's. Thus, 1991 is a turning point in India's foreign policy—the result was India's decision to establish diplomatic ties with Israel [early 1992] and also establish political, strategic and military ties with the US. All Indian governments since then have strived to establish close relations with the USA. It is now virtually taken for granted that the US and India are natural allies. Pakistani supported Kashmir militancy, Babri Masjid demolition, Mumbai bombings and killing of Muslims in Gujarat communal riots all added to complications in Indo-West Asian ties. After the 1998 Pokhran nuclear tests, although India's image improved in the region it soon got balanced by the Pakistani tests.

The 9/11 events brought home the issue of global terrorism and violence closer to India via Pakistan's support to Kashmiri militancy. India sought to invest through ONGC [VL] all over the world to ensure its energy security as dependency on Gulf oil and gas was seen as risky as also due to growing Indo-Israeli and Indo-US ties. Israel was also perceived as an important player to develop closer ties with the US. Despite opposition to the US invasion of Iraq, India could hardly do anything to prevent this blatant aggression in clear violation of UN Charter and international law and opinion. Due to massive opposition from the Indian public, Left, Congress and other parties the BJP led NDA government was forced not to send Indian troops to Iraq at the behest of the US and Israel. India did achieve some "strategic autonomy" by this bold decision. But there is no doubt of the fact that India's ties with the USA in many fields have improved rapidly. India has shown keen interest in buying US military equipment. This has long term implications world wide as the US tends to strengthen ties with the military structures ultimately leading to coups and military interventions and threats to democracy. The Indo-US 123 nuclear agreement and the EUMA arrangements are likely to restrict India's room to manoeuvre.

It is in this background that one should look at the US invasion of Iraq in March 2003 despite universal opposition and lack of UN authorization which was seen by many analysts as the confirmation of Pax Americana in the Gulf region. Due to the political and strategic significance of the Gulf region, the US since the end of First World War has been taking keen interest in this region. During the interwar period it made serious attempts to extend its influence but the British kept the US at a distance. Since the end of the Second World War the US with single minded determination has been planning and executing its strategy to extend its influence in the entire Gulf region largely due to the huge oil and gas resources and the commerce related to it.

It is the oil factor which pushed the US to intervene in Iran by overthrowing Mossedeq's government in 1953. The Shah of Iran became an important pillar of US policy in the Gulf. US saw Egypt's Nasser as a threat and after the Suez Crisis the 'Eisenhower Doctrine' was used to consolidate its influence in the area. After the 1962 revolution in Yemen and Egypt's military intervention, Saudi Arabia became another pillar of US policy in the area. Soon Israel received full US support which led to its victory in the 1967 war defeating Egypt, Syria and Jordan.

Thus, Iran, Saudi Arabia and Israel became US pillars in the region since then looking after its strategic interests. The 1973 Arab Israeli war and Saudi Arabia's decision to join other Arab States in oil embargo against the US and other supporters of Israel, was a turning point for the US policy in the region. The special relationship between the US and Saudi Arabia was ruptured. Soon King Feisal was assassinated in March 1975 and the US threatened to occupy the oil rich Gulf region if the Western economies were "strangulated". The 1979 revolution led by Ayatollah Khomeini led to the complete collapse of one pillar of US policy in the region. The Soviet Union's intervention in Afghanistan in December 1979 led the US President Carter to develop a Rapid Deployment Force (RDF). The Carter Doctrine called for use of direct military force to protect "vital interests" of the US in the Gulf region. [1]

Soon the RDF became CENTCOM to safeguard US strategic interests in the Gulf region. In addition, the US encouraged Iraq to invade Iran in 1980 and sustained the eight year Iran-Iraq war not only by supporting Saddam Hussein but also encouraging GCC states to help Iraq in its war against the Islamic Republic of Iran. The dual containment policy of Iran as well as Iraq was supplemented by huge transfer of arms to Saudi Arabia and other GCC states. US military presence increased in some GCC states especially Qatar, Oman, Bahrain and Saudi Arabia. Soon after the end of Iran-Iraq war in 1988, the US created perfect conditions to trap Iraq under Saddam Hussein and the result was the Iraqi invasion of Kuwait in August 1990.

It is well known that the US aborted all peaceful means to get Iraq out of Kuwait. The US decision to go to war against

Iraq in 1991 was in fact a "deliberate choice" aimed at crippling Iraq's military and economic infrastructure. The US had grown apprehensive over the emergence of Iraqi military power coupled with Iraqi efforts at modernization including the creation of an impressive infrastructure and an impressive industrial and technological base. The Iraqi President Saddam Hussein's linkage theory which demanded Israel's withdrawal from occupied Arab lands for his own withdrawal from Kuwait annoyed the US. Moreover, Israel also feared Iraq's WMD capability and it had attacked the Iraqi nuclear reactor near Baghdad in 1981. In fact, the destruction of Iraq's military capability and its advanced infrastructure served US-Israeli interests. Iraq's military capability had posed a strategic threat to Israel's domination in the area.

The US did great harm to Iraq's ability to support itself as an industrial society by UN sanctions, no fly zones, inspection by UNSCOM and later UNMOVIC, almost daily bombings since 1991 to further cripple Iraq's military infrastructure and capability by supporting opposition forces in and outside Iraq to remove the Iraqi leader Saddam Hussein and his Baathist regime. The neo-conservatives in the US led by Dick Cheney, Paul Wolfowitz and others called on the US to engage Iraq militarily as UN sanctions had failed to remove the Iraqi leader. They openly propagated a US invasion of Iraq as the panacea to international political terrorism especially after September 11, 2001.

It is also interesting to note that an arch imperialist group called the Project for the New American Century (PNAC) was established with Dick Cheney, Donald Rumsfeld, Paul Wolfowitz and others. This group brought out a document in September 2000 which called for the creation of a "Global Pax Americana" including an attack on Iraq to secure regime change even before George W. Bush took power in January 2001. The group also called for US global military supremacy and the use of pre-emptive military force to defeat any challenge to that supremacy. The September 11, 2001 attack on World Trade Center (WTC) and Pentagon enabled the Bush administration to declare war on international terrorism.

It should be noted that the doctrine pushed by Dick Cheney and others in the PNAC had no serious takers until 9/11. It is well-known that Saddam Hussein had nothing to do with Al- Qaeda but the PNAC this group insisted on invading Iraq. Asked by Bush's chief speech writer, Michael Gerson, why he supported the Iraq invasion, Henry Kissinger replied, "Because Afghanistan wasn't enough". In the conflict with radical Islam, he said, they want to humiliate us. "And we need to humiliate them". What Condoleezza Rice said in 2004 was similar. She explained, "While Saddam Hussein had nothing to do with the actual attacks on America, Saddam's Iraq was a part of the Middle East that was festering and was unstable [and] was a part of the circumstances that created the problem in 2001". Obviously, Iraq was seen as an easy target.

So, Saddam's secular regime was to stand in for all radical Islamists, all terrorists, and the states that sponsored them". By early 2001, West Asia and the Gulf region had come to see violence on a large scale not only due to the Palestinian Intifada but also as a fallout from Afghanistan's Taliban and other groups opposed to US, Israel and its Arab allies. Even countries like Saudi Arabia had come to witness greater violence within its territory. All this led to the 9/11 events in the US, which linked global violence/terrorism to the region. The new Bush administration propounded a new National Security Strategy (of the US) whose main feature was pre-emptive strikes and offensive counter-proliferation strategies. Under this the US wants to restore nuclear weapons to the centre stage of national security policy. All these led to the undermining of multilateralism especially the UNO. Soon after 9/11, the Doctrine of the War on Terror was proclaimed by President Bush.

This unlimited war on terror is based on the twin doctrines of hegemony and pre-emption. The US attacked Afghanistan and overthrew the Taliban government. Then the US Nuclear

Policy Review identified seven countries against which nuclear weapons may be used in the US national interest in certain cases. These are Asian countries–China, Iran, Syria, Iraq and North Korea. Russia a Eurasian power is the sixth. The doctrine of the war on terror is primarily focused on Asia from West Asia-Gulf region to East Asia which is seen as the 'theatre of war'. After Afghanistan, Iraq became the next target of the US. It was invaded in March 2003 and Saddam toppled on the pretext of WMD's, human rights violations and support to terrorism. All of it was in violation of UN and International law.

The US invasion and occupation of Iraq and Afghanistan has given new boost to Islamic groups who are resorting to violence. Shia-Sunni-Kurdish sectarianism has led to civil war in Iraq with fear of its disintegration. Soon the US threatened Syria via Lebanon and Iran on the nuclear issue. Regime change which was applied in Afghanistan and Iraq was being threatened in Iran and Syria. This led to greater violence in Iraq as both Syria and Iran supported the Iraqi resistance which is fighting US occupation. Religious groups from Hamas, Hezbollah, Islamic Jihad, Al-Qaeda and many more have emerged which preach violence to counter the US-Israeli hegemony. In order to ensure its place as the sole superpower as also for its energy security, the US invaded Iraq defying UN, world public opinion and in breach of international law.

As long as it remains in Iraq and manipulates Iraqi governments, the spill over is likely to be felt in the entire Gulf region, where violence by extremist groups could lead to instability and insecurity. As former US Ambassador to India Robert D. Blackwell said, "Asia's century is now underway… because Asia is poised to become the strategic centre of gravity in international politics. Although the US will not face an Asian peer competitor in the foreseeable future, regional powers are developing sufficient capabilities to threaten American vital national interests, and those of its friends and allies". The ultimate goal of the US is to contain China,

Russia, Iran, India and other potential powers. [2]

US Invasion of Iraq for Oil

The "Axis of Evil" speech of US President George W. Bush made on January 29, 2002 identifying Iran, Iraq and North Korea was a clear signal to Iraq about the impending focus on Iraqi Weapons of Mass Destruction (WMD). With legal (international law, UN, conventions etc.) and moral principles abandoned, the debate focused on US "national interest" and its ability to use force to punish its enemies. Another report "Rebuilding America's Defences: Strategy, Forces and Resources for a New Century" also showed that George W. Bush's cabinet intended to take military control of the oil rich Gulf region whether or not Saddam Hussein was in power. It said: "The US had for decades sought to play a more permanent role in Gulf regional security.

While the unresolved conflict with Iraq provides the immediate justification, the need for a substantial American force presence in the Gulf transcends the issue of the regime of Saddam Hussein". No wonder the US became more strident in its demands for the return of UN weapons inspectors the Iraq. Due to persistent pressure, and lobbying from the US, UNSCR 1441 was adopted in November 2002 allowing for far stricter time bound weapons inspections of Iraq. When Iraq allowed UN inspectors under Hans Blix (UNMOVIC) and Dr. Mohamed el Baradei of IAEA, the US refused the three months extra time needed to complete the inspections.

Bush and his team feared that UNMOVIC chief might certify that if Iraq didn't have WMD's the UN sanctions could be lifted. US interest in prolonging UN sanctions on Iraq was among other reasons to prevent foreign investments in Iraq, as also rehabilitation of the country's oil industry. UN sanctions became an important instrument for the US to prevent other powers from getting a foothold in Iraq. Saddam was presented as a ruler who was bent on dominating the Gulf region and its vast oil resources. The removal of Saddam Hussein's regime from power became imperative otherwise "a significant portion of the world's supply of oil will all be put at hazard".

The neo-cons argued that in order to avoid this, the USA "should establish and maintain a strong US military presence in the region, and to be prepared to use that force to protect our vital interests in the Gulf and if necessary, to help remove Saddam from power". Since Iraq had the second largest global oil reserves–an estimated 115 billion barrels, or 9.5 percent and was believed to possess as yet unexplored equal amount, controlling Iraqi oil was only a part of US motive for invading Iraq; far more significant was the geopolitical objective of maintaining control over the entire oil-rich Gulf region. So Saddam Hussein had to go and Iraq had to be occupied so as to implement US strategic objectives. [3]

As early as in December 1983 during the Iran-Iraq War, Donald Rumsfeld was sent by US President Ronald Reagan to meet Saddam in connection with a proposal to build an oil pipeline to Jordan's Aqaba and onto Israel, to be built by Bechtel. Saddam Hussein pondered over this proposal for two years and ultimately rejected it. In fact, since then itself Saddam Hussein became US enemy but more so after Iraqi invasion of Kuwait and a mortal danger since 9/11. There were other reasons as well apart from Iraq's second largest oil reserves. He was seen as a threat to his neighbours such as Kuwait and Saudi Arabia, which have huge oil reserves. The Gulf region holds nearly two thirds of the world oil–some 740 billion barrels of proven oil reserves [as of 2007] and nearly 2000 trillion cubic feet of gas. Moreover, 90 percent of excess world oil production lies in the Gulf region. For US strategic power, Iraq was absolutely central to it.

To control Iraq means to be in a very strong position to determine the price and production levels, not too high, not too low, to split OPEC and to use this power in US global strategy. It is not so much with access to it as it does have to do with actual physical control of oil. After 9/11, the US began to have serious doubts about Saudi Arabia's political stability due to the Al-Qaeda threat as also concern over Saudi-Iranian rapprochement. Crown Prince Abdullah's support for an increase in oil price shook the US as also the struggle for power in the Saudi royal family. So US attention shifted to Iraq from Saudi Arabia as Iraqi oil reserves could rival those of Riyadh's. Moreover, Iraqi oil is also the cheapest in the world to extract at below US$ 1 a barrel compared to Saudi Arabia which is around US$ 2.50 a barrel. [4]

The US national energy plan–the so called Cheney Report-released in early May 2001 called for a major increase in US engagement in Gulf region in order to secure future oil supplies. The reason why oil is so very important to the US is that it uses more oil than any other state—nearly 25 mbpd, i.e. almost the entire OPEC oil production in a single day. The US badly depends on imported oil to over 60 percent and its dependence is growing. Michael Renner of the World Watch Institute says, "The Bush energy policy is predicted on growing consumption of oil, preferably cheap oil".

In 1970, US was virtually self-sufficient in oil, but now it imports 60 percent of its needs and by 2025 it will import more than 75 percent of oil. Since the Gulf region is the main energy-producing region of the world, and non-OPEC oil production is declining fast, US imports have to come from the Gulf region. In fact as early as September 11, 1990, Cheney as Secretary of Defence in the first Bush administration testified before the Senate Armed Services Committee and highlighted the importance of Gulf oil for US.

We obviously have a significant interest because of the energy that is at stake in the Gulf. Iraq controlled 10 percent of the world's reserves prior to the invasion of Kuwait. Once Saddam Hussein took Kuwait, he doubled that to approximately 20 percent of the world's known oil reserves. Of course, within a couple of hundred miles of the border of Kuwait, in the Eastern Province of Saudi Arabia, reside another 24-25 percent of the world's known reserves. So, we found ourselves in a situation where suddenly, as a result of his invasion of Kuwait on August 2, he was indeed in control of the Persian Gulf's key reserves without ever having actually taken any more territory than Kuwait itself. Once he acquired Kuwait and deployed an army as large as the one he possess, he was clearly in a position to be able to dictate the future of worldwide energy policy, and that gave him a stranglehold on our economy. [5]

Dick Cheney repeated this argument more forcefully just before the US invasion of Iraq. Delivering a speech to the Veterans of Foreign Wars on August 25, 2002, he said: "Armed with an arsenal of [WMD] and a seat atop 10 percent of the world's oil reserves, Saddam Hussein could then be expected to seek domination of the entire Middle East, take control of a great portion of the world's energy supplies [and] directly threaten America's friends throughout the region". In fact, since 2001, the US Energy Department has been regularly warning that America has to increase its oil imports sharply in order to meet galloping domestic demand.

For the US, Iraq offers the last great oil boom. Hence, US invasion and occupation is fuelled by oil, a domination that has to control oil, a domination that has to have energy security. To have security for its economy, America has to have a "secure source of oil". It is also linked to a deeper economic struggle that the US is waging to preserve its economic supremacy in the world. It is a war between Euro and the US dollar and Iraq has become the military battle field.

The war over Iraq may be a war for oil, but at a deeper level, it is also a war for the defence of the continued control of the world oil economy through the US dollar. It is worthwhile to remember that in 1999 General Anthony C. Zinni, US head of CENTCOM, testified before Congress that the Gulf region with its huge oil reserves was a "vital interest of long standing for the US and that the US must have free access to the region's resources".

The Executive Director of the Global Policy Forum, James Paul wrote in December 2002, "For all the talk about terrorism, WMD and human rights violations by Saddam Hussein, these are not the core issues driving US policy. Rather, it is free access to Iraqi oil and the ultimate control over that oil by US and UK companies that raises the stakes high enough to set US forces on the move and risk the stakes of global empire". A special military task force was created whose primary task was to seize Iraqi oil fields in the initial hours of the invasion of Iraq. "Without going into great detail" a senior Pentagon official explained on January 24, 2003, "it's fair to say that our land component commander and his planning staff have crafted strategies that will allow us to secure and protect these fields as rapidly as possible".

No wonder the first thing US forces did after invading Iraq was to seize two important off shore terminals that transfer two million barrels of oil to tankers along with the Rumailyah oilfields. "Swooping silently out of the Persian Gulf night", an overly excited reporter for the New York Times wrote on March 22, 2003, " Navy Seals seized two Iraqi oil terminals in bold raids that ended early this morning, overwhelming lightly armed Iraqi guards and claiming a bloodless victory in the battle for Iraq's vast oil empire".

On reaching Baghdad in April 2003, US soldiers headed straight to the oil ministry building and secured Iraqi oil records, even while allowing the rest of the city to be sacked by mobs and looters clearly revealing their objective behind the invasion. General Richard Myers, Chairman of the Joint Chiefs of Staff, had an explanation, "I think its' as much as anything else, a matter of priorities". Steve Kretz'mann of the Institute for Policy Studies in Washington in June 1, 2003 said, "The Bush administration, not to mention the Blair government was at great pains to say that the war was about WMD that no one has been able to find. The critics are simply saying that the war had everything to do with what everyone knows Iraq does have–the world's second largest resource of oil". Moreover after US invasion of Iraq, funds earmarked for rebuilding basic municipal infrastructure were diverted to protect oil pipelines, refineries and oil loading facilities and terminals. No wonder Iraqis clearly saw US invasion in terms of oil as the primary reason. [6]

Much to the surprise and shock of its allies in the invasion of Iraq, including the UK, the US restricted the UN role primarily to minimal humanitarian tasks, while it worked to have full say in the new Iraqi set up. It opposed a robust UN role, which would restrict US ability to put pressure on Iran. It soon became very clear that the US intended to stay longer in Iraq than many had thought otherwise. With unlimited access to Iraqi oil, it's easier to undermine OPEC and with US energy security nearly complete, the US policy makers especially the neo-cons were getting ready to put pressure on Iran and Syria and then to reorder the map in the Gulf region. Until recently fierce Iraqi resistance to US occupation had not only intensified but the US confirmed that far from being sporadic attacks by the Baathist elements, a full scale guerrilla war and a well organized sophisticated resistance was underway against US forces. Despite the arrest and execution of Saddam and his key advisers, the Iraqi people have not buckled to US dictates and it is unlikely they will meekly surrender to US led occupation of their country.

The US invasion and occupation of Iraq seen as illegal, unjust and unnecessary is fuelling deeper anti-US feelings not only in the Gulf region but worldwide and this would surely lead to wider complications for the US and its allies. Also, since the US does nothing to restrain Israel's monstrous policy towards Palestinians and since people worldwide know that only the US could apply effective pressure on Israel, the Pax Americana established by force and suffering of the people will be increasingly challenged and no amount of talk about terrorism and WMD's will work in future. [7]

West Asia in general and Gulf region in particular has seen over the last thirty plus years several wars and perpetual instability. The implications flowing from the 1973 Arab Israeli war and the oil embargo imposed by OAPEC on US and its allies to force Israel to withdraw from Arab lands captured in the 1967 war are still being felt. The oil shortage and sudden price increase led to supply disruptions. The Arab oil embargo lasted for nearly six months and the loss of oil supplies was estimated at 4.4 mbpd. Barely had the world recovered oil supplies were again disrupted due to the 1979 Iranian revolution for about six months with a loss of about 3.7 mbpd. The subsequent Iran-Iraq war which continued for eight long years not only disrupted oil supplies from two major oil producers but also pushed oil prices from US$ 14 to 35 US$ per barrel. Then followed the Iraqi invasion of Kuwait in August 1990, and soon UN embargo was imposed on Iraqi oil supplies. Of course, Kuwait was able to resume its oil supplies soon after its liberation in early 1991, but the invasion, war and UN sanctions pushed oil prices to record levels. [8]

India and the Gulf Oil

All the above crises in the Gulf region which disrupted oil supplies and led to increase in oil prices were related to US policies in the region and all especially linked to its support to Israel and the [Arab] autocratic regimes. The 1973 oil crisis pushed India's oil bill by over fifty percent. The Iranian revolution and the Iran-Iraq war also affected India's economy both by disruption of oil supplies and hike in oil prices. During 1990, Kuwait had agreed to sell India about 1.5 million tonnes of oil and Iraq 6.25 million tonnes, which included about 4.5 million tonnes that Iraq was transferring to India on behalf of the USSR against rupee payment. Before Iraqi invasion of Kuwait, India had received only half the oil from the total of about 7.75 million tonnes and it's was difficult for India to procure the rest. Moreover, increase in oil prices in the international spot market increased from about US$ 16-17 per barrel in July 1990 to over US$ 35 per barrel upset India's budget/economy.

According to one estimate, the direct overall adverse impact of the 1990 Iraq-Kuwait crisis on India's balance of payments was estimated at ₹ 5,180 crore. According to another conservative estimate, India lost nearly US$ 3 billion (US) in foreign exchange alone. This includes US$ 2.36 billion (US) as extra import of oil; US$ 200 million to evacuate Indians from Gulf; US$ 200 million as loss of exports to Iraq and Kuwait and about US$ 200 million as loss of remittances sent by Indian workers from both the countries. India (for 2002-2003) needs about 110 million tonnes of oil of which only about 32 million tonnes is produced domestically. India imports oil from about 30 countries, but it imports about 75 percent from five countries—Saudi Arabia, Nigeria, UAE, Kuwait and Iran. India imports over 72 percent of its oil needs and from the Gulf region alone more than 67 percent.

India's oil demand is expected to grow by over five percent annually from 2.4 million barrels a day (mbd) in 2003 to 6 mbd in 2025. India's Planning Commission's estimates are that oil import dependence could go up to between 90-93 percent of oil demand in 2031-32 from the current level. As seen before India's domestic oil production is gradually declining. India's import of oil and products costs the economy over ₹ 1 lakh crore and imports from GCC countries alone is over US$ 10 billion. As seen above any disruption of oil supplies or increase in oil prices due to uncertain situation in the Gulf region will adversely affect Indian economy both in the short and long term. Nearly five million (fifty lakh) Indians are gainfully employed in the GCC states alone who send over US$ twenty billion dollars annually as remittances. Not only this, foreign exchange is important but the safety and security of Indian workers is of uppermost concern for Indian governments.

The minority government of V.P. Singh in 1990 was mainly concerned with the evacuation of more than lakh Indian citizens from Kuwait and about 25,000 from Iraq. Mounting public pressure as also the decision of Members of Parliament from Kerala to sit on hunger strike at the Parliament House on 16 August 1990 to protest against the "inaction of the government regarding the plight of Indians" in both the Gulf states also forced the V.P. Singh government to accord the safe evacuation of Indians top priority. This was one of the crucial reasons why India did not condemn the Iraqi invasion and occupation of Kuwait as it could have adversely affected the evacuation of Indians from the Gulf. US-Israeli policies in the West Asian/Gulf region and more particularly US support to authoritarian regimes has, allowed Islamic groups to grow but this is also allowing these groups to use the Palestine issue to resort to greater violence.

Growing US military presence in the region, control of oil resources and blind US support to Israel is leading to religious extremism and most resort to terror not only against the US but also against US allies in the region. Since bulk of the Indian workers live and work in GCC states which are slow in initiating genuine democratic reforms and where US influence is predominant, hence some Indians are likely to be affected due to mounting religious extremism preached by religious groups thereby impacting India's secular/domestic stability. The Gulf region is equally important to India in terms of trade especially exports (about 16 percent of India's total valued at over US$ 100 billion) which fetch us valuable foreign exchange. Investments from the Gulf-both official and private are also significant for the Indian economy.

The US domination of the Gulf region is slowly elbowing India out from the region as witnessed by sanctions (and now chaos) in Iraq, Iran, so on which has led to reduced trade, winding up of joint ventures, return of Indian workers, and declining investments from the region. India should actively encourage the process of political change and modernization because once the Gulf regimes become democratic and responsive to popular demands, not only their legitimacy would be enhanced but their absolute (abject) dependence on US would be reduced. This would lead to reduction in US military presence and thereby maintaining security and stability that are so very essential to protect India's vital interests as also contain the growing violence in this volatile region from spreading to India in future. [9]

Strategic Importance of Gulf

India after having consolidated its ties with the ASEAN countries especially after the FTA is now gradually focusing on its energy security with the GCC states. The key factors driving its policy apart from India's quest for energy security are trade, investment, security of workers and their remittances. Despite global search for oil/gas resources, the focus remains on the Gulf region to ensure adequate supplies to sustain its high economic growth. Thus, the Gulf region has become an important foreign exchange earning zone from the standpoint of growing trade, workers remittances, and investment opportunities and tourism.

One can notice numerous steps being taken both by India and the GCC states to strengthen bilateral ties in all of these areas. All the GCC states have security agreements with the United States and with their consent the presence of United States troops and a huge naval fleet in a string of air and naval bases in all the GCC States/region. The need for security and stability in the Gulf region is gradually bringing India and United States closer. There is no doubt of growing convergence between the two countries and both are closely cooperating with the GCC states. Gulf region being extended neighbourhood of the Indian sub-continent makes India pursue pragmatic policies taking into consideration the sensitivities of the United States, GCC states and India's own strategic interests.

The economic-commercial content in India-GCC relationship is growing and has more potential to expand for mutual benefit. The new strategic development with far reaching implications is that in the very near future India would be working in tandem with the United States in the GCC region, to further promote its core interests. Major highlights in GCC–India Relations have been the steps both have taken towards initiating negotiations for a free trade pact. India considers the GCC region as its "natural economic hinterland". The presence of nearly five million Indian workers in the GCC states is an important link as also the growing remittances which act as a cushion to the increasing oil prices. This has led to Air India, Indian Airlines and Air Arabia among others rapidly expanding air services to new places in both the regions.

Growing competition among airlines has led to better services and cheaper fares for passengers. As the job profile of Indian workers is changing and switching over to white collar jobs, salaries are increasing and with it the need for new financial institutional cooperation. UTI, Baroda bank, State Bank of India, ICICI and other financial institutions from India are seeking cooperation with financial institutions in GCC states so as to cater to the growing financial needs of both the peoples. More and more recruiting agencies are coming into the picture, as getting skilled people to GCC states become lucrative. Along with these, problems are also multiplying, like non-payment of salaries, and other restrictions, which recently led to a major strike by Indian workers in UAE and Qatar. The Indian Embassy had to intervene in the matter, which was resented by the recruiting companies. There is need for more rigorous monitoring and regulation of labour as manipulation has led to unhealthy practices.

There is also in India growing concern about the religious extremist groups in the GCC states targeting Indian workers due to developments in Iraq and elsewhere in the region as also due to India's close proximity to the United States and Israel and the now strain in Indo-Iranian ties due to India's vote thrice against Iran at the IAEA on the nuclear issue. This has divided the country's public and the UPA government is under pressure to support Iran due to India's energy predicament. All the efforts towards Iran-India-Pakistan gas pipeline appear to have been undermined. Undoubtedly, US opposition to the above pipeline due to its hostile policy towards Iran and massive presence in the Gulf region are contributory reasons.

Due to this uncertainty over Iran, Qatar has emerged as a reliable supplier of Liquid Natural Gas [LNG] to India. Qatar has agreed to supply 7.5 million tonnes of LNG annually for 25 years with the first shipments arriving early in 2004. Qatar had also agreed to supply additional LNG over and above the already contracted for supply over the 25 year period [from 5 MT to 20 MT in next ten years]. More and more seminars and conferences held both in India and GCC states are recollecting the close ties both had and the potential for future. From India's perspective, Qatar has emerged as Liquid Natural Gas supplier, Bahrain for financial cooperation, UAE for educational and cultural contacts, Oman for naval, security cooperation, Kuwait for oil and petroleum products, trade and investments; and Saudi Arabia for (hajj) pilgrimage, oil, trade and Indian workers. All the GCC states have retained their diverse ties with India amid special areas. [10]

Security and Stability in the Gulf

Most Gulf Arab regimes are on the defensive due to internal challenges and India has been supporting conservative Arab [GCC] regimes lately than earlier. For New Delhi, to fight terrorism in Kashmir and other parts of India and in the larger context of South Asia, it needs cooperation with West Asian states. But it has become clear that India must work with the secular and democratic forces in the region and also the dominant world powers which have vast stakes in the region to maintain security and stability. So it is very essential to protect our vital interests and also to prevent the spread of violence and terrorism from this volatile region to India in future. Hence, India needs to enhance its interaction with other countries to seek greater role in cooperation with the states that vital to our interests especially to enhance our energy security.

India should actively encourage the process of political change and modernization because once the Arab regimes become democratic and responsive to popular demands, not only would their legitimacy be enhanced but more significantly their dependence on outside states especially the US would come down and this may lead to reduction in outside military and political intervention which has periodically undermined peace, security and stability in the region thereby adversely affecting India's interests as well. Genuine political reforms would give the politically oppressed people a stake in the running of the political system and also the much needed political stability and smooth transition. The abundant oil resources could then be used to advance economic development so as to engage the Arab people in the process of political and economic progress.

Undoubtedly for India, the threat of religious extremism and terrorism from these regions would be contained if this democratic process takes shape. Along with these steps towards democratic transformation, steps to resolve the thorny Arab- Israeli conflict would also be debated and discussed at all forums, thereby allowing Arab leaders to take initiatives for meaningful steps along with serious US-Israeli steps (which are very essential). Both these steps would reinforce the momentum for change and India could then look forward to greater peace, security and stability in future. In certain Arab countries, Islamic parties have gained substantial seats in legislature or come to share power through democratic process but such groups have learnt how to be responsible and accountable.

It is far easier to control terrorism and religious extremism in liberal democratic political systems which have high level of legitimacy and strong domestic control than the present political set up where the rulers want to remain in total control of all state affairs. The long over due change has now become inevitable but if it is not coming soon, internal and regional violence may be directed against such autocratic regimes unwilling or unable to initiate meaningful reforms. Instability, religious extremism and terrorism could spill over into South

Asia as security and stability in both the regions are mutually interlinked through a number of factors. The most credible option to tackle this twin menace which is posing a new challenge to India's composite culture, liberal democratic structures and also national security, is to adopt a political course that prevents alienation of any segment of the population especially religious minorities–so that they do not take recourse to unlawful activities or violence. Thus, instability, religious extremism, border conflicts, Arab-Israeli tension over Palestine, authoritarian regimes in control of affairs and US support to them is complicating factors for India's energy security. [11]

Urgent Need for Genuine Political Reforms

In GCC States, legitimacy is side stepped in favour of coercive power, itself dependent on an unequal relationship with the US. In all likelihood, the much suspected link with the US will continue to promote repressive policies and discourage genuine political participation until at least abundant oil and its revenues are available. The GCC regimes with US support have become confident, bold and thus more repressive. They use security and intelligence apparatus to perpetuate their undemocratic rule. This structure of the state presided over by the Minister of Interior [invariably by a ruling family member] in most cases, is the most modern, efficient and perhaps highly developed and is being widely used or abused.

The technology of repression has been upgraded by leaps and bounds with severe implications for popular participation and human rights. Thus, democracy has become a victim of a political process in which legitimacy and consensus politics are truly wanting. Under such circumstances dissent is seen as unacceptable. The concept of a loyal opposition is not even known in GCC states. Suspicion, paranoia, fear of assassination and of being overthrown are leading to expulsion, assassination, repression, incarceration, including torture and in some cases execution of dissenters under fake trials. To a very large extent, this sad state of affairs is also due to the ongoing Arab-Israeli conflict.

More and more people in the Gulf now believe that their governments, due to the authoritarian nature of the political system and also under US influence, cannot do anything to relieve their humiliation and improve their lot and hence the emergence of Islamic groups which employ violence and suicide bombings. Moreover, secular groups also follow this strategy under popular support. One writer says, "suicide bombings take root because they free the desperate from the need to rely on governments. Rather than being sponsored by states, this form of violence challenges states." Al-Qaeda and other religious groups may be ultimately contained, but newer groups would emerge and may follow their methods. Lack of democracy and suppression of political opposition invariably drives people to join Islamic groups and repression alone cannot eliminate terrorism. "Any successful counter terrorism strategy must thus address both the opportunities available to militants and the level of their motivations". [12]

US and Emerging Regional Factors

There is clearly no doubt that US-Israeli policies in the Gulf/West Asia are undermining peace, security and stability leading to periodic threats of military intervention or wars or to prop up threatened fragile regimes against their own population who are demanding political participation. The US invasion and occupation of Iraq and the continued instability [fear of split] in many parts of Iraq, in addition to US accusations of Iranian interference in Iraqi affairs is used by the US to put pressure on Iran to cease its ideas and programs. This has also put pressure on Indo-Iranian ties. US attempts to reshape Afghan affairs to increase Pakistani influence also strains Indo-Pak and Indo-Iranian ties. US determination to stay in Iraq and its attempts to put pressure on Iran for regime change is partly linked to help project its power into Central Asia, due to the oil and gas reserves.

From the Indian perspective, increasing bilateral ties with Gulf/West Asian states is not only important due to trade, oil and gas, but also due to the unique proximity of these states to events in Afghanistan, Central Asia, and the Gulf region. The common political and strategic concerns of India and these states will reinforce and strengthen mutual cooperation. If India, in cooperation with the US, reassures the GCC states of its desire to work for peace, security and stability in the region, outside interference could be contained, which many perceive to be the root cause of much of the problems which India and the GCC states face. The 1990s saw the reassertion of regional identities in the face of external interference.

The critical space is widening and it is in this context that India and the GCC can create opportunities for mutual benefit and jointly prepare to meet emerging domestic and external challenges in the Gulf region. Instability in the region poses a greater threat than ever before, as India's reliance on Gulf oil is growing. Although the issue of terrorism is also important and as imported arms from Israel are vital for India's security, there is no need for India to place undue emphasis on bilateral relations between India and Israel as the NDA leadership did. The United Progressive Alliance [UPA] government's common minimum program stated that it will maintain the independence of India's foreign policy stance on all regional and global issues even as it pursues closer strategic and economic engagement with the US. But the reality is that in the context of Gulf/West Asia, US policy is actually affecting India. Pax-Americana in Gulf/West Asia has serious implications for India.

The US control of Gulf oil may in the future affect our quest for energy security, especially as India imports over 70 percent of its oil from outside especially the Gulf. US support to undemocratic regimes in the region is encouraging the Islamic groups to use violence in the face of reluctance of the rulers to initiate political reforms. The security and future of Indian workers in the region in the wake of continued wars and instability has become an issue of concern. Peace, security and stability in the region are crucial for India's own security and prosperity and these calls for new initiatives, dynamism and recognition of the traditionally close historical relationship with the Islamic world. India's economic ties are unlikely to suffer with these states in the immediate future, but one needs to be cautious in developing closer ties with Israel until the process of reconciliation gets under way between the Arabs, especially Palestinians and Israelis.

The UPA coalition should attempt to balance the traditionally close ties with the West Asian states with that of Israel. Security and stability in the region is linked with early resolution of the Iraq crisis, (withdrawal of US forces) establishment of a viable Palestinian state and encouraging political reforms and democratization which alone can contain the growing slide towards religious resurgence, violence and terrorism leading to instability in the region. But what we witnessed recently are record oil prices of over US$ 150 per barrel. US policies to put pressure on Syria and Iran and the 2006 Israeli invasion of Lebanon and Gaza 2008-09 have made the situation much worse. Not only have oil prices gone up but the region is sliding towards more extremism, hatred and growing animosities which are bound to affect security, stability in the region. [13]

Mounting Challenges from the Gulf

Any disruption of oil supplies or increase in oil price due to an uncertain situation in the Gulf will adversely affect Indian economy both in the short and long term. US-Israeli policies in the wake of occupation of Iraq and attacks on Lebanon and more particularly US support to authoritarian regimes, has allowed Islamic groups to grow but this is also allowing these groups to use the Palestine issue in order to resort to greater violence. US talk of further fragmentation of the area into smaller states based on sectarianism and ethnicity and the emergence of the so-called Shia crescent is likely to further destabilize the already volatile region.

Growing US domination and military presence in the region and control of oil resources and blind US support to Israel is leading to religious extremism and most resort to terror not only against the US but also against US allies in the region. India should therefore actively encourage the process of political change and modernization because once the Gulf regimes become democratic and responsive to popular demands, not only their legitimacy would be enhanced but their absolute (abject) dependence on US would be reduced. India can help the GCC states in establishing the election commissions, train officials for elections, help in drafting electoral laws, preparing constituencies, preparing mechanisms to resolve electoral disputes, and so on.

This would lead to reduction in US military presence and thereby maintain security and stability so very essential to protect India's vital interests as also contain the growing violence in this volatile region from spreading to India in future. The big question is: Are the GCC monarchies willing to share power with their own people and reduce their dependence on US? The other big question is: Will the US allow them to become truly democratic and independent from US influence? The area of armed resistance to US-Israeli policies has only widened with violence spreading to new areas in the region. US and Israel would like to tackle the peripheral groups first before launching all-out attacks on Iran and Syria–two states still holding out in West Asia–a region which has largely been subjugated to US-Israeli domination.

The developments in Iraq, especially growing violence and sectarianism are pushing the country (until recently secular) towards religious chaos and perhaps fragmentation. US pressure on Iran may lead to greater violence in Iraq. Together with the lack of infrastructure, growth of religious groups and their militias and US inability to handle the developments, the implications flowing from Iraq are likely to impact the region as a whole if not beyond. Shia-Sunni tensions are rising in the

GCC states especially Saudi Arabia, Bahrain and Kuwait, in view of developments in Iraq. If the US or Israel attacks Iran, Tehran may retaliate on oil tankers in the Gulf or Strait of Hormouz. Oil terminals, platforms may also become vulnerable thereby pushing oil prices.

If violence spreads in the Gulf region, Indian workers in the GCC states may have to be evacuated from some places. India should prepare contingency plans to move the workers to nearby safe places. In this, effort India may need Iran's assistance. India must also keep an eye of the impact of religious groups preaching extremism to Indian workers. US ability to dictate terms to India on our energy security like that in the case of Iran and Syria are bound to increase in future. As the US pressure on Iran mounts, Tehran will urge the GCC states to remove or reduce US presence like bases and troops. India need not share Iran's view on this issue entirely but actively work to have autonomy for Iran and the GCC states. India's energy needs are growing and everything possible has to be done to have the closest ties with oil producers in West Asia.

This has become vital for India's growth and prosperity. Of course India must have good ties with the US but our policy in West Asia should be autonomous of US and not subservient to the dictates of the dominant power in the region. After 9/11, it has become obvious that some countries in West Asia are looking to the East especially Saudi Arabia and they find India an attractive partner in some areas. India should extend support to such countries which are willing to stand up to US hegemony as the US doctrine of pre-emption is likely to destabilize the region still further. US domination is clearly restricting the role of India and the room for autonomous engagements is narrowing. Under the notion of unlimited war on terror the US is justifying its military intervention to contain terrorism. All of this is mounting pressure on the states in the region as also on India.

Not only have the West Asian rulers become nervous due

to US incited developments but despair and discontent among the unemployed youth in the region is also mounting. India should quietly urge the leaders in the region to move ahead with democratic reforms leading to political participation in the decision making process, thereby enhancing regime legitimacy. This will help reduce the Arab regime's dependence on outside powers, and tackle the dependency syndrome. It is clear that most regimes are going through severe loss of sovereignty and threat of disintegration, civil war and identity crisis. While continuing the fight against terror, problems like Israeli occupation of Arab lands and ending US occupation of Iraq and other local concerns need to be addressed. [14]

Case for a Proactive Indian Approach

There is need for greater Indian interest and initiative in the Gulf area so as to ensure peace, security and stability in the region. Indian interests in the Gulf include safety and security of Indian migrant workers residing in the GCC states, and continued supply of oil and gas from the region. Besides, political stability is a precondition to ensure mutual cooperation through trade, aid and investment opportunities in the region. From the strategic point of view, both India and Iran can work towards reducing the role of non-regional states whose policies, especially those of the US and Israel, are undermining peace, security and stability leading to periodic threats of military intervention or to prop up threatened fragile regimes against their own population who are demanding political participation. US occupation of Iraq and the continued instability in many parts of Iraq, and US pressure on Iran are putting pressure on Indo-Iranian ties.

US determination to stay in Iraq and its attempts to put pressure on Iran for regime change is partly linked to help project its power into Central Asia for energy. GCC states and India face the menace of terrorism and religious extremism and the need to combat such forces has assumed urgency. A modest beginning has been made for cooperation in the field of security with the GCC states, which has a rich potential field ahead. Many also emphasize the need to fulfil the growing aspirations of the Gulf people to play a greater role in the sphere of political participation and decision making process. Political systems which allow more space for civil society and work for enhancing their legitimacy would prove to be more enduring and also develop stake in peace and stability.

Of course, outside support will continue to be a major factor in Gulf politics but it is internal support which will eventually decide the final outcome especially major issues concerning peace, security and stability. So far, Indian diplomacy has been fairly successful in containing the negative impact flowing from domestic issues on India's relations with the GCC states but things are rapidly changing in the region. Lest we become complacent, there is urgent need to do hard thinking how best to keep our house in order and not give others the chance/opportunity to harm our interests. It would be foolhardy to assume that things would remain the same despite serious developments domestically and that any disturbance of status quo would hurt the GCC more than India.

We must be vigilant and not allow domestic developments to get out of hand due to electoral politics and posturing and allow outsiders to interfere in our domestic affairs. The key factor driving our policy is India's quest for energy security. Despite global search for oil/gas resources, the focus remains on the Gulf region to ensure adequate supplies to sustain its high economic growth. As seen earlier, this region has become an important foreign exchange earning zone from the standpoint of growing trade, workers remittances, and investment opportunities and tourism. One can notice numerous steps being taken both by India and the GCC to strengthen bilateral ties in all of these areas.

All the GCC states have security agreements with the United States and some NATO members and with their consent the presence of United State troops and a huge naval fleet in the region. As new threats emerge in the Gulf region which would destabilize the area, it is imperative for India to further engage all the states in the region at a much broader level. It would be in the long-term interest of India to have a balanced relationship with all the Gulf States. Any over-identification with one group of states is not in our long-term interest. Of course there are bound to be pulls and pressures between the US and GCC and Iran and India.

But an independent Indian approach has much greater chance to broaden and deepen our relationship with the Gulf States. In this connection, India should quietly but forcefully urge the leaders in the Gulf region to move ahead with gradual but meaningful democratic reforms leading to political participation. At the same time, India must also keep in touch with some of the civil groups advocating democratization in the GCC states. We must keep in mind EU's example of allowing groups from the Gulf that propagate democratization of the GCC regimes. It is obvious that most GCC regimes are going through severe loss of sovereignty and some even face threat of disintegration, civil war and identity crisis.

Outside support to religious minorities, ethnic groups and to members of former ruling families is becoming sharper in the Gulf region. Should India be in different to these momentous developments which have a direct bearing on its future interaction with this vital region? While continuing the fight against terror, and focusing on problems like ending Israeli occupation of Arab lands and US occupation of Iraq among many other local concerns, we need to constantly review our policies emerging from a strategic and volatile area and explore new ways of overcoming the mounting constraints which need to be addressed with a sense of urgency. [15]

Need for a Balanced Approach

When the former US President Bush was visiting the Gulf region [early 2008] to drum up Arab support against Iran, IAEA chief Mohammed El Baradei was in Iran where Tehran rolled out a red-carpet welcome and where he said Iran's ties with the IAEA have entered a new phase. He said, "Iran has made some breakthrough in [resolving] it's nuclear program". Due to its duplicitous policy in the region, the US stands accused of fomenting wars leading to instability and insecurity. Shielding Israel (with its nuclear arsenal) and targeting Iran will raise several crucial issues. US-Israeli policies of invasions, assassinations, bombings, massacres and torture are creating fertile grounds for extremist's violence and growth of religious groups and terrorism. US-Israeli occupations in Palestine, Afghanistan and Iraq have to be ended soon so as to spare the region from more suicide attacks, bloodshed and destruction with obvious implications for India.

Also, India's interests have, to some degree, been affected by wars, revolutions, instability, and terrorism in this volatile but strategically important region. India needs to work closely with the GCC states towards greater political participation, reduction in foreign military presence and withdrawal of huge naval fleets whose presence can spark off war any time. The US never imagined Iraqi resistance would be so fiercely strong and that governments in Baghdad will be run by allies of Iran, as also the growth of numerous Islamic groups. But instead of making amends to its policy, the US plans to stay in Iraq for long years. Growing corporate interests will compel the US not to abandon Iraq, despite sharp rise in the world price of oil. Also, the US appears in a strange way to be preparing to say that whatever needs to be done should be done on Iraqi terms to bring order to a chaotic state.

To conclude, we need to keep in mind three facts. First, despite US pressure on India not to go ahead with the gas pipeline project with Iran via Pakistan, India should not give up this important energy security project. India failed to support Dr. Mossadeq in 1953 and we have seen the consequences in the Gulf since 1979 when the Shah was toppled. India should do everything to prevent an invasion or attack on Iran either by the US or Israel. In future, Iran could be very useful to our interests in Central Asia, Afghanistan, Gulf and even Pakistan. As the Iranian Ambassador to India said, "any Israeli attack on Iran's nuclear facilities would be devastative for countries of the region (as well)".

Secondly, during the NDA government's tenure, there was talk of an axis between India, US and Israel especially attributed to National Security Advisor Brajesh Mishra. There was very little doubt of the close ties NDA established with Israel especially when L.K. Advani visited the Jewish state and Israeli PM Ariel Sharon was invited to India. But many expected the Congress led UPA government to follow a balanced policy between Israel and the Muslim states. Contrary to this, not only defence, but security ties with Israel are also growing and India, by launching an Israeli spy satellite to track activities in Iran and the region is perceived differently [negatively] by the Iranians and Arabs. Moreover, as the CPI [M] mentioned, UPA's "collaboration" and "shameful silence" over Israel's "criminal" blockade of the Gaza strip is harmful to India's interests.

Lastly, the Indian Ambassador to the US Ronen Sen is right when he said India and US cannot be "allies in the traditional military sense" and are more of "strategic partners" given their cooperation in diverse areas. India's purchase of six C-130 J Hercules planes for US$ one billion will be useful to evacuate Indian workers from the GCC states in emergency. India's PM should visit GCC states to further strengthen ties with them. From the Indian perspective, increasing bilateral ties with Gulf States is not only important due to trade, oil and gas, but also due to the unique proximity of these states to events in the wider WANA region.

The common political and strategic concerns of India and these Gulf states will reinforce and strengthen mutual cooperation. Given the close GCC-US relations and also growing Indo-US ties, India in cooperation with the US and others vitally interested in Gulf security should, work out a harmonious approach which reassures the Gulf states of the need to work for peace, security and stability in the region Outside interference could be contained, which many perceive to be the root cause of much of the problems which India and the GCC states face. The 1990s saw the reassertion of regional identities in the face of external interference. The critical space is widening and it is in this context that India and GCC can create opportunities for mutual benefit and jointly prepare to meet emerging domestic and external challenges in the Gulf region. [16]

Putting Mutual Anxiety in Context

Instability in the Gulf region poses a greater threat than ever before, as India's reliance on Gulf oil is growing. Although the issue of terrorism is important and imported arms from Israel are vital for India's security, [given US reluctance to sell arms directly to India] there is no need for India to place undue emphasis on bilateral relations between India and Israel as the NDA did. The United Progressive Alliance [UPA] government's common minimum program stated that "it will maintain the independence of India's foreign policy stance on all regional and global issues even as it pursues closer strategic and economic engagement with the US".

But the reality is that in the context of the Gulf, US policy is actually affecting India. Pax-Americana in the Gulf has serious implications for India. US influence over Gulf oil may in the future affect India's quest for energy security. All of this calls on India for new initiatives, dynamism and recognition of the traditionally close historical relationship with the Gulf States. India's economic ties are unlikely to suffer with these states in the immediate future, but one needs to be cautious in developing closer ties with Israel until the process of reconciliation gets under way between the Arabs, especially Palestinians and Israelis. The UPA coalition should attempt to balance the traditionally close ties with the GCC states and with Israel.

Security and stability in the region is linked with early

resolution of the Iraq crisis, (withdrawal of US forces) establishment of a viable Palestinian state and encouraging political reforms and genuine democratization which alone can contain the growing slide towards religious resurgence, violence and terrorism leading to instability in the region. [17] Thus, India should actively encourage the process of political change and modernization and it is in this connection New Delhi has welcomed the recent elections in Kuwait and other similar elections in the GCC states and return to rule of law and constitutional means especially in Bahrain. Indians look upon Kuwait as a model of democracy which needs to be emulated by its other GCC neighbours sooner than later. It is in this background, India can help the GCC states in establishing the Gulf elections commissions that, train officials for election, help them in drafting electoral laws, assist them in preparing constituencies and delimiting them, and prepare institutional mechanisms to resolve electoral disputes, supply stationery for elections so on.

Also there are a number of rules and regulations needed to initiate the electoral process and India can assist the GCC states. The fact that these are essentially Islamic states and Sharia has to be complied, needs to be kept in mind while devising electoral support structures. The big question again is: are the GCC monarchies willing to share power with their own people and reduce their dependence on the US? The other equally big question is: Will the US allow them to become truly democratic and independent from US influence? [18]

The UPA soon after assuming charge on 24th May 2004, among other things emphasized the importance of India's relationship with the Islamic world that went back many centuries. The MEA said, "We greatly value our relations with our Islamic friends. There are over 50 countries (in OIC) whose religion is Islam. A large number of our people work and prosper in West Asia...Our foreign policy is not linked to any doctrine or dogma and we take decisions keeping in mind our vital national interests". The absence of reference to Israel clearly suggested that there would be a reassessment of foreign policy on this front. Pax Americana in West Asia has serious implications for India: (a) The US control of Gulf oil sources may in future affect India's quest for energy security especially as we import over 70 percent of our oil mostly from the Gulf; (b) the US support to undemocratic regimes in the region is encouraging the Islamic groups who are increasingly using violence in the face of reluctance of the rulers to initiate political reforms; (c) the security and future of Indian workers in the GCC states in the wake of continued wars and instability has become an issue of concern; and US desire to involve Pakistan in its strategy in West Asia has implications for India's security and influence in the region. India's ties with Iran and Syria have come under pressure as the US intensifies its pressure on these two states while doing nothing to restrain Israel, which seeks to increase its influence in the region with US help.

It is imperative to maintain close ties with Iran in the context of Afghanistan, Central Asia, gas from Iran and the Pakistani factor. India's relationship with Iran is also vital for Iraq and stability in the Gulf region. President Mubarak of Egypt was awarded the 1995 Nehru Award for International Understanding in 1997 but he could visit India only in 2008 to take the award. Why? The answer probably lies in India's pro-Israeli tilt which has become a burden and its high time India pursues a more vigorous policy to strengthen its relations with the Arabs in Gulf and West Asia in general. Peace, security and stability in West Asia are crucial for India's own security and prosperity and these calls for new initiatives, dynamism and recognition of the traditionally close historical relationship with the Islamic world. [19]

Dealing with Iraq Repercussions

The developments in Iraq especially growing violence and sectarianism are pushing the country (until recently secular) towards religious chaos and perhaps fragmentation. US pressure on Iran is leading to greater violence in Iraq. Together with the lack of infrastructure, growth of religious groups and their militias and US inability to handle the developments, the implications flowing from Iraq are likely to impact the region as a whole if not beyond. Shia-Sunni tensions are raising in the GCC states especially in Saudi Arabia, Bahrain and Kuwait, in view of developments in Iraq. India's former special envoy to West Asia, Ambassador C.R. Ghare Khan has already spoken of the spill over of Shia-Sunni acrimony into India. If the US or Israel or both attack Iran on the nuclear issue, Tehran may retaliate by attacking US ships or oil tankers in the Gulf or Strait of Hormouz. Oil terminals and platforms may also become vulnerable thereby leading to oil shortage which would be push oil prices still higher.

If violence spreads in the Gulf region, Indian workers may have to be evacuated from some places. India should prepare contingency plans to move some of the workers to nearby safe places and we may need Iran's help to tide over any such emergency. India must also keep an eye on the impact of religious groups preaching extremism to Indian workers. US ability to dictate terms to India on our energy security like what it is doing in the case of Iran and Syria are bound to increase in future. As the US pressure on Iran mounts, Tehran may redouble its efforts to get WMD's. Iran would also urge the GCC states to remove or reduce US presence like bases and troops.

Although, India need not share Iran's view on this issue entirely, India should actively work to have autonomy for Iran and the GCC states. India's energy needs are growing and everything possible has to be done to have the closest ties with oil producers in the Gulf. This has become vital for India's growth and prosperity. Of course India must have good ties with the US as well, but our policy in the Gulf should be autonomous of US and not become subservient to the dictates of the dominant power in the region. [20]

Conclusion

Many feel the space for independent foreign policy to suit the strategic interests of the country is shrinking. Apparently some of the decisions and promises [terms and conditions of the deal India has acceded to with the US] made are not disclosed and shared with the public for fear of being exposed. As Rajiv Sikri argued, "India's ruling elite and its supporters, who are ecstatic after the signing of the India-US nuclear deal, have failed to appreciate that a lasting strategic partnership cannot be crafted by stealth and subterfuge". He points out that it appears "that there is more to the deal, perhaps even confidential agreements or understandings, than the Indian government is willing to admit". Sikri argues that the real US policy goal is to ensure that India's foreign policy is 'congruent' with that of the US. We must keep in mind the fact that US will never abandon Pakistan as a strategic ally in favour of India.

The US will consolidate its grip over Pakistan and would like to have India also as an additional strategic partner as also try to use India's huge military assets especially naval facilities. The US needs these Indian facilities to contain China and Russia. Indirectly India is likely to get sucked into the US strategic plans at least in Asia. Also India's ties with Iran have become hostage to US policies towards Iran as India [under US pressure] additionally has to confront the issue of Iran's quest for nuclear technology. But more than ever it has become imperative for India to keep our lines of communications wide open and follow a wise and judicious policy at home and strive to reduce the number of flash points in the broader West Asian and Gulf region, where accumulation of sophisticated arms, lack of democracy, growth of religious extremism and availability of oil/gas and enormous wealth has drawn global attention to our extended neighbourhood.

Ever since India's decision to establish diplomatic ties with Israel, Indo-Israeli ties of course have improved quite rapidly, especially during the BJP led NDA when there was talk of a strategic alliance with the Jewish state. This has led to India and Israel closely cooperating on the war on terror. India's increased dependence on Israel for "defence supplies and advanced defence technologies" is obviously under US pressure. The so-called war on terror and the policy of exporting democracy have led to unilateral military action by the US to fulfil its global ambitions and to keep the world unipolar. But there is no doubt that the Palestine issue remains fairly popular in India with overwhelming support from all sections of Indians for an early end to the misery and sufferings of the Palestinians.

Many Indians see the continuing Israeli violence in Palestine mainly due to the inflexible Israeli policies. Although India is keen to join the Arab-Israeli peace process, it has become imperative to coordinate its efforts with Russia, China and the regional states like Egypt, Turkey, Saudi Arabia and others. This calls for strengthening efforts towards a multipolar world, making the UN and other multilateral structures and non-aligned movement truly effective. But with India taking a "less strident position against Israel in the UN forums much to the chagrin of the Palestinians" and having "made considerable attempts to moderate anti-Israeli resolutions" at the NAM meetings, it is obvious that the expectations of many especially in the West Asian region that the Congress-led UPA government would restore the balance it had pursued in its policy towards West Asia earlier, remains largely elusive.

Any contention that Israel is a major arms supplier to India and hence the government should soft pedal any firm stand against Israel will obviously affect India's credibility in the West Asian region [and also the wider Islamic world] where bulk of India's interests lie. India must continue to wholeheartedly support the Palestine cause and ensure that justice is given to the Palestinians and other Arabs struggling for freedom. Suicide bombings, lack of democracy, dependency syndrome, growing clout of religious groups especially non-state actors, narco-terrorism, maritime security, WMD's, arms race and mounting outside military interventions are matters of growing concern to India as threats from all of these factors are bound to increase in future from West Asia.

Undoubtedly, the US domination in the Gulf region is restricting the role of India and the room for autonomous engagements is narrowing. Under the notion of unlimited war on terror the US is justifying its military intervention to contain terrorism. All of this is mounting pressure on the states in the region as also on India. Not only have the Gulf rulers become nervous due to new and unexpected developments but despair and discontent among the unemployed youth in the region is also mounting—to take the example of Arab Spring in Tunisia, Libya, Egypt, Syria, Bahrain, Oman, Yemen and elsewhere in the region. As new threats emerge in the Gulf region which would destabilize the area it is imperative for India to further engage all the states in the region at a much broader and higher level.

The US has mounted pressure on India to reduce its trade especially oil imports from Iran due to its policy to isolate Tehran on the pretext of the latter's nuclear program. India must not only resist US pressure in this regard but try to resolve by mediation the thorny issues between US and Iran. It should also work with the BRICS group to achieve this goal. Since India had established close ties with Saudi Arabia, Qatar and Oman in the GCC, we must leverage our ties to reduce the areas of friction between Iran and the GCC states over Iran's nuclear issue and the islands issue with UAE. Also it would be in the long term interest of India to have a balanced relationship with all the Gulf States and also other nations like Iran, Iraq and Turkey. Any over-identification with one group of states is not in India's long term interest. Of course there are bound to be pulls and pressures between the US and GCC and Iran and India. But an independent Indian approach has much greater chance to broaden and deepen our relationship with the

Gulf States. In this connection, India should quietly but forcefully urge the leaders in the Gulf region to move ahead with gradual but genuine democratic reforms leading to meaningful political participation.

At the same time, India must also keep in touch with some of the civil groups advocating democratization in the GCC states. We must keep in mind EU's example of allowing groups from the Gulf which propagate democratization of the GCC regimes. It is obvious that most GCC regimes are going through severe loss of sovereignty and some even face the threat of disintegration, civil war and an identity crisis. Outside support to religious minorities, ethnic groups and to members of former ruling families is becoming sharper in the Gulf region. Should India be unaware of these momentous developments which have a direct bearing on its future interaction with this vital energy rich-region?

While continuing the fight against terror, and focusing on problems like ending Israeli occupation of Arab lands and US occupation of Afghanistan among many other local concerns, we need to constantly review our policies emerging from a strategic and volatile area and explore new and dynamic ways of overcoming the mounting constraints which need to be addressed with a sense of urgency. It needs to be emphasized that India needs to charter its energy security policies independent of the US and other Asian powers so as not to compromise its long term energy and security interests.

Despite the challenges [as discussed above like the US factor, Arab-Israeli conflict, ambitions of Iran, border conflicts, instability due to dependency syndrome, Pakistan's attempt to isolate India in the region, emerging challenge from China among other factors], it is surely possible for India to strive for good ties not only with all the WANA states especially with the Gulf states but also with the US and Israel (without of course over-identifying with their agenda in West Asia and elsewhere). Indian diplomacy needs to rise to the occasion as it has both challenges [hidden and known] and opportunities [discovered and emerging] in the energy rich but unstable Gulf region which is after all India's extended neighbourhood.

End Notes

1. Charles W. Hamilton, Americans and Oil in the Middle East, [Houston: Gulf Publishing Company, 1962]; Peter R. Odell, Oil and World Power, [London: Penguin Books, 1970]. Since the Carter administration [1977-1981] US policy has been to employ military force to prevent any hostile power from achieving a position from which it could threaten the safe flow of Gulf oil to the US or its allies. The Carter Doctrine was first applied when USSR invaded Afghanistan in 1979 and has been used since then to any nation that appeared to pose a threat to the flow of Gulf oil. According to one estimate the global enforcement of the Carter Doctrine would run to about US$ 100 billion per year or approximately one-fourth of the US defence budget. This excludes the direct costs of the war in Iraq but encompasses operational costs of the Central Command forces. M.T. Klare, "A Motive Hiding in Plain Sight: War for Oil", in Miriam Pemberton and William D. Hartung (ed.), Lessons from Iraq: Avoiding the Next War, [London: Paradigm Publishers, 2008] pp. 35-37.
2. Gulf Energy and the World: Challenges and Threats, [Abu Dhabi: The Emirates Centre for Strategic Studies and Research, 1997]; Michael Klare, Blood and Oil: How America's Thirst for Oil Petrol is Killing US, [London: Penguin Books, 2004]. The neo-cons and future architects of Iraq war delivered its recommendations as early as in February 1992 as a draft of the Annual Defence Planning Guidance. The draft, leaked to New York Times, asserted that the US mission was to ensure that no rival emerged in any part of the world. The US, the document stated, "must maintain the mechanism for deterring potential competitors from even aspiring to a larger regional or global role". Frances Fitzgerald, "Ideas Floating Free: War as Demonstration Model", in Miriam Pemberton and William D. Hartung (ed.), Lessons from Iraq: Avoiding the Next War, [London: Paradigm Publishers, 2008], pp. 26-28.
3. Paul Roberts, The End of Oil: The Decline of the Petroleum Economy and the Rise of a New Energy Order, [London:

Bloomsbury, 2004]; Michael Youssefff, America, Oil, and The Islamic Mind: The Real Crisis is the Gulf Between our Ways of Thinking [Michigan: Zondervan Publishing House, 1991]. After 9/11 US focused on Al Qaeda but soon they found new reasons to invade Iraq. One of their reasons, according to Richard Clarke, the senior advisor to the National Security Council [NSC] on counterterrorism, was "a felt need to do something big" to respond to 9/11, "a fast, bold, simple move that would send a signal at home and abroad that said,' don't mess with Texas or America". Another, according to those attending NSC meetings in this period, was "to create a demonstration model to guide the behaviour of anyone with temerity to acquire destructive weapons or, in any way, flout the authority of the US". Yet another, according to Douglas Feith, deputy secretary of defence for policy, was that US military action against Iraq "would register with other countries around the world that are sponsoring terrorism, and would perhaps change their cost-benefit calculation". Frances Fitzgerald, "Ideas Floating Free: War as Demonstration Model", in Miriam Pemberton and William D. Hartung (ed.), Lessons from Iraq: Avoiding the Next War, [London: Paradigm Publishers, 2008], p. 28.

4. Matthew R. Simmons, "Twilight in the Desert: The Coming Saudi Oil Shock and the World Economy", [Hoboken: NJ; John Wiley and Sons, 2005]; Dilip Hiro, Blood of the Earth: The Battle for the World's Vanishing Oil Resources, [New Delhi: Penguin Books, 2007].
5. Larry Everest, Oil, Power and Empire, [Monore ME: Common Courage Press, 2004]; David Goodstein, Out of Gas: The End of the Age of Oil, [New York: WW Norton, 2004]; Sanju Gupta, Indian Security Environment and West Asia. The Challenge of Energy Security (Lambert Academic Publishing, Germany, 2011].
6. Vaclav Smil, Energy at the Crossroads: Global Perspectives and Uncertainties, [Cambridge, MA: MIT Press, 2003]; Daniel Yergin, The Prize: The Epic Quest for Oil, Money and Power, [New York: Simon and Shuster, 1991, "Ensuring Energy Security", Foreign Affairs, Vol. 85. No. 2, March-April 2006, pp. 69-89; Alan Greenspan, the former chairman of US Federal Reserve wrote in his book The Age of Turbulence: Adventurer in a New World, [New York: 2009] that indeed oil was the

driving force behind the 2003 US invasion of Iraq, [p. 463]; MT Klare, "A motive Hiding in Plain Sight: War for Oil", in Miriam Pemberton and William D. Hartung ed., Lessons from Iraq: Avoiding the Next War, [London: Paradigm Publishers, 2008] pp. 34-35; James Dao, "Navy Seals Easily Seize 2 Oil Sites", New York Times, March 22, 2003.

7. Aijaz Ahmad, Iraq, Afghanistan and the Imperialism of our Time [New Delhi: Left word Books, 2004].
8. K.R. Singh, "Energy Insecurity and Military Misadventures in the Persian Gulf Region", International Studies [JNU], Vol. 44, no.4, October-December 2007, pp. 283-304; Arun Kumar Banerji, The Gulf War and the Energy Crisis in India, [Calcutta: K.P. Bagchi, 1993].
9. Pierre Audinet and others (eds.), "India's Energy: Essays on Sustainable Development", [New Delhi: Manohar Books, 2000]; S.R. Dadwal and U.K. Sinha, "Equity Oil and India's Energy Security", Strategic Analysis, Vol. 29, No.3, July-September 2005, pp. 521-534.
10. Joe Barnes and Amy Myers Jaffe, "The Persian Gulf and the Geopolitics of Oil", Survival, Vol. 48, No. 1, 2007, pp. 143-162.
11. Javed Ahmad Khan, "India's Energy Security and the Arabian Gulf", [New Delhi: Arise Publishers, 2005]; Rajiv Sikri, Challenge and Strategy: Rethinking India's Foreign Policy, [New Delhi: Sage, 2009]; A.K. Pasha, "11 September 2001 Attack on US and West Asia", in M.A. Saleem Kidwai (ed.), *US Policy Towards the Muslim World: Focus on Post-9/11 Period*, [New York: University Press of America, 2010], pp. 77-178; A.K. Pasha, "India and Iran: Areas of Cooperation [1947-2005] in A.K. Sinha and A.K. Singh (ed.), *Cultural Parallels: India and Iran,* [New Delhi: Anamika Publishers, 2011] pp. 245- 253.
12. Chintamani Mahapatra, "The US Approach to the Islamic World in Post-9/11: Implications for India", [New Delhi: Academic Foundation, 2009]; M.S. Roy, (ed.), International and Regional Security Dynamics: Indian and Iranian Perspectives [New Delhi: IDSA, 2009].
13. B.K. Singh, "India's Energy Security: The Changing Dynamics", [New Delhi: Pentagon Energy Press, 2010]; G. Pant, "Energy Security in Asia: The Necessity of Interdependence", Strategic Analysis, Vol. 31, No. 3, May 2007, pp. 507-526; A.K. Pasha, "India-Saudi Arabia Relations: Fresh Perceptions", *World*

Focus, Vol. XXXI, Nos. 11-12, November-December 2010, pp. 561-567; A.K. Pasha, "Lessons from Egypt", *Diplomatist* [New Delhi], Vol. III, No. 2, February, 2011, pp. 22-25; A.K. Pasha, "Ferment in Egypt", *Africa Quarterly*, Vol. 50, No.4, November 2010- January 2011, pp. 26-33; A.K. Pasha, "Turmoil in the Arab World: Arab Spring or Hot Summer", *Journal of Peace Studies*, Vol. 18, Issue 3&4, July-December, 2011, pp. 3-21.

14. Gulshan Dietl, "New Threats to Oil and Gas in West Asia: Issues in India's Energy Security" in Strategic Analysis, Vol. 28, No. 3, July-September 2004, pp. 373-389; I.P. Khosla, (ed.), Energy and Diplomacy, [Delhi: Konark Publishers, 2005].
15. S.D. Muni and Girijesh Pant, India's Search for Energy Security, [New Delhi: Rupa and Co., 2005]; Girijesh Pant, India: The Emerging Energy Player, [New Delhi: Pearson, 2008].
16. Gary Sick and Lawrence G. Potter, Security in the Persian Gulf [New York: Palgrave, 2002].
17. A.K. Pasha, "Iraq: Sanctions and Wars" (New Delhi: Sterling Publications, 2003); A.K. Pasha, "Pax-Americana in the Gulf Region: Implications for India's Quest for Energy Security", in S.N. Malakar (ed.), "India's Energy Security and the Gulf" (Delhi: Academic Excellence, 2006) pp.116-122.
18. A.K. Pasha, "India's Policy towards the Persian Gulf" in A.K. Pasha, "Turmoil in Libya and India", *World Focus*, Annual Number, Vol. XXXII, No. 11-12, November-December 2011, pp. 922-930; A.K. Pasha, "New Directions in India's Role in West Asia and the Gulf", *International Studies* [JNU, New Delhi], Vol. 47, Nos.: 2-4, April-December, 2010, pp. 333-346; A.K. Pasha, "Democracy in the GCC States", *Journal of the Centre for Southeast Asian and Pacific Studies*, Vol. 2, No. 2, July-December 2008, pp. 30-42; G. Kishore Babu, (ed.), India's Foreign Policy: Continuity and Change, [Delhi: Academic Excellence, 2008], pp. 215-247, World Focus Series-Two; A.K. Pasha, "Recent Developments in the Gulf Region: An Overview", World Focus, Vol. 29, No. 2 [338] February 2008, pp. 43-47.
19. A.K. Pasha, "India and the Gulf states: Challenges and Opportunities", in Rajen Harshe and K.M. Seethi (ed.): Engaging with the World: Critical Reflections on India's Foreign Policy (New Delhi: Orient Longman, 2005), pp. 389-424.

20. A.K. Pasha, "Emerging Challenges to India in the Gulf: Nature and Consequences", in I.P. Khosla, (ed.), India and the Gulf [New Delhi: Konark Publishers, 2009] pp. 100-145; A.K. Pasha, "India and West Asia: Challenges and Opportunities" in Anjali Ghosh, et al. (ed.), India's Foreign Policy, [New Delhi: Pearson, 2009], pp. 301-356; A.K. Pasha, "Violence in West Asia: Implications for India's Federalism and Security" in G. Gopa Kumar (ed.), *Foreign Policy, Federalism and International Treaties*, [New Delhi: New Century Publications, 2011], pp. 192-254; A.K. Pasha, "India and the GCC States: Political, Economic and Foreign Relations" in Kingshuk Chatterjee (ed.), *India and the Middle East: Problems and Prospects*, [New Delhi: Knowledge World Publishers, 2012], pp. 25-65; Rajiv Sikri, "Challenge and Strategy: Rethinking India's Foreign Policy", [New Delhi: Sage, 2009].

11

India's Search for Energy Security: The Way Forward

Dharitri Parija and Mohanan B. Pillai

Introduction

The question of energy security has been under discussion in India ever since we reformed our economy on neo-liberal principles two decades back. To keep the economic growth on a fast track we have to ensure uninterrupted supply of energy either taping domestic sources or importing it from other countries. In fact, India's energy resource endowments are not sufficient enough to ensure energy security for a fast growing economy. Here comes the question what do we mean by energy security? Succinct answer has been given by our planning commission. According to the Planning Commission of India, "we are energy secure when it can supply lifeline energy to all its citizens as well as meet their effective demand for safe and convenient energy to satisfy various needs at affordable costs at all time with a prescribed confidence level considering shocks and disruptions that can be reasonably expected". (Planning Commission, 2006) In fact, India's rapid economic growth has made it the second fastest-growing energy market in the world. India's intensified search for energy security is a by-product of the liberalization, privatization and globalization of the Indian economy.

Low level of domestic production of energy and high per capita consumption of energy are major hurdles in the way of India's emergence as a major player in regional and global politics. In our villages, many people still do not have access to electricity for their basic needs. In fact, energy security in India is enmeshed with growth and poverty. On the one hand, the country has to provide enough commercial energy for growth and on the other hand it has to bridge the inequality gap between the urban middle class and rural poor's consumption level of energy. So, a clear articulation of long term goal is essential for prioritizing short-term activities for building the path to a sustainable future.

Against this backdrop, the present paper makes an assessment of India's increasing energy demand and the challenges, opportunities and success or otherwise of India's attempts to gain access to alternative energy sources to maintain consistency in economic growth.

India's Energy Security Scene: An Overview

As we all know, in recent years, the Indian economy has emerged as one of the fastest growing economies of the world with a population of 1.25 billion. As a result, India faces twin challenges of meeting its energy needs to maintain economic growth and to achieve the development targets of its rising population. In the past couple of decades, energy related issues and policy challenges have grown in colossal terms due to economic development, population growth, lifestyle changes, rapidly growing automobile sector etc.

At present, substantial portion of India's energy basket is filled in by coal. But, being a signatory to the Kyoto Protocol, India is committed to cater its burgeoning energy needs of urbanization, modernization and rapid growth in transportation through cleaner fuels. Furthermore, if economic growth continues to register at five per cent rate per annum as it is doing now, proven reserves of coal, as per the estimation, will not last more than 40 years. Secondly, 90 percent of India's commercial energy requirement is precariously dependent on fossil fuel, which the country is not well endowed with it. On current consumption rate, domestic reserves of crude oil are estimated to be sufficient only for about eight years or 33 years at current production levels. (Nanda, 2009:51)

Major Sources of Energy Consumed in India

According to the International Energy Agency (IEA), hydrocarbons account for a major share of India's energy use. Together, coal and oil represent about two-thirds of the total energy use. Natural gas now accounts for seven percent share. Combustible renewable and waste constitute about one fourth of the Indian energy use which include traditional biomass sources such as firewood and dung, which are used by more than 800 million Indian households for cooking. Other renewable sources such as wind, geothermal, solar and hydroelectricity represent a 2 percent share of the Indian fuel mix and nuclear energy holds only one percent share. According to B.P. Statistical Review of World Energy 2011, coal, oil, natural gas, nuclear power and hydroelectricity account for the bulk of the total primary commercial energy consumed within India.

Coal Resources: As has already been noted, coal is the most important energy source for India. More than 40 percent of its total energy needs are met from both domestic and imported coal. About 70 percent of the total coal consumed is used for power generation. India's coal consumption is growing by 10 percent every five years. Because of low productivity and high cost of coal production has made imported coal cheaper and more attractive Moreover, high ash content and low calorific value of Indian coal causes considerable environmental degradation. (Chellaney, 2005:63)

Oil Resources: The position of India in the nmatter of oil reserves is not as comfortable as coal. India has limited oil resources and have to import oil to meet the growing energy requirement. According to the CIA World Factbook, 2011, of proven oil reserves, India ranks 21st in the world. The proven oil resource with India is estimated to be 8.9 billion barrels. Oil, which contributes roughly 24 percent of India's energy need is very crucial to Indian economy and its secure and reliable supply at affordable price will shape up the over all economic growth. The demand has been steadily increasing and is likely to rise in the time to come but the overall oil production is not growing along with the growth in demand. Thus, rising oil consumption and relatively flat production has left India increasingly dependent on imports to meet its petroleum demand. In 2010, India was the world's fifth largest net importer of oil, importing more than 2.2 million bbl/d, or about 70 percent of its consumption. (Sahu, 2010:24)

Table 11.1: Resource Endowment: Proven Oil Reserves

Country	Oil Reserves	Rank
Russia	60 billion bbl	8
US	20.68 billion bbl	11
China	14.7 billion bbl	14
India	8.935 billob bbl	20
Germany	276 million bbl	57
Japan	44.12 million bbl	80

Source: CIA, The World Factbook, 2012; accessed on 13-03-2013.

Substantial portion of India's crude oil imports come from the Middle East, Saudi Arabia and Iran. Africa adds 22 percent to Indian oil imports.

Natural Gas: The situation in regard to natural gas is not much different from the oil sector. India ranks 26th in world's proven natural gas reserves having an estimated gas reserve of 38 trillion cubic feet (TCF).

Though, India's internal production of gas has increased substantially, the demand for gas, however, has increased much faster than the production. As a result, India has become an importer of gas. India's natural gas demand is driven by power and fertilizer sectors, which consume roughly three fourth of the total demand. Natural gas demand is expected to grow considerably, largely driven by demand in the power sector. Moreover, natural gas is expected to be an increasingly important component of energy consumption as the country pursues energy resource diversification to attain the goal of energy security. It is emerging as an alternative to oil in the transportation sector in the form of compressed natural gas because of firstly, environmental reasons and secondly, the effort of the Government to reduce increasing dependence on oil.

Table 11.2: Resource Enndowment: Proven Natural Gas Reserves

Country	Natural Gas Reserves	Rank
Russia	47.57 trillion cu m	1
Iran	33.07 trillion cu m	2
Qatar	25.2 trillion cu m	3
Saudi Arabia	8.028 trillion cu m	4
US	7.716 trillion cu m	5
China	3.1 Trillion cu m	14
India	1.154 Trillion cu m	25
Germany	175.6 billion cu m	48
Japan	20.9 billion cu m	76

Source: CIA, The World Factbook, 2012; accessed on 13-03-2013.

Nuclear Power: Nuclear power accounts for a small portion of the total commercial energy consumed in India. Though, right now, nuclear power contributes a small quantum, it bears the potential to be India's reliable energy source. The future development of nuclear power within India is dependent on civil nuclear commercial engagementwith the international community. According to the Indian Energy Handbook 2011, Indian nuclear market is estimated to be worth US$100 billion, and planners hope to build 40,000 MW of nuclear capacity by 2020. The GoI wants the share of nuclear in the overall fuel mix to increase from around 3 percent to 25 percent by 2050. The signing of the Indo-US nuclear deal in October 2006 has opened up opportunities for India in the field of civilian nuclear trade and cooperation. (India Energy Handbook, 2011:14)

Hydro Power: Hydro electricity accounts for 5-6 percent of the total commercial primary energy consumption in India. In recent years, hydropower has contributed to 23 percent of the total electricity generation in India. The country is endowed with many large rivers and two close neighbours having enough hydro potential from which barely a quarter has been tapped till now. Controversies with regard to the hydal projects indicate that India faces serious ecological, social and political challenges in developing its hydel power. But hydroelectricity cooperation at the regional level in south Asia has important implications for India's energy security.

According to the Report of the Ministry of New and Renewable Energy, India occupies 2.4 percent of the world's land area but supports 16.2 percent of the world's human popualtion with an expected GDP growth of average 8-9 percent annually which needs more and more energy to sustain the growth paradigm. It is the fourth largest energy consumer in the world after the US, China and Russian Federation. However, the per capita energy consumption in comparison with the other global powers is very low. Out of 72 percent of rural population, 45 percent of rural households are yet to be provided with electricity and 14 percent of the population lives in unelectrified villages. (Maithani, 2011) Therefore, India needs an uninterrupted and secure supply of energy to meet its global power aspiration as also to bridge the rich-poor gap. Therefore, India has to diversify the energy sources and develop and tap every possible alternative sources on a war-footing basis.

In this context, it is imperative to have a look at India's energy diplomacy and international engagement.

Energy Diplomacy: The Way Forward

There is a geographical mismatch between the major centres of oil and gas productions—primarily the Middle East, Central Asia and the Caucasus—and the centres of consumption, i.e. the US, Europe, China, Japan and India. The large energy consuming nations of the world have been pursuing foreign relations in the energy resources rich regions with the objective of keeping the supply channels in their favour. (Pardesi and Ganguly, 2009:102) To meet the rapidly growing energy needs through imports from various nations having energy in surplus involves finest form of diplomatic skills. Diplomacy becomes imperative because the energy exporting nations have the liberty to choose the buyer with a view to accrue the best possible benefits from the buyer country.

As a re-emerging power, energy security has always been a foreign policy priority area for India as the country has been traditionally dependent on imports. The hydrocarbons sector plays a vital role in the economic growth of the country. Therefore, in order to have a long-term policy for the hydrocarbons sector, which would facilitate meeting the future needs of the country, the formulation of Hydrocabon Vision, 2025 is an important step by the Government of India in right direction. The Hydrocarbons Vision, 2025 lays down the framework to guide the policies relating to the hydrocarbon sector for the next 25 years which reads as follows:

1. To focus on oil security through intensification of exploration efforts and achievement of 100 percent coverage of unexplored basins in a time bound manner to enhance domestic availability of oil and gas.
2. To secure acreages in identified countries having high attractiveness for ensuring sustainable long term supplies.
3. To pursue projects to meet the deficit in demand and supply of natural gas, and facilitate availability of LNG.
4. To maintain adequate levels of self-sufficiency in refining (90 percent of consumption of middle distillates).
5. To establish adequate strategic storage of crude and petroleum products in different locations.
6. To create additional infrastructure for distribution and marketing of oil and gas.
7. To open up the hydrocarbon market so that there is free and fair competition, between public sector enterprises, private companies and other international players.
8. To create a policy framework for cleaner and greener fuels.

9. To have a rational tariff and pricing policy, which would ensure the consumer getting the petroleum products at the most reasonable prices and requisite quality, eliminating adulteration?
10. To announce a long-term fiscal policy to attract required investments in the hydrocarbon sector.
11. To restructure the oil sector PSUs with the objective of enhancing shareholder value and disinvest in a phased manner in all the oil sector PSUs.
12. To develop regulatory and legislative framework for providing oil or gas security for the country (Hydrocarbon Vision, 2025).

To put it in other words, India has reassessed its energy related foreign policy objectives and energy strategies to address the issue of energy security in the following ways: (i) diversification of suppliers, (ii) diversification of sources of energy, (iii) the purchase of equity stakes overseas, (iv) the security of its hydrocarbon supplies, (v) ensuring adequate storage of energy, and (vi) cooperation with neighbouring countries within South Asia as well as outside South Asia.

Regional Dimensions

Though, India has been actively trying to engage its Himalayan neighbours to harness hydroelectricity to reduce its dependence on fossil fuels for electricity generation, there are various domestic problems associated with it. Nepal and Bhutan currently harness merely 1.2 and 2.6 percent of their total hydroelectricity potential respectively. The financial and tecnological assistance from India in hydropower cooperation have become an important consideration for both Nepal and Bhutan. At present, 15 joint hydroeletricity projects with four of its neighbouring countries i.e Bhutan, Nepal, Myanmar and Afghanistan are under discussion. But India's image as a 'Big Brother' among the small countries of South Asia has created some kind of flutter in the way of meaningful cooperation. For instance, Nepal thinks that India cheated it in the Mahakali

Treaty of 1996. Alongwith this we have to consider whether increasing involvement of China in Nepal's development programmes is fueling the fire.

Similarly, gas pipeline proposal from Myanmar to India's North-East marked the potential of bilateral energy co-operation in Southern Asia. If materilised properly, Myanmar could become an important source of energy supply to India's eastern states. But unfortunately, India has been too slow and is not having a clear long term vision on how to engage Myanmar and to deal with Chinese influence there. (Lall, 2008) India's pipeline proposal was finally rejected by Myanmar after China's state-owned company got the project.

According to Sreeradha Datta (2008), as quoted by Panwar, "One ONGC official conceded that, China matched India's offer very aggressively and they made every effort to ensure that this gas project is wrapped up. We lacked that kind of aggressive strategy and also suffered from delays in decision-making". (Panwar, 2009:14). Furthermore, it is noteworthy that the 'Look East Policy' has not added much to improve the relationship. The same is the case with Bangladesh. Bangladesh can earn substantial foreign exchange by selling natural gas to India. (Chellany, 2005:75) But because of Bangladesh's unwillingness to export gas to India and India's unwillingness to link trade-related issues in its negotiation with Bangladesh, the cooperation is not materialising as desired. One fact is clear that India's energy diplomacy has been restricted by its conflicting interests to the extent to which it is hampering its energy security efforts. Furthermore, India's oil diplomacy with a few countries for acquisition of oil and gas assets abroad through the construction of pipelines, are hindered by certain strategic factors, including the US factor. Quite naturally, India seems to run into conflict of interests with the US while trying to cooperate with potential energy suppliers like Myanmar, Sudan and Venezuela.

It is very much discrenible that India's quest for energy

supply is being met with road blocks in the form of tense border relations with energy suppliers, energy transit countries as also from other buyers in the energy market. Unlike China, which has either resolved or shelved its border disputes, India has unsolved conflicts with almost all of its neighbouring states. India's sensitive relations with Pakistan is standing in the way of the proposed gas pipeline from Turkmenistan or Iran to India, which will have to pass through Pakistani territory. Furthermore, India's not so good relations with natural gas-rich Bangladesh and Myanmar who are very much China friendly have again hampered its energy quest inside South Asia. Thus, India has to deal with more serious geopolitical and security challenges before it can realize its overland pipeline dreams. (Hong, 2009) Moreover, China is always there as a strong competitor in the regional as well as global energy market. Needless to say US strtegies to have a monopoly control over the energy resource rich regions of the world has its own bearing on India's energy diplomacy.

Another important factor to be considered at this jencture is the absence of institutional structure to develop an integrated energy policy. India, now has seven or eight different ministries that are currently involved with energy security. The result is obviously the absence of a single holistic framework which can frame an ingegrated energy policy. (Mehta, 2011) It is noteworthy that China has established a high level energy entity in charge of formulating and implementing its overall energy development strategy. China established the Energy Leading Group in 2005 as a supra-ministerial coordinating body headed by Chinese Premier. In March 2008, China established another national-level energy institution called the National Energy Administration. All this shows China is adept at dealing with energy security issues. It has evolved an integrated energy sector management mechanism by improving coordination between industries and ministries in the matter of the formation, implementation and enforcement of energy policies and strategies. (Hong, 2009)

India has become increasingly conscious about the importance of diversification of energy sources particularly with regard to oil and gas. Oil and gas reserves are concentrated in the unstable Middle East, Persian Gulf, Central Asia and Russia. Over 70 percent of natural gas reserves are located in Russia, Iran and Qatar.

In this new energy world order of intense competition between the developed and emerging countries, Iran, Russia and the energy resource rich Persian Gulf states have reclaimed their advantageous positions as popular energy suppliers. At the same time, India and China have emerged as the biggest consumers of Eurasian energy resources in general and Middle Eastern in particular. (Coşkun, 2011:73)

Middle East

Of late, India's policy towards the Middle East has often been assessed through the lens of Indo-Iranian relations which have come under intense scrutiny. Pakistan has already signed a pipeline deal with Tehran.

China is trying to play a major role in the geo-politics by undertaking massive investments in the country and by becoming Iran's largest trading partner. Recent years have marked India's shrinking presence and China's growing engagement with Iran when firms such as Reliance Industries withdrew due to western pressure.

Moreover, a number of important projects with Indian businesses and the Indian government have either been rejected by Iran or have yet to be finalized due to last minute changes in the terms and conditions by Tehran which shows the unreliability of Iran and the short-sighted diplomacy from the Indian side. The nuclear issue is also equally complicated for Indian-Iranian relations. Iran was not supportive of the Indian nuclear tests in 1998 and was in favour of the UN Security Council's resolution asking India to sign the NPT and CTBT. (Pant, 2011:63, 64) Moreover, the Iranian nuclear issue where US pressure on India was clearly visible. The case of I-

P-I pipeline is another issue. However, India's support for the security of Afghanistan is a crucial point in Indo-Iranian relations.

At the same time, India also wants to secure energy supplies and consolidate economic and trade relations with the Gulf States i.e. Bahrain, Kuwait, Oman, Qatar, Saudi Arabia, and the UAE, or the members of the Gulf Cooperation Council. India is now the fourth largest recipient of Saudi oil after China, the United States and Japan. Both India and Saudi Arabia are having their own strategic interest in themselves. Other than oil, India wants Saudi Arabia's partnership to counterweight its traditional ally Pakistan in the Islamic world. Having the third largest Muslim population in the world, India possesses an advantage. Likewise, the Iranian Islamic Revolution of 1979 which added a new phase of rivalry between Iran and Saudi Arabia, the relationship with India is having another advantage for Saudi Arabia.

Therefore, India must use the opportunity of engaging Saudi Arabia in a mutually beneficial manner. However, energy has become the major driving force in Gulf-Indian relations. The GCC countries supply 45 percent of India's petroleum consumption and out of which Saudi Arabia is exporting a quarter of those supplies and Kuwait, Oman, and the UAE are other major suppliers.

Moreover, Qatar is the exclusive supplier of natural gas, annually supplying five million tons of LNG to India. India is also engaging Israel bilaterally by becoming Israel's second largest trading partner for non-military goods and services in Asia. In essence, India is in a good position in its relationship with the Middle East. The security consequences of a rising Iran in the Arab Gulf states, Tehran's nuclear drive, its interference in neighbouring Iraq, and President Ahmadinejad's aggressive rhetoric are raising anxieties in Arab states about a resurgent Iran, forcing them to reorient their diplomacy accordingly where an emerging India becomes a better option (ibid). For India, it is the 65 percent of Middle

Eastern oil which has become the diplomatic priority. However, India also has to face China and the US as strong competitors in the Middle Eastern chessboard.

Central Asia and Russia

Central Asian and Russian oil and gas are another source where India can diversify its energy security thrust. However, India has not yet entered into any long term energy import agreement with the countries of Central Asia but it is trying to enhance its own political, economic and military influence there. The proposed gas pipeline from central Asia, i.e. Turkmenistan-Afghanistan-Pakistan-India (TAPI), if it is successful, would be able to supply gas from Central Asia and the Caucasus region to India through an interlinked region connecting Turkmenistan. In addition to central Asian hydrocarbon, India is also trying to access hydroelectricity from Tajikistan and Kyrgyzstan to supply to its northern Indian states. However, this path is also not free from any difficulty. India faces strategic competition from China and the US who is an old player in this part of Eurasia. (Blank, 2009:302) China with its durable energy strategy has built its oil and natural gas pipelines from Central Asia faster than other countries.

It has signed agreements with the central Asian countries with a long term vision. Through massive investments, Chinese influence and visibility is growing significantly in a positive way in the region. However, China is not much comfortable with Russia where it will face strategic competition. (Pop, 2010) Russia's resurgence as a major energy power in the world stage has again changed world politics. As an old ally, India expects Russia to play a major role as a global power. At the same time, a rising India can play a great part for a multipolar world ambition of Russia. So, in this new global system, it has become necessary to diversify their respective interest and engage each other in a mutually beneficial manner. India must have to frame a long-term

Central Asian energy vision to face a great deal of competition and to project itself as a major player in the region.

Africa

The energy deposits in Africa have generated a great deal of interest all over the world including India. India opted to establish relations with more remote regions in order to secure its energy supplies. The African continent holds 9.4 percent of the world's oil reserves. Angola is Africa's largest oil producer having superior grade oil with low sulphur content. The United States is the single largest buyer of Angolan crude followed by China. Angola is the third largest source of Chinese imports. Mozambican coal has attracted Indian companies and has seen growing investment. India's historical linkages and diplomatic relations brought these countries closer and helped in promoting investment. India and Mozambique have closer diplomatic relations and in Mozambique, Indian companies have invested in coal. India also has invested in SaoTome and Principe and Indian companies have secured shares in oil blocks. However, competition from international oil companies especially Chinese oil companies in Angola has kept India out of the oil sector. In 2004, the ONGC through its international arm ONGC Videsh Limited (OVL) made a bid to buy Shell's fifty percent share in Block 18 of Angola. The deal was important for India as it could have yielded about 5 million barrels of crude oil daily. But Chinese company's last minute intervention and much higher aid package made India lose the bid. (Sahu, 2010)

United States

In an article entitled 'Nuclear power is our gateway to a prosperous future' India's nuclear scientist and ex-President A.P.J. Abdul Kalam has argued that India is blessed with a very rare and important nuclear fuel called Thorium which is considered to be the nuclear fuel of the future. Nuclear power, when compared with other sources of energy, provides a relatively clean, high-density source of reliable energy with an international presence. He argues, "There is a need for better technology and more stable plant design across the world, but the occurrence of four failures in six decades cannot be made out as a case for completely disbanding the technology." He assures, "it is poor judgment and a deliberate act of spreading fear to compare a nuclear bomb with a nuclear plant. The bomb is designed to deliver a large amount of energy over a very short period of time, leading to explosions, firestorms and massive heat energy generated to obliterate every object in its path. That is what a bomb is supposed to do! Civilian nuclear applications in the form of a power plant, on the other hand, are designed to deliver small amounts of energy in a sustainable manner over a far larger time frame. It is designed with systems to control and cool the nuclear reaction. There are safety procedures and back-ups, and even in the event of failures, as in the 2011 disaster, the destructive might will never be even a fraction of what happens in the case of a nuclear bomb." Since July 2005, Indo-US relationship has accelerated a new point of strategic engagement. Nuclear power which is an affordable, clean and abundant energy source, if developed completely, can lead us to a healthy future. (Kalam and Singh, 2011)

To this end, the Indo-US Civil Nuclear Deal marked an end in India's nuclear isolation. The deal if unsuccessful will hamper India's energy security as well as rising strategic profile. But this relationship is having its own rhetoric from both the sides and that has to be managed carefully by taking into account each other's expectations.

Concluding Observations

From the above analysis certain important points are clearly emerging. Firstly, India does not enjoy self sufficiency in the matter of domestic energy sources whether it is oil, natural gas or coal. We have to buy it from the international market which is mainly controlled by the US and India's attempts to make inroads into a difficult terrain are curtailed by an insurmountable presence of China. It is also note worthy that India's energy diplomacy is fine tuned to diversify market access. At the same time lack of an integrated energy administration mechanism has been neutralizing the diplomatic initiatives of the Indian foreign policy establishment for diversification of the energy procurement market. In the present day energy world order it is a daunting task to maintain cordial relations with traditional suppliers in the Gulf region as also making forays into new regions which are blessed with abundant supply of energy resources like Central Asia and Africa. In addition to the diversifying of supply sources India has to concentrate on tapping hither to a little tapped sources of energy within the country. Our research in the field of renewable energy sources have to come out with commercially viable technology to tap wind and solar energy. As it has rightly been pointed out by our former president A.P.J. Abdul Kalam, "nuclear power is our gateway to a prosperous future".

Neo-liberal globalization and rapid industrialization and urbanization in China and India have added a new dimension to security discourses in the form of energy security, which has become the prime concern of every state in the international arena. In this complex scenario, India needs a very careful strategic move towards its regional neighbours as well as global friends. India needs to rearticulate its energy strategies and engage regional as well as global players through bilateral and multi-lateral mechanisms.

There is also a growing need for diplomatic and economic support for ways to minimize the Middle East's influence by developing alternative supply sources and alternative energy routes from Central Asia and Africa by engaging them for a long term relationship. Furthermore, energy cooperation and proactive energy diplomacy in its South Asian neighbourhood would allow India to transform into an important global player who could shape its regional environment. By emerging as a secured country in its energy sector, India can retain its dominant position in South Asia. Moreover, well-planned pragmatic energy diplomacy towards Central Asia, limited but healthy relationship with China and strategic friendship with the US would enable India to emerge as a major player in international politics.

References

Blank, Stephen (2009), "India and Central Asia: Part of the New Great Game" in Harsh V. Pant (ed.), *Indian Foreign Policy in a Unipolar World,* Routledge, pp. 277-304.

Chellaney, Brahma (2005), India's Future Security Challenge: Energy Security" in *India as a New Global Leader,* The Foreign Policy Centre.

Coşkun, BezenBalamir (2010), "Energizing the Middle East: Iran, Turkey and Persian Gulf States", *Turkish Policy Quarterly*, Vol. 9, No. 2, pp. 71-80.

Energy Information Administration, *Country Analysis Briefs*, www.eia.doe.gov.

Energy Outlook 2030, *BP Statistical Review 2011*, London, January 2011.

India Energy Handbook, 2011, *International Energy Consulting Corporation (IECC)*, PSI Media Inc., Las Vegas, Nevada (USA) www.iecc-us.com.

India Hydrocarbon Vision, 2025 (2001), *Ministry of Petroleum and natural Gas*, Government of India, petroleum.nic.in (accessed on 13-3-2013).

Integrated Energy Policy: Report of the Expert Committee (2006), Planning Commission of India, Government of India.

Kalam, A.P.J. Abdul and Srijan Pal Singh (2011), "Nuclear power is our gateway to a prosperous future", Special Essay, *The Hindu*, Sunday, November 6.

Lall, Marie (2008), "India-Myanmar Relations-Geopolitics and Energy in Light of the New Balance of Power in Asia", *ISAS WorkingPpaper*, No. 29.

Maithani, P.C. (2011), "The Private Sector and Climate Change: Opportunities and Challenges in Emerging Economies", *Renewable energy in India-A Policy Perspective,* Ministry of New and Renewable Energy.

Mehta, Vikarm (2011), "India's Energy Options: New Sources, Innovations and Areas of Cooperation" Remarks at the Center for Strategic and International Studies (CSIS) B1 Conference Center.

Hong, Zhao (2009), "China and India: The Energy Policies", *EAI Background Brief No. 462.*

Misra, Kishlaya (2012), "Energy Diplomacy for Energy Security" *Ninth AIMS International Conference on Management.*

Nanda, Nitya (2009), "Trading in the World Energy Market" in Ligia Noronha and Anant Sudarshan (ed.), *India's Energy Security*, Routledge, pp. 51-63.

Pant, Harsh V. (2011), "India's Relations with Iran: Much Ado about Nothing", *The Washington Quarterly*, No. 34:1, pp. 61-74.

Panwar, Namrata (2009), "India and China Competing over Myanmar Energy Resources", *Working Draft for BISA Conference*, University of Leicester, Leicester.

Pardesi, Manjeet S. and Sumit Ganguly (2009), "India and Energy Security: A Foreign Policy Priority" in Harsh V. Pant (ed.), *Indian Foreign Policy in a Unipolar World,* Routledge, pp. 99-127.

Pop, Irina Ionela (2010), "China's Energy Strategy in Central Asia: Interactions with Russia, India and Japan", UNISCI *Discussion Papers*, No. 24 (October).

Roadmap for Upscaling and Mainstreaming Renewables, *DIREC 2010 Report*, Ministry of New and Renewable Energy, Government of India

Sahu, Manendra (2010), "Energy Resources in Lusophone Africa and India's Energy Demand", *African Current*, Volume XXX No. 46.

Part IV
Maritime Security

12

India's Maritime Security

Harvir Sharma

We are aware of the changes that are taking place on the globe. Due to the break-up of the Soviet Union and the emergence of Central Asian republics, the Cold War between United States of America and the USSR is almost over. Eastern Europe and the Soviet Union have opted for multi-party politics and mixed economy. The unification of Germany has changed the geo-political scenario of the entire Europe.

In a military sense, with the reduction of NATO's significance, the equations are changing in Europe which is likely to emerge as a strong entity in global affairs. New relationships are emerging between Japan and the Soviet Union in terms of revised economic relations. Since more littoral states are there than ever before, there are more navies and maritime interests. The Arabian Peninsula and the Gulf region will continue to remain an area of competitive struggle and world focus due to vast oil reserves. To meet the current crisis, the US and the Western Powers have reinforced their naval presence in the region to safeguard their economic interests and if required, in support of their friendly littorals in the region.

It is essential to assess the geo-strategic and geo-political environment in our neighbourhood. The mobility of naval forces ensures that they can move rapidly into an area of confrontation to provide fire power where none existed earlier. If it is desired to maintain a low key posture, it will help to do so. If the task be such that there is a requirement for projection of sea power, it will just as easily switch to that option. It is appropriate to examine India's capabilities and weaknesses and clearly define the nation's role and identify the maritime strategy to sustain this role in the coming years. Traditionally, analysts of naval power have understood its economic foundation. Modern experts have traced the economic power of continental states and maritime empires and have opined that in modern technological situations, it is the socio-economic well-being of a nation which is closely associated with its abilities as a maritime power. The growth of maritime power depends on the socio-economic well-being of a country. It would be relevant to appraise the socio-economic and technological challenges which will be faced by India in the future.

Maritime strategy cannot be viewed in isolation. It forms part of the national strategy as it takes into account, besides naval forces, several other factors relating to maritime strategy could be defined as the capability to exploit all resources which are essential for meeting the maritime goals of a nation during peace and war. Maritime strategy is but a small part of the overall strategy of a nation which in turn, is a reflection of its national policy. Article 51 of the Constitution, talks about the promotion of international peace and security and specifies a need to evolve a strategy on national security or in other words, a defence strategy.

Now, let us take a closer view of the Indian Ocean Region and examine some aspects of its oceanic geography which has given India an advantageous maritime position location. The Indian Ocean covers 72 million square kilometres and extends 10,500 kilometres across the continents of Africa, Asia and Australia. It encompasses one-fifth of the world's sea area, washes the shores of 36 littorals and 11 hinterland states. Most of the littoral states on the periphery of the ocean are developing nations and economic constraints make them susceptible to intervention and influence by super powers. India dominates the Indian Ocean and due to her size and relation with the littorals, commands considerable respect in the region. Sub-continental India has a coastline of 6,300 kilometres with the island territories of Lakshadweep and Andaman and Nicobar adding another 1,100 kilometres.

To a maritime strategist, the significance of island territories, particularly those who overlook busy sea lanes or choke points, are obvious. In the case of India, we have seaboards. The new emerging laws of the sea when applied to our coast line and island territories give us an Exclusive Economic Zone (EEZ) of a staggering 2.2 million square kilometres. Geography and demographic compulsions and the profile compels us to harness these vast resources for our national well-being.

India's Maritime Security Environment

Innovative use of technology and human intelligence for coastal security, warrants the highest priority and piece meal acquisitions by individual department will be counter-productive. For instance, virtual coastal fence (akin to the barbed-wire fence along the Indo-Pak land border) comprise static radar chains with S-band radars. The lateral induction of naval and coast guard personnel into the state marine police is long overdue. Coastal states would be well advised to appoint individual maritime advisers. The vast coast line and EEZ give rise to India's maritime interests which in turn are a function of her politico-economic and military interests.

The economic rise of Germany, the political implications of a united Germany, the restructuring of NATO and a broader European unit are of immense significance. These have profound effects not only on Europe but also on the Afro-Asian region. Keeping this in view, the development of the Indian Navy has been aimed towards an all-round balanced growth. In the long-term perspective, India would have to progressively develop her naval capability and establish her credentials in the Indian Ocean as a 'balancing power'.

If India is to envisage a future role for herself as a maritime power in the region, then the subtleties of sea power as an expression of her politico-economic interests as the most effective tools of diplomacy must prevail. With changing relationships between the great powers, with power bloc in rivalries having receded into the background and the economic imperatives impinging on the ability of nations to divert funds for massive defence spending, the international order is slowly moving towards a state of diffusion of power in several regimes. Mutually opposing stands of the super powers at every pressure point or conflicting regional issues are giving way to the growth of new power patterns.

The issue of the emergence of a united Germany occupies the European scene. Similarly, rise of Japan as an economic power and the rise of China and India as new power centres in Asia cannot be ignored. A changing global scenario has been initiated to recast great power relationships. Factually, its effects are extending to our neighbourhood. Inherent instabilities and traditional rivalries have admittedly something to do with these developments. Specifically, the Indo-US relations show signs of relatively marked improvements in coming years. It is pertinent to quote that the US has categorically stated that "India is a responsible nuclear State". It is yet to show improvements in reduction of sophisticated American weapons in our immediate neighbourhood inimical to our interests. The client status of Pakistan seems still etched in the strategic perception of the United States. Military overtures of Pakistan and her ambitions to seek a bigger regional role with US military aid appears to be around for few years in the foreseeable future. There are arguments that the new strategic environment may be hospitable and helpful to large developing countries which are stable and express dynamism in their approach to external affairs.

Flow of Energy through Strategic Sea Lanes

As a commodity of strategic importance, energy has been the object of geo-strategic confrontation for its access, control and distribution, as fossil fuels remain the main power engine of industrial development. To ensure a constant and uninterrupted oil supply, the strategies of industrialized countries have been articulated by the use of military force, economic incentives and uneasy alliances with oil producers, namely in the Persian Gulf. Access to Persian Gulf as the key strategic location, is likely to be the most important factor of contemporary energy geopolitics.

The geo-strategies of maritime petroleum circulation involves six major chock points—Strait of Hormuz, Strait of Malacca, Bab-el-Mandeb, Suez Canal, Bosporus and Panama Canal. These are in fact the strategic passages of the world. Two of these strategic passages are of extremely high importance—Hormuz and Malacca—since they account for more than 60 percent of oil transits. This is particularly the case of China, as its oil imports stretch from the Strait of Hormuz, Malacca and the South China Sea, most of which are patrolled by the United States. It is argued that as there is no multilateral approach to energy security in Asia, the competition for energy resources may spark regional and international conflicts.

The internal instability in Pakistan and its armed forces intent to exploit the internal and external situation to advantage, the rise of Islamic fundamentalism in Afghanistan, particularly, spread of terrorism through Wakhan corridor, are serious security concerns. As such, Pakistan is an important factor in Indo-Afghan relations. An Islamic alliance to checkmate pan-handled Afghanistan does not appear to be taking shape. However, an arrangement of a loose alliance of Persian Gulf states with Pakistan playing the proxy for the United States may become a reality.

If it is so, the Western theatre on land, sea and air will continue to witness the introduction of sophisticated arms through the United States of America. To ensure constant and uninterrupted oil supplies, the strategies of industrialized countries have been articulated by the use of military force (mostly by the United States), economic incentives and uneasy alliances with the oil producing countries, mainly in the

Persian Gulf. Access to the Persian Gulf (because of its key strategic location), is likely to be the most important factor of contemporary energy geo-politics.

China's Initiatives

As far as China is concerned, her internal situation indicates the competing politico-economic claims to control the shape of things to come. Sanctions that followed the Tiananmen Square incident reportedly appear to have hurt the economy. Another demographic factor is dominating in the Sinkiang Province of China. The natives of this region namely, Uighurs, Khirghiz and Kazaks with their pastoral economy, are demanding for autonomy. The three Central Asian Republics—Kazakhstan, Khirghizstan and Tajikhstan are bordering China. Even when these Republics were part of the then Soviet Union, Russia had extended a railway line from Tashkent to Alam Atty, a new town of Kazakhstan and the people of Sinkiang used to get all supplies from Kazakhstan and not from main land China. China is worried about the Islamic ring in this region. In the regional context, China's sale of ballistic missiles to Saudi Arabia, an active defence co-operation with Pakistan and Bangladesh and possible talks between Pakistan and China over sharing of nuclear submarine technology are serious concerns to India.

In the Sino-Pak nexus, Pakistan is providing dry-port facilities to China through Pak-occupied Kashmir, especially via the Karakoram Highway which the Chinese built in 1968. Both the countries named this China-Gilgit Road as a "friendly communication link" between Pakistan and China. Through this highway, Chinese are more successful in gaining entry to the Arabian Sea through Karachi port than their Russian rivals. As usual, India has been very late in realizing China's seriousness about Maldives. India continued to have faith that like her neighbours–Nepal, Myanmar and Sri Lanka, the island country Maldives will remain loyal to New Delhi. The main problem for India is, that Maldives has become another pearl in China's string of facilities around its periphery.

China's politico-economic and diplomatic investment in Maldives is significant and has given India a run for its money and even left it behind in some areas in Maldives. China became the first non-South Asian country to have a diplomatic mission in Maldives—a nation of about 4 lakh people. China's trade with Maldives reached early US$ 4mn in 2010, up 56 percent against 2009, while that of India declined from ₹ 608.21 crore in 2008-09 to ₹ 395.57 crore in 2009-10. China is spreading infrastructure with a Chinese company constructing 1000 houses in Maldives. She also built the Foreign Ministry and National Museum buildings in Male in July 2010.

In the same year, direct charter and commercial flights were launched between the two countries. China's probing and expansion into the Seychelles and Maldives are of concern to India. Chinese port projects around India in Bangladesh, Myanmar and Sri Lanka are commercial ventures with strategic and military potentials. These ports are seen as part of Beijing's far-sighted policy to choke India. China is also reportedly, constructing its first overseas military base in Seychelles, not far from Maldives.

However, in a friendly shift towards India, Maldives extended friendship with India and permitted India to deploy coastal radar patrol in its territorial waters and Exclusive Economic Zone in 2009. An Indian company was also allowed to refurnish an airbase there to host Indian reconnaissance and surveillance aircraft. This shift is part of a strategy since smaller states like to play the China card against India and Maldives has also benefited from it. India also extended its support worth US$ 140mn to Maldives and is likely to develop a port there. Indian influence in the Indian Ocean grew larger when the Indian giant company GMR took over Male international airport. Many believe it as a broader Indian policy to have control in the Indian Ocean. Indian Ocean's geopolitics may become quite complicated.

It further added that the India-China fight over the region

is hurting Maldives. But then, politics is the art of survival. China is spreading its wings and is sharpening its claws rapidly from deadly long range nuclear missiles and is expanding blue-water navy to potent space and cyber warfare capabilities. China will have a modern military capable of prolonged high-intensity combat operations in near future. India can ill-afford to ignore China's increasing trans-border military strength, its assiduous strategic encircling of India and hardening its posture in the Sino-Indian border talks. India remains concerned over China's close military affiliations with Pakistan, Sino-Pak nexus in Pak-occupied Kashmir and Beijing's growing foot print in the Indian Ocean, Central Asian Republics and Africa.

Power Struggle in the Indian Ocean

Once an economic giant of Asia, Japan's economic power, favourable balance of payments and trade and status as one of the big aid donors, makes it a main actor in global politics. Though termed as a maritime self defence force, Japan's military and naval capabilities are substantial. Their naval assets are modern and superior in qualitative terms. There are discussions on whether Japan, encouraged by its economic strength, and can embark on a militarization process.

If so, will their reach extend beyond the 1,000 miles zone and into the Indian Ocean Region. Indications are there that Japan will have a major role to play in our region either directly or indirectly because of the Persian Gulf oil, investments and economic interests in this region. Going through the above, the following observations emerge:

1. Due to China's initiatives in the Indian Ocean rim countries, she continues to retain an active influence in the Indian Ocean which may be inimical to India's security and maritime interests.
2. Japan has emerged as a new economic power capable of exerting sufficient military pressure in the Asian region.
3. Should the United States of America decide to reduce or

withdraw from the Indian Ocean region, the following scenario may emerge:

- A limited security arrangement with a few Islamic countries to checkmate Iran with the United States playing a supportive role in the Gulf region.
- A US-Japan alliance to maintain an active presence to keep open Japan's sea-lanes of communication.

4. Rise of India's maritime power to provide a stable influence in the sea areas surrounding the Indian Sub-continent.
5. China's active participation to play a leading role in the Indian Ocean region.

Since the growth of India's maritime power will only enhance the stability of this region, a period of active and tacit support from several quarters can be expected. Our active maritime posture, however, may have to overcome some of the traditional regional irritants. The new phase in super power relationship will also permit the United States to view our naval strategy in the right perspective. Our legitimate maritime interests and commensurate naval growth will be rightfully acknowledged by the United States and will not be viewed as an extension of Soviet influence as has been done in the past. The conversion of strategic thoughts into necessary naval hardware involves the application of technologies. It has been realized that during the last 40 years, some areas of naval warfare have recorded relatively overwhelming technological progress. These are satellite capabilities for intelligence, extended ranges and accuracies in naval missilery, electronic warfare and underwater nuclear propulsion.

Looking ahead, India's first concern must be with its neighbourhood–South Asia and the Indian Ocean regions. Its next concern should be with the Indian Ocean littoral states, the Gulf, East Africa, South East Asia, the Asia Pacific and the island-nation states. Thereafter, comes the great powers–Western Europe, Africa and Latin America. In the immediate neighbourhood, while seeking friendly and mutually beneficial relations with Nepal, Bhutan, Bangladesh, Maldives and Myanmar, we must be aware of certain objective factors that will condition the relationship. We must expect a level of continuing apprehension on their part about India's size and dominant political, economic and military presence in the sub-continent. Sri Lanka and other immediate neighbours will remain our security concerns.

Alongside this, must actively encourage regional economic integration through SAARC and bilaterally reinforce greater complementarily with our neighbours. Pakistan is a significant neighbour and India has to deal with it cautiously and carefully. We must not make the mistake of considering Pakistan as a strategic, economic or power echo. Our foreign policy concerns must reflect our larger objectives. We would wish to have friendly and economically vigorous relations with Pakistan but this may not be possible till Pakistan returns to proper democratic functioning and till its national identity is further consolidated.

Till then they will find cause to fear our political system, secular society and economic potentials. China has been accepted in the club of nuclear weapon states. Its capacity to act as a major power will be dependent on its economic and technological modernization. India has an edge over its powerful neighbour. India's democratic and open system is better equipped to handle the consequences of technological change and rapid economic growth. India and China are two big powers of Asia and must inevitably contend for political and economic advantage in South East Asia, Indo-China and South Asia. China has resolved the border issues with most of her neighbours except India. China is not in hurry to solve the border problems with India.

They do believe in the existing reality. The Chinese are not going to vacate the areas under their possession. China's cartographic and demographic aggression to claim Arunachal Pradesh is falsely offensive. It is unlikely that the border problem will result in hostilities. Both the countries need peace to pursue their economic development and both have to respect each other's military capabilities. China will remain active in its support for Pakistan as its strategic ally and will keep its options open for Nepal, Myanmar and Bangladesh, just as India could continue to support Vietnam, seek a role in the Cambodian settlement and keep options open in South East Asia. Both India and China would further strengthen their naval forces. Since China is taking more initiatives in the Indian Ocean and India hopefully, in the South China Sea, India's policy towards China must have dexterity to combine a tension-free bilateral political relationship with aiming at economic advantage in Asia and in the global pecking order.

India and Africa share an enviable geographic proximity in the western Indian Ocean. The piracy threat along the Somali and East African coast provides the Indian Navy a grand opportunity to evolve in a regional security protectorate. India could escalate this by keeping sea-lanes of communication like the Gulf, Aden, Beb El Mandeb and the Mozambique channel secured, and by developing the naval capabilities of the East African States through increased joint naval exercises, new listening posts and the supply of vessels.

The Indian Ocean Naval Symposium (from which China is excluded) and revival of the Indian Ocean Rim Association for Regional Cooperation are important steps in this regard. Tactical triangulations with other partners, such as the India-Brazil-South Africa (IBSA) naval forces, the US AFRICOM, the European Union or NATO could further leverage this advantage over China. India could start thinking of developing its democracy and human rights discourse in Africa. As a founding member of the Community of Democracies, Delhi could explore this regime advantage and supposed popularity of the "Beijing consensus".

Some African countries have shown their interests in learning from India's successful experience with federalism. India needs to explore its diplomatic capital as a "bridging power". India's role as a non-aligned power and consistent support to the African independence movements has also earned it a persisting respectability as a "Southern Power". India is also a member of the Commonwealth Organization and is at the heart of the impressive tri-continental IBSA axis that provides it an advantage to engage the Southern Africa Development Community and Sub-Saharan Africa.

Strategic Sea Lanes

India's geo-strategic location confers upon it unique strategic advantages. Its peninsular shape makes it the natural contender to dominate the Indian Ocean, the hub of commercial activity of the world. Our area of influence clearly extends well beyond the geographical borders i.e. from the Persian Gulf in the west to across the straits of Malacca in the east and from the Central Asian Republics in the north to the Equator in the south. The geo-strategy of maritime petroleum circulation involves six choke-points: Strait of Hormuz, Strait of Malacca, Beb-el-Mandeb, Suez Canal, Bosphorous and Panama Canal. In fact, these are the strategic passages of the world. India's vast coast line of 7,683 kilometres, through which 97 percent of her overseas trade and 80 percent of oil transit, along with island territories, provide it with an exclusive economic zone of over two million square kilometres—an area endowed with rich and rare minerals and still relatively unexploited.

Given its large size, geo-strategic location, trade links and enormous exclusive economic zone, India is the natural leader in South Asia. Geographically, India must dominate the Indian Ocean, since the region is very significant for us. Our long coast-line, island territories, sizeable economic zone, tremendous economic potential of the ocean's resources, growing sea-borne trade and the presence of extra territorial powers are known to us. We must continue to oppose the presence of these extra-regional powers but such opposition can only begin to be credible if we can forge together an alternative. India's foreign policy should aim at mobilizing the littoral states to put together in a regional arrangement that could, in time, provide such an alternative.

India could work with Indonesia, Malaysia, Australia, Iran, the Gulf states and hopefully, Pakistan to ensure the security of the sea-lanes and monitor the activities of outside presences. This could enable outside powers to minimize their presence in the Indian Ocean region but still not ensure their withdrawal. Even more provocatively, the United States could consider working with India or other NATO countries on functioning bilateral relations with Iran, and to move goods from either Chah Bahar or Bandar Abbas. Iran and India have built a substantial infrastructure, linking Iranian ports to Afghanistan.

The peninsular India is flanked to its east, west and south by the Bay of Bengal, Arabian Sea and the Indian Ocean, respectively. The Andaman and Nicobar Islands are located 1300 km. away from the nearest point of its east coast and are strategically significant in relation to the entrance to the Malacca Strait. The Lakshadweep and Minicoy islands lie about 450 km. from the nearest land point on the West Coast in the Arabian Sea, on the east-ward sea lane of communication, the Persian Gulf and the Red Sea. India's geographical area, geo-strategic location, trade links and its exclusive economic zone connect its security environment directly with its extensive neighbourhood, particularly neighbouring countries and the regions of Central Asia, South-East Asia, the Gulf and the Indian Ocean.

In an increasingly globalised environment, these factors involve concomitant security concerns, responsibilities and challenges. The rise of countries like China, Brazil, South Africa and India are developments of global significance. The trend holds promise and opportunities, as well as challenges. Even though the probability of conventional full scale inter-state wars is reckoned by several defence analysts to have reduced, the security environment has become complex and tense, with incidence of low intensity conflicts and asymmetric threats taking various forms, including domestic and transnational terrorism, narco-terrorism, cyber warfare and piracy.

The threat of piracy and terrorism to international trade and safety of the sea lanes of communication have emerged as a major problem. The spread of piracy to the areas close to India's western sea board has made this a cause of grave concern. With regard to the regional security environment, the security situation in India's' neighbourhood continues to be a cause for concern at present, owing to continued insurgency in Afghanistan, spread of terrorism, growing Islamic fundamentalism and radicalism in the region. The dynamic regional and global security scenario depict a wide spectrum of challenges to India which must be faced rapidly and effectively, in order to sustain and support the growth and rise of the nation and development of its people. Nonetheless, the country and our security forces remain fully prepared to tackle all eventualities.

Conclusion

Geopolitically, the Indian Ocean Region is immensely diverse in its complexion. It owns enormous sub-regional personalities and several local conflicts exist at this level. The vacuum in the region is filled up by the presence of Western powers.

Global terrorism, religious orthodoxy and drug-trafficking have emerged as geo-strategic problems in the region because of the location of the hub of these international threats. It is a long-term agenda since solutions would need drastic changes in regional situations and external approaches. The Gulf region is exceptionally very rich in seabed resources which are very significant for great consumer countries inside and outside the region. The issue of energy supplies through the strategic sea-lanes is a basic concern and the sensitive choke-points on the western and eastern edges of the region have a major geo-strategic significance in this regard, and of trade flow in general. India's central location in the Afro-Asian region, its dependence on the sea-lanes and its maritime capability enable her to pursue cooperative maritime policies which are in the interests of all littoral states.

India at first sight seems an unlikely global power. It has a hostile neighbour to its North-West, a 50 year old Maoist insurgency, corrupt political governance and over 445 million poor people who live on less than ₹ 26 a day. India's economy and markets are growing despite political mis-governance. To play a role in global affairs in line with its size, population resources and economy, India needs to realize and act like a major power. It must fix governance at home, build a strategic foreign policy and leverage its demographic and economic assets with strong political will. In the emerging world order, the India-US partnership will be pivotal. As one of the pivots in the new world order, India has four priceless assets and three damaging liabilities. The assets are its growing economy, strong military power, advanced scientific approach and plural democracy. The liabilities are mis-governance, poor domestic politics and social inequality.

Unless good governance overlays our economic growth, poverty will persist. No nation can become great if nearly half of its people live in penury. Inclusive growth follows from good governance. Without that, India's rise as a great power will falter.

As a maritime nation, one of India's national interests is the free and open use of the seas for communication and trade. Since defence technology and weapon systems are developed over the years, the security of sea-lanes of communication has to be taken into account. Threats arise from sub-surface, air and space dimensions. The continuing progress of off-shore oil extraction and the living and non-living resources in the seas around India influence the manner in which India needs to look at the sea for economic well being. Accordingly, the application of any credible maritime strategy must encompass and exercise the judicious use of the seas for legitimate commercial, scientific, economic and security interests. This is not only in terms of the sustenance of India's economic growth and development, but also for her overall national security.

It cannot be ruled out that the action is being taken by great powers in the oceans of the developing nations to hurt the maritime interests of the developing nations. We have to look at it from the point of view of the changing environment, and we should also view the probability of the nature of wars in which we would like to be involved and whether we are likely to be involved in a war with any major industrialized power in the world. Creation of naval assets not merely takes time but involves appropriate technologies and costs.

It enables us to the point of resources and technical co-operation. Escalating costs of equipment and weapon systems have imposed strains on our ability to add requisite capabilities. However, with certain judicious planning it should be possible to attain the required capabilities. It would be advantageous to us in future. Since we are not self-sufficient in most of the areas of naval technology, co-operation with certain select countries in this regard would be fruitful. The Indian Navy is passing through fundamental determinants and transformation in relation to its force structure and doctrines along with its expanding maritime security concerns. A synthetic politico-maritime approach may secure the essential co-operation. In the emerging geo-political and strategic environment with socio-economic challenges, India will certainly go ahead with its strong Maritime Strategy in future.

India's power status seems to be the logical conclusion of its geo-strategic thrust that includes its geographical location at the 'Centre of Asia' and as a sentinel anchor in the Indian Ocean. More than the geo-strategic thrust, it is India's economic dynamism, political stability, military capability and over-growing pool of skilled and enterprising manpower, that contribute to India's aspirations and projections as a great power of this new millennium. It requires no emphasis that now the main global dynamic is economics and the interdependent technological and scientific innovations. It is a universal fact that economic development does not ever translate into military effectiveness; still all great power shifts in the world's military power balance have followed alterations in the productive balances of countries. In case, we can enhance the economic strength of India which is the world's largest democracy and also modernize its defence management to counter the emerging maritime security challenges that have been thrown up by a resurgent India by providing the cutting edge to its security forces to counter the threats to our national security and to defend our national marine interests, the nation would become a power to reckon with.

In history, a nation's pursuit of friendly and mutually beneficial ties with a globally dominant power has hardly translated into securing a trustworthy friend. The implications for India of China's growing relations with the Indian Ocean rim countries present India's policy-makers with the classic dilemma of balancing geopolitical compulsions with geo-economic objectives. Geography is central to national security, it cannot be wished away. North-east India has been a hostage to geopolitics for far too long. It is now time to cautiously open up to the forces of geo-economics, while at the same time taking measures to ascertain that there are no rude surprises emanating from the maritime geo-strategic front.

The Indian Naval forces, due to their multidimensional abilities, strategic positioning and robust presence in the regions of interest have been catalysts for peace, tranquility and stability in the Indian Ocean. In recent times, the Indian Navy has engaged other maritime countries to help national initiatives of cooperation and engagement and our naval fleets have sailed and exercised successfully in the South China Sea and the African and Mediterranean waters. Such exercises have strengthened bilateral relationship, enriched inter-operability and supported in sharing useful practices from other navies. Such overseas deployments assure our overseas Indian people. To perform its mandated tasks, the Indian Navy is escalating its capabilities, cooperation and inter-operability with regional and extra-regional naval forces.

The Indian Navy has ever responded swiftly and carefully to various challenges, like safeguarding our frontiers and sea trade, combating piracy and terrorism at sea, conducting hydrographic surveys in Indian Ocean Region and in the waters of friendly foreign countries, coordinating navigational warnings over vast oceanic and littoral areas and providing search and rescue facilities for those in distress. India's proactive response and professional handling of situations has encouraged a number of countries of the Indian Ocean Region in seeking its help and advice to counter maritime challenges in their respective exclusive economic zones. India continues to support and augment efforts towards capacity building and surveillance, thereby enhancing overall maritime capabilities in Afro-Asian region.

Creation of capability and modernization of the force is being pursued with valour, based upon threat perceptions, prevailing external strategic security environment and emerging innovations in the field of science and technology. The Indian Navy is immensely committed to the process of indigenization by inducting capabilities from the public as well as private sectors. To ascertain the security of sea lines of communications from piracy attacks, the Indian Navy has deployed one war ship regularly in the Gulf of Aden with effect from October 3, 2008.

Our long-term and immediate security interests lie in encouraging greater multi-polarity in the evolution of the international community. This requires the emergence of economically strong and stable countries, secured within their legally defined borders and interacting with each other and the major powers from a position of mutual benefit, respect and equality. It would be proper to including the following facts towards India's maritime security imperatives:

1. To maintain a balance with regard to our relations amongst the US, China and Russia to enhance our maritime interests.

2. Relations with our neighbours especially with the island nations and Indian Ocean's rim countries, are immensely desired. Diplomacy without geo-strategic and geo-economic understanding is meaningless.
3. India's growing economic strength and market potential.
4. India's maritime strategy in the Afro-Asian region and India's approach to making use of strategic sea-lanes.
5. Maintaining a nuclear balance in the sub-continent.
6. Internal security is threatened by an interplay of domestic politics, corruption and the absence of good governance. We require internal cleaning.

In short, India has to examine the prognosis of the geo-strategic and geo-economic compulsions in the foreseeable future to visualize how the nation should play its role to shape the regional security environment so as to emerge as an economic power. In doing so, the short long-term national interests of all leading players in the Indian Ocean Region have to be taken note of, so as to understand how these match or mismatch our maritime interests. The focus on India's continental and maritime strategies would be of great significance in assessing a geo-strategic appraisal of the nations on the periphery of the Indian Ocean and the options that India would seek in near future. India needs to work on her own policy for regional stability, economic strength, maritime thinking and modern innovations in weapon technology and defence capability.

13

Global Dimensions of Maritime Piracy

R.S. Vasan

The recent developments in the maritime neighbourhood of India have caused great concern to all the stake holders and security agencies. The uppermost concern today is related to the acts of piracy in the west Arabian Sea that has kept the naval and coast guard forces around the world occupied in chasing the pirates and protecting the vulnerable logistic chains along the sea lanes of communication. Some of the recommended measures to protect shipping by making them sail close to the Indian coast have caused enormous problems for fishermen who are dependent on the fish stocks in the Exclusive Economic Zone (EEZ) for livelihood.

The case of Enrica Lexie, an Italian tanker that shot at a fishing boat mistaking it for a pirate boat that resulted in the killing of two innocent fishermen is an example of this. This has opened up a Pandora's Box that has brought out legal and jurisdictional issues for prosecution of the offenders in recognized areas of the oceans such as the high seas, the contiguous zone and the territorial waters. There are also issues of the efficacy of the surveillance, reconnaissance and information systems that assist the authorities in ensuring that they are in a position to intervene in time to prevent a security/safety breach.

Close on the heels of this shooting incident five more fishermen lost their lives in the waters off Kerala coast again due to the carelessness of another Singapore flagged, Indian owned vessel MV Prabhudeva. While investigations are still being conducted, these two cases clearly bring out the lacunae in our maritime safety and security architecture. The paper will discuss the impact of such actions that affect legitimate activities in the Indian EEZ. The challenges faced by the merchantmen, fishermen and law enforcement agencies as a result of a global phenomenon leading to regional implications, are indeed enormous.

Introduction

Maritime piracy is as old as civilization itself and history is replete with accounts of piracy in many parts of the world including India. The 1990s saw a phenomenal rise in the number of attacks particularly in the Malacca Straits. The increased threat to shipping and crew prompted the international community to establish the Piracy Reporting Centre in Kualalampur to keep a tab on the number of incidents. However, the statistics were skewed as even petty robbery attempts at anchorages were counted as acts of piracy resulting in the numbers going up. It may be noted that Chennai in India and ports in Bangladesh were considered as the most dangerous just based on the methodology of accounting for piracy/robbery attacks.

The piracy attacks in Malacca straits took a heavy toll of shipping in those areas and the Lloyd's War Committee had declared the Malacca Straits as high risk area which led to increase in insurance rates and avoidance of the ports in the area by sea farers. This brought the littoral states of Singapore, Malaysia, Indonesia and Thailand together to work out strategies to combat the menace to ensure that the trading profits did not dwindle. It led to many initiatives by the littoral countries. Some of the important measures adopted are listed below:

1. The right of hot pursuit (chasing an offender in to the territorial waters of a neighbouring country without seeking permission) was provided to ensure that there were no time delays.
2. The nations in question decided to mount a joint air patrol by pooling in resources and ensuring that the

representatives' of all the countries were represented in the aircraft under the Eyes in the Sky (EiS) project.

3. There was greater institutional arrangement to ensure free flow of information and streamlining of response mechanisms.

Also, the tsunami of 2004 dealt a severe blow to the infrastructure of the pirates in Aceh province and also took a heavy toll of many of the pirates and their bases. It is also impossible not to acknowledge the changes brought about to ship and port security since the implementation of the International Ship and Port Security Code in July 2004. The cumulative effect of all this concerted action resulted in bringing down the acts of piracy to single digit from a three digit figure and also ensured that the declaration by the Lloyds committee was reviewed bringing relief to the ship owners plying these routes through the Malacca Straits.

Scene in Somalia

The period from 2004 onwards in the Gulf of Aden witnessed phenomenal increase in the number of incidences of piracy off the Somali coast. Many of the reasons ascribed to this increase in the acts of piracy have their origins in land. Without going in to all the reasons, it would be worthwhile to record some of the more important causes for piracy. Somalia has remained a lawless country and is administered by a Transitional Federal Government (TFG). However, the country has faced numerous spells of droughts and famines leading to unemployment, lack of amenities, funds and even basic minimum amenities. While the country has many tribes who do fight for control over one another, the threat of Jehadi terrorists and practice of extreme fundamentalism by Al Shabaab with links to Al-Qaeda has been a source of serious concern for the TFG and the international community.

The existing state of affairs has forced a constant exodus of refugees from Somalia moving in to the adjoining states. Kenya has borne the brunt of such refugee influx and has declared war against Al-Shabaab. Al-Shabaab which wants to establish the Sharia laws is getting its monetary support from Al-Qaeda and other radical groups and is fighting for controlling areas in Somalia.

The levels of property and mal nutrition compelled the United Nations to implement the Food for Aid programme. However, Al-Shabaab cadres have insisted that the food distribution be done by them as it gives them the power to control people in the country. This has led to clashes and one witnesses Somalia as an unstable country without a future.

Root Cause

Another complaint that is regularly received is about the indiscriminate dumping of toxic waste in Somalian waters that has led to shrinking of the rich fishing grounds. Traditionally, some of the areas around Somalia provided good opportunities for the Somali fishermen to make a decent living from the fisheries catch. The rich fishing grounds were the envy of foreign poachers and apparently they would regularly fish in the Somali waters and did not even allow the Somali traditional fishermen to fish in their own waters.

This happened due to the absence of a declaration of an Exclusive Economic Zone (EEZ) and the means to protect the resources. In the absence of a Navy or a Coast Guard, the Somali fishermen were compelled to protect their own interests and it has been assessed that therein lay the seeds of piracy. The fishermen started defending their fishing areas by taking to arms and soon realized that not only were they able to protect their back yard but if a vessel was taken over then it provided the leverage for demanding ransom. This became the easy way and the Somali fishermen had found a new way as means of livelihood. Unfortunately, on realization that there is a lot of money, the targets became bigger and with the busy shipping routes carrying merchandise and energy products, there was no shortage of targets for the now full fledged pirates.

The escalation of the ransom demands can be realized by the fact that in 2005 a ship would be released for a sum of US$ 15000 and in 2011, a ransom of US$ 13.5 million was paid for release of ship, crew and cargo. The easy money and the modus operandi succeeded in establishing a complete business venture. Many unscrupulous people joined the business venture and were controlling the piracy operations from ashore with use of sophisticated command and control architecture. The supply of arms and ammunition, employment of youth even from hinterland who came looking for easy money, ensured that the threat of piracy grew in proportion and posed serious challenges to the maritime nations and to the seafarers who were now at the mercy of the well established piracy networks.

The problem lay ignored and was by and large left to the shipping companies and the insurance companies to sort out. Invariably it is common for the owner of the vessel to have a flag that is not his nationality. So the owner, the Flag State and the operator could all be in different parts of the globe separated by many time zones. The gravity of the problem was not clearly understood by the nations and the international community at large. It is only from 2008 onwards that there was a greater focus on this region and the UNSC also started getting involved and interested in the happenings that had enormous impact on the concept of the freedom of the high seas and right to safe navigation in the global commons.

Towards the end of 2008, the UNSC indicated that nations who have a stake in the safety of the merchantmen could dispatch their own navies to protect the large volume of shipping that was moving in and out of the straits of Hormuz and the Gulf of Aden. Hence, one witnessed an enormous increase in the number of nations dispatching their own naval units for protection of the merchantmen. The US Navy which has always maintained a presence in the region for energy security and to watch over the developments of Iran, Iraq and Afghanistan was quick to deploy the Combined Maritime

Force (CMF) with rotational command to monitor the seas and to provide help and succor to the merchant ships.

India was also compelled to dispatch its own naval units particularly after the families of the crew members of a Maersk ship highlighted the plight of the sea farers through media and through staging of demonstrations in the capital of the country. The organized grouping of ships besides the CMF consists of the grouping from NATO, and the European Union. Many other navies of the world including, China, Malaysia, Russia, India, Korea, etc., have added to the numbers and have made a slow but steady impact in bringing down the incidents of piracy in the region by better policing coordination and assertive action at sea.

Industrialisation of the Phenomenon

The analysis and the extent of expected investments and turn over in piracy has brought out the bitter truth that it has become an industry. The following has been established:

1. Escalation, considering the ever-growing number of pirates who today even hail from the hinterland (currently totalling at least 1,500, according to the Transitional Federal Government). The escalation is both in terms of the number of mother ships and also the employees if one could call them by that nomenclature.
2. Intensification of the violence of attacks (first weapons of choice are AK-47 automatic assault rifles and RPG-7 rocket launchers); Also, with the efforts of the sea farers to protect themselves in the citadels, there is fear that greater fire power would be brought to bear on the hapless victims and the ships.
3. Sophistication of the modus operandi (increasing use of "mother ships" to backstop attack skiffs, global positioning satellites (GPS), automatic identification system (AIS) data, satellite telephones and counterfeit detectors; organization of re-fuelling at sea of captured ships for the trip to Somalia).

4. Logistic and organisational capacity both over sea and land for negotiations and for holding on to their hostages to provide continuous income even during monsoons. It is assessed that the high level of profit generated has drawn many mercenaries to Somalia and surrounding countries with a view to making a quick buck and the like minded criminals are getting together to establish a fiefdom to control all aspects of piracy.

Action by UNSC

Concerned by the increasing attacks on sea farers, the UN Secretary General, Ban Ki-moon ordered a detailed study by Jack Lang who has come out with the detailed recommendations for addressing the problems both over land and at sea. Some of the key findings of Jack Lang include the following:

1. The violence escalated.
2. The periods of detention became lengthier.
3. The modus operandi became more sophisticated.
4. The area of attacks extended farther to the south (as far as Mozambique) and east in the Indian Ocean.
5. The pirate economy, which has its epicentre in Puntland, is having a destabilizing effect on Somalia and the entire region, owing to rising prices, insecurity of energy supplies and loss of revenue.
6. While world seaborne trade appears to be handling the threat better thanks to naval operations, which play a crucial role in providing security, the number of victims is nevertheless rising, with 1,900 persons taken hostage since the end of 2008. In the long term, the entire world economy could be affected.
7. There are numerous gaps in the counter-piracy effort.

There were many recommendations made by Jack Lang including the setting up of separate courts, improving the economy in Somalia and helping the country to manage its own affairs. While that was the action initiated by the UN, the merchant men who were directly affected started putting in place a slew of measures through the IMB. The Best Management Practices to be adopted while at sea to thwart a developing piracy attack were promulgated. The present edition that governs such practices is designated as BMP 4.

However, there is a need for the BMP to also include the local authorities in the list depending on the area of operation. International Maritime Organisation (IMO) has promulgated a document called Best Management Practices (BMP) that provides clear directives to ship owners and the, ship's crew on the methods that would enhance the safety of the ship and help in preventing any attacks. As per statistics, it has been established that the ships which comply with the BMP are less susceptible to attack.

While it is also true that the presence of the Armed guards also deters pirates, any action to neutralize a developing threat if any, demands greater responsibility, professionalism, training and calibrated responses. It is obvious that the security guards did not assess the situation correctly and also have not complied with the provisions of BMP. BMP clearly indicates that deployment of armed guards is not a substitute for BMP. According to the BMP, the standard actions required are to increase speed, alter course and also deploy fire hoses, barbed wire, acoustic devices etc.

The issue of arms to sea farers and or armed guards that has been debated for centuries was resolved to a certain extent by allowing the carriage of private guards on board ships. However, this has resulted in certain complications including the death of two innocent fishermen off the Kerala coast in February this year. The case of Enrica Lexie is discussed separately subsequently. The figures for 2011 does show that all the measures implemented has shown some results in bringing down the number of incidents. However, there is lot more that needs to be done to eliminate the threat from sea and also resolve all the issues over land in Somalia where the root causes lie. Before making recommendations for elimination of piracy, it would be of interest to study the Enrica Lexie case that highlights the regional implications of a global disorder.

Case Study of Enrica Lexie Shooting Incident

The cold blooded murder of two Indian fishermen by the armed guards on the Italian ship Enrica Lexie on February 15th, clearly illustrates that all is not well in the response structures against piracy and armed robbery. From the proceedings thus far, it is clear that the security guards and the master failed to read the developing situation correctly and ended up in killing the fishermen who were fishing in the exclusive economic zone of India that extends up to 200 nautical miles from the coast. The Italian authorities claimed that they fired warning shots and the alleged pirate boat moved away. The carrying of armed guards was permitted only after the phenomenal increase in the piracy attacks particularly in and around the horn of Africa including the Somalian waters.

For centuries, armed guards, by and large have been not allowed for various reasons. However, there were compelling reasons in the recent years that forced the IMO and the UNSC to permit trained armed guards for protection. This saw a mushrooming of many security solution providers who knew that there was plenty of profit to be made. While sizeable numbers employed do have a marine background, there are some who may have not operated in the trying and harsh marine environment. Even India allowed deployment of armed guards by the end of August 2011 and recommended stringent recruitment standards. It also has made it compulsory for the details of the security guards to be provided to the concerned authorities in a port.

In the case of India, while it has allowed the armed guards, it does not allow bringing in of unlicensed/unregistered arms in to a port and has stringent regulations that prohibit the movement of arms and ammunition in and out of India. The armed guards have found a solution to this by dumping such arms prior to entering a port or by disembarking at a port which allows arms. Many ships resort to this action by going to Colombo which does allow the arms to be brought in by the security guards. The profit of margins is so high that the security companies can afford to dump the arms and yet make huge profits.

Coming back to the shooting incident on 15th evening, it is clear that the security guards and the crew of the ship misread the intentions of the fishing vessel which was legitimately engaged in fishing with in the EEZ of India. Apparently, the hasty action was precipitated due to the hijacking of a sister ship by pirates some 460 nautical miles from L&M Islands. Here are some issues that need to be understood prior to analyzing the actions of the trigger happy security guards.

Increasingly, merchant ships moving in the Arabian Sea are being advised to move closer to the coast as the areas are patrolled regularly by both the Indian navy and the Indian Coast Guard. It is obvious that the ships plying through these routes are aware of the agencies like the Navy or the Coast Guard to be contacted for instant response. The ship was transiting quite close to India and should have alerted either the Coast Guard, the Navy or the Port authorities about suspicious actions if any. It may be recalled that the Indian Navy thwarted an actual piracy attack on a Chinese vessel in May 2011 by quickly deploying its maritime aircraft which buzzed around the pirates who abandoned their effort on being warned by the long range maritime aircraft TU142 which remained in the area till the arrival of other warships deployed for anti piracy missions.

In that case, the TU142 was in the area within 30 minutes of the warning. The crew onboard had locked themselves in a citadel to deny being taken over by the pirates. Similar action would have been taken by the naval or CG authorities as the area was less than 15 minutes of flying even for a helicopter carrying commandos. It is also noteworthy that the timing of the shoot was at 1630 hrs. providing adequate time for recognizing that it was a genuine fishing boat and not a skiff which is the standard boat for such attacks. Sound seamanship practices have clearly been given the go by, that led to this tragic incident. A little more care and caution in drawing the right inferences would have prevented the loss of innocent lives.

The Indian Coast Guard has an effective system for Search and Rescue in which the ships entering the Indian Search and Rescue Region (this area is over 4 million square kilometres) are required to report to the concerned CG authorities as specified in the INDSAR system. The system has been effective as it allows the Coast Guard to monitor the progress of a ship, entering its area of responsibility and is able to provide any assistance to this ship should it be faced with an emergency.

While it was essential for the provision of the SAR cover, the system post Mumbai terror attacks has enabled law enforcement authorities to keep track of the vessels that are plying in an area that is twice the size of India's EEZ. There is a need to establish if any such voluntary reporting was made by the ship in question and also whether they were aware of the system. As per the BMP, the ship that faces a potential threat is required to report to UKMTO based in Dubai and other organizations. Most ships have resorted to hugging the Indian coast before shaping course towards their final destinations in Africa or Middle East.

The BMP also clearly indicates the modus operandi of pirates who move in pairs in high speed skiffs fitted with two OBMs and also carry RPGs and AK-47s besides a ladder that they use to board a ship. The fishing boat that came under attack was a slow speed vessel which apparently was just waiting for the ship to pass before continuing with tuna fishing. The claims by the Italian ship that they came under fire has been proved to be wrong after a physical inspection of the merchant ship by the Indian Navy which saw no evidence of any bullet marks on the ship's structure.

The global community is quite clear about the concept of

the freedom of the high seas where all vessels have a right of innocent passage and are not to be interfered with. What needs to be understood is that this freedom is not the exclusive prerogative of such vessels but also available for any vessel including smaller fishing vessels which are engaged in legitimate activity in their own EEZ or the high seas.

Legal Issues and UNCLOS

That the Italian authorities agreed to hand over the two Italian naval personnel for further investigation regarding the shooting incident on 15th February, that killed two innocent fishermen after a gap of four days paved the way for the Kerala police to go ahead with the investigation in to this murder for which the crew have been charged under Indian Penal Code (IPC) 302. The ship was allowed to leave Kochi after due bonds were executed. There are also certain legal issues and the responsibility of the master of the vessel. India is a signatory to the United Nations Convention on the Laws of the Seas (UNCLOS) that was promulgated in 1982.

As far as the provisions of the UNCLOS are concerned, the territorial waters up to 12 nautical miles allow application of the laws of the land in this defined area. The contiguous zones are another 12 nautical miles from the territorial waters and allow for limited control in this area for violation of sanitary laws, customs, fiscal, immigration and other defined violations. The Exclusive Economic Zone which extends up to 200 nautical miles allows the state in possession of this area the right for harnessing the living and non living resources in this area. It is quite clear that all vessels do enjoy the right of innocent passage even in the territorial waters of a country as long as it is peaceful and does not cause infringement to the laws of the land which extend up to the territorial waters.

If the vessel was not guilty or maintained that the incident committed was on the high seas, then technically it was possible for the ship not to stop or be diverted. It is clear that the master and the crew were aware of their mistake and therefore agreed to come to Kochi for investigation when confronted by the Navy. If the vessel had disregarded the directives of the Navy/Coast Guard, maintaining that it was on the high seas, the incident could have escalated leading to possible use of force by the Indian Navy. This would have brought the relations between India and Italy to greater stress in addition to creating an international situation.

Role of Master

As per reports, it has been indicated that the Master was not aware of the firing at all. According to certain other inputs, it has been indicated that the Master had a meeting onboard prior to taking a decision to engage the fishing vessel St. Antony. If it happened without the knowledge of the master, this is a serious situation where the master is not in control of the happenings on board. As per the international conventions, a master of a vessel cannot be absolved of his responsibility for the conduct of his ship and crew members under all circumstances without exception.

Even according to a set of rules called the Rules of the Road (RoR, surprisingly not called the Rules of the Seas) that govern the passage and crossing of ships at sea, rule number 2(a) clearly stipulates that nothing in these rules shall exonerate any vessel, or the owner, master or crew thereof, from the consequences of any neglect to comply with these Rules or of the neglect of any precaution which may be required by the ordinary practice of seamen, or by the special circumstances of the case.

According to rule number 5 of RoR, every vessel shall at all times maintain a proper look-out by sight and hearing as well as by all available means appropriate in the prevailing circumstances and conditions so as to make a full appraisal of the situation and of the risk of collision. It is obvious that full appraisal of the situation was not carried out by a thorough analysis of all inputs including radar plot to establish the position and speed of the fishing vessel and visual inputs through binoculars that would have indicated that there were no arms or any other means that would be used against the ship for boarding.

Sub-clauses of rule 18 while establishing the responsibilities between vessels of different description, clearly includes that a power driven vessel underway shall keep out of the way of vessel, engaged in fishing. It is again clear that the master of this power driven vessel, who could manoeuvre, was guilty of not keeping out of the way of the fishing vessel.

Also, while the courts have allowed the search of the ship for the fire arms used for shooting, since a lot of time has elapsed in recovering the weapons after the search, the joint ballistic examination could be misleading as the right weapon may not have been handed over. There was enough time to tamper with material evidence or even dump the weapon involved in the firing to ensure that the investigation reaches a dead end. This would require lengthy investigation to establish the number of weapons and ammunition carried by the ship and all the records related to their carriage, transfer, maintenance and use.

By all the above accounts and the application of the relevant laws, it is clear that the master of the vessel is blameworthy and is to be tried for his neglect that has resulted in the shooting of two innocent fishermen. There is another important centuries old obligation of the master which is to render help to those who are distressed at sea. In this case, it is clear that the master had no intention of helping out the fishermen who were shot in the mistaken belief that they were pirates. Without the trial of the master and his deposition in a court, it would not be possible to establish the role of the master and the crew and not complying with international codes of conduct. By not being arrested, and only targeting the marines, the master is likely to walk away scot free. There is an immediate need to prevent this from happening.

As this case is still being investigated, two more fishermen have been killed due to a collision at 0200 hrs on March 1, 2012 in a classic case of hit and run. While two have been reported dead, three more are missing and others injured. So we have a case of 'shoot and scoot' on 15th February followed by a 'hit and run' case on March 1, 2012. Both the cases clearly illustrate that the merchantmen plying close to our waters are being reckless and irresponsible and are not even conforming to the norms of code of conduct at sea. There have been increased violations of the Rules of the Road. India has apparently lodged a protest about the classification of the entire Arabian Sea including areas under its control as high risk areas.

Most of the shipping companies are being advised by the security service providers (who are paid hefty amounts) to hug the coast as there are no acts of piracy close to the Indian coast due to the proactive assertive action by the maritime forces of India. As such there is no justification for the concerned authorities to include areas of Indian waters under risk areas. The reason for the ships coming closer to the Indian coast is to prevent the piracy attacks which are happening in the mid seas at extended ranges from Somalia. So it is ironical that the ships that sail closer to the Indian shores to be safe are endangering the safety and lives of Indian vessels and crew in Indian water.

By all accounts it is clear that the security guards and the master have over reacted and have failed to assess the intentions of the fishing vessel and have caused death by negligence. The detailed investigations would bring out the lacunae if any in the reporting systems and also focus on the deficiency of training and preparation of the security guards who are deployed on ships in different parts of the world. The inputs would be vital in reviewing the BMP and also issuing additional Maritime Security Circulars by IMO which should highlight the need for caution while employing armed guards.

Conclusion

The issues highlighted above clearly are illustrative of the potential of a global phenomenon to induce regional imbalances in the maritime arena and leading to loss of lives and affecting the stability of a region. There is a reason for better coordination with international agencies to ensure that the areas of interest to India including the EEZ are not converted in to disaster sites due to lack of regulation, monitoring and enforcement by the concerned agencies.

While there are no doubts that piracy needs to be eliminated, it will take a lot of sustained effort as it contains both short term and the long term measures. The increased dependence on the sea routes for development, commerce and livelihood brings in many stake holders in a dense environment that is challenging to say the least. The proceedings in the case of Enrica Lexie would hold special significance from the point of establishing legal and jurisdictional precedents for trying of offences in the Exclusive Economic Zones of India. It also is evident that the maritime community and the law enforcement agencies at sea need to engage in greater dialogue to arrive at mutually agreed points to promote safety and security at sea.

References

Best Management Practices (BMP4).

DG Shipping notification on armed guards on Indian flagged vessels.

Economic Cost of Somali Piracy, One Earth Future Organisation, 2011.

Indian Coast Guard web page.

Indian Navy web page.

International Maritime Bureau notifications about piracy.

Jack Lang report by United Nations.

Joint War Committee of Lloyds London, *Declaration of Risk Prone Area in the Arabian Sea.*

Live Piracy and Armed Robbery Report 2012, International Chamber of Commerce.

Maritime Zones of India Act of 1976 promulgated by the Government of India.

Ministry of Defence, *End of Year Report 2011,* Government of India.

Oceans beyond Piracy Deliberations in New Delhi, November 2011.

Rules of the Road as promulgated by International Regulations for Preventing collisions at Sea.

Safety of Lives at Sea, SOLAS Conventions.

Stimson, Indian Ocean Region-Maritime Security and Policy Challenges.

Stimson, Environmental Security-Maritime Security, Briefing #2 Spring, 2012.

United Conventions on the Laws of the Seas (UNCLOS), 1982.

14

China, US and the South China Sea Dispute

C. Vinodan

The South China Sea is a strategic waterway providing the key maritime link between the Indian Ocean and East Asia. Sea lines of communication (SLOC) of the South China Sea are a matter of life and death for the Asia Pacific countries, and SLOC security has been a fundamental factor contributing to regional economic development. Maritime significance in the South China Sea are increasing for several reasons: higher volumes of shipping traffic, protection of exclusive economic zone resources, piracy, terrorist threats, greater international scrutiny of ports and shipping, and the modernization of regional naval and coast guard forces. Coastal states and international user states have many overlapping interests in the South China Sea, for example, in promoting safe navigation through its busy sea-lanes. (Rosenberg and Chung, 2008)

The strategic geography of the South China Sea invited more specific challenges, including the potential for conflict between regional states over territory or marine resources and the possibility of conflict between major powers. At the highest level of the threat spectrum, the possibility of conflict between major powers is also rarely absent from such an important sea area, which involves some of the world's busiest and most important sea lines of communication (SLOC). There are many reasons why efforts to address and ameliorate challenges to order, security, and well-being in a semi-enclosed sea area, within which many of those challenges are transnational, ought to be shared cooperatively between littoral states.

However, the political sensitivities involved in Southeast Asia, where national interests often clash, or at least diverge, as much as they are shared, make the achievement of a "stable maritime regime," extremely unlikely. [1] It is in the South China Sea that the components of Asia's changing power dynamics are most concentrated and on display. These include: China's growing strategic heft and paranoid sense of entitlement; its Southeast Asian neighbour's hopes and misgivings about China's regional dominance; and the United States' compulsion to meet China's strategic challenge.

This paper examines the dimensions of the growing tension in the region especially the potential involvement of the United States and a rapidly growing and assertive China in the dispute. The impasse over territorial sovereignty and control of natural resources in the South China Sea represents an increasingly serious challenge to regional security. (Clayton, 2012) The South China Sea territorial dispute increasingly looks like a point of strategic friction between the United States and China. The US Department of State criticized China for its plan to base a new military garrison in the Paracel Islands, saying this would increase international tensions. Beijing shot back that the United States should mind its own business.

Many observers wonder why Washington and Beijing are allowing a new irritant to emerge in the incalculably important US-China relationship. US officials have named several specific US concerns about China's policies and activities in the South China Sea, the US concern most widely understood and repeated one being the potential threat to "freedom of navigation": the PRC might be moving toward imposing restrictions on foreign ships sailing in the South China Sea. (Roy, 2012) The situation demonstrates the need for more effective and transparent regional security mechanism than what currently exists.

Strategic Significance of South China Sea

The South China Sea is a large space linking southern

China and Taiwan to peninsular and archipelagic Southeast Asia and peninsular and continental Southeast Asia to archipelagic Southeast Asia. The South China Sea is categorized as semi-enclosed sea under the United Nations Convention on the Law of the Sea (the LOS Convention). [2] The importance of the South China Sea, which borders eight nations—China, Vietnam, Taiwan, Malaysia, Brunei, Indonesia, and the Philippines—has grown as the trade that passes through the area has become integral to the global economy. The merchant vessels sailing the waters form a 'super waterway' that connects the busiest shipping ports in the world—Shanghai, Singapore, Hong Kong, Guangzhou—to all corners of the globe. Almost half, in terms of tonnage, of all commercial goods pass through the South China Sea, including over US$ 1.2 trillion in US trade each year. [3]

The South China Sea also constitutes a vital section of the seaborne trade route linking: both Europe and the Middle East to Northeast Asia; Southeast Asia to Northeast Asia; and much of Southeast Asia to the Pacific Ocean and North America. [4] Its complexity ensures both physical dangers for the safety of navigation and political dangers as a source of international dispute. A leading factor in the South China Sea has been the disputes over the territorial features and, as a consequence, the potential maritime jurisdiction to which such features may be entitled, including the related living and nonliving marine resources. Questions exist over the extent of possible hydrocarbon resources in the central South China Sea.

Another factor often overlooked in South China Sea diplomatic discussions is the South China Sea's importance as a fishing ground, accounting for 10 percent of the global catch, [5] with the annual harvest of around 5 million tonnes representing the fourth largest of the world's 19 major fishing areas. [6] The South China Sea provides the habitat and spawning grounds for the world's most valuable fisheries of shrimp and tuna, among others. [7] Over 500 million people live within a hundred miles off the shores of the South China

Sea and the importance of the fishing industry that feeds and employs this population cannot be overstated. [8]

In fact, the political tensions in the South China Sea are more often about fishing rights than military manoeuvres or oil drilling operations. However, the latter is more likely to spark international skirmishes and possibly war. But, at the heart of South China Sea maritime boundary disputes are not today's economic activities like fishing, but the promise of tomorrow's resources. The petroleum passing through the strait, the lifeblood of all nations, is the major source of oil for Japan, South Korea, and the growing economies of Singapore, Indonesia, Malaysia, and the Philippines.

Estimates of oil reserves vary. The Chinese government estimates that the South China Sea sits upon nearly 200 billion barrels of oil and 266 trillion cubic feet of natural gas. [9] The U.S. Geological Survey's conservative projections estimate far less: 4.8 billion barrels of oil and 64 trillion cubic feet of natural gas. Keep in mind that the smaller, conservative estimate is still equivalent to Alaska's discovered oil reserves, and more than the discovered gas reserves under the Gulf of Mexico. [10]

Survey data is scarce due to the Chinese government's efforts to prevent governments and corporations from conducting survey operations in the South China Sea. Even without solid evidence, several oil corporations (e.g., ExxonMobil, Shell, and Chevron) have expressed an interest in making major investments in oil exploration efforts. The South China Sea, on the western edge of the Pacific Ocean, is vast, over 1.4 million square miles (3.6 million sq. km.) but the two major island groups (Spratly and Paracel) that cover less than six square miles (15.5 sq. km.) are at the centre of many disputes. Yet, China, Brunei, Malaysia, the Philippines, Vietnam, and Taiwan have been positioning themselves to claim control over the islands, reefs, and in many cases, some protruding rocks, so as to claim sovereignty, which gives them underground excavation and fishing rights.

This has resulted in disputed maritime claims that have existed in the South China Sea for almost a generation. However, the current global recession and a growing demand for oil and natural gas have caused some players to become more aggressive. According to the Southeast Asia Program at the Centre for Strategic and International Studies, twenty-three confrontations have occurred in the region over the last three years. [11]

The centrality of China's role as a claimant state, and the linkages between its interests in the South China Sea and the development of Chinese maritime power and its overall ambitions for regional hegemony, make the disputes important beyond the limited face value of a few small, scattered islands, rocks, and reefs—or even potential energy resources. China has long been wary of the strategic presence of opposing hegemonic powers in Southeast Asia, who might exploit Chinese weaknesses at sea to apply pressure on China from its southern maritime periphery. China's strategic ambitions in the South China Sea therefore involve the extension of its defensive perimeter, countering the presence of other major powers, countering threats to its territorial and maritime interests by other claimants, and, ultimately, seeking some measure of maritime command over the area to enforce its hegemonic pretensions.

Furthermore, China also has an interest in being able to exert control over East Asian sea-lanes, both to safeguard its own oil supplies and to threaten the economic lifelines of Taiwan and Japan if necessary. A permanent strategic presence in the South China Sea, particularly if it can successfully enforce its territorial claims, might conceivably provide China with such ability in the future. The establishment of bases, staging, and surveillance posts along the vital sea-lanes has been described as China's "string of pearls" strategy. [12] China has over a period of more than three decades slowly built up its military facilities throughout the South China Sea, including in the Spratlys. In recent years, it has significantly enhanced bases, in particular, on Hainan Island and in the Paracel archipelago.

There have also been reports that the People's Liberation Army (PLA) Navy intends to bolster its forces in the area, with a senior PLA officer suggesting that the security situation was "very grim," requiring China to deploy more ships to the disputed region, and to enhance the militarization of occupied features in the Spratlys, including constructing a port for naval vessels and an airport on Mischief Reef, a Chinese occupied reef that lies inside the EEZ claimed by the Philippines. [13] Chinese strategists also noted the geopolitical importance of controlling Taiwan and the Taiwanese-occupied islands in the Spratlys if China is to establish a dominating position into the "southernmost reaches of the South China Sea."

Another driver of naval modernization is the likelihood that these factors have led to a degree of hedging by the Southeast Asian littoral states against strategic uncertainty or the possibility of a significant conflict. Although rarely stated by the regional states, it is fair to suggest that the most likely contingencies that might directly affect the South China Sea area involve China. The possibilities include a conflict over Taiwan, with Japan *or* the United States, Chinese moves in the Spratlys or against Vietnam, or the external consequences of internal instability within China itself. Although less likely to lead to armed conflict, the region is also rife with longstanding local rivalries. [14]

Naval modernization in the South China Sea states thus cannot be attributed to any single factor. While each individual state may have its own priorities, all of the issues discussed above influence most of the littoral states of the South China Sea to a greater or lesser extent. However, the fluid state of great power relations and the rise of China should not be discounted as a leading driver of at least some of the higher end war fighting capabilities being procured, such as submarines.

China's Shifting Strategy in South China Sea Dispute

The dynamic rise of China as a global economic and political actor is a major topic of current academic and political debates around the world. This global power shift will be one of the most important transformations in international politics in modern history. The direction that China and US-Chinese relations take may well "*define the strategic future of the world for years to come*". (Bergsten et al., 2006,1) Most governments in the region perceive some degree of strategic peril in a militarily strong China with an assertive foreign policy. Also in question is the continued viability of certain accepted international norms which the Chinese government does not support.

As China becomes stronger, the government appears to be more ambitious in its efforts to control its surroundings. The Chinese may believe that they are defending legitimate interests, but much of the region perceives some Chinese policies as overly assertive and bullying. The South China Sea symbolises rising China's larger maritime dilemma. The country's major population and productive centres cluster along China's coastline, and are therefore vulnerable to major attack from the sea. Naval strategists see China as being hemmed in along its sea coast by a chain of states or territories hostile to Beijing: Japan, Korea, the Ryuku Islands, Taiwan, and the Philippines.

The overriding goal of Chinese naval strategy is to establish dominance over the waters within this 'first island chain'. [15] China is both a coastal state with an extensive coastline and EEZ resource claims as well as a user state with a large shipping fleet and a growing dependence on energy imports. An energy importer since 1993, China's high energy demand has prompted it to intensify offshore exploration, including a tripartite seismic survey in the South China Sea with the Philippines and Vietnam; to acquire or invest in exploration and production projects overseas; to enter into supply contracts with countries as diverse as Angola,

Australia, Iran, Sudan, and Venezuela; and to establish a strategic oil reserve.

China considers any interruption of tanker traffic through the South China Sea to have immediate negative effects on China's industrial, urban, and transport sectors. The economic dimension of China's maritime security interests, including in the South China Sea, is underscored by the fact that 90 percent of its foreign trade is seaborne. (Sakhuja, 2001) The South China Sea also presents a potential opportunity for China to use its territorial claims to gain control of oil/natural gas reserves to deny access to or disrupt supplies.

The region contains the heavily disputed Paracel and Spratly Islands with overlapping claims to various areas and energy exploration blocks by China, Taiwan, the Philippines, Vietnam, Indonesia, Malaysia, Brunei, and Thailand. [16] Over the last 20 years, there have been at least 10 documented disputes over energy exploration rights and 17 military confrontations in the South China Sea and its territories. [17]

Some confrontations have resulted in deaths while most have merely jeopardized attempts to exploit energy resources, most significantly between China, Vietnam, and the Philippines. Ultimately, China's extensive claims raise US suspicions over its intent to potentially control the South China Sea and its resources. Such suspicions have evoked strong criticism from the US which espouses "to intercede to ensure safe passage through international waters" as prescribed by the 1982 United Nations Convention for the Law of the Sea (UNCLOS). [18]

Under the UNCLOS, states have sovereign rights to explore, exploit, conserve, and manage the natural resources within an EEZ which can range to 200 nautical miles (nms) beyond a state's territorial sea. [19] China's loose interpretation of the UNCLOS has permitted it to claim territory and establish an EEZ that stretches to nearly 1,000 nms beyond mainland China and encroaches upon the sovereignty of its neighbours. Notably, most of the Spratly

Islands are submerged at high tide and don't meet the legal criteria necessary for EEZs. [20]

Furthermore, although a signatory to the UNCLOS, China unilaterally established its own measure through its 1992 Law on Territorial Waters and their Contiguous Areas. This solidified the Chinese claim to the Spratly and Parcel islands as well as empowered the People's Liberation Army (PLA) to employ force to defend the islands. [21] Citing this, UNCLOS, and historical records, China claims ownership of roughly 80 percent of the South China Sea including areas that encompass existing oil fields operated by Brunei and Indonesia. China bases such claims on historical references to exploration, naming, utilization, government jurisdiction, and acceptance of the Japanese surrender following World War II to validate its sovereign control of the area, yet this isn't codified anywhere in international law. [22]

The rise of China to global prominence and its ambition to assume superpower status prompted it to enhance its economic, military and diplomatic activities in the larger East Asian region. For China, the South China Sea dispute represents the kind of challenge that could determine whether or how China will indeed ascend to superpower status. Regrettably, China does not yet recognize the extent to which its aggressive course in the South China Sea is damaging its diplomacy with neighbouring countries.

First, sovereignty disputes with some ASEAN neighbours have severely weakened China's standing in the region and beyond. The deterioration of China's relationship with the West after the 1989 Tiananmen Square incident should be a strong reminder to Beijing of its recent strategic errors in judgment. During that period, ASEAN played an important role as a conduit for China to the outside world. Indeed, it is in large part due to China's relationship with ASEAN that China was able to gradually resume normal diplomatic relations with the West. China's current assertiveness in the South China Sea is now slowly but surely eroding its positive image with its

ASEAN neighbours as a peacefully rising power.

Without exception, countries within Southeast Asia and beyond are very cautious of China's rise. Even as China's national economic and global stature increase, its influence, image and "soft power" abroad is declining dramatically. China's aggressiveness has resulted in the United States reprioritizing its global strategy with its "pivot" or "rebalance" toward the Asia-Pacific region. This policy adjustment by the United States has given Chinese policymakers serious reason for concern and activated the fear that China might again end up being contained in much the same way as the former Soviet Union was during the Cold War. China now sees "US hands" in both its internal and external affairs.

Throughout the region, US allies including Japan, South Korea and the Philippines have all upgraded their already strong military cooperation with the United States. If China continues to ignore the interests or concerns of its neighbours who have a stake in the South China Sea, its aggressiveness is likely to galvanize increased regional cooperation with the United States. Troubles with close neighbours also affect the image and position of China in the world. The most important condition for any country aspiring to ascend to global power status is to maintain good relations with its neighbours.

However, if China is unable or unwilling to maintain a cordial relationship with its closest neighbours, how can countries further afar trust and respect this aspiring superpower? As long as China is unable to maintain a significant level of trust and friendship with its neighbours, benevolent global power status for China is likely to remain a pipe dream. China's dramatic assertion of unilateral sovereignty over the South China Sea has adversely affected the peaceful environment China desperately needs to become a global power.

If conflict does break out, it is likely to have a sustained, widespread and long-term detrimental impact on the regional economic and security situation in the region. China itself would severely be impacted as nearly 80 percent of its oil imports and the majority of its goods, imports and exports, flow through the Strait of Malacca and other South China Sea routes. Central to the dispute is China's claim of sovereignty over the U-shaped line that it claims to have inherited from the Kuomintang government, and which was only officially submitted to the UN Commission on the Limits of the Continental Shelf in 2009.

As the lines are not based on any legal foundation and have no specific geographical coordinates, they leave room for inconsistent explanations from China. It should be noted that the Chinese U-shaped line covers 80 percent of the South China Sea, while China only administers 15 percent of that area. China's unilateral claims of sovereignty over the years to the South China Sea has made the majority of Chinese citizenry mistakenly believe that China does indeed own the entire area within the U-shaped line and that the line makes up China's southern border.

However, newly discovered maps in 1904 dating from the Qing Dynasty do not show the Paracel and Spratlys Islands. Instead, it is Hainan Island that is depicted as China's southern most borders. Unfortunately, this U-shaped line is now very much like a bone of contention in the emerging security environment. How China overcomes its miscalculations in its South China Sea policy will significantly influence China's rising profile in the emerging world order. Its handling of sovereignty disputes with some of its neighbours, however, has already weakened its standing in the Far East and beyond.

United States Interests and Response to the Dispute

The United States has developed unprecedented strategic interest in the South China Sea dispute in the context of the rapidly changing global political and security order. [23] The rise of China to global prominence is perhaps the most consequential security issue of this century. The US strategic planners consider a stronger China to challenge important aspects of the long-established Pax-Americana, including the US interests across the globe, the US alliance system, and American involvement in regional issues. A struggle for regional leadership between China and the United States is slowly emerging in different parts of the globe. This is particularly visible in both parties' claims in the South China Sea dispute.

Throughout 2010 and into 2011, disputes in the South China Sea were at the forefront of regional tensions involving China, the United States, and neighbouring countries. The focal point of such tensions was the 2010 Association of Southeast Asian Nations (ASEAN) Regional Forum where the United States along with ASEAN countries confronted China over its "assertive" behaviour in the South China Sea. This episode demonstrated clearly the troubled situation in the South China Sea and the potential for conflict in East Asia. [24] The US is also concerned about China's efforts to keep U.S. military ships and aircraft out of its waters and airspace in its Exclusive Economic Zone (EEZ), and more recently, about China's more vigorous assertions of sovereignty over disputed maritime territories in the South and East China Seas, and the potential for these disputes to spin out of control.

It is in the South China Sea that Southeast Asia's anxieties about China overlap with American anxieties about Beijing's naval build-up. Over the past two years, the United States has taken an active interest and position in what had formerly been a dispute between China and the other claimants. This means there are now in effect two layers to this dispute: a basic stand-off between the territorial claimants; and an overarching strategic contest between Beijing and Washington. For the United States, what's at stake in the South China Sea is the viability of its entire presence in the western Pacific. The US Navy's access to the South China Sea is contested by Beijing.

China claims it will respect the freedom of *passage* of ships and aircraft through the area, on the condition that they are en route to another destination, and do not conduct military exercises or collect intelligence or militarily useful data. Washington is adamant that the South China Sea's sea lanes are international waters, and are therefore subject to freedom of *navigation*, which in international law allows the conduct of military exercises and the collection of intelligence and militarily useful data. [25]

Tensions among rival claimants to territory in the South China Sea (SCS) have emerged as a major US security concern in the Asia Pacific. The United States had developed a strong alliance system with major countries of the region under the Asia-Pacific umbrella since the end of World War II. The United States has signed defence treaties with Australia, Japan, South Korea, Thailand, New Zealand, and the Philippines. U.S. military relationships have been strengthened with many ASEAN members including Brunei, Cambodia, Indonesia, Laos, Malaysia, Vietnam, and Singapore.

Recent negotiations have enabled the United States to base warships in Singapore and the same is expected to occur in the Philippines. With regard to China, diplomatic relations have significantly improved over the last twenty years, but various military incidents indicate shortcomings in Sino-US relations. The US EP-3 reconnaissance aircraft's collision with a Chinese Shenyang J-8 fighter aircraft followed by a crash landing on Hainan Island in April 2001, cancellation of a planned port visit in Hong Kong by the aircraft carrier USS Kitty Hawk and two minesweepers by the PRC Ministry of Foreign Affairs in November 2007, the harassment of U.S Navy ocean surveillance ships USNS Victorious and USNS Impeccable by multiple Chinese vessels and aircraft in March 2009, and the "inadvertent encounter" (collision) of a Chinese submarine with the towed sonar array of the USS John McCain off the Philippine coast in June 2009 are a few examples of incidents that have sparked US concern in the South China Sea (SCS). [26]

The SCS is also bordered by a US treaty ally, the Philippines, and is a key strategic waterway for the US Navy.

Recent examples of tension over the SCS include a protracted standoff between China and the Philippines in the spring and summer of 2012 over a shoal known in English as Scarborough Shoal and in Chinese as Huangyan Dao. The confrontation, which began with the Philippines sending a warship to confront Chinese fishing boats near the shoal, followed a series of confrontations between the two countries in 2011.

Among the 2011 incidents was a face-off over Reed Bank, known in China as Liyue Tan, in which Chinese Maritime Surveillance ships reportedly harassed a Philippine ship conducting a seismic survey in the area. Confrontations between China and Vietnam have included two 2011 incidents in which Chinese ships cut the cables of Vietnamese oil exploration vessels. Other provocations have involved efforts to embed sovereignty claims in domestic laws and administrative structures. In June 2012, Vietnam passed a law claiming jurisdiction over two sets of island chains in the SCS, the Paracels and Spratlys, known in China as the Xisha and Nansha. On the same day, China announced the establishment of a new city on an island in the Paracels chain, Woody Island, known in China as Yongxing Dao, that it said would administer the Paracels, Spratlys, and the Macclesfield Bank, known in China as the Zhongsha. The city has its own military garrison. [27]

The strategic significance of the disputes has been raised by the fact that rising China is a major claimant. Beijing's U-shaped, nine-dashed lines lay claim to about 80 percent of the South China Sea. Washington considers Beijing's attitude and behaviour in relation to the disputes should be viewed as a gauge of how a strong China may behave in the future. Such perceptions, combined with Chinese rhetoric and actions, have the potential to fuel anti-China sentiments and competitive nationalisms, reinforce historical antagonisms, and affect strategic alignments in the region. Smaller claimant countries may turn to more powerful countries like the United States to deter and counter Chinese assertiveness. China has extensive, though imprecise, claims to large parts of the SCS, which is believed to be rich in oil and gas deposits as well as fisheries, and through which a major portion of the world's trade passes by sea.

Territory claimed by China is also claimed in part by Brunei, Malaysia, the Philippines, and Vietnam, and in entirety by Taiwan, with the fiercest territorial disputes being those between China and Vietnam and China and the Philippines. In July 2010, Secretary of State Hillary Clinton explicitly declared a US "national interest" in the SCS. The State Department defines that national interest as being in "the maintenance of peace and stability, respect for international law, freedom of navigation, and unimpeded lawful commerce" in the sea. [28] The United States has said that it does not take a position on the competing sovereignty claims, but opposes "the use or threat of force by any claimant."

In her July 2010 comments at the Association of Southeast Asian Nations Regional Forum in Vietnam, Clinton said the United States was "prepared to facilitate initiatives and confidence building measures" in the area, consistent with a 2002 agreement between China and the Association of Southeast Asian Nations (ASEAN), the ASEAN-China Declaration on the Conduct of Parties in the South China Sea. [29] The United States has since supported efforts by China's rival claimants to place the issue of the tensions in the South China Sea on the discussion agenda for regional meetings, and publicly urged ASEAN and China to move forward with long-stalled negotiations over the text of a code of conduct.

On August 3, 2012, the State Department criticized China's establishment of the new city and military garrison in the South China Sea, saying the moves "run counter to collaborative diplomatic efforts to resolve differences and risk further escalating tensions in the region." [30] The United States has also stepped up military cooperation with both the Philippines and Vietnam, in addition to announcing its policy of strategic rebalancing toward the Asia-Pacific, which includes plans to increase the proportion of U.S. warships in the Asia Pacific from 50 percent to 60 percent of the US fleet, and strengthen defence ties with many of China's neighbours.

China has long sought to manage its territorial disputes in the South China Sea on a bilateral basis with rival claimants, and has resisted a multilateral approach in which it might face an opposing coalition of some of these other countries. It has made clear its unhappiness with US involvement on the issue, accusing the United States of complicating the situation by "internationalizing" it. Chinese commentators have also suggested that US support has emboldened China's rival claimants to be more assertive in asserting their sovereignty claims. The twenty-first century will be America's Pacific century, a period of unprecedented outreach and partnership in this dynamic, complex, and consequential region. [31]

Conclusion

The rise of China as a global economic and political actor is rapidly transforming the global political and security order. This global power shift will be one of the most important transformations in international politics in modern history. The rise of China is undoubtedly one of the most consequential security issues of this century. A stronger China is challenging important aspects of the long-established American world order, including the US interests across the globe, the US alliance system, and American involvement in regional issues. The rise of China towards global prominence and its ambition to assume superpower status prompted it to enhance its economic, military and diplomatic activities in the larger East Asian region.

For China, the South China Sea dispute represents the kind of challenge that could determine whether or how China will indeed ascend to superpower status. A struggle for regional leadership between China and the United States is slowly emerging. This is particularly visible in both parties' claims in the South China Sea dispute. The South China Sea territorial dispute increasingly looks like a point of strategic friction between the United States and the rising China in the Asia Pacific region. Washington and Beijing are allowing a new irritant to emerge in the incalculably important US-China relationship. To be sure, the United States is a strong proponent of freedom of navigation in international waters.

This stance reflects not only America's commitment to the general principle of liberty but also the interests of a trading nation with the world's most capable navy. There is every possibility of a US involvement in the South China Sea dispute if freedom of navigation was in jeopardy in the South China Sea. Competitive strategic alignments, if they do occur, will make power politics more prominent in the Asian security region working to the detriment of an ASEAN-centric rules-based order in Asia. There will still be rules but power would feature more prominently than principles in the making of order. The disputes could also undermine ASEAN as an institution and its peace and security role in Asia. There is an urgent need for addressing the issue through transparent and multilateral way to find an amicable solution to convince all stake holders in the dispute. Effective Confidence Building Measures and constructive dialogue among the various claimants to the dispute will certainly ease tension and pave the way for peace and security in this vital part of the world.

End Notes

1. Michael Leifer, "The Maritime Regime and Regional Security in East Asia," *Pacific Review* 4 (1991): 126-136. See also, more recently, Sam Bateman, "Building Good Order at Sea in Southeast Asia: The Promise of International Regimes" in *Maritime Security in Southeast Asia*, (eds.) Kwa Chong Guan and John K. Skogan (London: Routledge, 2007), 97-116.
2. United Nations Convention on the Law of the Sea, 1833 *U.N.T.S.* 397, Article 122.
3. Eric Talmadge, "Battle for Control of Asia's Seas Goes Underwater," *The Straits Times*, 19 January, 2012, available at, http://www.straitstimes.com/BreakingNews/Asia/Story/

STIStory_757506.html.

4. John H. Noer and David Gregory, *Chokepoints: Maritime Economic Concerns in Southeast Asia* (Washington, DC: NDU Press, 1996), Figures: 17-20, 63-66.
5. Clive Schofield, "Dangerous Ground: A Geo-political Overview of the South China Sea" in *Security and International Politics in the South China Sea: Towards a Cooperative Management Regime*, (eds.) Sam Bateman and Ralf Emmers (London: Routledge, 2009), 14, 18.
6. United Nations Environment Programme (UNEP), *Global International Waters Assessment. South China Sea: Regional Assessment 54* (Kalmar, Sweden: University of Kalmar, 2005), 40-41.
7. David Rosenberg, "Governing the South China Sea: From Freedom of the Seas to Ocean Enclosure Movements," *Harvard Asia Quarterly*, 26 December, 2010, available at, http://asiaquarterly.com/2010/12/26/governing-the-south-china-sea-from-freedom-of-the-seas-to-ocean-enclosure-movements/.
8. Ralf Emmers, *Geopolitics and Maritime Territorial Disputes in East Asia,* London, New York: Routledge, 2010.
9. John C. Daly, "China's Benign Foreign Policy Image at Odds with South China Sea Stance," *Refinery News*, 20 February, 2012, available at, http://refinerynews.com/chinas-benign-foreign-policy-image-at-odds-with-south-china-sea-stance/.
10. Steve Hargreaves, "Tensions Heat Up Over Oil, Gas in South China Sea," *CNN*, 26 April, 2012, available at, http://money.cnn.com/2012/04/24/news/economy/south-china-sea/index.htm.
11. Ibid.
12. This term was coined by a U.S. report, *Energy Futures in Asia*, produced by consultants Booz Allen Hamilton for the Office of the Secretary of Defence. A string of ports, bases, and listening posts stretching from the entrance to the Persian Gulf through to the South China Sea constitute the so-called "pearls." The report was first publicised by Bill Gertz, "China Builds Up Strategic Sea Lanes," *Washington Times*, 18 January 2005.
13. L.C. Russell Hsiao, "In a Fortnight: PLA General Advises Building Bases in the South China Sea," Jamestown Foundation, *China Brief*, 24 June 2009, 1-2.

14. Some of these are historically based, such as between Singapore and Malaysia; related to territorial or maritime disputes, such as that between Indonesia and Malaysia over the Ambalat offshore development area on the east coast of Borneo; or both, such as the nascent Philippine claim to Sabah or the long-standing enmity and distrust between Vietnam and China. Religious and ethnic factors may also play a role in some rivalries. Even though many of the rival states would never admit to it, such relationships are factors in military modernization.
15. Toshi Yoshihara and James R. Holmes, *Red star over the Pacific: China's rise and the challenge to US maritime strategy*, Annapolis, Naval Institute Press, 2010, pp. 51-53.
16. China's historical claims to the South China Sea date back to the Han and Ming Dynasties. For a detailed discussion on the Spratly Island dispute and territorial claims, see Michael W. King, *United States and the Spratly Islands: Six Actors, Which Stage?* Strategy Research Project (Carlisle Barracks, PA: U.S. Army War College, November 24, 2001) 1-21; Also, see Country Analysis Briefs, South China Sea, available at, http://search.usa.gov/search?affiliate=eia.doe.gov&v percent3Aproject=firstgov&query=spratly+islands (accessed January 17, 2011).
17. For a detailed listing see Country Analysis Briefs for the South China Sea, available at, http://search.usa.gov/search?affiliate=eia.doe.gov&v percent3Aproject=firstgov&query=spratly+islands (accessed January 17, 2011).
18. Daniel T. Kate, and Nicole Gaouette, "Clinton Signals U.S. Role in China Territorial Disputes After ASEAN," July 23, 2010, available at, http://www.bloomberg.com/news/2010-07-23/u-s-says-settling-south-china-sea-disputes-leading-diplomatic-priority-.html (accessed March 24, 2011).
19. Article 57 of UNCLOS prescribes a 200nm limit to any Exclusive Economic Zone (EEZ), available at, http://www.un.org/Depts/los/convention_agreements/convention_overview_convention.htm (accessed March 21, 2011).
20. "Why ASEAN Should Align Against China," January 31, 2008 available at, http://www.paracelspratly.com (accessed February 21, 2011).

21. Michael T. Klare, *Resource Wars: The New Landscape of Global Conflict* (New York, NY: Henry Hold and Company, LLC, 2001), 121.
22. Xavier Furtado, "International Law and the Dispute over the Spratly Islands: Whither UNCLOS?" *Contemporary Southeast Asia*, December 1999, 386-404.
23. The United States has had an extensive history with Asian nations over the past century, and every action in the South China Sea is viewed through this historic lens. The opening of Japan (1853), the Boxer Rebellion (1899-1901), the Philippine-American War (1899-1902), the Asiatic Fleet (1902-1942), The Flying Tigers (1941-1942), World War II (1939-1945), Sino-American Mutual Defence Treaty (1955), the Korean War (1950-1953), and the Vietnam War (1950-1975) are just a few historical events that shape US's role in and perception of Asia's geo-politics.
24. Robert D. Kaplan, writing on how the issue will be a major challenge for the future, states that "Just as German soil constituted the military front line of the Cold War, the waters of the South China Sea may constitute the military front line of the coming decades." Kaplan, Robert D. "The South China Sea Is the Future of Conflict," Foreign Policy, September/October, 2011.
25. Peter Dutton, Three disputes and three objectives: China and the South China Sea, *Naval War College Review*, 64 (4) Autumn 2011, pp. 54-55.) If Washington surrenders its ability to navigate the South China Sea on its own terms, it will lose a major foothold in the western Pacific.
26. Barbara Star, "Sub Collides with Sonar Array Towed by U.S. Navy Ship," *CNN*, 12 June, 2009, available at, ttp://articles.cnn.com/2009-06-12/us/china.submarine_1_navy-ship-sonar-array-chinese-vessels?_s=PM:US.
27. International Crisis Group, *Stirring Up the South China Sea (II): Regional Responses*, Asia Report No. 229, July 24, 2012, pp. 2-10, available at, http://www.crisisgroup.org/en/regions/asia/north-east-asia/china/229-stirring-up-the-south-china-sea-iiregional-responses.aspx.
28. U.S. Department of State, "Patrick Ventrell, Acting Deputy Spokesperson, Office of Press Relations: Statement on the South

China Sea," August 3, 2012, available at, http://www.state.gov/r/pa/prs/ps/2012/08/196022.htm.

29. Remarks at Press Availability, Hillary Rodham Clinton, Secretary of State, National Convention Centre, Hanoi, Vietnam, July 23, 2010. The text of the Declaration on the Conduct of Parties In the South China Sea can be found at http://www.aseansec.org/13163.htm. ASEAN comprises 10 Southeast Asian nations: Brunei, Cambodia, Indonesia, Lao, Malaysia, Myanmar, Philippines, Singapore, Thailand, Vietnam.
30. U.S. Department of State, "Patrick Ventrell, Acting Deputy Spokesperson, Office of Press Relations: Statement on the South China Sea," August 3, 2012, available at, http://www.state.gov/r/pa/prs/ps/2012/08/196022.htm.
31. Hillary Rodham Clinton, "America's Pacific Century," (East-West Centre, Honolulu, HI, 10 November, 2011).

References

Barton, B., Redgwell, C., Ronne, A., and Zillman, D.N. (eds.) (2004), *Energy Security: Managing Risk in a Dynamic Legal and Regulatory Environment*. Oxford: Oxford University Press.

Bergsten, F. (2006), China the balance sheet: What the world needs to know now about the emerging superpower, New York: Public Affairs

David Rosenberg and Christopher Chung, Maritime Security in the South China Sea: Coordinating Coastal and User State Priorities, Ocean Development and International Law, 39:51-68, 2008.

Denny Roy (2012), South China Sea: Not Just About "Free Navigation", Asia Pacific Bulletin, Number 17, August 14.

Hamilton, L.H. (2005), Foreword in J.H. Kalicki and D.L. Goldwyn (eds.) *Energy and Security: Toward a New Foreign Policy Strategy*. Washington: Woodrow Wilson Centre Press, p. xxi.

Hancher, L., and Janssen, S. (2004), Shared Competences and Multi-Faceted Concepts-European Legal Framework for Security of Supply. In B. Barton, C. Redgwell, A. Ronne, and D.N. Zillman (eds.) *Energy Security: Managing Risk in a Dynamic Legal and Regulatory Environment*. Oxford: Oxford University Press, pp. 85-119.

Hauser, Gunther/Kernic, Franz (eds.), China: The Rising Power Frankfurt am Main, Berlin, Bern, Bruxelles, New York, Oxford, Wien, 2009, 215, p. 1).

International Energy Agency (2007), *Toward a Clean, Clever and Competitive Energy Future-IEA Report to G8 Summit in Heiligendamm, Germany 2007,* available at, www.iea.org/Textbase/publications/free_new_Desc.asp?PUBS_ID=1920, accessed July 2, 2009.

Klare, M.T. (2008), *Rising Powers, Shrinking Planet: The New Geopolitics of Energy*. New York: Metropolitan Books.

Kleveman, L. (2003), *The New Great Game: Blood and Oil in Central Asia*. New York: Grove Press.

Marquis Clayton (2012), Uncomfortable Truths: Breaking the Impasse in the South China Sea, Asia Pacific Bulletin, Number 178, August 24, 2012.

Nye, J. (2005), *Understanding International Conflicts: an Introduction to Theory and History*. New York: Pearson/Longman.

Redgwell, C. (2004), International Energy Security, in B. Barton, C. Redgwell, A. Ronne, and D.N. Zillman (eds.) *Energy Security: Managing Risk in a Dynamic Legal and Regulatory Environment*, Oxford: Oxford University Press, pp. 17-46.

Vijay Sakhuja, "Maritime Power of People's Republic of China: The Economic Dimension," *Strategic Analysis*, 24 (2001): 2024.

Yunchang Jeffrey Bor and ZhongXiang Zhang (2010), Energy Economics: Asian Energy in the Context of Growing Security and Environmental Concerns, Amsterdam.

Zweig, David and Jianhai Bi (2005), China's Global Hunt for Energy, *Foreign Affairs*, 84 (5): 25-38.

15

Transformed Contexts and Complexities of India's Maritime Security

W. Lawrence S. Prabhakar

India's security paradigms have been in the throes of constant transformation since 1991 with the end of the Cold War. Three milestones have been etched in this transformation. The first milestone has been the shift from the overwhelming emphasis on traditional security concerns to non-traditional security issues and concerns that witnessed the collapse of the state security/regime security referents to the human security referent. The second milestone is the theoretical emphasis from the neorealist framework emphasis to a more complex social constructivist and identity lens by which security issues were identified and located in the social, cultural and ethnic matrix of the Indian society and polity.

The interdependence of the social, cultural, sectarian, economic and political issues complicates the security predicament of the Indian state. The third milestone of the transformation is the emergence of asymmetric warfare and the linkages with weapons of mass destruction that has resulted in the exposure of the state the perennial threats by radical groups of the potent use of weapons of mass destruction and the inability of the state agencies to locate and track them in real terms.

In the sinews of India's security lies the expansive domain of India's maritime security that is known for its complex labyrinth of varied challenges, complexities and threats. India has a critical contention with a vast array of challenges, threats and perils in its littoral-maritime space that spans about 7,516 km. of its maritime boundary line with an Exclusive Economic

Zone domain of 2,013,410 sq. km. with an expansive continental shelf to almost 2.9 million sq. km. equalling the landmass of India. This space confers India with sovereign rights and entitlements of its sea-bed resources of 1,50,000 sq. km. of sea-bed in the high seas. [1]

Securing India's maritime-littoral space is a colossal daunting task that cannot be achieved by mere technological implements alone or by operational rigour, or by constitutional provisions and institutional framework. None of these are stand alone responses to secure and safeguard the space. Instead, these are comprehensive efforts that would augur for the human security of the country that would call for investment into human development in the civic, political, social and economic realms of India's citizenry that would be India's empowered first respondents to any scope of symmetric and asymmetric threats.

The paper intends to analyse: (a) the contexts and linkages of India's Security thinking and praxis and its defaults; (b) the issues and challenges of India's Maritime Security viewed from the lens of traditional and non-traditional security foci; and (c) the matrices of capacities and responses that India needs to initiate and focus on.

Contexts and Linkages of India's Security Thinking, Praxis and Defaults

India's strategic evolution in the contemporary period has thus been an eclectic combine of diplomacy, economic development and the quest for technological know-how that caters to the needs of civilian economic development and defence needs.

The challenges to India's strategic evolution has been conditioned by the complexities of the vast and complex pluralistic social-ethnic order; its daunting demographic and economic challenges; the complex challenges of democratic governance; the vexatious internal security situation and the persistence of external threats and challenges. India's contemporary history reflects the varied experience of the nation building process built on stable, equitable political order; viable economic and industrial strengths and an optimal defence-development model that addresses its security concerns. The span and pace of India's strategic evolution has been over the past half-century and its profile has been built on its *élan vital* to weather the various internal and external threats and challenges. Its economic development, technological growth and its military capabilities reflect its steady and sure ascendancy to a major power status. [2]

The significant events of 1991 in India's economic and technological concourse have placed it in the trajectory of its strategic evolution marked by persistence in terms of its autonomy of action, assertion of its capabilities and the quest for its predominant role. Its outreach in the Southern Asia-Indian Ocean Region and growing extended role in Central Asia, South West Asia and South East Asia promises to confirm its evolution as a major power.

India's strategic thought and the *praxis* of its interests are based on the key issues that would determine its autonomy and capability. They are characterized as: (a) Territorial integrity; (b) economic development and growth; (c) autonomy in the strategic domain; and (d) the quest for technological capabilities and power. India's grand strategy is based on its realist strategic paradigm of being a *core state* encompassed with concentric circles of the immediate, intermediate and the extended strategic theatres. As the core state, India articulates on its strategic conduct and the sources of strategic conduct of states in the immediate, intermediate and outer concentric rings in proactive and reactive actions to changing regional and international security dynamics.

Strategic culture informs India a realist construct envisaging how states define and dynamically move in the spatial contexts of international relations, driven by the imperatives of strategic autonomy and strategic culture envisages for India—the dynamism of alliances by which states conduct themselves in relation to the changing regional and international setting. India's maritime grand strategy is based on its realist strategic paradigm of being a core state encompassed with concentric circles of the immediate, intermediate and the extended strategic theatres. It proactively articulates its strategic conduct and responds to the strategic conduct of states in the immediate, intermediate and outer concentric rings to changing regional and international security dynamics. India's strategic -realist construct envisages the imperatives of its strategic autonomy. It envisages the scope and dynamism of alliances by which states conduct themselves in relation to the changing regional and international setting.

The Indian strategic culture and its praxis are characterized by the following tenets of its conception and action.

Defensive-Defence Orientation: India's preferred strategic outlook and posture had always been inertly defensive in nature and its scope of actions have been built around this orientation *Ad hoc preferences* have been the mainstay of policy and decision making, with the political class preferring expediency over systematic planning perspective. This attitude has been persistent since the *civilian leadership's distaste for the technical-operational detail* had always been evident in peace and crisis times. Yet another persistent character of the security establishment has been the *lack of integrated vision and deficits in operational detail.* India's defence procurement policies and decisions have always been plagued by the significant lack of integrated vision with the over lording of the civilian leadership over technical services.

India's planning preferences have always been torn between the choices of *contingency planning vs. long-term planning* and the Indian bureaucratic system always relied on contingency rather than long-term plan perspective. Given the high intensity of inter-services and inter-ministerial rivalry, there have been persistent challenges in implanting a viable Joint doctrine and thus it has featured teething problems in jointness: (i) civilian/military; (ii) intelligence/military; and (iii) inter-services. Overall, the political class in India exhibited the innate potential of indecision and preferred the brevity of the administrative leadership's role in shaping policy. Thus, in every policy decision, the impetus has been for the preference of procedure over substance, and Preference of the routine rather than the "out-of-the-box".

Mismatch of resources outlay and capabilities developed has been the outcome of the flawed policy planning and decision making. India's resources have tremendously improved with the growing economy, but it always failed in the calibration of resources outlay to the development of indigenous capabilities and the quantum of resources available. *Mismatch of capabilities to contingencies on hand* have always been India's chink in the armour that has confronted the country every time new challenges and contingencies have outflanked the capabilities at hand.

Issues and Challenges of India's Maritime Security

India has a critical contention with a vast array of challenges, threats and perils in its littoral-maritime space that have revealed several critical deficits that India has contended for a long time. Among them the following factors expose the defaults of the Indian system:

1. India suffers from two serious deficits in its security apparatus that is now emblematic of its security and strategic culture. One has been the amateurish approach and response in matters of strategic and diplomatic issues and the open exhibit of the inter-services rivalry, inter-ministerial rivalry and the accusations that are being traded against one another in the aftermath of a national tragedy. The second deficit is the reluctance of the strategic elite civilian and military to conduct a serious strategic review and initiate a process of a strategic defence review that warrants not only for the armed forces but more importantly for the national strategic assessment.

India thus trudges along an ad hoc oriented defence spending that is hiked meaninglessly by knee jerk, reactions after a terrorist incident with no policy planning perspective or a white paper and worst still the complete forfeiture of the need to debate by an informed Parliament on the nuances of India's national security policy.

2. India is an interesting case study of how its strategic practitioners pay lip service and pontificate for the need for a rational strategic culture in podiums and plenary sessions but are in the act of denial in their praxis. Scholarship in academic and policy analysis has pointed out that India has been a *power adrift* with no defined paradigms of defence policy not to mention a strategic culture and vision to the enormity and the plethora of complex challenges and threats it faces.
3. India's maritime domain and its navy had been its "Cinderella Service" for too long with neglect and ignorance. Its day of reckon arrived with India's engagement in globalization and maritime trade that catalyzed the economy and poured in resources for the Indian Navy—long neglected for the obsession that we had with our land borders and boundaries. Periodic spurts of Indian defence spending had resulted in the haphazard growth of platforms that had no defined doctrinal attribution until 2004 when the Indian Maritime Doctrine INBR 8 was released and subsequently other doctrinal articulation followed.
4. What India lacks and perhaps its greatest deficit is a Maritime strategic thinking as a dimension of the Indian strategic thinking. The fact is that both are completely absent and that successive governments, civil servants and the higher defence command found it passionate to focus on ad hoc preferences rather than initiating a process of creating and nurturing a paradigm and process that would give them clarity and objective understanding of India's serious and complex security challenges. The institutional

macro-strategic response demands an imperative of maritime strategic and security thinking and process as a means by which the architecture of challenges, threats, responses and policy-strategic-resources issues could be meaningfully addressed.

In the context of securing India's maritime-littoral threat matrix, it is imperative to understand the complexities of the matrices of complexities, challenges and perils that are evident in India's long maritime boundary and coastline.

Addressing a profile of threats and challenges in India's maritime-littoral continuum, there is a need to examine the 'comprehensiveness of the 'littoral'. The littoral connotes a continuum of the territorial maritime boundary that has its seamless interface with the sea. The littoral also denotes the matrices of how the density of human demographics and the maritime-territorial geography are configured. The littoral is the fulcrum of how governance, maritime domain awareness and the operations of the agencies converge, determining the security calculus and the development index of the region.

A definition of littoral security could be the sum total of how littoral governance and littoral social economic development is harmonized with the national development.

The critical gravity of India's maritime-littoral matrix lies in the huge maritime territorial entitlements and assets of the nation of an area of 2.9 million sq. km. equal to the entire land mass of India.

The critical issues in this assessment lie in the following questions:

1. What would be the framework of a specific India-centric Maritime Domain Awareness and how would India contend the threat matrices in this framework?
2. What constitute the continuing operational lacunae and deficits and what have been the lessons learned? Does India have a good learning curve capacity from past incidents?
3. What constitutes the capacities-responses framework that

India has gained from its various maritime theatre operational experiences of its Maritime Low Intensity Conflicts?

4. What future awaits India in terms of how its maritime security praxis could emerge from the synergies of its institutional framework, doctrinal evolution and operational realities?

Maritime-Littoral Domain Matrices

In the age of globalization and the post-globalization phases of economic development and growth, the "maritime-littoral" has emerged to be hubs of development and transportation linking the seas with the hinterland. In its conceptual definition, the "maritime" refers to the "brown waters" or "green waters" from the coastal shelf. The "littoral" refers to the coastal strip of land 100 km. from the shore into the hinterland that's hosts 60 percent of the world's population while the next 350 km. hosts the world's 75 percent of the world's population. Cities with population exceeding 1 million are all littoral cities and 50 percent of global cities with populations exceeding 5,00,000 are all littoral cities (ports). [3]

The global maritime supply chains are the "principal drivers" of the maritime-based economic interdependence, while they constitute the maritime nations access to sea and trade. The maritime domain also has emerged as an arena of opportunity for various acts of violence at sea and on shore. In its physical and terrain geography, the "littoral" connotes a continuum of the territorial maritime boundary and its seamless interface with the sea.

In its social demographic salience, the littoral denotes the matrices of how the density of human demographics and the maritime-territorial geography are configured. In its political and governance salience, the littoral is the fulcrum of how governance, maritime domain awareness and the operations of the agencies converge determining the security calculus and the development index of the region. Therefore, the polyhedral importance of the littorals cannot be underestimated.

Globalization has spawned the growth of ports, and the growth of on-shore and offshore "critical maritime infrastructure" that are critical links to the economy of the state constituting vital pillars of the nation's economy and growth. It is these critical assets that are now being targeted by a variety of shore-based non-state actors from within the state and external to the state by a host of Low Intensity Maritime Operation (LIMO) of asymmetric non-state actors, viz. pirates, terrorist groups and other groups with maritime attack capabilities. [4] Securing the sea and its expanses is a formidable task as the capabilities are disproportionate to the tasks at hand.

The challenges evident in the maritime-littoral domain are not easily explained due to several complex factors that impact on them. It prompted a new definition termed "Chaos in the Littorals" that is defined by the following factors:

1. Porous territory is characteristic of the littorals in the developing world. The span of territory is long and thickly populated by the sea-faring communities. The stretch of the territory is usually porous owing to the easy access to shore by various users of the sea and the freedom of using the coastal waters. The task of securing this territory usually lies with the local communities who have a better territorial and domain awareness. However, with the onset of the variety of asymmetric challenges and threats, the porous scope of this territory is being exploited by various actors who have clandestine social and economic agenda of subversion.
2. Decreasing effect of governance is a concomitant consequence to the porous nature of territory. Until the impact of maritime asymmetric conflicts, the need for constant surveillance and reconnaissance was unknown as the seas were a commonwealth for all its users, benign and malafide. Governance of the maritime-littorals was more informal and voluntary, since the scope of threat was more

of crime conflation than the orchestrated dimensions of maritime terrorism. But with the onset of the complexities of the varied maritime asymmetric challenges and threats, these complexities have increased.

3. Cumulative social and civic conflicts over a long time had been festering in the littoral domains. There have been spates of communal, caste and ethnic conflicts and tensions that have often erupted into crisis proportions. These tensions have often affected governance and situations of social chaos have often been prevalent in the littorals.
4. Continued smuggling and infiltration of light and weapons, narcotics has been a phenomenon of the littoral regions. Smugglers, pirates, terrorists and insurgents have always been able to operate seamlessly in these regions. In the earlier periods, the thriving of smugglers and insurgents had been possible due to the heightened activities of the pirates who have used the littorals and the sea to exploit the maritime trade and shipping. In the present context, one could see new conflations of piracy and terrorism and the linkages between smugglers of humans, weapons and narcotics having close operational links with terrorists and pirates. Piracy and terrorism have been able to thrive on a political economy of smuggling. The 1998 Mumbai blasts and the numerous instances of infiltration have all relied on these illegitimate vehicles and felony.
5. Reigns of anarchy by armed gangs and the crime syndicates in the littorals have been the persistent trends even with the increasing span of state governance in the regions. Even as the state battles the piracy and maritime terrorism and the groups with maritime capabilities, there remains the "unholy nexus" between corrupt politicians, crime syndicates and their activities. Empirical evidence shows that increasing linkages between the criminals and politicians have often been strong with strong economic

support to party candidates during elections in return for the "blind eye" towards their nefarious activities. The "reign of anarchy" has been ably supported by the active connivance of several shady political and social elites with highly polemical involvement.

Littorals are thus the loci of porous territory, decreasing effect of governance, cumulative social and civic conflicts and the continued smuggling and infiltration of light and weapons, narcotics, armed gangs and the crime syndicates. The often argued factor of "violence at sea" [5] has always had an inevitable littoral access without which no violence in the sea could be possible. Therefore, the contexts of addressing the cumulative violence of piracy, maritime terrorism, insurgency, and smuggling that could all be addressed as Maritime Low Intensity Conflicts have their onshore access and established networks that exploit the maritime commons for violent means.

While various conceptual and operational frameworks on counterterrorism have been proposed to combat and contain "violence at sea", there has been no rationale of using these to address the littoral interface in this critical challenge and peril. Critical to the issue of combating and containing "violence at sea" is the imperative for a viable and robust "Maritime Domain Awareness" and the "Awareness of the Craft/Container"–both material and human contents of ships calling to ports and those in continuous transit or those who employ Crafts of Opportunity (CooP) to infiltrate and beach in the coasts. Maintaining sustained domain awareness is complex, given the opacity of the seas, the vastness of the terrain and the immense difficulties of the defenders to spot the intruders. An iron-clad regime of maritime counter-asymmetric operations is a hugely complex task. Such operations would hamper the freedom of the seas as well as the freedom of trade.

It is an evident fact that the economic opportunity of trade in the globalization and post-globalization phases in the developing world has produced the polarised sections of littoral populations of the affluent and the desperately poor. Social and economic human development profiles in the littorals have been either the noveau-rich or the poorest with severe deprivations. It is this huge disparity that has emerged as the levitating point of exploitation by the criminal syndicates and the gangs that have used social and economic discontent to their advantage.

The locus of solution to this problem therefore lies in investing in the littoral populations who are the primary stakeholders of the littoral-maritime commons.

The primary argument is that the critical need to secure the maritime-littoral from the threats and challenges is vital. It could be better addressed when the contradictions of social and economic disparity are directly proportionate to the level of social-economic development. Littoral regions lack in human security and human development. The development of these capacities could lead to better governance. Better governance is the prerequisite for better securing of the littorals.

The objective of good governance' is vital to the comprehensive development of human security that is the resultant of human rights, human dignity and human development. A comprehensive approach to tackle the asymmetric challenges and perils of the maritime-littoral regions could come from investing into human development and winning the hearts and minds of the littoral populations. This will go a long way in faction the perilous threats and challenges.

India-centric Maritime Domain Awareness

The importance of developing an India-centric Maritime Domain Awareness is the crucial investment that the country has to make prior to investing in resources and capabilities. What needs to be secured? What would be the benchmarks of the maritime asymmetric challenges? What would be the dynamically evolving patterns of the maritime asymmetric threats that have to be analysed. Understanding and analyzing India's maritime security needs "comprehensive" operational definition and parameters. India's vast profile is evident in the fact that the sub-continental geographic maritime boundaries are extensive and equal to the landmass of India–2.9 million sq. km. of maritime territory.

The post-colonial evolution of India's governance and security culture had always discounted the maritime boundaries of the nation given its focus on the border-boundary management of the contentious land borders and boundaries. Traditional sources of India's adversity had always given India an inward land-approach look with a clear lack of "comprehensiveness" of the land-maritime border/boundary management. Perhaps the only comprehensive strategic review that was attempted was the Kargil Review Committee Report, 2001 which made salutary mention of the importance of border management. But it is a matter of disappointment that there has been no substantive plan of action nor have been any developments in the follow-up reports.

Seven Challenges Persist in India's Maritime-Littorals

India's Maritime-littorals and the Exclusive Economic Zone hosts dense maritime domain of both native and alien maritime activity with little governance and regulation fraught with a wide- spectrum of maritime asymmetric threats of increasing incidence of piracy and maritime terrorism–porous boundaries and lack of governance due to lack of effective profiling and surveillance. The porous nature of littoral and maritime borders does not define and distinguish between the friendly and hostile interventions. Thus the possibilities of threats and attacks from asymmetric sources emerge. [6]

Secondly, the dense shipping sea-lanes of communication run adjacent to India's maritime-littorals in excess of 1,00,000 vessels exiting and entering the Indian Ocean-Arabian Sea-Bay of Bengal. It has spawned the ill-consequences of increased maritime pollution in to India's EEZ, ship ballast discharge, unobserved ship-based activities in this region that are not monitored and the covert infiltration of the region by Crafts of Opportunity. They represent the daunting weakness of maritime surveillance.

The third challenge is illegal infiltration in to India's littoral-maritime space and in the vast EEZ—poaching for fishing by foreign trawlers that have wrecked the delicate environmental balance of the diversified and rich marine life and resources of the Arabian Sea-Indian Ocean-Bay of Bengal areas.

The fourth challenge is the established nexus between organized crime in the hinterland with terror groups, added by the proximity of India's borders and boundaries with Sri Lanka, Myanmar, and Bangladesh. India's littorals are the staging points for the long chain of links in the smuggling process that are the basis of the challenges of crime-terrorism conflation and the complexity in responses.

The fifth challenge is the covert transit of components and sub-assemblies of Weapons of Mass Destruction in the Arabian Sea mainly based on North Korean-Pakistani shipping. This represents the unknown maritime domain activity and is not discovered until interdicted.

The sixth challenge is the colossal devastation of the littorals environment owing to ship-breaking yards and location of other toxic industries that are extremely hazardous to human life and ecology reflecting the ecological mal-governance of the littorals.

The seventh challenge has been the poaching of foreign states' agencies like the Sri Lankan navy and the Pakistani Maritime Agency apprehending and firing on Indian fishermen. It demands a response that would have to secure Indian fishermen.

The nature and complexity of these challenges have been quite tough for the Central and state governments in India. There is an evident lack of constitutional clarity with regard to maritime issues. Much time has been spent on how to manage the centre-state issues of organizational and operational overlap. The first task is therefore to devolve the centre-state overlap of operational jurisdiction of roles, powers and agencies in a seamless manner. It follows that there has to be an imperative to configure the importance of Maritime Domain Awareness, which could come as a result of effective governance of the littorals providing a meaningful engagement of the state in development and capacity building experiments, calling for seamless operations of intelligence, surveillance and operational responses.

The Mumbai attacks of 26 November, 2008 have exposed the daunting weakness of India's maritime-littoral operational matrix. There have been several lacunae, despite the various incidents of coastal infiltration and attacks that have preceded it but have not exploded. [7]

What are the Daunting Lacunae?

While location and equipment modernization of forces, training of forces is underway; what is not yet in place is the operational coordination of the Special Operation Forces with the civil agencies of the state. Several constitutional roadblocks are being cited as hindrances to the effective seamless overlap of central and state agencies interoperability. There have been responses that have been in place taking into consideration the Mumbai style patterns of infiltration. In the art and science of terrorism and infiltration, innovation is the key forte for the violent non-state actor. The violent non-state actor innovates for the next wave of attack and the state security forces simply react. This action-response sequence perennially places the terrorist as the strongest innovator of tactics and strategy.

Several responses are imperative. Some of the following issues need important consideration:

1. Imperative for Reverse Analysis by which state agencies need to shed the bureaucratic rigidity and adapt operational and tactical flexibility to simulate new

templates of threats and derive proportionate responses.

2. Safe-havens are important staging points along the littorals as the first point of landing and rendezvous. Safe havens could be detected only by Human Intelligence (HUMINT). The imperative is to have continuous surveillance of the littorals and their connecting routes and other villages in the hinterland. The build-up for a terrorist attack commences in the safe-havens since they are tactical reconnaissance centres for terrorist attacks.
3. Imperative to build lateral coordination to secure communication between the various agencies of operation. While responses and coordination are vital links and pivots for a robust defence against the next attack, there is a need to think out-of-the-box for new contingencies: Serious and critical introspection is essential for the following contingencies:

- What operational responses are in place if terrorists are armed with Weapons of Mass Destruction (WMD) possibly nuclear-radiological, chemical and biological weapons?
- What measures have been initiated to counter the radicalization of the home population with radical ideologies that propel them to be supporters of a possible terrorist attack? There is a priority need for a counter-information/communication strategy against the radicalization campaign of the radical groups.
- What is the Indian state's response to the media? While the media reports on terrorist incidents, it tends to sensationalize it and hamper operations onsite like in the Mumbai 26/11 and the IC-814 hijack incidents.

Capacities-Responses Framework

India has three levels in Capacities-Responses by which it has to configure its responses, viz. intelligence, operations and governance and development.

In the area of intelligence, there are critical imperatives to build seamless coordination of state and central intelligence avoiding duplication of agencies and work; essence to streamline and canalize intelligence with analysis, etc. It necessitates the need for a 24/7 Area Maritime Surveillance through the employment of Unmanned Aerial Vehicles which is already been mounted along with various means of national intelligence gathering and assessment methods. [8]

The objective would be to develop and monitor a national real-time digital mapping process of movements and surveillance assessments with a central head quarters as well as coastal stations that would be field outposts feeding into the digital domain. At present there various stations at Kochi (Kerala), Uchipuli (TN) and Porbandar (Gujarat). The need is to build a viable network of field posts. There is an urgent need to work out the Central-State intelligence sharing and operational coordination of civil-military; Navy-Coast Guard overlap. [9] Other vital initiatives include the increased investment in HUMINT (Human intelligence) that has to be ably complemented with ELINT (Electronic intelligence) and SIGINT (Signals intelligence).

The second area is in the realm of operations: Imperatives have to be in place for the training and modernization of equipment of NSGs, State Police, and Maritime Police. The imperative is to develop inter-agency interoperability through constant simulation and scenario building exercises. Investments in Inter-agency interoperability exercises are to be placed to be trained along with the Navy and the Coast Guard so as to develop common responses and coordinated flexibility. The strengths of constant interoperability would lead to the development of various situational response approaches. The imperative is also to evolve theatre command and operational flexibility even as forces and equipment are now in theatre deployments. Joint operations are to be made to ensue for robust and focused responses and civil-military coordination.

The third area is in the realm of governance and responses

to equitable development. Governance and Development are vital even as asymmetric threats gather momentum in exploiting local situations. Good governance and regulation of the littoral areas would address the problem of porous and ungovernable tracts of territory—the need to secure the littorals with good governance and development is important, otherwise we would have a Naxalite type ungoverned territory that fosters violence. Higher levels of inter-agency enforcement of order on one hand should be balanced with the confidence investment in littoral population, fishermen, coastal communities for their trust and confidence investment in the state. Coastal communities would be the primary sources of HUMINT (Human intelligence). Investment in human development is primary to securing communities in the littorals and the hinterland.

Capacity-building and awareness build-up of the coastal communities with the prevalent threat assessment is vital. It would create a stakeholdership of their civic participation in the counter-asymmetric threat response mechanism. The imperative is to address their social-economic and civic needs on a fair and equitable basis.

India's Emergent Maritime-littoral Security Praxis

India's praxis in building the security of its maritime-littorals could emerge from three responses: (a) governance and security; (b) enhanced domain awareness and responses; and (c) joint operations.

Governance and Security: The most vital investment that India should be doing is the human development paradigm that goes with good governance providing comprehensive security. Winning the hearts and minds of the poverty stricken coastal communities is highly important as they are the first stakeholders of the littoral maritime domain. Governance and development augurs well for equitable growth and invests the role of the state in constructive purpose in the public space. This would be the best "human hedge" that would keep the terrorists out and integrate the communities for meaningful, sustainable and appropriate development. Good governance and social economic development nurtures a vital stake of India's citizenry—the vital synergies as primary stakeholders in combating crime and terrorism.

Heavy handed security measures and draconian legislations have no appeal for a discontented populace. Human security from human development is the derivative of good governance yielding comprehensive security. Either India succeeds in ushering the due and deserving social and economic development of these communities or it cedes their loyalties to terrorists, criminals and insurgents whose sway on them could be by exploiting their poverty and disenchantment.

Enhanced Domain Awareness and Responses: Asymmetric challenges and threats are better handled with proaction and robust domain awareness—not from constitutionally mandated structures that have no operational and tactical utility. In the learning curve of counter-asymmetric operations, the degree of success in such operations rests in the robust awareness and the effective translation of intelligence into action. The fact is that there could be no actionable intelligence. The cry that there is no actionable intelligence is the most unprofessional admission of lapses and laxity and an escapist argument—No intelligence comes with a platter of accuracy.

Intelligence and its specific domain and theatre milieu do not await the lethargy of bureaucratic perception. Intelligence is tactical and extremely fungible and mutates into newer formidable threats in hyper momentum. Enhanced domain awareness and response is the linking of the sensor and the shooter that demands extreme agility that can come only from' Jointness' of perception and response, involves all levels of respondents, civilian, military, intelligence and communities—it has to be a mailed fist not an open hand

Joint Operations: In the age of highly coordinated asymmetric operations—"Jointness" is the strength and synergy of the terrorists, insurgents and organized crime syndicates combining Stealth, Surprise, Speed, Initiative and Manoeuvre (S3I&M) along with their state patron. That's how the LeT and the ISI ran the Mumbai operation 26/11. The imperative for India is to counter-intuit its operational response in a joint operations approach.

Littoral-maritime operations demand a single maritime agency that coordinates coastal and off shore security. It demands the need for a Joint Forces command model evident in the Andaman and Nicobar Island Command with its adaptive linkages with civil machinery.

The imperative for a strategic command and operational theatre commands with a single dynamically evolving digital scenario picture that would elicit robust responses, is the need of the hour; not lethargic bureaucratic archaic protocols instead, on-site operational robustness

In conclusion, India's grand strategic goal should be: (a) Its crucial address of the governance-security paradigm in the littorals; (b) Robust systemic and operational initiatives are the need of the hour; and (c) National consensus devoid of political fanfare, gaining political brownie points and the acrimony of the blame-game. A rising India should adeptly balance the imperatives of governance and security on one hand while accentuating growth and stability.

End Notes

1. "Maritime Statistics of India" Indian Maritime Military Doctrine, 2007, p. 56 and Indian Maritime Doctrine INBR 8, 2009, p. 62.
2. Nayar and Paul (2003), India in the World Order: Searching for Major Power Status, Cambridge: Cambridge University Press.
3. Samuel Huntington, "National Policy and the Transoceanic Navy", United States Naval Institute Proceedings, Vol. 80, No. 5, May, 1954.
4. Arabinda Acharya and Nadeeka Withana "Terrorist Groups with Maritime Terrorist Capabilities," in V.R. Raghavan and W. Lawrence S. Prabhakar, (eds.), *Maritime Security in the Indian Ocean Region: Critical Issues in Debate*, New Delhi: Tata

McGraw-Hill, 2008.
5. Peter Lehr (2006), Violence at Sea: Piracy in the Age of Global Terrorism, London: Routledge.
6. Vijay Sakhuja Securing India's Littorals Journal of Defence Studies Vol.3 Issue 2, April 2009, available at, http://www.idsa.in/system/files/jds_3_2_vsakhuja.pdf accessed on 27 August 2012.
7. "Intelligence Failure or Action Failure?", Times of India, December 1, 2008.
8. Amitav Ranjan, "Blue Water Blueprint Ready To Secure Nation's Coastline", Indian Express, December 28, 2008.
9. "New Ships, Radars Among Measures To Tighten Coastline Security", Press Trust of India, December 20, 2008.

16

India-US-China Trilateral Co-operation in the Indian Ocean Region

S.Y. Surendra Kumar

The Indian Ocean Region (IOR) continues to be significant in the 21st century for its strategic location–it is the world's third largest ocean, touching Asia, Africa, and Antarctica; the Ocean also connects the Middle East, Africa and East Asia with Europe and the Americas. Thus, it is surrounded by five continents, 40 countries, constituting 1/3rd of the world population and 25 percent of its landmass. Subsequently, it has 40 percent of the world's oil and gas reserves; [1] 60 percent of uranium, 40 percent of gold and 80 percent of all diamond deposits and is rich in raw materials like lithium, beryllium, thorium, coal, iron, copper, manganese, tin, bauxite, nickel, cobalt, vanadium, phosphates and so on. [2] Moreover, the region is the locus of important international Sea lines of communication (SLOCs) and has emerged as a major transport route and export supply area for oil and gas from the Middle East and coal from Australia and South Africa. As a result, the region is not just an important energy route for South and Southeast nations, but also for Japan and Italy, which imports 90 percent and 85 percent of their oil respectively, while the UK, Germany and France import 60 percent each of their oil.

At the same time, the region is considered to be the most troubled and dangerous region due to many political conflicts and non-traditional security threats, like weapons of mass destruction (WMD) proliferation, radical terrorism, unstable states, piracy, arms and drugs trafficking running from South East Asian terror hubs, posing challenges to the international community. Subsequently, it is surrounded by famine plagued nations of the Horn of Africa, and also faces geopolitical challenges of Iraq and Iran and maritime competition between India and China. Hence, from the energy, trade and security perspective, the region is now of prime interest not just to India, China and littoral states, but also for many far-off states in the world like the US, EU, Japan, Russia and Australia.

The geo-strategic interest of the Indian Ocean is well reflected in countries strategic planning documents. For example the US Pentagon's 2010 Quadrennial Defence Review emphasised for a "more integrated approach to the region across military and civilian organisation" [3], while the Australian Defence White Paper (2009) highlighted that by 2030, "the India Ocean will join the Pacific Ocean in terms of its centrality to maritime strategy and defence planning of Australia". [4] Thus, in addition to India and China's maritime interest in IOR, other countries also have developed Indian Ocean strategies. Overall, the IOR provides both opportunities and challenges in which India, China and the US have major roles. In this context, it would be interesting to examine the basis for the formation of a trilateral cooperation among India-China-US and also analyse its limitation and implications on IOR.

Areas Ripe for Trilateral Cooperation

Generally, both India and China have stakes in the Indian Ocean region due to its geographical proximity. Subsequently, the region being of great diversity and contrasts in terms of political, population, culture, economy, environment and complex geopolitical framework continues to have a vast impact on both the countries maritime policy. On the other hand, for the US, the IOR has only recently become a central focus of its strategic priorities, and the country is particularly concerned with the threats of non-state actors and fragile or failing states like Somalia, Yemen and Pakistan. Nevertheless, the US has emerged as an external actor in the Indian Ocean and has a more significant military presence than before in the

Persian Gulf and Arabian Sea, Pakistan, East and Northeast Africa, Singapore, and Diego Garcia.

In this regard, Robert Kaplan, emphasised the importance of IOR for US, "The Indian Ocean is the region in which the US will have to keep the peace and help guard the global commons-interdicting terrorists, pirates, and smugglers; providing humanitarian assistance; managing the competition between India and China". [5] Thus, over a period of time, all the three countries have developed exclusive policy towards IOR to achieve their strategic interest. In addition to the significance of IOR, there are other factors which can be the basis for the formation of a trilateral cooperation among the three.

Shared Strategic Interest: Although, the three countries have diverse strategic interests in the region, there are many shared strategic interests which can promote and strengthen trilateral cooperation, such as:

Economic and Energy Security: Economic and energy security are prime strategic interests for India and China, as both are large economies of the world and are keen on securing markets for exports, obtaining raw materials and energy resources and enhancing their international stature. The economic resurgence of these two countries are directly linked to their overseas trade and energy needs, most of which are transported by sea. In the case of India, the country's imports and exports have reached US$ 500 billion already and may well touch US$ 2 trillion by 2020. [6]

It also dependent upon 70 percent of its foreign oil and it is estimated to rise to 85 percent by 2020. Presently, India is the world's fourth largest energy consumer after the US, China and Japan and it is predicted that by 2025, it will overtake Japan as world's third largest net importer of oil. [7] As a result, many Indian security analysts believe that energy security will be India's prime strategic interest for the next 25 years. Similarly, China also depends on overseas resources and energy supplies, especially oil and natural gas from the Persian

Gulf and Africa. Subsequently, it is stated that the demand for oil will double by 2020 and its foreign supplies will be more than 75 percent by that time. At the same time, the consumption would also increase by 150 percent by 2020, in order to sustain the healthy economic growth rate. [8]

Unlike India and China, the US is partially dependent on the Indian Ocean region, except for 40 out of 54 types of raw materials used by its industry and are supplied through IOR. [9] Nevertheless, the US is concerned about the strategic interest of its allies in South East Asia and the Far East, who depend upon the IOR for meeting their economic and energy requirements particularly from the oil-rich Gulf States. In addition to protecting the interest of its allies, the region is vital to swing forces from the US Pacific Command to deal with challenges in Southwest Asia, as what happened during Operation Desert Storm (1991); Operations Enduring Freedom (2001) and Iraqi Freedom (2003). Moreover, the US Pacific Fleet with 180 ships, 1,500 airplanes and 1,25,000 soldiers operate from the Pacific coast of the US to the Indian Ocean, with some 50-60 of its ships in transit in this area every day, indicating the security significance of IOR for the US. [10] Overall, the three countries—India, China and the US share economic and energy security required for the prosperity of the region.

Protecting the SLOCs: There are many choke points in the Indian Ocean like the Strait of Hormuz, Suez Canal and Red Sea, Strait of Bab-el-Mandeb and Horn of Africa, Malacca Strait, Lombok Strait, Sunda Strait, Six Degree Channel, Nine Degree Channel, and Cape of Good Hope, [11] all of which are vital energy flow points. US$ 200 billion worth of oil comes out of the Strait of Hormuz and US$ 70 billion passes through the Malacca straits, which alone accounts for more than 25 percent of world's maritime trade, and is regarded as the world's busiest sea lane. [12] Subsequently, around 70,000 vessels transit the Malacca Strait annually and another 30,000 pass through the Gulf of Aden. [13]

Any disruption in traffic flow at these points will prove to be economically disastrous for both India and China, as it would hit the energy flows. For example 95 percent of oil used in China is transported by sea and 80 percent of that is shipped through the Strait of Malacca. Hence, if an accident occurs or the Strait is blocked by non-state actors or foreign powers, China will face tremendous energy security problems. China's sea-lane vulnerability was referred by Chinese President Hu Jintao, as the country's, "Malacca dilemma". [14] Similarly to China, India's prime strategic interest is to secure SLOCs.

The US policy towards IOR has been basically to ensure continued access to markets and smooth flow of global energy supply, trade and raw materials for its allies through SLOCs. However, in the recent times, Iran has threatened (December 2011) to shut down the Strait of Hormuz in response to the United Nations Security Council (UNSC) sanction on its nuclear programme, and if this happens, it would have a vast impact on both Asia and EU's economic and energy security. Thus, the US is also concerned about the safety of SLOC for its allies.

Presently, the major threats to the SLOCs are piracy, drug trafficking, gun running, human smuggling, pollution, accidents, mines, closure of choke points, inter-state conflicts and territorial disputes. Hence, the choke points of Indian Ocean during peace, tension or hostilities constitute the primary national maritime interest for the three countries.

Protecting Maritime-related Infrastructures and Investments

For the US, protecting the critical maritime-related infrastructures like physical and cyber networks, particularly the broadband communication connections between Asia, Europe, and the US, that are linked by undersea cables traversing the Indian Ocean are also of vital strategic interest. These infrastructure and key resources constitute a significant part of the national economy and security and it also functions as critical defence infrastructure. Apparently, these infrastructures are vulnerable to terrorist attacks in the form of piracy, transnational crimes, drugs and arms trafficking, illegal seaborne immigrations, and proliferation of WMD. [15] As a result, protecting the maritime infrastructures is vital to the US.

India and China in their quest for energy and to sustain economic growth have invested immensely in region. India needs to protect its offshore oil and gas field we have ongoing deep-sea oil drilling projects. India also needs to building infrastructure of shore and offshore oil and gas wells, pumping stations, telemetry posts, ports, pipeline grids, and refineries. [16] In addition, under the Public-Private Partnership (PPP), many oil companies have invested billions of dollars in the Exclusive Economic Zones (EEZ) stretching over 2.3 million sq. km., which will meet India's energy requirements. China also has invested in South Asian countries for development and upgrading of ports and also engaging with many littoral states, in December 2011, it signed an agreement with Seychelles for refuelling and re-provisioning of its naval vessels on anti-piracy runs. At the same time, International Seabed Authority, UN organisation awarded China exploration rights to polymetallic sulphide ore deposit in 10,000 sq. km. area of the IO over the next 15 years. [17] Thus, securing this infrastructure and investment is critical for the three countries, and it can be better achieved through trilateral cooperation.

Common Threat Perception

The region represents the most troubled and dangerous area of the world. In 2009 alone, a total of 170 political conflicts were recorded in the IOR, representing 46.6 percent of the 36 conflicts worldwide, with 50 percent of all the crises and severe crises in the world and 19 of the 31 high-intensity conflicts. [18] Of this, terrorism and transnational crime are perhaps the most prominent sources of non-traditional violence and instability in the region like the potential threats from Al-

Qaeda and its linkages, Jemmah Islamiah (JI), an umbrella organisation for a variety of terrorist groups in South East Asia and Islamist terrorism in the Horn of Africa. These issues could be well countered through trilateral cooperation, rather than unilaterally or bilaterally.

Although 30 navies are operating in IOR, piracy continues to be a major challenge, as in 2011 alone attacks by Somali groups were 237 compared to 219 in 2010. [19] According to maritime expert Anna Bowden piracy costs the world US$ 7-12 billion a year, plus the amount spent on re-routing, security equipments, additional insurance premiums and marinating of international forces. Thus, finding an amicable solution to this problem is a difficult task and it needs joint strategies by key players like India, China, the US and others to maintain the good order of the sea. In this regard, India, China and the US are working together along with the international community to combat piracy in the Gulf of Aden and off the coast of Somalia.

The Indian Navy in recent times has been successful in carrying out anti-piracy patrols like those in the Gulf of Aden (October 2008), effectively averted numerous piracy attempts and arrested several pirates and continue to provide protection and rendering assistance to merchant vessels irrespective of their nationality. In February 2011, American citizens were lost to an attack by Somali pirates and in the subsequent month, the Indian Navy neutralized a pirate mother ship and captured 61 Somali pirates, the largest such success in the ongoing anti-piracy operations, getting praise from the International Maritime Bureau (IMB). [20] Hence, the Indian Navy's success in the recent times can be further strengthened through cooperation with both the US and China, as they have lot of resources and technology to offer in combating piracy and terrorism.

The major threat to the collective interests of IOR countries and people is the non-traditional security risks such as the combined impacts of climate change and environmental degradation. In this regard, the Intergovernmental Panel on Climate Change (IPCC) has warned about rising sea temperatures and its impact on monsoon that can create drought, cyclone, intense storm and so on. [21] The rise of sea level, desertification, and the submergence of islands will lead to migration of millions of individuals and create environmental refugees, which would lead to additional problems such as health issues, scarce resource competition, and social and ethnic tensions. [22]

In addition, the region is prone to frequent natural disasters. Around 60 percent of the world's natural disasters take place in IOR. Subsequently, the ocean resource exploitation in the Indian Ocean also poses a major challenge, as there has been increasing competition for resources due to continued growth and prosperity globally. Apparently, the technological advances are enabling expanded marine activities such as energy development, resources extraction like sea food, minerals etc., and other commercial activity in and under the ocean. Subsequently, illegal fishing, toxic waste dumping and pollution continue to be major concerns. At the same time, most of the littoral states are confronted with regional instability due to ethnic, sectarian and religious dissensions, authoritarian regimes and many dependent on single product economies viz. energy resources. Thus, overcoming these problems needs a collaborative approach India, China and the US can assist IOR Island in mitigating these problems, as they have sufficient resources, technology and manpower to meet the needs of littoral states.

Over the years, there has been stronger maritime cooperation among the three countries, but most of the cooperation has been at the bilateral level, rather than any trilateral cooperation. Nevertheless, bilateral maritime cooperation can form the basis for trilateral cooperation.

India-US

India has always opposed the presence of major powers in

IOR, as it will exacerbate regional insecurity and threaten its regional hegemony. For instance, in 1970s, India rejected the Sri Lankan proposal of establishing 'Indian Ocean as a Zone of Peace' (IOZP), since it did not want the entry of the US and even Russia into the India Ocean after the British withdrawal. Subsequently, India also feared about the US and its alliances with China and Pakistan, which was a threat to India's security. Thus, India initially opposed US presence in Indian Ocean. However, with the transformation of the Indo-US relation into a strong strategic partnership under the Bush administration (2000-2008), Indian Ocean emerged as an area of common interest.

This was emphasised by the Secretary of State, Colin Powell in 2001 to the US Senate Foreign Relations Committee when he stated that, "India has the potential to help keep the pace in the vast Indian Ocean area and its periphery...and we should consistently help them in this endeavour". [23] In the process, in 2005, the Bush administration assured that it would help India become a major world power in the 21st century, seeking to build India's capabilities as an implicit balance to China. As a result, India signed the civil-nuclear deal and a 10 year Defence Agreement Framework with the US, which laid the foundation for stronger partnership in many key sectors.

In September 2011, Robert Blake, the Assistant Secretary of State for South and Central Asia stated, "New Delhi is a pillar of stability and prosperity in the Indian Ocean and beyond...India has long been a maritime power in Asia in its own right and only India itself can charter a path to navigate the geopolitical currents unfolding before us". [24] This statement indicated IOR as an area of convergence between the two countries. As a result, the US agreed on strengthening maritime cooperation by encouraging India's naval ambitions, expansion of its naval capabilities and coordinating its maritime strategy with the US in Persian Gulf, South-East Asia and as far as the Taiwan Strait. [25]

Apparently, under the larger strategic partnership, the US

has encouraged India to increase its naval presence in the north-east Indian Ocean and also assisted in building naval bases. Subsequently, the US conducted frequent joint exercises with the Indian Navy and sold an American warship for the first time—the 17,000 ton amphibious transport dock USS Trenton. At the same time, the US contactors have been offering India advance fighters jets and anti-ship missiles. From time to time, in order to expand and strengthen the US-India naval relationship, they undertook many bilateral naval exercises. After the end of Cold War, both nations have carried out 14 series of exercises, of which the last one was a 10 day joint naval exercise called Malabar 2011, in the Arabian Sea. [26]

The main focus of the operations was on anti-submarine warfare, surface firings and maritime interdiction operations, apart from humanitarian assistance and disaster-relief efforts. [27] The exercise included Indian Navy's advanced guided-missile destroyer, three guided missile frigates, one conventional submarine and several shore-based Sea Harrier fighters. From US Navy's side one guided- missile cruiser, two destroyers, one frigate, one nuclear-powered submarine along with two long-range marine patrol plane P-3s participated. [28] Interestingly, India now conducts more exercises with the US than with any other country.

In addition, both the countries have also undertaken naval exercises at multilateral levels like those in 2007 and 2009, involving Japan, Australia and Singapore. In August 2010, the 7th MILAN, biennial exercise of the Navies of Asia-Pacific littoral states, was held at Port Blair, in which 12 countries participated, the highest number since 1995, including Australia, Malaysia, Singapore, Indonesia, Thailand, Myanmar, Bangladesh and Sri Lanka and delegations from New Zealand, Vietnam and Brunei. [29] Thus, these developments have strengthened and deepened India and US maritime cooperation.

India-China

Although India is concerned about China's maritime power, in recent times, India and China's bilateral relations have improved, particularly in the sphere of trade and that of addressing transnational issues and now even in maritime cooperation. For instance, there are many instances of joint exercises undertaken by both the navies. However, it was only during the visit of Chinese Premier Wen Jiabao to India in December 2010, that new areas such as cooperation in maritime security were raised. Since then, both navies have deployed warships in the Gulf of Aden for tackling piracy and continue to be committed to freedom of navigation in line with international laws.

Most significantly, in March 2012, during the annual meeting of the India and Chinese Foreign Ministers, the Chinese Foreign Minister Yang Jiechi presented a proposal on maritime cooperation with India, which was accepted in principle by India. [30] But, the modalities of this cooperation are yet to be worked out. Nevertheless, mostly it would include joint operations against piracy, sharing of seabed research technology and other common areas concerning both the countries. Thus, these developments have laid a stronger foundation to secure the strategic interest of both countries and also to maintain the good order of the sea.

US-China

The maritime cooperation between the two countries dates back to 1974, when China joined the International Maritime Organisation (IOM) and designated 620 port facilities for port inspection. Apparently, only in 1998, both signed the military maritime consultative agreement and began to conduct consultation on military maritime security issues. In 2003, it formally joined the Container Security Initiative (CSI) and later also joined the related programs of CSI, such as the US coast guard program, the mega port, secure freight initiative, export control and related border security assistance program.

[31] Interestingly, since 2006, both have conducted joint maritime search and rescue exercises. From 2008, Chinese Navy conducted escort operation in the Gulf of Aden and waters of Somalia.

During these operations, it established mechanisms for regular intelligence exchange and also exchanged boarding visits with commanders from the US and other navies. All these steps have strengthened maritime cooperation and also promoted effective cooperation at the regional and global level in addressing their shared maritime interest. Thus, the prevailing strong bilateral maritime cooperation among the three has laid the foundation for the formation of trilateral cooperation in the IOR.

Overall, the three countries converge at defending critical maritime related infrastructures, protecting and facilitating maritime trade, protecting SLOCs, maintaining freedom of navigation, and safeguarding the ocean and maritime resources. Subsequently, all the three nations–India, the US and China face common threats and challenges like terrorist attacks; piracy; transnational crimes; drug and arms trafficking, WMD proliferation, illegal seaborne immigrants, illegal exploitation of resources, maritime disasters like typhoons, tsunami, earthquakes, shipwrecks, oil leaks and radioactive contamination and global warming. Given that none of the three countries alone have adequate resources to provide safety and security throughout the entire maritime domain, it is in the interest of all the three to form trilateral groupings.

Limits of Trilateral Cooperation

Although, there are adequate areas of convergence for the three countries, there are many issues that hinder the formation of trilateral cooperation, such as:

Concern Over Each Other's Maritime Power: First and foremost, all the three countries are concerned about each other's rising maritime power, which they feel would threaten their maritime interests. For instance, many Indian and US analysts have perceived China's policy towards the Indian Ocean as directed against India and the US, rather than being a legitimate reflection of Chinese interests in its SLOC across the Indian Ocean. China, in order to address its energy security needs, has established a substantial naval presence along vital maritime chokepoints, which is popularly known as China's 'String of Pearls", a plan to acquire several strategically placed ports, naval bases and listening posts in friendly countries like Gwadar (Pakistan), Hambantota (Sri Lanka), Sittwe (Myanmar), Chittagong (Bangladesh); electronic intelligence gathering facilities on islands in the Bay of Bengal; funding construction of a canal across the Kra Isthmus in Thailand; a military agreement with Cambodia and building up of forces in the South China Sea. [32]

Presently, an attempt is also being made to construct a submarine base in the Maldives, to protect the billions of dollars worth trade that pass through strategic sea lanes like the Strait of Hormuz or the Malacca straits to Middle East, Africa and Latin America. Thus, both India and the US argue that the string of pearls aim to counterbalance US power, check India's rise and monitor maritime activities carried on by these maritime competitors.

The Chinese government has justified this strategy by emphasising that it imports more than 50 percent of its oil consumption (2010) and the Malacca Strait is the key choke-point on China's oil supply routes. Hence, it is in China's interest to develop alternative ports and pipelines, such as 'string of pearls', to reduce the criticality of the Malacca Strait and build strategic ties with several countries along the sea lanes from the Middle East to the South China Sea in order to protect China's energy interests and security objectives. Furthermore, Chinese President Hu Jintao in September 2010 stated that "the growth of the Indian navy means that Chinese economic development is potentially at the mercy of India, as well as the US. The forging of Indian security links with Japan and the US is therefore a source of concern," [33] Despite the

Chinese justification, India and the US are concerned about Chinese naval presence, which poses a threat to their national security and maritime interest.

Apart from this, traditionally India and US have been a close partner of IOR islands and has always supported numerous endeavours to ensure 'good order at sea'. The Indian Navy has assisted the weaker littoral states of the Indian Ocean in building their own capacities by training, advising and providing equipment to safeguard its security such as helping Mauritius to operate coast guard, strengthening Sri Lanka's ability to control its waters, improving the ability of Mozambique, Madagascar and Maldives to monitor their maritime domain etc. [34]

However, in recent times, China has been strengthening relationships with Indian Ocean islands like Mauritius, Seychelles and also other African nations which is seen by India and the US as threat to its security and strategic interest. As a result, both India and the US are cautious in allowing China to establish security relationships with Indian Ocean islands. Thus, the increasing Chinese naval ambition and presence poses a great challenge to India's dominance in the region and is also a threat to US allies.

On the other hand, China from time to time has raised serious concern about India and the US maritime power in the IOR. For example, the Chinese naval analyst Zang Ming argues that the Andaman and Nicobar Islands could be used by India as a 'metal chain' or Iron Curtain to block Chinese access to the Straits of Malacca. Chinese also view India's moves to develop and increase military access to islands of Mauritius, Maldives, Seychelles and Madagascar and the rim states of South Africa, Tanzania and Mozambique, as having strategic imprints. The support includes transfer of offshore naval vessels and, imparting training and refit facilities. Moreover, China has concerns about India and US geopolitical ambitions beyond the India Ocean, i.e., India's look east policy towards ASEAN and both India and US's interests in South

China Sea carry maritime implication for China.

China from time to time, has raised objection to India's growing relations with the US, Japan and ASEAN cooperation on counter-terrorism, maritime security, and transitional crime fighting, which represents part of grand Indian strategy to control the IO particularly the Malacca strait. It is regarded that, once India commands the IO, it will not be satisfied with its position and will continuously seek to extend its influence, and its eastward strategy will have a vast impact on China. Furthermore, many Chinese strategists consider the Indian Ocean as one theatre in which Washington will work towards containing the broader aspirations of Beijing or even jointly with Tokyo, to seal off the strait as a coercive strategy against China.

The Chinese are concerned about the US Navy's dominance of the high seas stretching from the Persian Gulf to the Indian Ocean to South China Sea. They feel that American naval powers will hold China's sea dependent economy hostage in times of crisis, particularly the Malacca strait. There is a possibility that America might hypothetically interrupt Chinese oil supplies. Despite Indian and US justification of actions in IOR, China is concerned about Indian and US naval presence, which pose a threat to its national security and maritime interest. As a result, from time to time, China has exercised its diplomatic and economic instruments of national power to reduce the regional influence of India, US and Japan.

Interestingly, India is also concerned about the large U.S. military presence in the Indian Ocean to India's west—in the Arabian Sea and the Persian Gulf. This was stressed in India's *Maritime Doctrine,* that "the growing US and western presence and deployment of naval forces, the battle for oil dominance and its control in the littoral and hinterland are factors that are likely to have a long-term impact on the overall security environment in the Indian Ocean region." [35] Thus, India is also very much worried about the increasing US presence in region, which challenges India's regional hegemony.

As a result, many argue that the Indian government is deliberately excluding the US from membership into the Indian Ocean Naval Symposium (IONS) [36], on the grounds that the former is not a littoral state. As of now there are 35 members and 23 have applied for observer status, including the US and the UK. However, the meeting of INOS in Cape Town, South Africa (April 2012) did not discuss the granting of observer status. Nevertheless, sooner or later India will have no option but to grant the US observer status due to pressure from the INOS members and also due to its own growing strategic partnership with the US. Thus, India, China and the US are concerned that each others maritime power would limit the formation or hinder the growth of trilateral cooperation.

Diverse Strategic Ambition: The three countries have diverse strategic ambition in the region, which limits the formation of trilateral cooperation. By the virtue of geography, the Indian Ocean is India's backyard and it is both natural and desirable for India to have a predominant influence in this region. Moreover, India occupies a highly strategic position in the northern Indian Ocean, which allows it to control the key SLOCs to and from the Suez Canal, Persian Gulf and Malacca Strait.

As a result, many Indian strategic thinkers and Indian establishments have emphasised from time to time that India has a legitimate aspiration in emerging as regional hegemony in the region and should have greater role in the Indian Ocean. The K.M. Panikkar, popularly known as the father of Indian maritime strategy argued that a Indian Ocean must remain 'truly India' and even advocated the creation of a 'steel ring' around India through the establishment of forward naval bases in Singapore, Mauritius, Yemen and Sri Lanka. [37] Presently, many advocate this strategy as a counter to China's string of pearls'. Furthermore, the Indian Navy's *Maritime Doctrine* (2004), argues for India building maritime power "to control the choke points as bargaining chip in the international power game". [38]

Others like Jaswant Singh, the former Indian Foreign Minister called the Indian Ocean as India's 'sphere of influence' i.e., India could use the region to achieve its foreign policy objectives. This was further elaborated Prime Minister Manmohan Singh, who felt that Indian Ocean is India's 'strategic footprint', [39] connecting the South East Asia, Far East and beyond, which would strengthen India's successful rise, achieve security ambitions and become the predominant maritime security provider in the region stretching from the Red Sea to Singapore.

As a result, India has given greater importance to the Malacca Strait, since its ability to control the Strait is seen as a prerequisite of effective control of the eastern Indian Ocean. To achieve this, it has developed military facilities in Andaman and Nicobar Island as the base for a new tri-service far eastern strategic command. Subsequently, India is strengthening its strategic relationship with Singapore and Indonesia, and working on the same line with other external powers like the US, Australia and Japan. Thus, India's proximity to Indian Ocean has shaped its naval ambition to increase its sphere of influence across the IOR and also globally.

Similar to India's strategic ambition, China also has a long term quest for a presence in the Indian Ocean, in order to project its maritime power and protect its merchant and energy fleet. For the US, preventing new or established extremist groups from harming the interests of the US or allied Indian Ocean littoral states constitute the core interest. [40] The region is important for the US and its allies as it could become a secondary arena for a great power and strategic competition in Asia, particularly between India and China, where the US can play the role of balancer. Moreover, the US has a long history of alliances with other countries and alliance strategy, as can be seen from World War II, Persian Gulf War, Kosovo War, etc. and its has strong relationships with Japan, South Korea, Philippines, Thailand and Australia. Hence, to maintain the credibility of its defence commitments to allies, the US is prepared to help its allies militarily if there is a need. [41]

India and China Non-committal to US-led PSI: The US is unhappy with both India and China's response to the Proliferation Security Initiative (PSI), proposed during the Bush administration. This is a web of partnerships aiming to prevent proliferation of the shipments of WMD at sea, air and land, and their delivery systems to terrorists or countries suspected of trying to acquire them. Presently, more than 97 countries (as of January 2011) have supported the initiative, and there are 21 Operations Expert Groups (OEG). However, India and China have expressed their unwillingness to being part of this initiative. India's reservations are on the legitimacy of PSI, that it is not endorsed by United Nations (UN); political sensitivities, technical and diplomatic imperatives. [42]

Moreover, PSI is more of an extension of the existing US headed military alliances like North Atlantic Treaty Organisation (NATO). In addition, the PSI is aimed directly at Iran and North Korea. Apparently, India has a strategic cooperation with Iran and it imports 14 percent of its total foreign oil from Iran. Despite being non-committal, India has participated as an observer in three PSI exercises–Pacific Protector, hosted by Australia in 2006, Pacific Shield, hosted by Japan in 2007, and Maru, hosted by New Zealand in 2008. [43] Thus, India is reluctant in joining the US-led PSI and this continues to be an irritant in India-US relations, which would have an effect on maritime cooperation as well.

China on the other hand has made its stand clear of not joining PSI in near future on the grounds that there are many concerns in international community about the legitimacy and effectiveness of PSI interdictions and consequences that may arise from there. It is also of the perception that the proliferation issue should be resolved within the international legal frameworks by political and diplomatic means, rather than any unilateral initiatives.

Moreover, any non-proliferation measures should serve to promote international and regional peace, security and stability, rather than confrontation. At the same time, China's Foreign Ministry spokesperson also raised other concerns like "PSI might allow military intercepting, which is beyond the limits of international law". [44] Subsequently, this initiative might infringe upon the rights of innocent passage of Chinese ships through the territorial waters of PSI members, like the Malacca straits. Thus, both India and China's reluctance in joining PSI continues to be a major irritant which limits the formation of trilateral cooperation.

Concluding Observations

India, China and the US will continue to protect and facilitate their maritime interests. However, in the present complicated maritime environment, neither India, nor China, nor the US can cope with threats and challenges single-handedly. Hence, the formation of India-China-US trilateral cooperation in the IOR would be an important step towards ensuring peace, security and prosperity to the region. Furthermore, there is wide scope for the formation of trilateral cooperation, such as the following:

1. The shared common interests of the three in the region should lay the foundation for cooperation, as all the three converge to a large degree, with regard to uninterrupted access to shipping lanes, freedom of global commons, maintenance of the rule of law and an end to extremist violence.
2. The main threat to IOR is not from the presence of big powers, but from non-traditional security threats, which needs cooperation among these powers, and on this front, the three have already cooperated on the counter-piracy operation in the Gulf of Aden, which demonstrated that cooperation on regional strategic issues is possible, and so is the case for trilateral cooperation.
3. The three have much to lose from a conflict in Indian

Ocean, thus cooperation will be better for them and also for the region.

4. The formation of this trilateral cooperation will also discourage unilateral power plays in response to piracy, terrorism or other littoral challenges in the IOR.
5. The issues concerning effective maritime governance and security have been ignored by the existing multilateral forums like Indian Ocean Rim-Association for Regional Cooperation (IOR-ARC, 1997); BIMSTEC, (1997) consisting of Bangladesh, India, Myanmar, Sri Lanka and Thailand; South Asian Association for Regional Cooperation (SAARC, 1985); Southern African Development Community (SADC, 1975); Economic Community of West African States, (ECOWAS, 1975) and so on, all of which have an economic agenda and deals little with security issues. This gap can be effectively filled by trilateral cooperation. Thus, it is imperative for the three powers to maintain the global commons through their maritime power.

At the same time, there are vital limitations in the formation of trilateral cooperation, which can be addressed through dialogue. Nevertheless, the three countries should form and strengthen the trilateral cooperation based on the principles of equality, mutual respect, and mutual benefits. Secondly, they should strengthen the consultation mechanism to improve maritime security. Third, increase high-level exchanges to deepen strategic mutual trust. Fourth, continue to collaborate on humanitarian assistance and disaster relief operations. Finally, expand maritime joint military exercises and education cooperation. If all these happen, the formation of trilateral cooperation will go a long way in ensuring the growth and prosperity of IOR.

End Notes

1. Lee Cordner, (2010), "Rethinking Maritime Security in the Indian Ocean Region", *Journal of the Indian Ocean Region*, 6(1), June 2010, p. 69.
2. Amardeep Athwal, (2008), *China-India Relations:*

Contemporary Dynamics, London: Routledge, p. 31.
3. Michael Green and Andrew Shearer, (2012), "Defining US Indian Ocean Strategy", *The Washington Quarterly*, 35 (2): p. 175.
4. Australian Department of Defence, (2009), *Defending Australia in the Asia-Pacific Century Force 2030,* available at, www.defence.gov.au/whitepaper/docs/defence_white_paper_2009.pdf.
5. Robert D. Kaplan, (2009), "Centre Stage for the Twenty-first Century", *Foreign Affairs,* March/April 88 (2), p. 18.
6. Vice Admiral Das, (2011), "Maritime Power: Key to Indian Security Interest", *Policy Paper Series*, p. 9.
7. Robert D. Kaplan, (2011), *Monsoon: The Indian Ocean and the Future of American Power*, New York: Random House Trade, p. 8.
8. James Holmes, Andrew Winner and Toshi Yoshihara, (2010), *Indian Naval Strategy in the Twenty-first Century*, London: Routledge, p. 129.
9. Michale Green, op. cit. 3, p. 177.
10. Gaoyue Fan, (2011), "Maritime Interests: China-US Cooperation and Conflicts", *Issues and Insights*, 11(10), p. 4.
11. Ministry of Defence, (2007), *Freedom to Use the Seas: Indian Maritime Military Strategy,*", New Delhi: Integrated Headquarters Ministry of Defence (Navy).
12. Vidhan Pathak, (2009), "China and Francophone Western Indian Ocean Region: Implications for Indian Interests", *Journal of Defence Studies*, 3 (4):91 and Sheldon W. Simon, (2011), "Safety and Security in the Malacca Straits: The Limits of Collaboration", *Asian Security*, 7 (1): 27-43.
13. Vice Admiral Das, op. cit. 6, p. 9.
14. As quoted in Robert Kaplan, op. cit. 7, p. 10.
15. Gaoyue Fan, op. cit. 10.
16. Vidhan Pathak, op. cit. 12.
17. Praveen Swami, "No more at Sea" *The Hindu,* 6th March 2012, p. 12.
18. Christian Bouchard and William Crumplin, (2010), "Neglected No Longer: The Indian Ocean at the Forefront of World Geopolitics and Global Geostrategic", *Journal of the Indian Ocean Region,* 6 (1): 27.
19. Praveen Swami, op. cit. 17.

20. Sameer Saxena, "One Ocean, Two Shades: Perception about the Indian Ocean". James R. Holmes, (2010), "Tackling Somali Piracy Ashore: Maritime Security and Geopolitics in the Indian Ocean", *Strategic Analysis*, 35 (5):717-727.
21. Lee Cordner, op. cit. 1, p. 70.
22. Conference Report, (2010), *Maritime Challenges and Priorities in Asia, Singapore: S. Rajaratnam School of International Studies.*
23. Washgington File, (2001), 'Powell statement before Senate Foreign Relations Committee', 17 January, available at, http://usinfo.org/wf-archive/2001/010117/epf301.html.
24. "India Pillar of Stability in Indian Ocean Region: Robert Blake", 28th September 2011.
25. Ashley Tellis, (2002), "South Asia", in Richard Ellings and Aaron Friedberg (eds.), *Strategic Asia 2001-2002: Power and Purpose*, Seattle: National Bureau of Asian Research, p. 224.
26. The Malabar exercise was conducted in 1992, 1995, 1996, 2002, 2003, 2004, 2005, 2006, 2007 (twice), 2008, 2009, 2010 and 2011). Twelve exercises were conducted off Indian Coast and two in the Pacific Ocean. Although, this exercise is primarily a bilateral exercise, but Japanese Navy, Australian and Singapore Navies also participated on few occasions.
27. Balaji Chandramohan, "US courts India in the Indian Ocean", available at, http://www.atimes.com/atimes/South_Asia/LE06Df02.html.
28. "Indian Navy starts Annual Joint Exercise with U.S. Navy", 24 April 2010, available at, http://english.peopledaily.com.cn/90001/90777/90851/6962009.html.
29. "Indian Navy: 2010 Year-End-Review", 5th January 2011, available at, http://www.defencetalk.com/indian-navy-2010-year-end-review-31032/#ixzz1r3CITuuf
30. Praveen Swami, op. cit. 17.
31. Gaoyue Fan, op. cit. 10, p. 7.
32. Amardeep Athwal, op. cit. 2, pp. 30-76.
33. "India, US need to partner to balance China in Indian Ocean", *The Indian Express*, 2 September 2010, available at, www.indianexpress.com/news/india-us-need-to-partner-to-balance-china-in-indian-ocean/676275/2.

34. C. Raja Mohan, (2010), "India and the Changing Geopolitics of the Indian Ocean", *Maritime Affairs*, 6 (2):9.
35. Government of India, Ministry of Defence, *Annual Report, 2004-05,* New Delhi: Ministry of Defence, p. 46, available at, www.meaindia.nic.in.
36. The Indian Ocean Naval Symposium (2008) is a voluntary initiative consist of 35 members, seeks to increase maritime cooperation amongst navies of the littoral states of the Indian Ocean Region by providing an open and inclusive forum for discussion of regionally relevant maritime issues and, in the process, endeavours to generate a flow of information between naval professionals that would lead to a common understanding and possible agreements on the way ahead.
37. K.M. Panikkar (1962), *India and the Indian Ocean: An Essay on the Influence of Sea Power in Indian History*, Bombay: George Allen and Unwin, p. 15.
38. David Brewster, (2010), "Australia and India: the Indian Ocean and the Limits of Strategic Convergence", *Australian Journal of International Affairs*, 64 (5): 554.
39. Ibid., p. 555.
40. James R. Holmes, Andrew C. Winner and Toshi Yoshihara, op. cit. 8, pp. 106-125 and Bronson Percival, (2010), "Growing Chinese and Indian Naval Power", in Sam Bateman and Joshua Ho, (eds.), Southeast Asia and the Rise of Chinese and Indian Naval Power, London: Routledge, pp. 46-47.
41. Michael J. Green and Andrew Shearer, op.cit.3, p.178.
42. Sameer Sexane, op.cit.20, p.19.
43. Charles Wolf, Brian G. Chow and Gregory S. Jones, (2008), *Enhancement by Enlargement: The Proliferation Security Initiative,* Santa Monica: Rand Corporation, p. 36.
44. Ibid., p. 20 and also see Mary Beth Nikitin, (2011), *Proliferation Security Initiative (PSI),* Washington: CRS Report for Congress, pp. 1-9.

PART V
Human Security

17

Human Security and Climate Change in South Asia

A. Subramanyam Raju

The concept of security is extended from military to political, economic, environment or human security. It is equated with security of individuals. Mahbub-ul-Haq in the UNDP's Human Development Report of 1994 observed that, "Human security is a child who did not die, a disease that did not spread, a job that was not cut, an ethnic tension that did not explode in violence, a dissident who was not silenced. Human security is not a concern with weapons–it is a concern with human life and dignity...It is concerned with how people live and breathe in a society, how freely they exercise their many choices, how much access they have to market and social opportunities–and whether they live in conflict or in peace." [1] He argued that "The search for human security lies in development, not in arms." [2]

Thus, the state has to reorient its policies to address the problems of human beings. The threats to human security are far more numerous and complex than the threats to state security. The UNDP has called for "a transition from the narrow concept of national security to the 'all-encompassing concept of human security." [3] There are two approaches to human security i.e. UNDP and Canadian approaches. Both approaches oppose traditional instruments of security–force, deterrence and balance of power. [4] The UNDP's emphasis is on economic development, whereas the Canadians focus is on political development. [5] It argues that freedom from want is essential whereas the Canadian approach argues for freedom from fear. Both are equally important for ensuring the security of human beings. Freedom from fear would be meaningful only when freedom from want is ensured and freedom from want is possible only when freedom from fear is achieved. [6]

Several states have initiated a number of policies from the human security point of view. They tried to follow a new model of developmental strategy for the last one decade. Thus, one witnesses lack of affordability to have food resulting in hunger and starvation, inadequate water, poor primary health care, deprivation of basic needs increasing, poverty, unemployment, environmental degradation etc.

No doubt the governments of respective countries in South Asia are concerned about these issues but they are unable to address them adequately due to various reasons and constraints. Since environmental threats are being seen as greater threats than terrorism in South Asia, an attempt is made in this paper to examine climate change and its impact on human livelihood in South Asia.

South Asia and Climate Change

South Asia represents one fourth of the world population with low gross domestic product, low per capita and low literacy rate coupled with high birth and high death rates. In 2005, the South Asian region was home to forty four percent of the world's poor [7] and contained the largest number of the world's hungry of about 350 million people. [8] Disputes, mutual distrust, misunderstanding and suspicion still prevail in the region. It is clearly evident that absence of a collective identity, lack of trust and lack of a sense of belongingness do exist among the countries in the region.

The discourse on climate change [9] reveals that the entire humanity would face numerous problems [10] such as rise of sea level, migration of people who live in low lying areas, environmental hazards, cyclones, droughts, impact on health and crop yield, water scarcity etc. in the near future due to the emission green house gases (GHGs-Co_2, methane, nitrous oxide, hydro fluorocarbons, fluorocarbons and sulphur hexafluoride). Though, the developing countries were in no way responsible for global warming, they have to be part of the solution. Impact of climate change would be more on them than on developed countries. [11] Climate change cannot be addressed without addressing the issue of energy.

Total global energy consumption will expand by seventy one percent between 2003 and 2030. Increase in energy demand will occur in developing countries that depend upon the combustion of hydrocarbons such as coal to produce the electricity to meet their energy needs. Carbon dioxide emissions from developing countries are projected to exceed those of the industrialized nations soon after 2010. Oil and gas are not as abundantly available as coal. Projections indicate that under current policies and trends fossil fuels will remain the dominant source of energy in the future. The International Energy Agency forecasts that between 2004 and 2030, fossil fuels will account for eighty three percent of the overall increase in global energy demand. There is a need to find alternative sources of energy that can supply the burgeoning energy needs of the world. Further development and deployment of sustainable energy technologies on an unprecedented scale is needed.

South Asia's commercial energy mix in 2002 was forty six percent coal, thirty four percent petroleum, twelve percent natural gas, six percent hydroelectricity, one percent nuclear and one percent other resources. There is a disparity in terms of availability of energy resources across the region. For instance, in 2002, Bangladesh's energy resources is dominated by natural gas (66.4 percent), India depended greatly on coal (54.5 percent), Sri Lanka and the Maldives are mostly dependent on petroleum (82 percent and 100 percent respectively); Pakistan on petroleum (42.7 percent) and natural gas (42.2 percent) and Bhutan and Nepal have access to hydroelectric power (80 percent and 31 percent, respectively). [12] Mostly, South Asian countries are depending on importing energy resources. Thirty percent of the energy demands of the South Asian countries can be met through energy cooperation.

South Asian countries, on one hand, have to provide enough commercial energy for growth and on the other hand they have to minimize the inequality between urban and rural people's consumption levels of energy. [13] For instance, it realized the need for coherent and enduring foreign energy security policy to secure energy imports at affordable price and without any disturbance.

It is expected that oil will be available for about forty to sixty years, and natural gas for and her hundred years. If this is going to be the reality, then India, which is depending heavily on imports, should explore alternatives to secure its energy need viz. renewable energy (wind energy, solar energy, hydroelectricity power etc.) and nuclear energy. India has a renewable capacity of over 11,000 Mw, of which 7,000 Mw is based on wind power. India is projected to expand its nuclear capacity significantly over the next twenty five years to increase the diversity of its energy supplies, improve energy security and provide a low-carbon alternative to fossil fuels.

Through the India-US nuclear energy cooperation agreement, India is expected to produce about 20,000 Mw by 2020 and double this by 2030. India's main focus on nuclear energy is not only to meet its demands but also to reduce its green house emission. In Pakistan, nuclear power makes a small contribution to the total energy production and requirements, supplying only 2.34 percent of the country's electricity. The total generating capacity is 20 GWe and in 2006, 98 billion kWh gross was produced, thirty seven percent of it from gas and twenty nine percent from oil. [14] Bangladesh had a deal with Russia to construct a nuclear power plant in the former for energy production by the latter.

Rise in Sea Level

Energy consumption contributes to climate change and climate change contributes to the rise in sea level. Oceans too, are a major heat-transfer engine in the Earth's climate system. Oceans absorb more than half of the solar energy reaching the Earth's surface. Tropical oceans, especially, are big absorbers of solar energy. The ocean surface is heated by the Sun, i.e. heat is redistributed by a complex global system of ocean currents. The movement of ocean currents, however, is much slower than the movement of atmospheric circulation currents. The water in the oceans is structured in layers and these layers are important to circulation patterns. The uppermost layer, where heat is first absorbed, is well mixed by wind and waves, and exchanges heat and gases with the atmosphere on the shortest time-scales.

Much of the energy absorbed by the ocean's upper layer goes to evaporate water, resulting in warm, humid air that contains extra heat energy. The convective updrafts of this air can be a major force driving weather systems. Large-scale migration from coastal zones is expected due to submergence of coast-lines after sea levels have risen. This will create large numbers of environmental refugees especially from low-lying regions in poor countries. Intrusion of sea-water in the ground water and changes in temperature can reduce agricultural and fishing incomes. Climate change could represent an additional stress on ecological and socioeconomic systems that are already facing tremendous pressure.

Climate change impacts include sea level rise, changes in the monsoon, increased severe storms and flooding and drought. Sea level rise will damage aquaculture industries, fish productivity and cause of increased frequency and intensity of coastal surges and cyclones. It is estimated that the rate of global sea level rise was between 0.1 and 0.2 meters (about 3.9 to 7.9 inches) during the twentieth century and this rate of sea level rise was ten times that of the previous 3,000 years. Since the end of the ice age, transfers of mass from ice sheets to the oceans have raised sea level by 120 meters. The global ocean heat content, according to the IPCC (Intergovernmental Panel for Climate Change), has increased since late 1950s.

Due to the impact of climate change, it is expected that the sea level will increase. As a result, people who live in coastal areas/low-lying areas, will have to suffer. It is estimated that by 2050, about 250 million people may leave their places due to intensifying monsoon flooding, desertification and reduced food production. Most of the developing countries, which are dependent on coastal fishery and agriculture, are likely to be affected. If a one-meter sea level rise were to take place today, it would displace seven million persons in India. [15] In the future many more may be displaced. Further, intrusion of sea-water in the ground water and changes in temperature can reduce agricultural and fishing incomes.

With changes in temperature, precipitation and humidity, main sectors such as agriculture and rural development are likely to be severely affected in the coastal regions of India, Pakistan, Bangladesh, Sri Lanka and Maldives. [16] Impacts are already being seen in heat waves, cyclones, floods, salinisation of the coastline and their effects on agriculture, fisheries and health. The ocean has the largest heat capacity of any single component of the climate system and over the past forty years, it has been the dominant source of changes in global heat content. Global ocean heat content, according to the IPCC, has increased since the late 1950s.

The IPCC projections reveal that by the mid 2090s, the global sea level will reach 0.22 to 0.44 m above 1990 levels, and is rising at about 4 mm/year. Thermal expansion is projected to contribute more than half of the average rise, but land ice will lose mass rapidly in the future. Besides causing a sea level rise, ocean heat content may cause changes in the occurrence of extreme events such as cyclones. Emission of carbon dioxide, sulphur and hexafluoride into the atmosphere is a matter of global concern. Due to the impact of climate change, it is expected that the sea level will grow up.

Then, people who live in coastal areas, will have to suffer. An increase in cyclone intensity of 10-20 percent for 2-4 degree celsius of warming is predicted. These cyclonic storms will particularly affect the poor in coastal areas. A rise in sea level would result in the gradual submergence of coastal states and cities (the Maldives, Jakarta, Bangkok, Manila and Shanghai). Tens of millions of people in Asia may have to be resettled and massive expenditures to be incurred to protect the coastal cities from sea level rise, which may range from about 20-70 centimetres (about 8 inches to 2 feet) by the end of this century.

India has a 7,500 km. coastal line and it needs to protect the people who live in the coastal areas. Some predict that the sea may rise to 1-2 m by 2100. India needs to take steps on property loss and damage, relocation and evacuation plans. However, India failed to think about the negative implication of constructing the Sethusamudram Canal [17] in the Tamil Nadu coast. The livelihood of fishermen [18] in 138 fishing stations along the five coastal districts would be severely affected. There is also concern over the impact on the environment. Dredging of the Pamban channel is required, where coral reef is in abundance, which would lead to the depletion of fish and the destruction of the marine ecology.

It would break the continuous limestone formation which would cause sudden tilting drift and gravitational pull setting in motion various other violent processes. The areas where dredging is required, are prone to high rates of sedimentation. There are incidents that the canal is also threatened by cyclones. About sixty four cyclones had hit the Tamil Nadu coast during from 1891 to 2000 of which thirty six were severe. The December 1964 cyclone that wiped out the entire island-town of Dhanushkodi is a classical example.

The tsunami of 2004, extensively transformed the landscape of the eastern coast. If the sea level rises to one metre in Tamil Nadu, it is estimated that about five districts in the Cauvery delta region and other states like Andhra Pradesh, Orissa and West Bengal will be affected. [19] After the tsunami of 2004, there was hardly a study on the impact of the Canal. It is to be noted that the coastal stretch between

Nagapatnam and Pamban is a high risk zone and the area is prone to tsunami and cyclones. About sixty four cyclones hit the Tamil Nadu during 1891-2000 of which thirty six were severe. Around the Bay of Bengal, an estimated 1.3 million cyclone related deaths have been reported over the past 200 years. [20]

A one degree celsius rise in temperature would contribute to ten percent productivity loss in farming. For Bangladesh, according to Bangladesh's Prime Minister Sheikh Hasina, it is about 4 million metric tonnes of food grain loss, amounting to about US$ 2.5 billion. In other words, it is about two percent of its GDP, [21] whereas for India it would be more than 5 percent loss. [22] It is to be noted that most of the developing countries are going to be vulnerable as they face drought, water shortages, crop failure, poverty and disease. More than 100 million people would die and the global economic growth will be cut by 3.2 percent of the GDP by 2030 if necessary steps are not be taken in tackling climate change, according to a report commissioned by 20 governments. [23]

The coastal states in South Asia must show concern in coastal hazards. There are various factors that are responsible for recurring coastal disasters: non implementation of existing policies, breakdown of enforcement, lack of post disaster redevelopment guidelines, etc. People living in poverty will not be able to cope with the challenges posed by climate change. It is to be noted that a majority of the people who live in coastal areas in South Asia are poor. It is expected that there will be a large-scale migration from coastal zones due to rise of sea level, which will lead to submergence of coast-lines.

This will create a large number of environmental refugees who are living in low-lying areas. Further, it will reduce agricultural and fishing incomes due to intrusion of sea-water in the ground water and changes in temperature. People who are depending on coastal areas for fishery and agriculture, will be adversely affected. For instance, eighteen percent of the land in Bangladesh would be submerged by a one-meter rise. It will be difficult for Dhaka to take protective measures, and as a result tens of millions of people will be displaced in Bangladesh and many of them could spill over into India. Evacuation is not easily implemented, because of the reluctance of governments to order mandatory evacuations and unwillingness of residents to leave their unprotected property. [24] Mumbai is the tenth largest city in the world and the economic capital of India with 12 million inhabitants. It was estimated that the cost to Mumbai of a one meter sea level rise will be US$ 71 billion, indicative of the huge economic cost of climate change faced by Asia's coastal city. [25]

Floods of the Kosi river drove million from their homes in Nepal and Bihar. Cyclones Aila and Nargis have killed thousands and displaced millions more in Myanmar, Bangladesh and West Bengal. On the other hand, drought threatens millions of farmers in India, Bangladesh and Nepal. It is to be noted that the tsunami of 2004 did not have a direct link to climate change. Though none of these natural disasters can be directly attributed to climate change, there are predictions that there will be more severe consequences due to global warming.

Severe floods along the Ganges and Brahmaputra rivers in 2007 affected more than 13 million people in Bangladesh and economic loss was US$ 1 billion. Floods in Pakistan in 2010 affected 20 million people and the loss was US$ 10 billion. [26] Similarly, India too suffered due to extreme rainfall, floods and droughts. Climate change will lead to rise in temperature and this would require more irrigation facilities for crops. According to some reports, India's GDP may suffer a 2 percent loss, while Bangladesh, Maldives, Nepal, Pakistan and Sri Lanka may suffer even more. [27] Countries in the region would suffer from insecurity of food, water and health.

There is a need to invest more in constructing dams and canal lining to address the floods. For instance, "Pakistan's Tarbela dam produced more benefits than was projected. It generates 3,000 Mw of power" but otherwise it was planned to produce only 2,400 Mw and it irrigated 17.5 million ha. against the planned 15 million ha. and it reduced flood damages from US$ 43 billion to US$ 10 billion. [28] The recent "disrupt power supply for hundreds of millions of people in North India in August 2012 was due to global warming, shortages in hydroelectric power, failure of the monsoons and the absence of grid discipline". [29]

A two degree rise in average global temperature will cause a ten to forty percent crop loss and hundreds of billions of rupees in loss of revenue from agriculture. Rise of sea level contributes to damage to land and livelihoods, coastal erosion, morbidity, and mortality, forced displacement and property loss from flood. [30] Even the land locked countries (Afghanistan, Bhutan and Nepal) too will have problems due to droughts and shortage of rainfall. Due to climate change, India's GDP may lose two percent and other South Asian countries may suffer even more.

Conclusion

South Asia, particularly India, must take initiatives to limit GHGs emissions through initiatives like improving the efficiency of the energy and industrial production capacity, as well as energy development, both conventional and renewable, which target improved environmental quality and limit human health hazards from air pollution.

South Asian countries have to join with other countries in a collaborative effort to bring about a strategic shift, across the globe, from production and consumption patterns based on carbon-based fossil fuels to those based on renewable energy and non-carbon fuels, because it is question of life and death for every human being in the world. They must prioritize areas such as: energy efficiency in lighting, transport, power generation and reduce the energy-intensity of industrial production.

For instance, India is about 4½ times more inefficient than the US in production and even more so than some European countries. For every unit of consumption, India generates about two to three times more CO_2 emissions than other industrial countries. The US' per capita consumption of energy is forty nine times that of India and with regard to transport it is 146 times that of India. Though the South Asian countries were not part of the problem they have to be a part of the solution. The South Asian countries have to focus on energy efficiency, clean energy, prevention of air pollution, afforestation and wasteland development and population reduction. Since, the obligation of a State is to protect the welfare of the people, the South Asian countries need to collectively work towards mitigating global warming.

End Notes

1. *Human Development Report, 1994*, New York: Oxford University Press, 1994, p. 22.
   Some of the definitions for human security are:
   Kofi Annan describes human security as, "Human security in its broadest sense embraces far more than the absence of violent conflict. It encompasses human rights, good governance, access to education and health care and ensuring that each individual has opportunities and choices to fulfil his or her own potential. Every step in this direction is also a step towards reducing poverty, achieving economic growth and preventing conflict. Freedom from want, freedom from fear and the freedom of future generations to inherit a healthy natural environment-these are the interrelated building blocks of human and therefore national security". See Kofi Annan, 'Secretary-General Salutes International Workshops on Human Security in Mongolia', Ulaanbaator, May 8-10, 2000. Press Release SG/SM/7382, available at,
   http://www.Un.org/News/Press/docs/2000/2000508.sgsm 7382.doc.html.
   Amartya Sen and Sadako Ogare define it as, "Human security means protecting fundamental freedoms-freedoms that are the essence of life. It means protecting people from critical (severe) and pervasive (widespread) threats and situations. It means using processes that build on people's strengths and aspirations. It means creating political, social, environmental, economic,

military, and cultural systems that together give people the building blocks of survival, livelihood, and dignity.
The vital core of life is a set of elementary rights and freedoms people enjoy. What people consider to be 'vital'–what they consider to be 'of the essence of life' and 'crucially important'–varies across individuals and societies. That is why any concept of human security must be dynamic. And that is why we refrain from proposing an itemized list of what makes up human rights.
Cited in Sabina Alkire, "Concepts of Human Security", in Lincoln Chen, Sakiko Fukuda-Parr & Ellen Seidensticker (ed.), *Human Insecurity in a Global World*, New Delhi: Viva Books Pvt. Ltd., 2005), p. 32.

2. *Human Development Report,* Ibid., p. 1.
3. Ibid., p. 24.
4. I.P. Khosla, "Evolving a Theoretical Perspective on Human Security", P.R. Chari and Sonika Gupta (ed.), *Human Security in South Asia,* New Delhi: Social Science Press, 2003, p. 24.
5. Kanti Bajpai, *Human Security: Concept and Measurement,* Kroc Institute Occasional Paper, No. 19, August 2000, p. 35.
6. A.K.M. Abdus Sabur, "Evolving a Theoretical Perspective in Human Security: The South Asian Context", in Chari and Gupta, n. 4, p. 44.
7. See Tushaar Shah and Uma Lele (eds.), *Climate Change, Food and Water Security in South Asia: Critical Issues and Cooperative Strategies in an Age of Increased Risk and Uncertainty*, Workshop Discussions, www.gwp.org, p. 3.
8. www.fao.org/hunger/en/, p. 3.
9. Earth Summit (1992), Kyoto Protocol (signed in 1997 and ratified in 2005), Bali Road Map (2007), Copenhagen Agreement (2009) are some of the agreements/conventions focused on mitigating climate change under the United Nations Framework Convention on Climate Change.
10. Some scientists argue that greater concentration of Co_2 is good for life on Earth, as they make for higher crop yields and faster regeneration of forests. There were periods in the history of the Earth when Co_2 levels were a million times higher than today, and life continued to evolve quite successfully. The Europeans are diverting the world to improve the competitiveness of European products and slow down economic growth in emerging economies. In 1970s when global temperature began

to dip, many warned that we faced a new ice age.

11. In temperate latitudes a rise in temperature would help developed countries increase food productivity, while it will have adverse effect on countries like India in the tropics. See Editorial, "Climate Change and Agriculture", *The Hindu*, 30 June 2009, p. 8.
12. EIA (US Energy Information Administration), Country Brief, available at, http://www.eia.doe.gov/emeu/cabs/nepal.html, accessed on 20 September, 2006.
13. For disparity between rural and urban people in terms of energy consumption levels, see Anant Sudarshan and Logia Noronha, "Contextualizing India's Energy Security", in Logia Noronha and Anant Sudarshan (ed.), *India's Energy Security*, London: Routledge, 2009, p. 3.
14. http://www.world-nuclear.org/info/inf108.html.
15. ADB, 1995, cited in Jyoti K. Parikh and Kirit Parikh, *Climate Change: India's Perceptions, Positions, Policies and Possibilities*, Organization for Economic Co-operation and Development (OECD), 2002, p. 7.
16. Coastline of India (7,500 km.), Pakistan (1,050 km.), Bangladesh (580 km.), Sri Lanka (1,340 km.) and Maldives (644 km.).
17. For more details see A. Subramanyam Raju and S.I. Keethaponcalan, *Maritime Cooperation between India and Sri Lanka* (New Delhi: Manohar Publishers, 2006); "Sethusamudram Ship Canal Project: Environmental Issues", in Rajesh Anand (ed.) et al., *Disaster Management and Sustainable Development: Emerging Issues and Concerns,* New Delhi: Pentagon Press, 2009, pp. 78-87.
18. A. Subramanyam Raju, "The (In)Security of Fisheries in South Asia", in Dennis Rumely, Sanjay Chaturvedi and Vijay Sakhuja (eds), *Fisheries Exploitation in the Indian Ocean: Threats and Opportunities,* Singapore: ISEAS, 2009, pp. 163-176.
19. *The Hindu*, 9th December 2010, p. 5.
20. C. Small and R.J. Nicholls, "A Global Analysis of Human Settlement in Coastal Zones", *Journal of Coastal Research,* Vol. 19, No. 3, 2003, pp. 584-599.
21. http://www.reuters.com/article/2012/09/25/us-climate-inaction-idUSBRE88O1HG20120925.

22. *Ibid.*
23. *Ibid.*
24. Roland J. Fuchs, *Cities at Risk: Asia' Coastal Cities in an Age of Climate Change*, Asia Pacific Issue, East-West Centre (Honolulu*)*, No. 96, July 2010, p. 8.
25. TERI (The Energy and Resources Institute), "The Economic Impact of a One Metre Sea Level Rise on the Indian Coastline: Method and Case Studies", report submitted to the Ford Foundation, 2006, cited in ibid, p. 4.
26. See n. 7, p. 3
27. See, n. 7, p. 7.
28. See n. 7, p. 19.
29. Sujatha Byravan and Sudhir Chella Rajan, "Warming Signs for the Economy", *The Hindu*, 22nd August 2012, p. 11.
30. *Ibid.*

18

Human Rights and Human Security: Reflections on India's Policy Initiatives

Kadloor Savitri

A broad understanding of the notion of human security requires an appraisal of a country's commitment to international human rights norms and domestic efforts in meeting the needs and social well-being of its citizens. Hence, in ascertaining the policy initiatives adopted in India to augment human security, India's efforts in furthering human rights, particularly social and economic rights, operate as an important signpost to fulfilling its promise of enhancing human security. In this context, the following broad policy initiatives will be taken up to measure the performance of India's policy initiatives.

1. India's international obligations in implementing the various human rights treaties.
2. MGNREGA as an employment guarantee scheme to fulfil the economic right to sustenance (Article 7 and 8 of ICESCR).
3. Food security as an area of social and economic security (Article 11 of ICESCR).

While the first category points towards a broad umbrella of treaty obligations that India has endeavoured to honour, the next two aspects are, in the main, pertaining to socio-economic rights. Needless to say, any understanding of national security, and human security, will be diminished if it does not factor in the need for a robust human rights regime.

Situating Human Rights and Human Security

The notion of security policy has long transcended the

narrow, conventional limits of state security to include the various non-state security aspects that contribute to fulfilling an individual's needs; the latter have assumed salience and moved to the centre-stage of security dialogue in a way that has significantly altered the kernel of discussion on the subject. In fact, it is this shift in the understanding of security–from state to a non-state dimension–that has enabled the non-state actors to proactively campaign for the social dimension of the security dialogue and act as a check on the unilateral actions of the state.

One of the most important developments of the twentieth century has been the interweaving of human rights in every conceivable intellectual and socio-political discussion with attendant impact that has been a phenomenal game changer. The effects of economic globalization on human rights has been both good and bad, has been both beneficial and challenging, but its benefits are most evident in the way member states have been compelled to accede to international human rights instruments and harmonize their domestic laws in line with them. In doing so, member states are experiencing unprecedented external pressure from the international institutions to implement the human rights standards. (Savitri, 2008:172)

Added to this, internally, civil society and non-governmental organizations are exerting never-before influence on states, both directly and via the international bodies, to demand adherence to international norms and standards. In this context, globalization presents newer challenges to the states striving to establish and maintaining a human rights regime and complicates the understanding of precarious interrelationship between human rights and human security. The challenges of globalization to achieving a robust human rights regime are two-fold. One set of challenges flows from the fact that the arena of state control and regulation is constantly shrinking under the impact of globalization. As a result, state activity and expenditure in the social sector has receded considerably in the recent years in most countries, notably the developing ones. Structural adjustment policies (SAP) delimit the capacity of states to independently determine their development priorities.

Moreover, economic and social policies driven by the directives from international institutions like the World Bank and IMF erode the avenues of participation of local communities in decision making on socio-economic policies and thus create a democratic deficit that has negative implications for human rights. In countries where SAP has been initiated, there is an element of disenchantment with the lack of the state's involvement in social sectors, be it education, health, housing or social security. Interestingly, these are precisely the areas that form the nerve-centre of interplay between human rights and human security.

The second set of challenges emanates from the fact that the state has increasingly come under scrutiny for its role in the protection and promotion of human rights. The agents of such scrutiny are both the international and intra-national actors. International donors and lending agencies impose on the recipient countries, mostly developing countries reeling under debt burden, such non-economic conditionalities as good governance and respect for human rights even as the states are pursuing severely restricted policy choices. Within the state, civil society organizations, political and social groups, and NGOs are raising uncomfortable questions and issues related to survival and dignity of those marginalised by the shift in policy choices initiated by the state. As a spin-off of the international and intra-state pressures on the state, human rights issues have re-emerged and have come to occupy the centre-stage of the discourse on an individual's relationship with the state.

Thus, there is a serious shift in the way policies are formulated and objectives are delineated in India and elsewhere, an honest attempt to incorporate the prevailing international policy framework in the domestic setting. In order to understand the impact of human rights discourse on securing human security in India, one must look at the trajectory of human rights influences on domestic policy choices in the light of India's external orientation on human rights issues and how international obligations are sought to be incorporated, applied and implemented within the country.

India's International Obligations

India is a signatory to most of the international human rights instruments, particularly those that concern with social-economic rights. A country's commitment to international instruments automatically obligates it to implement the provisions of treaties and conventions which have been ratified. India's obligations towards social and economic rights emanates from the provisions of the International Covenant on Economic, Social and Cultural Rights (ICESCR) which it has ratified in 1978. Most importantly, the right to gainful employment, right to food and right to education are the rights incorporated in this Covenant. Moreover, right to free and compulsory education up to the age of fourteen years, right to food and nutrition in childhood are also part of the Convention on the Rights of the Child (CRC) to which India is a party. Besides these UN human rights instruments, there are certain other conventions and binding instruments of the ILO to which India is a signatory and which obligate the member states to ensure the delivery of these rights to its citizens.

The international human rights instruments monitor the implementation of its provisions by the member states through consideration of periodic reports of the member states by the respective committees and offering critical inputs and suggestions on future implementation. India makes a curious case in terms of its commitment to international obligation. While India has been generally enthusiastic about participating in human rights bodies and representing on Commission on Human Rights continuously since its inception in 1946, the same enthusiasm has not resonated in ratifying treaties or instruments adopted by those very bodies.

Any instance of sudden spurt in ratification has been largely owing to international pressure, the immediacy of the situation or unique domestic compulsions. One can see a similar trend in terms of national legislations related to incorporating international human rights standards. Thus, repeated reminders and highly critical inputs from the international treaty bodies on India's periodic reports have prompted the Indian government to establish NHRIs in the field of human rights protection, women's rights, rights of the children and minorities. Also one is able to see a string of domestic legislations that guarantee a right (education, food, information) or grant protection from violation (DVA). Each of these is an instance of follow up after ratifying international instruments.

The NHRIs have also, in turn, helped in building consensus and highlighting the urgency of some of the social rights such as NCPCR for food, education and NCW for protection from domestic violence. Thus a concert of interests exists between international treaty bodies, NHRIs, NGOs and civil society organizations in pressing for increased commitment of the state to making these rights legally binding and constitutionally entrenched (education, for instance). It can be asserted here with a modicum of certainty that India's need for projecting a greater image in the world and its desire to play a larger role in international institutions have fuelled the domestic activism seen in terms of legislations guaranteeing some of the social and economic rights. The international approval and currency enjoyed by human security concept, albeit sceptically and critically in some quarters, has further prompted India to pay attention to human rights standards. In the next section, the concept of human security and its linkages with rights based approach (RBA) and human rights is established.

Concept of Human Security: Problem of Definition

The concept of human security came into prominence with

the human development report in 1994. "The concept of human security emerged out of the recognition that individuals and communities' security does not necessarily follow from the security of the state in which they are citizens". (Bilgin, 2003:213) UNDP's Human Development Report, 1994, heralded a clear formulation of the concept of human security. Amartya Sen linked human security to threats to "the survival, daily life, and dignity of human beings and to strengthening the efforts to confront these threats." (Sen, 2000:1)

It signified two major shifts in the way in which security was cognized. Firstly, it broadened the notion of security to include socio-economic issues like employment, health, food and nutrition, housing, education. These issues were beyond the traditional notions of security. Secondly, human security altered the primary referral point in security discourse from state to the individual or community (human-centric instead of state-centric). The traditional notion of security was more amenable to the Westphalian conception of international order where states were the dominant actors. In the post-Cold War era, this had to undergo a radical shift so as to accommodate international actors other than states in formulating and implementing new security policy. Since the shift is from state to the individuals and communities, this approach is often referred to as individualist or popular approach as against the statist approach.

According to HDR, 1994, seven elements comprise human security. They are: economic security, food security, health security, environmental security, personal security, community security, and political security. (UNDP, 1994:24-25) The concept of human security offers a moral justification and analytical prioritization of individuals over states. There are two aspects of protection that human security is expected to afford: (a) threats, such as hunger, disease, and repression; and (b) sudden and harmful disruptions in the patterns of daily life. One must also pay attention to linkages between these two, that is, threats emanating from disruption to social security policies since those also constitute disruptions in the pattern of daily life.

In the human security paradigm, the threats are not external, to be managed by the military forces. Rather, threats are internal, manifested in gross violation of human rights (sometimes induced by the state itself), economic failure reflected in problems of underdevelopment or lopsided development, discrimination at various levels and on many counts, mass migration, hunger, infectious diseases, and so on. While human security broadly alludes to all the above parameters, there is no single definition of human security (Tajbakhsh, 2005: 5) that crisply encapsulates all that has been mentioned above. Hence, one has to take a long detour to make sense of the term for our analysis here.

One of the things the term human security means is that it is a broad policy framework that includes just about everything that makes human life secure in the public domain, a referral point for looking at the orientation of public policies. Public policies are formulated by the state but state is not the only actor in its implementation or, sometimes, even in its formulation. Nor are there any short and sudden measures to fix the problems of human security in the sense in which the realists emphasize on military solutions. 'Interventions' do and should involve longer-term engagements (Tajbakhsh, 2005:8) revolving around development and reform.

It is in this sense of a criss-cross between policy orientation and promotion of human rights that the term human security is used here. If human security relates to freedom from fear and want (of gainful employment, food, health, housing and education), this paper focuses on issues concerning freedom from *want*, that is, a discussion on social and economic rights.

Human security also resonates with 'concerns about how globalization rendered traditional notions of sovereignty and security are less relevant.' (Kim, 2010)

Human Security and Human Rights: Convergence, Confluence or Clash?

Until 2000, human development (human security is seen as a dimension of this, hence introduced first in HDR 1994) and human rights followed separate paths—both in concept and action. Human development was dominated by economists, policy makers and social scientists whereas the concern for human rights was punctuated more by political activists, lawyers and philosophers. The two streams also adopted divergent strategies of analysis and action; while human development promoted economic and social progress reflected in cogently quantifiable terms, human rights movement was inclined towards applying political pressure, seeking legal reform and even ethical questioning. (Alston and Robinson, 2005: 27)

The activism associated with the global human rights movement and its confrontation with disorder and havoc caused by globalization has augmented the human security concept further. The threats to human security enumerated above have gained a transnational character that in a swift, dramatic snapping of fingers reduces the relevance and the responsibility of state system to protect its citizens from those threats. The contribution of human rights movement and its progeny, the rights based approach, is that it changed this divergent trajectory and helped the development practitioners in absolving some of the blame and guilt that they did not integrate human rights concerns in their development work.

Development agencies, UN bodies and independent researchers have increasingly adopted RBA to tread a common ground between human rights, security and human development. Amartya Sen's 'Development as Freedom' has a strong accent on social rights based approach to economic development. It is now a commonly held idea based on compelling evidence that policy initiatives and governance models or choices that did not pay adequate attention to human rights have not been able to deliver long-term improvements in well-being of target groups, be it in the area of forest management, poverty alleviation, education or housing. Since these are constituent part of the MDGs, it can be cryptically asserted that MDGs cannot be accomplished 'without giving attention to rights'. (Colchester, 2007:3)

Rights Based Approach

Rights based approach (RBA) signifies a significant shift in the social science discourse in general and human rights discourse in particular. It was developed in the context of development and human security to denote human rights-centric approach wherein every individual can claim services as a matter of right before the public authorities and not as a mere passive recipient. It is this insistence on right that alters the notion of RBA from other approaches that seek to achieve development and human security. RBA alters the position of the individual in one swift stroke, almost spectacularly, from being a passive, helpless individual to an active bearer of rights; from being an object of international efforts and national planning to a subject of international and national law. RBA does not merely change the position of the individual.

It lends legal, political and social capital that enables an individual to become a *bearer of rights* while making the state a *bearer of duty* towards its citizens. RBA in the context of human security is important as an approach because it incorporates the international human rights standards, principles and norms into planning and policy initiatives undertaken at home.

In recent years, RBA has been used to analyze the various policy initiatives undertaken by the state to deliver public goods and services and thereby alleviate the position of the poor and marginalized in the developing world. From the standpoint of the state, RBA imposes certain principles as responsibility, accountability, transparency, non-discrimination and rule of law. RBA lays emphasis on an undeniable link between human rights and issues of human development and security. It looks at human security beyond the traditional framework of physical, infrastructural security as reflected in the defence paraphernalia of a state.

The question that crops up in one's mind at this point is, does human rights and human security need each other for sustaining its momentum? Or is it merely a linear linkage, a marriage of convenience? The answer to this question lies in the way these two concepts have interacted in the past decade. International human rights activism has helped human security to find a foothold in the conceptual and implementational realm. The scepticism associated with human security found a favourable subscription in human rights discourse by establishing linkages between 'freedom from want' on the one hand and on the other, basic undeniable individual rights that was the hallmark of post-Second World War development of international human rights norms.

Human rights also dramatically retrieved human security from the core of development paradigm to make it intellectually and practically appealing to interpret human rights standards. If this justification sounds conclusively tilted in favour of the contribution of human rights in augmenting human security, one needs to only look at the linkage between MDGs and human security to be convinced to the contrary. MDGs appear to be the meeting point between human rights and human security. Human rights and MDGs require human security to bring them within the development fold that alone can ensure resource allocation and policy attention in immediate and long-term planning.

More critically, human security legitimized the demand of international human rights movement to look beyond state—and to make individual the subject, not merely the object—toward 'globalizing' of policy initiatives. It gives "political voice to the otherwise politically marginalized". (Osler Hampson's idea summarized in Owen, 2004:377) Lastly, human rights abuses and violations are recognized as one of the main sources of threats to human security. A sound normative and policy-oriented convergence between human rights and human security is imperative for the success of both.

Thus, the above discussion reveals that over a period of a decade-and-a-half, a web of interdependencies and linkages has been created between development, human rights, rights based approach, MDGs and human security that appears difficult to untangle both in policy analysis and policy implementation. While the linkages are deep and enmeshed, they are by no means linear and uncomplicated. In fact, the kind of ambivalence that signified the interrelationship between globalization and human rights in the early 1990s has also afflicted the interdependence between human rights and human security. The intense activity in the field of human rights has made international NGOs and human rights institutions to eventually move away from traditional civil-political rights to bring socio-economic rights and standards in sharper relief in the form of corporate social responsibility and insistence on state activity in social sectors.

There has been a phenomenal increase in the number of NGOs active in the human rights field, and the level of their participation, in the last decade-and-a-half. The new-found vigour and resurgence of NGO participation is a positive outcome of the free flow of information and ideas, avenues of communication, and cooperation across the borders made possible by globalization. Many of these NGOs have a consultative status with the Economic and Social Council (ECOSOC) of the United Nations and are therefore able to voice their concerns and record their protests before the various international monitoring bodies.

They also submit alternative reports to the treaty bodies to counter a state party's laudatory reports and grand representation of the human rights situation at home. In fact, NGOs have been instrumental in internationalizing human rights violations and demanding their redress. NGOs are an important component of global civil society and they share a commitment to values and universal human rights norms. In their quest for global human rights standards, they have augmented the cause of human security. In another context, it has been acknowledged that NGOs and international civil society organizations have brought pressure on "the state to accept responsibility for the poor and dispossessed and on the corporations to accept social responsibility in their global dealings." (Shelton, 2004: 340)

An alternative view suggests that the linkages between human rights and human security are not always beneficial and that it scuttles the focus away from human rights and dilutes its efficacy. Howard-Hassmann points to the dangers of overemphasizing human security concept that can undermine the cause of human rights. Insofar as identifying threats to human security, victims of those threats, "or new mechanisms to deal with those threats at the inter-state level, it adds to the established human rights regime". But the attempt by human security supporters to rephrase state obligations toward its citizens into policy initiatives of human security makes the two as competing discourses. (Howard-Hassmann, 2012:89) She conclusively argues that indivisibility and interconnectedness of human rights encompasses common solutions for human insecurity. In fact, human rights regime requires states to be the primary duty bearers if rights can be claimed as entitlements that are given and not there that have to be earned. (2012; 94-95)

Moreover, human rights as a concept and as a movement has had to contend with several challenges and obstacles in the past and human security, rights based approach to development and governance have only added to that list of challenges. The institutional challenges encountered in the protection and promotion of human rights is partly couched in rights based approach to development and governance. It means that human rights are becoming a focal point of governance at the international and national level to be effected through the formation of national human rights institutions (NHRIs). However, NHRIs, on their part, have not been very effective in implementing social and economic rights. (Raj Kumar, 2011) This implies that the institutional challenges faced by human rights reflect in weaker efficacy of NHRIs in augmenting human security agenda. The problem gets further magnified if one looks at the inability and inadequate response of institutions of governance in India to the problems of poverty and increasing incidences of farmers' suicide.

Critics of human security point out that it is too broad and obscure a concept, and there is no single unified approach which presents difficulties in its application. Its scepticism about international organizations and state system has also come for criticism although the concept itself is a child of 'post-Cold War scepticism toward the dominant traditional security paradigm'. (Owen, 2004a:16) Hence, its scepticism toward Westphalian institutions such as international organizations is only an extension of its intellectual roots. The concept of human security can be interventionist in that it looks into the domestic affairs of the state to assess and assist, question and even intervene (militarily, e.g. cry for humanitarian intervention in Darfur to stem starvation deaths there and the R2P response). Asian countries do not accept such justification for intervention or other sovereignty-eroding, interference-inducing characteristics of human security. That makes critical policy analysis within a state extremely difficult.

In fact, some Asian scholars like Sumit Ganguly and Sung Won Kim argue that predicting the trajectory of human security in an Eastphalian order (Asian perspective on international law and governance, and an increased accent on Asian influence on international system) presents a difficult task even as the Asian region might prove to be an "interesting laboratory for the human security project". (Kim, 2010:85; Kim, Fidler and Ganguly, 2009) Traditionally, Asian societies have placed trust in ideas of sovereignty and non-interference. Kim argues that human security picture is most complicated in

India not in the least because it has been reluctant to adopt this concept in its foreign policy. There is a general reluctance to accord primacy to human security in the foreign policies of China, Japan and India. (Kim, 2010:95)

In spite of such reservations, there is overwhelming support for the concept of human security more due to the evident crumbling pie of traditional security paradigm and its inability to discharge its primary responsibility to protect its people from death and disaster. (Owen, 2004:374)

India's Policy Initiatives: Baby Steps to Cover Miles

The present paper takes a synoptic view of two policy initiatives, namely, MGNREGA and the Food Security Bill, in providing economic and food security to situate them in the larger context of debate on interdependency between human rights and human security. In India, as in many developing countries, freedom from want equals if not exceeds the issues of freedom from fear, which are no less important. In doing so, one central government program that was introduced in 2007 and the other that is fairly nascent in its inception have been chosen to see how these two present a case for evaluating human security in India.

The common thread linking these two programmes is that they overtly acknowledge and build on the rights based approach to right to subsistence and right to food. This appears to be a mundane idea until one is compelled to notice how remarkably different these programmes are from their predecessors in various avatars. While there have been as many programmes and centrally sponsored schemes for employment, poverty eradication and eliminating hunger in the past, they fall short in policy foresight and orientation in comparison to what is sought to be achieved by the two policies under consideration here.

The current critical debate in India regarding the determination or definition of poverty reflects a complete lack of understanding of the ground situation and the lowering of the threshold by the Planning Commission of India to an abysmal level is in fact an attempt to help the state to retreat from its responsibilities further. By statistically and artificially bringing the BPL down, the Planning Commission, typically dominated by developmental economists, overlooks the non-economic and non-statistical aspects of human security that does not augur well either for human development indices or for the regime of human rights in India.

MGNREGA, 2006, was a flagship programme introduced by the Ministry of Rural Development that aimed to enhance livelihood security in rural areas. Right to shelter, security of livelihood has been considered as a part of right to life itself since the Supreme Court expanded the definition of right to life in *Olga Tellis vs BMC* judgment. Its linkage with right to life makes it doubly important as an individual right and as a collective right to human security and durable asset creation. The programme was introduced in three phases beginning with 200 most backward districts in 2006. 130 more districts were added in 2007 and in 2008, the remaining 274 districts were included. Hence, it is now truly an all India programme.

In keeping with the broader interpretation of right to life, the main objective of MGNREGA was to augment wage employment, enhance wage-earning capacity of the rural poor, create durable assets in rural areas, and lastly, financial inclusion of the poor. These objectives also had certain auxiliary aims such as strengthening natural resource management thereby encouraging sustainable development. Natural resource management was expected to address the causes of poverty, deforestation, non-availability of bio-mass and soil erosion. It also sought to strengthen processes of democracy and transparency in governance at the grassroot level.

A remarkable feature that set it apart was that it was the first social welfare programme to directly allude to RBA as the guiding approach and human security as its declared objective. BPL families were no longer to be seen as mere passive recipients of central schemes. It is the responsibility of state that believes in social welfare and human security. The moment we perceive it as a right, it seriously alters the position of the individual as a legitimate claimant of a right upon state or society. Hence, there is an element of 'empowerment' and 'encapacitation' in RBA which was absent in earlier employment schemes like Jawahar Rozgar Yojna (JRY).

The scheme is demand-driven. Wherever, there is demand for avenues of livelihood and concurrently a demand for creating durable assets, the scheme is supposed to take root and grow. It is expected to lead to twin policy impact of capacity building of the community while empowering the individual.

It also marked a shift in the dependence on agriculture as the sole source of livelihood to other sources of unskilled manual labour related to construction and asset creation. The need however is to have a convergence approach to sustain the benefits in future.

There has been absolute lack of coordination among the various departments that has undermined the capacity of such livelihood guarantee schemes to optimize the multiplier effects by integrating watershed development programme, Horticulture Mission, providing better small-credit system for rural entrepreneurship, etc. As a result, there is a splintering of benefits wherein the sum is not greater than all parts. Secondly, the parliamentary standing committee on rural development found the initial momentum has not been sustained in the later years. In effect, this remains a well-designed livelihood scheme that has failed to translate into a human security project due to lack of long-term sustainability and inclusion in participation which should be the hallmark of 'freedom from want' framework.

Food Security Bill

This has been another forward-looking scheme that appears to adopt RBA for the social security schemes. Although the cabinet cleared the Bill in December 2011 and tabled it in the Parliament the following day (22 December 2011), it has run into rough weather almost immediately. This Bill aims to provide subsidized food grains to people, predominantly to the BPL population in rural and urban areas. Most states already provide for PDS and the food security bill was supposed to alter the image of PDS as a sluggish scheme and provide an extra safety net. Like MGNREGA, the Food Security bill, if implemented, alters the nature of the hitherto existing notion of PDS.

For one, this is a centrally sponsored scheme that aims to achieve uniformity in the level of human security even while taking into account regional and economic disparity among the population. Existing nutrition and select social security schemes would also be brought under the legislation as an entitlement. While PDS was a state welfare scheme, the Food Security Bill is couched in terms of human right to livelihood. This is exactly in line with article 11 of the ICESCR to which India is a signatory. In fact, experts wrote an open letter to the PM in September 2011 (Times of India, 27 September 2011) rubbishing the Planning Commission's estimate of poverty threshold and pointed out that that this estimate should not be linked to the entitlements of the poor. "It is unacceptable and counterproductive to link the official poverty estimates to basic entitlements of people, especially access to food". Targeted PDS was introduced in 1997 that has done more harm than good and has created artificial divisions leading to massive errors of exclusion. Evidence has established that states that have moved towards universalisation of PDS have performed much better in reducing leakages.

The linkage of food security bill with our discussion stems from the idea that the proposed bill could cater to those who are in the danger zone although they might be technically just out of the BPL category. This buffer category between poor and non poor would be typically vulnerable to changes in environment like drought or economic slowdown for they are not rich enough to be excluded but also not poor enough to be automatically included in BPL category.

Universalization of food security would 'protect them from sudden disruption of patterns of life' as defined in human security paradigm and provide a 'zero deprivation' band for the poor. Mihir Shah, Member, Planning Commission, said the idea of *zero deprivation* is crucial to ensuring *justice* in identifying families for subsidies. This would reconcile the demands of social justice in Rawlsian terms for the least advantaged, the state obligation to provide socio-economic rights and the needs of individual and community for human security.

States like Tamil Nadu, Odisha and Bihar have opposed the poverty cap imposed by the Centre. Southern states already run food schemes parallel to the proposed bill and many states have been providing cheaper grains in the past. The Centre gains upper hand in that states cannot provide subsidized food to anyone that the centre rules out of its beneficiaries' list.

Conclusion

Human rights and human security concepts have found common ground in more ways than one. The development of the concept of human rights and its widespread acceptance as international standard has encouraged the supporters of human security to moor their demand in terms of human rights. There are several areas of convergence between human rights and human security but three of those are important to re-emphasize here. Both human rights and human security seek to prioritize individual over the state and have thus revolutionalized the way in which individual is juxtaposed vis-à-vis the state. Secondly, both human security and human rights recognize that the threats to security are not external but internal in nature, often rooted in violations of core human rights. Thirdly, RBA appears to be the common link between human rights and human security.

While these linkages are accepted and lauded, it is pertinent to note the challenges and dangers of overemphasizing the inter-relationship between the two concepts. Human security discourse poses the danger of overtaking and usurping the political and policy space hitherto enjoyed by human rights. It can seriously scuttle the balance between civil-political rights and socio-economic rights. In India, the NHRIs have not been very effective in delivering social and economic rights and have thus tilted the balance in favour of civil-political rights.

It is argued here that a lot still needs to be done to secure a better human security regime in India by way of eliminating poverty, preventing suicides by debt-ridden farmers, and a better implementation plan for right to education. However, some encouraging shifts in policy orientation have thus far been initiated because of the pressures exerted by the external and internal human rights actors on the Indian state. In developing countries like India, international human rights standards hold the key to furthering human security mainly due to a broad consensus and moral justification enjoyed by them. It also shows that the rights based approach to development that has gained currency worldwide is now beginning to reflect more explicitly in policy statements and objectives. Thus, globalization as a process is pushing the human rights agenda internationally and this, in turn, is driving the human security issues. The readily available human rights platform has been used to justify and negotiate human security issues with the member states.

India presents a curious laboratory because of a string of policies where the centrality assumed by the state augurs well for human rights supporters and those more hopeful of human security paradigm. They also show that the willingness of the Indian state remains the main interlocutor in the implementation of rights which is a good sign for those placing their bet on human rights as the primary vehicle through which human security can be, and has to be, achieved.

Social rights within these schemes are important to create concentric circles of human rights, for instance, access to drinking water and nutrition as part of right to education, or provision for health and other insurance benefits to unorganized labour in MGNREGA. Thus, human rights, particularly social and economic rights, can prove to be a useful parameter to gauge and channelize human security initiatives to secure 'freedom from want'.

References

Alston, Philip and Robonson, Mary (2005), (ed.), *Human Rights and Human Development: Towards Mutual Reinforcement*, Oxford University Press.

Bilgin, Pinar (2003), 'Individual and Societal Dimensions of Security', *International Studies Review*, Vol. 5, pp. 203-222.

Colchester, Marcus (2007), *Beyond Tenure: Rights-based Approaches to People and Forests,* Paper for RECOFTC, Bangkok, September 3-7.

Howard-Hassmann, Rhoda E. (2012), 'Human Security: Undermining Human Rights?', *Human Rights Quarterly*, Vol. 34, pp. 88-112.

Kim, Sung Won (2010), 'Human Security with an Asian Face?', *Indiana Journal of Global Legal Studies,* Vol. 17, No. 1, pp. 83-103.

Kim, Sung Won, Fidler, David P. and Ganguly, Sumit (2009), 'Eastphalia Rising-Asian Influence and the Fate of Human Security', *World Policy Journal*, Vol. 26.

Owen, Taylor (2004), 'Human Security–Conflict, Critique and Consensus: Colloquium Remarks and a Proposal for a Threshold-Based Definition', *Security Dialogue*, Vol. 35, No. 3, pp. 373-387.

Owen, Taylor (2004a), 'Challenges and Opportunities for Defining and Measuring Human Security', *Disarmament Forum,* available at, www.unidir.org/pdf/articles/pdf-art2138.pdf.

Raj Kumar, C. (2011), "Challenges to Human Rights", Keynote address, National Seminar on *Emerging Paradigms of Human Rights: Issues, Challenges and Prospects,* organized by the Department of Political Science, AMU, Aligarh, 19-21 October.

Savitri, K. (2008), 'Implementing International Human Rights Standards in a Globalizing World' in Rumki Basu, (ed.),

Globalisation and the Changing Role of the State: Issues and Impacts, New Delhi/Illionois, New Dawn Press, pp. 171-192.

Sen, Amartya (2000), 'Why Human Security?', *International Symposium on Human Security*, Tokyo: Commission on Human Security.

Shelton, Dina (2004), 'Protecting Human Rights in a Globalizing World' in Charlotte Ku and Paul F. Diehl, (ed.), *International Law: Classic and Contemporary Readings*, Lynne Reiner/Viva Books, New Delhi.

Tadjbakhsh, Shahrbanou (2005), 'Human Security: Concepts and Implications with an Application to Post-Intervention Challenges in Afghanistan', *Les Etudes du CERI,* 117-118, September.

UNDP (1994), *Human Development Report, 1994: New Dimensions of Human Security.*

19

Indo-International Initiative for Billions of Fruit Trees (IIIBFT)

R. Alagu Perumal Ramasamy

Food Security impacts human security and global security. Climate change, changing lifestyles, land loss, shrinking water resources, rising fuel prices and fertilizer costs have already resulted in rising food prices all over the world. In 2008 as many as twenty countries experienced unrest that were fuelled by rising food prices and some governments collapsed as well. Also research on Causes of War in the post-Cold War period finds resource short nations involving in wars with neighbours.

In this scenario, India is poised to become the world's most populated country, replacing China, within the next two decades, which means that India will have to feed a lot more people than what it already does. Given the changing conditions mentioned above, feeding another half a billion is going to be a huge challenge. Solutions to the challenge require active involvement of not just the governments and political leadership, but also civil society organizations, industries, the scientific community, farmers and citizens.

In this paper, the author provides an inexpensive and workable solution to address food security. As we know, food security is fundamental impacting human security, national security and global security. The article suggests urgent measures to be taken to promote food security in the region.

Introduction

In the 2008 meeting of the G-8 nations, in response to the rising food prices across the world, the leaders of the eight major economies Canada, France, Germany, Italy, Japan,

Russia, the United Kingdom, and the United States declared, 'We are deeply concerned that the steep rise in global food prices coupled with availability problems in a number of developing countries is threatening global food security. The negative impacts of this recent trend could push millions more back into poverty, rolling back progress made towards achieving the Millennium Development Goals. We have taken additional steps to assist those suffering from food insecurity or hunger, and today renew our commitment to address this multifaceted and structural crisis'. (Ministry of Foreign Affairs of Japan, 2008)

Food price rise in 2008 sent shockwaves across the world. It caused food riots in fifteen countries with the Food and Agricultural Organization (FAO) declaring 1.5 billion people from thirty seven countries as facing starvation. Several governments collapsed unable to handle the situation. Yet the food price rise of 2008 was only the tip of the iceberg. (Cribb, 2010)

The real food crisis is imminent and within a span of a generation the world would be threatened by a major crisis which has not been faced by humanity in all of its existence. In this scenario, the work done by Indo-International Initiative for Billions of Fruit Trees (IIIBFT) gains significance for its role in promoting food security which in turn promotes human security. As human security improves, relations with the national neighbours are bound to improve as well. In the rest of the paper, an attempt is made to explain the above argument. But before discussing the role of IIIBFT in promoting food security, we take a bird's eye view of Indian relations with China.

Food Security, Human Security, Global Security and India

Food security is integral to human security. The 1994 Human Development Report, considered as a landmark document by many scholars working on human security defines human security as people's "safety from chronic threats and protection from sudden hurtful disruptions in the patterns of daily life". Seven types of security were listed as components of human security: economic security; food security; health security; environmental security; personal (physical) security; community security; and political security.

As one of the fundamental components of human security, food security requires our urgent attention.

Although, at the moment India is food sufficient, it is important to keep in mind the pressures exerted on our natural resources for producing food for the entire country when we would be surpassing China and becoming the world's most populated country.

Why is the Food Crisis Imminent?

World population would cross 9 billion by 2050 (United Nations, 2005); nearly thirty percent more than the size of the population today. Feeding such a huge population is going to be an enormous pressure on the fragile ecosystems. The Food and Agricultural Organization in its report *'How to Feed the World in 2050,'* estimates that the world will have to raise its annual cereal production from 2.1 billion tons to 3 billion tons and annual meat production should rise from 200 million tons to 470 million tons in order to feed the ballooning population.

Even though the rising population and the threat to food security is not new to humanity and on earlier occasions, solutions to food shortages have been found through effective use of technology and the consequent productivity rises, the crisis that is looming large upon us currently cannot be easily solved as was done before. There are various reasons such as land scarcity and declining quality, nutrient losses, depleted oil resources, falling ocean livestock, water crisis, diminishing returns to technological applications, climate change and politics all coming together to aggravate the crisis.

Impact of the Crisis on India

The impact of the crisis would be very severe in India as

by 2050 she will have the largest population in the world. The Chinese government, through its one child policy has managed to control the population and soon India would be occupying the number one position in the world in terms of population. Unfortunately, India will also have a significant percentage of the population living under poverty line. This would be so because the vast majority of Indians still do not have access to college education.

According to the National Knowledge Commission, only 7 to 14 percent of Indian children in the age group of 18-24 enrol in colleges. (National Knowledge Commission, 2006) In the absence of college education, the vast majority of them will not be in a position to have access to a fair means of livelihood. So it is clear that India will be over populated and poor unless there is a change in the governmental policies. The poor obviously will not be able to buy food at the prices that could be many times the current levels. Given this scenario, it is highly likely that India will be affected adversely by the coming food crisis.

Human Security and International Relations

An analysis of the causes of war in the post-Cold War era points to resource constraints as causes of conflicts. Conflicts linked to agriculture, according to Peace Research Institute, Oslo, dominate the projections for the future. "The causes of armed conflict are perpetuated by conflict itself. People fight over vital necessities such as food, to protect a livelihood, for economic and political justice, and to obtain safety from violence and want. States that can provide such necessities also create conditions conducive to peace and prosperity; they gain legitimacy, and they strengthen the social bonds crucial for socio-economic and political stability," say Indra de Soysa and Nils PetterGleditsch (1999).

Secure nations promote peaceful relations with neighbours. In the current scenario where India and China are competing with each other for resources and space in the international arena, it is imperative to develop human security in our society.

What is IIIBFT?

Many organizations have come up with solutions. These solutions generally revolve around liberalizing trade of agricultural goods, raising productivity through increased use of fertilizers, reducing wastages in food production, reducing loss due to pest attacks, changing food habits, raising awareness about nutrient recycling and others. Some of these solutions are expensive and unlikely to be achieved due to acute shortage of resources of production, expensive technologies, and degradation of soil and water resources. Expensive solutions may not be in the best interests of the poor who amount to as much 80 percent of the world population.

No single body, be it government or private, has the power to solve the crisis. Co-creation (as phrased by C.K. Prahalad, 2006), of solutions with the involvement of one and all would be necessary to meet this challenge–governments, businesses, non-governmental organizations, and universities together with the public will all have to be part of the solution.

One such solution to the crisis would be to plant *Billions of Fruit Trees*. Fruit trees could be viewed as land multipliers and food reservoirs. While we are losing land to various forces of globalization and urbanization, fruit trees rising above the ground, produce fruits at various layers of the tree, which can be in other words viewed as having multiplied the area of land. Secondly, they are food reservoirs. They produce every year at the same time, year after year, with little or no human intervention. There is no other man-made item that could be such a reliable source of food.

Fruits can act as supplements for nutrition when cereal production cannot meet the demands of the population, while also being able to contribute to other forms of life such as birds and animals, thus sustaining the eco-systems. Supply of fruits will help as fodder to boost milk production, while also supporting other industries which have a direct impact on health and personal care.

Thus, one could look at an initiative that proposes to plant a *Billion Fruit Trees* in order to mitigate or moderate the impact of the coming food crisis. The initiative includes raising saplings of various fruits native to India and which can be transplanted easily. The author is actively involved in maintaining a nursery where saplings are raised and nurtured. These are later shared and distributed to be planted in different areas—gardens, parks, school and college grounds, temples and other public spaces.

What does IIIBFT Propose to Do?

IIIBFT proposes to plant billions of Fruit Bearing Trees which will contribute to humanity and all other forms of life by providing food supplements. The idea has a simple logic behind it. Let us assume that due to food shortage only 300 grams of rice/wheat is available instead of the 400 grams needed by a small family for a meal. The shortage of 100 grams could be compensated if the family had a fruit bearing tree such as a mango or jack fruit in its backyard. Fruits are rich source of vitamins and also have a positive impact on health. With this idea at the centre, we have grown thousands of saplings of Fruit Bearing Trees and are planting them in rural as well as urban areas. We believe that in the next ten to twenty years, this IIIBFT Project will contribute immensely to the benefit of the society.

Objectives of IIIBFT

1. To plant billions of fruit bearing trees around the world.
2. To promote alternative sources of food.
3. To promote food security.
4. To minimize the effect of global warming and climate change.
5. To promote co-existence among all forms of life.
6. To conserve and raise water table and minimize soil erosion.

Guiding Principles

1. Hunger should be removed from the face of the Earth.
2. To employ the principles of management to mass produce to serve the people at the base of the economic pyramid (the poor).
3. To involve local communities at all levels.
4. To work with governments at all levels to promote IIIBFT.
5. To take minimum from the Earth and return maximum to enrich it.
6. To employ green and sustainable methods.

Strategies Adopted by IIIBFT

Central to the success of the project is community participation. To create awareness we propose to conduct various forms of information campaigning and train communities in the art of tree cultivation and management. The following are the strategies we propose to employ in the execution of IIIBFT:

1. To employ management techniques for mass fruit tree plantation by efficiently and judiciously utilizing the resources from the earth while enriching the Earth.
2. To engage in advocacy and lobbying with the government to bring new laws to prevent deforestation, implement them effectively and to involve every Panchayat and Grama Sabha to plan fruit trees at the village level.
3. To collaborate with government departments, local and international agencies and the governments that work in line with similar objects.
4. To promote, organize and to hold seminars at national and international levels on issues related to tree plantations and forestry development.
5. To make tree plantation a mass movement involving each and every citizen.
6. To protect and promote bio-diversity in all the regions.
7. To educate people about the importance of trees and forestry.

8. To promote natural methods of fruit bearing trees cultivation.
9. To take necessary steps to prevent deforestation.
10. To train people to cultivate and maintain trees.
11. To develop private forests.
12. To turn waste land into forests.
13. To promote green, bio-degradable and environment friendly materials for daily use.

Stages of IIIBFT Implementation

There are four different stages in the execution of IIIBFT.

1. Stage one is the initial stage wherein the newly grown saplings are protected and maintained.
2. Seeds production, maintenance and distribution.
3. Involving schools and colleges for mass production.
4. Involving communities for seed production.
5. Development of distributed sapling production centres in urban or semi-urban areas.
6. Stage two involves identification of lands for plantation and transportation of the saplings.
7. Developing low cost fencing.
8. Identifying lands for cultivation.
9. Developing sustainable methods of distribution.
10. Stage three mainly involves maintenance and monitoring of trees.
11. Developing systems for watering and maintaining plants.
12. Developing monitoring mechanisms.
13. Involving local communities for monitoring and maintenance.
14. Stage four is about sustainable utilization of the fruits borne.
15. Sustainable utilization of products from fruit trees.
16. Maintenance and monitoring.

Benefits of IIIBFT

The main objective of this project is to promote food

security. Apart from providing food security, IIIBFT will provide all the benefits such as shade, controlling soil erosion, minimizing global warming, soil enriching, promoting co-existence, reducing carbon levels in the environment, etc.

Many industries will also benefit from this project. Some of the industries that would benefit:

1. Dairy industry.
2. Food and food processing.
3. Animal fodder industry.
4. Cosmetics.
5. Organic chemicals and fertilizers.
6. Meat and leather industry.
7. Healthcare.
8. Plastic wastage reduction and recycling.

Conclusion

Food security is fundamental to Human Security. Secure nations build more positive relations with their neighbours and others. Such nations also build the conditions for prosperity and growth in the long run. They have stable societies free from want and fear. The role played by Indo-International Initiative for Billions of Fruit Trees in promoting human security is through providing alternative and supplementary sources of food and its impact can be assessed objectively as the idea begins to produce results.

References

Cribb, J., (2010), "The Coming Famine: The Global Food Crisis and What we do to Avoid It" University of California Press.

Ministry of Foreign Affairs of Japan (2008), *G-8 Leaders Statement on Global Food Security,* [online] G8 Hokkaido Toyako Summit, available at, http://www.mofa.go.jp/policy/economy/summit/2008/doc/doc080709_04_en.html[Accessed on 30-Jan-2012].

National Knowledge Commission (2006), *National Knowledge Commission Note on Higher Education.*

Prahalad, C.K. (2006), *The Fortune at the Bottom of the Pyramid,* Pearson: Wharton School Publishing.

Soysa, I. and Nils Petter Gleditsch (1999), *To Cultivate Peace: Agriculture in a World of Conflict,* PRIO, Oslo, available at, http://www.prio.no/

United Nations (2005), *World Population to Reach 9.1 Billion in 2050, UN projects*, [online] United Nations News Centre. available at, http://www.un.org/apps/news/story.asp?NewsID=13451&Cr=population&Cr1; accessed on 30th January, 2012.

20

Human Security and Gandhian Ethics in a Globalised World

Mohanan B. Pillai and Dharitri Parija

Introduction

The concept 'security' has undergone fundamental changes from that of a narrow military-strategic one to a broad and multi-dimensional understanding of human security. The term human security encompasses areas that are determined by people's need starting right from political, economic, social, technological and environmental factors to basic individual freedom. Though economic development is always a vital and immediate concern for individual development, the negative impact of globalization has caught our attention to re-think the mainstream development paradigm. Much of this have been brought about by an unsustainable economic system, driven by the corporate world—imperialism in a new form supported by Government policies based on consumerism, militarism and an unregulated economy. Treating nature as a resource to be plundered, food as a commodity and agriculture as an industry is degrading the Earth, causing water shortage and desertification, polluting water and the air we breathe and poisoning the food we eat. In this scenario, the end user of this development paradigm, the common man, is not even assured of his basic needs. Keeping this dilemma in mind, the present paper tries to deal with the relevance of Gandhian ethics in economic development in the present crises prone world.

Much has been debated about the far reaching consequences of neo-liberal globalisation which has touched the life of every one directly and indirectly ever since the last quarter of the 20th century. In fact, the neo-liberal policies have intensified both interdependence and competition among the economies of the world and it has in turn made the life of common man vulnerable and insecure. Rising inequality, exploitation, poverty and environmental degradation are the net outcome of neo-liberal reforms in every country of the Third World. (Zifcak, 2005) India is also very much within the clutches of this growth paradigm where more than half of its population still live in the villages. The government in its efforts to turn India into a leading global exporter and technology hub is not paying proper attention to the basic issues of poverty and mal-development.

The idea of holistic development, which is still a distant dream, was an integral element of the philosophy of Indian freedom movement and it got well enshrined in the Constitution of India. However, Gandhi and his ideology are treated as redundant by the new generation politicians and policy makers who are the apostles of neo-liberal globalisation. In this context, the present paper attempts to reinvent the Gandhian legacy with a view to reconstruct the concept of human security. Accordingly, this paper has been divided into three sections. The first section briefly highlights the consequences of liberalisation in the life of the common man. The second section conceptualises human security against the backdrop of the new growth paradigm of liberalisation, privatisation and globalisation. The third section analyses the Gandhian legacy and in the light that the concept of human security is redefined.

Effects of Globalisation: An overview

The 21st century, according to several studies, belongs to China and India in particular and Asia in general. The end of the Cold War and the growing impact of globalisation through economic liberalisation influenced India to redefine its position and role both at the regional and global level. The liberalisation of the economy since the early 1990s led to growth rates of 6-7 percent p.a., and India's global presence has been steadily visible since then. (Bava, 2007)

But this is an ongoing process, not a signpost, and so it is important to examine how industrialization and liberalisation which have created a new world order are most hotly-debated topics. This has come to dominate the world since the nineties of the last century with the end of the Cold War and the break-up of the former Soviet Union. With increased reliance on the market economy and renewed faith in the private capital and resources, a process of structural adjustment spurred many of the developing countries as guided by the World Bank and other multilateral organisations. In the words of Samir Amin, the post-war period inaugurated a new phase of world system followed by massive economic, political and social transformations in all parts of the world which were the products of social regulations imposed on capital by the popular classes. However, they were the products of a false liberal ideology of market expansion which has defined a new framework for the challenges that confront the people of the world now in the twenty-first century. (Amin, 2000)

Many scholars noted that liberalisation did not benefit the masses in any significant manner. This new state apparatus helped to create a market for Western consumer goods. The manipulation of Third World economies by large scale multinational companies with the encouragement of local elites was part of a wider malaise which some identified as the domination of the periphery of the global economy by those who lived in the core areas of Europe and America. Neo-liberalism can best be described as a discourse and practice which aimed to curtail the powers of labour and to construct a society of capitalists and entrepreneurs. (Read, 2009)

David Harvey has interpreted neo-liberalization as a utopian project which is intended to create a theoretical design for the reorganization of international capitalism or as a political project to re-establish the conditions for capital accumulation with a view to reposition the economic elites.

Though it has not been much effective in revitalizing global capital accumulation it has succeeded well in restoring and in certain instances creating the power of the economic elite. The volatility of uneven geographical development has enabled certain territories to advance at the expense of others. (Harvey, 2005:19) The current economic downturn has witnessed the fact that neo-liberal policies and globalization put the burden of the economic and fiscal crises unto the common mass where as the benefits go primarily to the transnational corporations and to the political class.

Moreover, economic policies give priority to save big businesses and banks and neglect the needs of the vast majority which in turn is definitely re-intensifying the class divided contemporary society and widening gap in income distribution. And the capitalist societies have become polarized between a small group of powerful owners where as repressed masses are suffering due to ever increasing economic inequalities. These capitalist economies are undoubtedly exploiting both human beings and nature with new types of policies and deepening social and environmental crises the world over. (Itoh, 2001:121)

Undoubtedly, globalisation has brought new opportunities for developing countries through greater access to the developed country's markets and new technology. This in turn has improved productivity and ensured higher living standards at least for a section of the people. In almost every area of human activity, the international interconnectedness of peoples, institutions, states and systems, has increased exponentially. This applies to whether or not the activities are political, economic, social, cultural, technological or environmental. But globalisation has also thrown up new challenges like growing inequality across and within nations, and volatility in financial markets and environmental deteriorations.

Another most important aspect of globalisation is that a majority of developing countries remained isolated from this so called development process. An eminent scholar Guy Brainbant says that "the process of globalisation not only includes opening up of world trade, development of advanced means of communication, internationalisation of financial markets, growing importance of MNCs, population migrations and more generally increased mobility of persons, goods, capital, data and ideas but also infections, diseases and pollution". (as quoted in Goyal, 2006:166) The huge cross-border flow of people, massive movement of capital, the spread of diseases, environmental degradation, the widening poverty gap between North and South, the proliferation of terrorist networks, and the abuse of human rights are some notable examples.

While economic inequality, rural poverty, and hunger seem to have been exacerbated for many by economic liberalization, the end user of this developmental process, the common man has been particularly affected. Economic liberalization has not improved the lives of the millions of rural poor. In fact, these neo-liberal policies have created a kind of apartheid in the economy where the wealthy seems to have separated their lucrative sectors from the rest of the economy. The government also seems to care less about rural redistribution and still the poor are available as cheap labour in both rural and urban India.

As the Indian government has reduced state support for agriculture, rural development programmes and food subsidies, the rural poor has lost some of the most essential means of survival. Farmers can no longer access to affordable credit and find themselves competing in the international markets against heavily subsidized competitors. The truth of the matter is that economic liberalization has favoured a small class of commercial farmers, multinational corporations and urban service sectors. Neo-liberal policies have driven the poor to a vulnerable state in rural as well as urban areas and this in turn aggravated social division (*Ibid*).

Higher levels of poverty, higher levels of illiteracy, lower levels of nutrition and health care, unemployment, cross border migration, terrorism have made the lives of the people more miserable. Despite economic progress, a large part of the population in the country continue to face serious problems concerning social and economic security, health care, education as well as food and housing all of which remain in an unsatisfactory condition. One does not feel safe at home, in the office, at a public place or while travelling or even while surfing the net. Each of these threats can cause large scale deaths, socio-economic disruption, prolonged human misery and massive demoralization. In a clearer sense, we can say that globalisation has placed the very simple but difficult question of 'human security' in the epicentre of the entire gamut of discussions on growth and development.

Human Security

Before coming to the term human security we have to revisit the concept of security per se. In fact, the term security carries with it different meanings and values for scholars, policy makers and analysts. We need to understand and broaden the concept of security keeping in mind our own social structure. Traditionally, the concept of security has been associated more with the state than with the people. With the emergence of the modern state system in the 17th century, international security has been understood and practised with reference to the needs and interests of the states. For a long period of time, security has been equated with threats to a country's borders and nations have sought arms to protect their security.

The changes that came into effect from the days of Cold War to the notion of security, which was based on the East-West stability and its maintenance through nuclear deterrence and nuclear power, could not address properly the security requirements and interests of the third world countries. It was based on the military dominated understanding of national security. Most of the Third world countries gave importance to their domestic security through state-building and establishing a secure system for dealing with food, health, trade and commerce as much as it was about building up the military.

In the post-Cold War era, the traditional conceptualisation has been revisited by security scholars and more attention was paid to the threats emanating from non-state actors i.e. the individual, social groups, global civil society. The post-Cold War era, accompanied by a series of developments and followed by a series of growing disparities in economic opportunities both within and between states, witnessed increasing marginalisation of the people of developing countries by a globalising world economy, diminishing recourses and violence leading people to become refugees, growing inter-state conflicts and pressure for humanitarian intervention. These developments have led to an exploration of individual and societal dimensions of security. As a result, the term human security has got a place in the broader conception of security.

During the last decade, human security has become a central concern to many countries, institutions and social actors searching for innovative ways and means of tackling the many non-military threats to human life, peace and security. Of late, the term human security has got wide currency. Even though the term itself was in circulation earlier, the particular phrase, "human security", was coined and popularised by Mahbub-ul-Haq, who was associated with the 1994 *Human Development Report* on human security. The basic intent of human security was to provide the people the freedom from want and freedom from fear.

The Report identified five steps: a human development conception with emphasis on equity, sustainability and grassroots participation; a peace dividend to underwrite the broader agenda of human security; a new partnership between North and South based on justice and equitable access to global market opportunities and economic restructuring; a new framework of global governance built on reform of international institutions such as the IMF, World Bank, and the United Nations; and finally, a growing role for global civil society.

Again, the UNDP Report listed seven components or specific values of human security. These are: economic security, food security, health security, environmental security, personal security, community security, and political security. (Upadhyaya, 2004:76) As long back as June 1945, the then U.S. Secretary of State reported this to his government based on the results of the San Francisco Conference, "The battle of peace has to be fought on two fronts. The first is the security front where victory spells freedom from fear. The second is the economic and social front where victory means freedom from want. Only victory on both fronts can assure the world of an enduring peace. No Provisions that can be written into the Charter will enable the Security Council to make the world secure from war if men and women have no security in their homes and their jobs". (as quoted in Sabina Alkire, 2003:13) It recognizes that people and communities are fatally threatened by events well beyond their control: a financial crisis, a violent conflict, AIDS, a national policy that undercuts public and private investments in health care, a terrorist attack, water shortages, chronic destitution, or pollution in their country.

Various attempts have been made to conceptualize the term human security. There are two main contemporary theories of international relations which have contributed in broadening its scope. The first one is the neo-realist theory which is called 'new security thinking' approach and which emphasises the primacy of the state within a broadened conceptualization of human security. Secondly, the Postmodernist or 'critical human security' approach rooted in the pluralist theory of international politics talks about the interdependence and trans-nationalisation of non-state actors without giving priority to state.

The neo-realist theory advocated by Barry Buzan (1992)

broadened the scope of human security by including political, economic, social and environmental threats, in addition to militaristic threats. Buzan examines security from three angles .i.e. the international system, the state, and the individual, and concludes that the most important and effective provider of security is the sovereign state. In the 'critical' or postmodernist approach to human security, Ken Booth (1994) advocates a broadened conceptualization of security which goes beyond a military determination of threats. The advocates of the postmodernist approach stress and encompass a wide range of non-state actors, such as individuals, ethnic and cultural groups, regional economic blocs, multinational corporations (MNCs), non-governmental organizations (NGOs) and just about all humankind. In expanding the concept of security, Booth argues that human security is always more important than state security. (Naidoo, 2001:2)

Today, in this globalized world, the most pernicious threats to human security emanate from the conditions that give rise to genocide, civil war, human rights violations, global epidemics, environmental degradation, forced and slave labour, and malnutrition. All the current studies on security thus have to integrate the human dimension of security. (Tabyshalieva, 2006) This has been explained in the UNDP Report (1994), "For too long, security has been equated with threats to a country's borders. For too long, nations have sought arms to protect their security.

For most people today, a feeling of insecurity arises more from worries about daily life than from the dread of a cataclysmic world event. Job security, income security, health security, environmental security, security from crime, these are the emerging concerns of human security all over the world". (UNDP, 1994:3) To make it more clear, the former UN Secretary General Kofi Annan, in his 2000 Report to the United Nations, gave a broad description of human security. He said, "Human security in its broadest sense embraces far more than the absence of violent conflict. It encompasses human rights, good governance, access to education and health care and ensuring that each individual has opportunities and choices to fulfil his or her own potential. Every step in this direction is also a step towards reducing poverty, achieving economic growth and preventing conflict. Freedom from want, freedom from fear and the freedom of future generations to inherit a healthy natural environment—these are the interrelated building blocks of human security—and therefore national security". (As quoted by Alkire, 2003:14)

In this highly complicated world order which generates human insecurity, Gandhian thought system which focuses on the development of the human being as the basic unit of the developmental paradigm, is highly relevant. His ethics deal with a sustainable way of life, an economic system based on trusteeship for universal welfare and a society in which everyone gains, rather than a few becomes rich at the expense of the many. At a conference in Delhi, which was held to mark the centenary of the start of Gandhi's non-violent movement, in a video message, Nelson Mandela said "in a world full of violence and strife, Mahatma Gandhi's message of peace and non-violence holds the key to human survival in the 21st Century". (Nixon, 2007:5) Despite the great advancement of science and technology, Gandhian ideals still fit very well into economic, social and political fields. Gandhi realised that the soul of the Indian economy rests on its rural heartlands.

In this materialistic world, where economics has become all important, the present generation has begun to consider Gandhi and his principles as totally irrelevant in the present context. Here, we will analyse how Gandhi is more relevant today and his ideas are required to be urgently practiced more than ever before.

Human Security and Gandhian Ethics: A Synthesis

Gunnar Myrdal remarks that "my Indian friends will not be offended when I say, that if Indian planning has not been more successful than it has actually been, the main explanation is that they have not kept so close as they should to the fundamentals of the teaching of the Father of the Nation". (Myrdal, 1974)

Gandhian ethics basically deals with the maximization of social welfare and for this he gives prime importance to the welfare of the individuals by reducing inequality in income and wealth. In the views of Gandhiji, every person should be provided with bare minimum necessities i.e. food, shelter, and clothing. Concentration of wealth among a few certainly will shatter the dream of a society which will be socialist in nature. However, for attaining smooth development of the economy, it is imperative to develop all the regions of the country simultaneously. Bhuimali describes that overall progress of the entire economy depends on the balanced development of all the regions. But in India, there exists a huge regional disparity due to neo-liberal globalisation and industrialisation. While some states in India are advanced economically, others are backward. Even within a state some districts are more backward than the rest. As a result, this problem gives rise to the problem of socio-economic inequalities and further leads to depression, conflict and violence and the ultimately human insecurity.

In this context, Gandhian economics is relevant which supports the attainment of self-sufficiency level of industrialisation or uniform economic development for each region. Gandhi's views on economics reflect the common man's perception about his well-being. In his views, every man should increase his personal income and standard of living by utilising the existing natural and human resources fully in an eco-friendly manner. (Bhuimali, 2004)

The increasing craze for material progress in developing countries is based on the Growth Oriented Development Model. Today, economic growth has become the standard measure of power, strength and virtue at all levels i.e., individual, national and global. The IMF, World Bank, WTO and other multilateral institutions are trying to impress upon nations to accelerate their growth rate in order to integrate themselves into the process of globalization, despite the fact that it has brought about ecological imbalances, environmental problems and increasing disparity of economic well-being among nations. In this scenario, Gandhi's ideas appear to be rejecting the capital intensive growth model which is based on greed and selfishness. When we are experiencing war between man and nature through global warming, melting of glaciers, rising of sea levels etc., Gandhian ideas are required to be seriously studied and implemented by every state and individual human being. Industrialisation and urbanisation are no doubt placing India in a club of global power. But this is at the cost of the human life as is evident from increasing farmer suicides and the selling of children in order to get basic common necessities.

In the *Hind Swaraj*, Gandhi critiqued the modern western development paradigm and its resultant civilization. Gandhi said that this civilization is enslaving men by offering temptation of money and luxuries as its fruit. Alternatively, Gandhi propounded the model of Sarvodaya—the good for all. He said that economics has to be infused with spiritual values. It should create social prosperity in terms of cordial relationship, among different layers of society rather than accumulation of wealth in certain pockets only. (Lele, 2006) Today, it is a growing realization that even the so-called affluent societies created by the growth based economic model are experiencing isolation, emptiness and are losing their own perspectives. At the personal level, it is causing acute stress, depression and insecurity. Gandhi says that an economy based purely on material considerations and totally devoid of any value base would not bring happiness to mankind. Only that economic system which is regulated by ideals, rooted in permanent order of things would achieve the vision of a sustainable world.

Gandhi favoured the self-sufficient village economy where the villages would be independent economic units. Gandhian approach has always emphasised upon need based self-sufficient village communities and wanted to maintain a balance between man and nature. So, he proposed the application of appropriate technology in agriculture and small scale industries which would not deplete the soil and pollute the environment. Farmers should use eco-friendly production techniques by using lesser and lesser amount of fertilizers, insecticides and pesticides. However, in Gandhi's view, the agricultural sector alone cannot solve the problem of rural poverty and unemployment. That's why he specified on the growth of the rural industries like khadi, handlooms, sericulture and handicrafts.

He is often criticised for his stand on industrialisation. But what he taught was that machinery, being capital-intensive, displaces labour and naturally augments unemployment and under-employment. Replying to a question whether he was against all machinery, Gandhiji said, "How can I be when I know that even this body is a most delicate piece of machinery? The spinning wheel is a machine; a little toothpick is a machine. What I object to is the craze for machinery, not machinery as such. The craze is for what they call labour saving machinery. Men go on 'saving labour' till thousands are without work and thrown on the open streets to die of starvation. I want to save time and labour not for a fraction of mankind but *for all.* I want the concentration of wealth, not in the hands of a few, but in the hands of all. Today, machinery helps a few to ride on the backs of millions. The impetus behind it all is not the philanthropy to save labour, but greed. It is against this constitution of things that I am fighting with all my might...The supreme consideration is man. For instance, I would make intelligent exceptions. Take the case of the Singer sewing machine. It is one of the few useful things ever invented, and there is a romance about the device itself." (Gandhi, 1938:7-8)

In fact capital intensive production benefits a few at the cost of many unfortunate rural people leaving them unemployed and exploited. Therefore, it is a situation of two-person zero sum game. But what is disappointing is that it reduces the welfare of a large section of the rural population. Concentration of industries in a few cities has led to a number of problems. Large scale industries generally grow in the big cities which creates major problem of overpopulation in industrialized areas. With this there arises the problem of pollution of air and water of which the ultimate consumer of insecurity is the common man. In addition, large-scale industries promote monopolistic trends and unequal distribution of income.

Gandhi's idea of rural industries, on the other hand, helps decentralization of economic activities and a large proportion of income generated in these industries get distributed among the workers and among a very large number of people. However, his economic ideas are not completely based on cottage industries and handicraft. He visualises that industrialization leads to maximum exploitation of man and nature. Though it is based on large scale and highly sophisticated technology it leads to unemployment, poverty, urbanization, deforestation, desertification, pollution etc. So large scale industries should be owned by the state and administrated wholly for common good and development of the state as a whole. The effects which we are experiencing out of large scale industrialisation remind us how Mahatma had visualised it quite a long time before. According to him, an increase in personal income is an indication of the growth of national income. But the growth of national income is not always benefiting every man in the society.

In a nutshell, Gandhi is above all a champion of human dignity. All his ideas revolve around the betterment of the common man. It does not mean we should stick to traditional behaviour but it means that we should reject the ways of life and practices which is not in the true interest of mankind. The nature of global security has changed. However, climate change, financial instability, trade, food, energy security etc., require different thinking and different responses. There is a need to enquire into the fundamental causes of today's problems. Traditional way of thinking has no answers to these problems.

There is no military solution to any of these problems. It should be recognized that behind each of the present day problems lies the question of ethics and values. These have to be addressed. We should analyse the root causes behind the present day insecurities. Exploitation of resources without thinking of nature, maintenance of luxurious life style, differentiated activities pave the way for climate change and global warming. Likewise deprivations, clash of ethnicities', identity, moral superiority, intolerance, injustice, inequality etc., are leading to terrorism and secessionist activities. Socio-economic inequalities, greed, selfishness, financial instability, competition for resources etc. are causing poverty, organised crime and the end result is human vulnerability.

Mahatma Gandhi thus offers us an integrated approach and solution to the calls and cries of the present times. Gandhi says that science and technology should be so regulated to work for public good and not as tools to exploit hapless masses. In Gandhi's words, "True economics never militates against the highest ethical standards, just as all true ethics to be worth its name, must also be good economics". (as quoted by Lele, 2006) However, in this scenario, what is needed is to work upon our own social structure which is quite different from that of the West.

As rightly pointed out by Schumacher, "Development does not start with goods, it starts with people..." (as quoted by Choudhury, 1998) Amartya Sen also argues that, there is evidence that even with relatively low income, a population that guarantees health care and education to all can actually achieve remarkable results in terms of longevity and quality of life for the entire population. He called it as human capital which can contribute more in this developmental pattern. Human development has extraordinary social and demographic reach. The creation of social opportunities, expansion of education, health care etc. contribute to the expansion of human capabilities and the quality of life of the masses which in turn also greatly facilitates economic and industrial expansion and improves efficiency and wide reach of market economy. (Sen, 1999)

Gandhiji's message to the world was to build a federation of free nations in a world without war and hatred. He called upon nations to abjure violence against one another and to fight the dreaded enemies of poverty, ignorance, disease, human suffering and social injustice. He advised nations to employ scientific and technological knowledge to further the ideals of a peaceful world order respecting and promoting human rights and human welfare. (George, 2010) However, David Harvey has rightly pointed out the need to initiate a political process that can lead the world to a point where feasible alternatives, real possibilities become identifiable. In this critical situation he further discuses three alternative visions for getting out of the market ethics imposed by the neo-liberalisation.

Firstly, the primitivists who believe that the only hope for humanity is to return to that stage of hunter-gathering that preceded the rise of civilization and, in effect, start human history all over again.

Secondly, those who are influenced by movements like Crime Think and authors such as Derrick Jensen, who seek to purge themselves of all traces of incorporation into the capitalist market logic.

Thirdly, those who seek a world of mutual support through the formation of local economic trading systems (LETS) with their own 'local moneys' even in the very heart of a neo-liberal capitalism. (Harvey, 2005:186)

The third one seems to be practical, relevant and the most viable alternative in the present world of poverty, hunger, disease and despair. This is very much a recreation of Gandhian ideas. Though Gandhian ethics are the products of a particular historical setting, they find themselves to be the best possible solution in the present world order. We have been able to create prosperous countries, but we have failed to create better human beings, a better future and a better world. Therefore, again we have to keep faith in our villages and rural masses. By creating local industries and local market, the poor will get the actual value for his labour. In this way, Gandhian thought system can be of eminent relevance for the attainment of a better world. His ideas are by no means outmoded; on the contrary it can be well applied in today's context.

Concluding Remarks

To sum up, the eye catching economic growth followed by globalization in the world reflects only one side of the whole picture. The period of globalization that allows the capital to move around freely within and outside a country has widened income disparity and poverty among the populations. Not only have the products of the growth not been shared equally but most of them have been left behind without the opportunities to catch up with the main stream. In this manner a single problem is leading to a series of sufferings for the common man, making life more vulnerable. Excessive reliance on market economy for satisfying the greed of a few has become the root of all economic and social problems. For a large section of people who have been left outside the market system without the support and protection of social structures, poses the urgent need of theoretical and practical inquiries into our existing condition and seek to derive possible alternatives. In this context Gandhian economic ideas appears to be the most pragmatic one to address the question of human security.

References

Alkire, Sabina (2003), "A Conceptual Framework for Human Security", *CRISE Working Paper 2*, University of Oxford.

Amin, Samir (2000), "The Political Economy of the Twentieth Century", *Monthly Review*, Vol. 52, Issue 2, June.

Bava, Ummu Salma (2007), "New Powers for Global Change?

India's Role in the Emerging World Order", *FES Briefing Paper 4,* New Delhi.

Bhuimali, Anil (2004), "Relevance of M.K. Gandhi's Ideal of Self-Sufficient Village Economy in the 21st Century", Sarvodaya, Vol. 1, No. 5, January-February.

Chaudhuri, Ranjit (1998), "Towards Understanding Gandhian Economics", *Essays on Gandhian Thought,* Institute of Gandhian Studies, Wardha.

Coutinho, Sharon (2007), "Gandhiji's views on Economics", the paper presented at a Nasik Camp, October 2007, available at, www.mkgandhi.org/articles/gview_eco.htm.(accessed on 23-12-10).

Gandhi, M.K. (1938), "Hind Swaraj or Indian Home Rule", Navajivan Publishing House.

George, Joseph (2010), "Tribute to the Illustrious Son of the Soil", *The Hindu,* Sunday, October 3, 2010.

Gupta, Arvind (2008), "Global Security and the Role of Ethics and Values", available at,
www.worldacademy.org (accessed on 23-12-10).

Harvey, David (2005), *A Brief History of Neo-liberalism*, Oxford University Press.

Itoh, Makoto (2001), "Spiral Reversal of Capitalist Development: What does it Imply for the Twenty-First Century?" in Robert Albritton, Makoto Itoh, Richard Westra and Alan Zuege (ed.) *Phases of Capitalist Development: Booms, Crises and Globalisations,* Palgrave Publications, pp. 110-124.

Lele, M.P. (2007), "Gandhian Perspective on Convergence of Values: Spiritual, Political and Economic", Anasakti Darshan Vol. 2, No. 2, July-December.

Malik, Tanveer, "Impact of Globalization on Indian Economy-An Overview", available at,
http://www.fibre2fashion.com/services/article-writing-service/content-promotionservices.asp, (accessed on 27-09-2010).

Mathue, J.S. (ed.) (2006), "Gandhi: In the Mirror of Foreign Scholars", Gyan Publishing House, New Delhi.

Naidoo, Sagaren (2001), "A Theoretical Conceptualization of Human Security", Institute for Global Dialogue, Johannesburg.

Nixon, Bruce (2007), "All Rise-How Gandhi's Thinking Can Help us in the 21st Century", Schumacher Institute for Sustainable

Systems, Challenge Paper No 3, April.

Read, Jason (2009), "A Genelogy of Homo-Economicus: Neo-liberalism and the Production of subjectivity", Foucault studies, February, No. 6, pp. 25-36.

Ronaldo Porto Macedo Júnior: "Globalisation, regulation and consumer law"

Sen, Amartya K. (1999), "Beyond the Crisis: Development Strategies in Asia", in Pamela J. Noda (ed.), *Sustainable Development and Human Security: Second Intellectual Dialogue on Building Asia's Tomorrow*; Tokyo: Japan Centre for International Exchange, pp. 15-37.

Sungkawan, Decha: "Southeast Asian Human Security: A Regional Citizenship Approach", *Thammasat Review.*

Tabyshalieva, Anara (2006), "Promoting Human Security: Ethical, Normative and Educational Frameworks in Central Asia" UNESCO, available at,
http://www.unesco.org/securipax (accessed on 06-09-2010).

Zifcak, Spencer (2005), (ed.), "Globalisation and the Rule of Law", Routledge, New York.

PART VI
Environmental Security

21

Environmental Challenges for Policy Formation and National Security

Venkateshwaran Lokanathan

In a globally competitive neo-realist world, modern states, in their interactions with one another, have always sought to maximize their interest by increasing their power and influence. Interestingly, the emergence of technology has led to an inter-connected world in the twenty first century which has in turn led to the globalising of local issues. Globalisation has also simultaneously widened the traditional boundaries of competition, challenged competency and increased the urge for technological innovations. The pace at which the International environment has evolved over the last century has created considerable concern over its sustenance in the long-term.

An offshoot of this development is the wider ramifications posed by problems such as climate change which transcend the traditional boundaries of States. The emerging patterns of climate change and its impact on the environment will have serious consequences for the international community in the future. There is growing concerns over its impact on the global landscape which in turn will pose new challenges to state sovereignty. This paper will explore various ways by which climate change will affect geopolitics and its corresponding influence on foreign relations, national security and economic policies. There are some critical questions that need to be analysed at length.

This research paper will assess the impact of climate change on traditional borders of nation states. Whether the impact of climate change will lead to a potential loss of complete sovereignty for a nation state in the future will form a major part of the analysis. A modest attempt will be made to understand the larger implications for the connectivity and infrastructure of nation states. Understanding the complexities of the geo-political/geo-strategic implications of climate change will provide key critical insights for nation states to evolve cooperation among themselves in an effort to address this issue effectively.

Interestingly, the twenty first century has witnessed the emergence of an interconnected world, fuelled by the advent of the World Wide Web and advances in technology. Simultaneously, the advent of globalisation, characterised by cross border interactions, have blurred the traditional boundaries of competition, challenged competency and increased the urge for technological innovations. [1] (Friedman, 2005) Crucially, this inter-connectedness has pushed local agendas and issues to the global arena. An offshoot of this development is the wider ramifications posed by challenges like climate change which transcend the traditional boundaries of States.

Challenges like climate change are no more purely local or regional issues. They transcend the traditional boundaries of states and have become a larger part of international relations thereby requiring global solutions. This will require states to adopt a neo-liberal perspective based on cooperation and coordination of consensual policies. However, there are significant roadblocks to finding effective answers, partly as the result of a long-standing trust deficit between states. [2] (Vajpeyi, 2012) In a globally competitive world, from the Waltzian neo-realist perspective, modern states, in their interactions with one another, have always sought to maximize their interest by increasing their power and influence over one another.

Complexities over Terminology

The definition provided by the Inter-Governmental Panel on Climate Change (IPCC) and the United Nations Framework

Convention on Climate Change (UNFCCC) is a significant indicator to the terminology currently in use, which is often confused or inaccurate. The UNFCC defines climate change as–"a change of climate which is attributed directly or indirectly to human activity that alters the composition of the global atmosphere and which is in addition to natural climate variability observed over comparable time periods". [3] (UNFCCC, 1992) The IPCC definition, "refers to a statistically significant variation in either the mean state of the climate or in its variability, persisting for an extended period (typically decades or longer). Climate change may be due to natural internal processes or external forcings, or to persistent anthropogenic changes in the composition of the atmosphere or in land use." [4] (IPCC, 2007)

The UNFCCC specifically focuses on human induced climate change while the IPCC provides a wider connotation by drawing the distinction between changes in climatic patterns due to human interference and natural causes. There is, hence, an urgent need for clarification as to whether efforts are being largely addressed towards understanding natural causes or human induced or both when it comes to changes in patterns of climate. It will go a long way in providing clarity towards understanding the problem and assist in making efforts towards solving it more effective.

What needs to be clearly identified at the outset is that climate change is only one component of the larger problem of direct, man-made environmental change. The emerging patterns of climate change and its impact on the environment will have serious consequences for the international community in the future. Humans are making direct and major alterations to the environment creating considerable concern over its sustenance in the long term. As the carrying capacity of the planet is being pushed rapidly, a smaller degree of environmental variation has larger repercussions.

In the more recent past, massive population increases have had a dramatic effect on global sustainability. At the turn of the 20th century, there were around 1.65 billion people on the planet. The first decade of the 21st, has already seen this jump to 7 billion. The result will be an increased usage of groundwater, cutting of forests for human habitation, increased migration from rural to urban areas thereby creating social and cultural disruptions, land abuse leading to increased soil erosion, environmentally unsecure and faulty development of infrastructure and ultimately a changed environment.

There is an urgent necessity to explore the various ways by which climate change will affect geopolitics and its corresponding influence on foreign relations, national security and economic policies. Crucially, this needs to encompass an assessment of the impact of climate change on traditional borders of nation states. There are critical questions that require attention. One, will the impact of climate change lead to a potential loss of complete sovereignty for a nation state in the future? Second, what are the larger implications for the connectivity and infrastructure of nation states? Understanding the complexities of the geopolitical/geo-strategic implications of climate change will provide crucial impetus for nation states, obsessed with state sovereignty and territorial integrity, to cooperate in an effort to address this issue effectively. [5] (Paskal, 2007)

Warming Planet: The Domino Effect

It was the Club of Rome, an informal organization established in 1968, which for the first time in a book titled "The Limits to Growth" published in 1972, expressed increasing concerns over the sustenance of the planetary resources in the face of growing demands fuelled by a burgeoning population. Subsequently, the Stockholm Conference in 1972 highlighted the importance of sustainable development keeping in mind environmental concerns. Although the Brundtl and report and the IPCC Assessment Reports of 1990 and 1995 highlighted varying concerns over increasing global temperatures, it was the third assessment report of the IPCC in 2001 that significantly highlighted the emergence of global warming due to a combination of natural variability and human interference.

Based on observed, including palaeoclimatic data, it dwelt at length over an increase of approximately 0.6 degrees celsius over the twentieth century in global average surface temperature since 1861. It also inferred that extreme warming has occurred during the periods from 1910-1945 and 1976-2000 and identified the 1990s as the warmest decade of the twentieth century. Significantly, it observed that the three hottest years since 1861 is in the first decade of the twenty first century. [6] (Dash, 2007) The Fourth Assessment Report of IPCC released in 2007 further observed that eleven of the last twelve years (1995-2006) ranked among the twelve warmest years in the instrumental record of global surface temperature (since 1850). [7] (IPCC, 2007)

Decreasing Sea Ice

Sea ice plays a critical role in the natural maintenance of climate. It acts as an effective insulator by decreasing the amount of heat lost from oceans to the atmosphere. It also reflects a lot of solar radiation back into space there by playing a critical role in maintaining the thermal budget of the earth. The bacteria in the sea ice are also critical to the food chain of different marine species. Additionally, sea ice plays a vital role in converting complex organic matter back to C_o2. Crucially, satellite data has indicated a decrease of about ten percent in extent of snow cover since the 1960.

There is similar inference based on ground data which indicates a reduction of about two weeks in the annual duration for lake and river ice cover in the mid and high latitudes of Northern Hemisphere over the twentieth century. This is accompanied by widespread retreat of mountain glaciers in non-polar regions. The sea ice extent has decreased by ten to fifteen percent in the north hemisphere spring and summer since 1990. There are also records of a forty percent decline in artic sea ice thickness during late summer to early autumn in recent decades. [8] (Ibid)

Melting Glaciers

Mountain regions from the Andes to the Himalayas are warming faster than global average under climate change. Ice will turn into water and glaciers in the process will slowly reduce to being lakes. Glaciers ranging from Chile and Argentina to Alaska are showing double the rate of melting since 1975. There have been reports that the average temperature in the Himalayan region has risen by one degree Celsius since the mid-1970s. There are some 20,000 glacial lakes spread across varying altitudes across the Himalayas. There is increasing concern over increasing human activity on glaciers including the Gangotri which might result in major meltdown by 2023.

The environmental degradation of Siachen, a seventy six km long river of ice which feeds river Nubra that in turn flows into Indus, due to its militarization is a growing cause of concern. It is estimated to have receded by nearly 800 meters over the last twenty years. The Space Applications Centre (SAC) of the Indian Space Research Organisation (ISRO) and the Snow and Avalanche Study Establishment (SASE) of the Defence and Research Development Organisation (DRDO) have analysed the effect of melting glaciers in Beas and Baspa basins in Himachal Pradesh on the winter stream run-offs during December using WiFS data of Indian Remote Sensing Satellite.

The research has indicated an overall increase in stream-runoff by seventy five percent since 1966. A steady rise in global temperature has led to a steady rise in stream run-off. Warmer winters are also causing snowmelt and retreat of snow cover especially in the months of December and January at altitude of 5,400 m. The data of available temperature in the two towns of Manali and Shimla in Himachal Pradesh have confirmed the unusual warm winter. It has also indicated a fall in precipitation and considerable decrease in snowfall since the 1990s.

The glacial lakes in Nepal and Bhutan, for example, are filling rapidly with water due to the melting of glaciers and surrounding snow areas. One such example is the Tsho Rolpa Lake in Nepal which has grown from 0.23 sq. km. in the 1950s to 1.8 sq. km. in the first decade of the twenty first century. Once peak levels are reached, it will burst banks suddenly and travel many kilometres downstream thereby causing flooding, acute shortage of drinking water, increase in threat from water borne diseases and silting in the surrounding hydropower plants. Flooding of this Tsho Rolpa Lake, for example, will affect 10,000 people up to 108 kilometres downstream. [9] (Ibid)

The Imja Glacier Lake, another case in point, is situated at an altitude of 5,100 m above sea level. The lake is about 600 meters wide at the centre and up to 96.5 meters deep in some places. It is growing by forty seven meters a year and stretches for 1.5 miles down from the glacier spawning three small ponds. The chunks of ice falling due to the melting of surrounding glaciers can cause the lake to break through its walls of glacial debris known as moraine. This could release a deluge of water, mud and rock for almost 100 kilometres swamping houses and fields leading to the loss of valuable land. The International Centre for Integrated Mountain Development has begun making efforts to decrease water level by thirty meters and also a warning system for surrounding villages. However, mobilizing engineering equipment and expertise to lakes including the high costs involved at such high altitudes makes the task of meeting such challenges extremely daunting. [10] (Goldenberg, 2011)

Rising Sea Level

The rising sea level is another indicator of global warming. Based on tide gauge data—0.1 to 0.2 meters rise in global average sea level estimated during the twentieth century.

Although there have been no specific trends in global rainfall, it is believed to have increased by 0.5 to 1 percent per decade in the twentieth century. There has been also a two to four percent increase in frequency of heavy precipitation events in the mid and high latitudes of northern hemisphere in the last half of the twentieth century. Simultaneously, the El Nino and South Oscillation have been reported to be more frequent, persistent and intense since mid-1970s as compared to the previous century. The break-up of ice shelves by itself is a natural process of renewal.

However the cause for alarm in recent years is the size and rate of production of icebergs. In April 2002, a 500 billion tonne chunk of Larsen B ice shelf that was 200 m thick with a surface area of 3,240 sq. km., broke off in Antarctica in the Weddell Sea due to sharp rise in temperature by 2.5 degree celsius over the last fifty years. Similarly, the National Ice Centre, Maryland had spotted the collapse of the Ross Ice Shelf in Ross Sea in May 2002. Both the collapses were identified to a process of calving in which constant motion of polar ice cap fractures the ice into fragments.

These huge icebergs may float loose into the sea and result in further break-ups in the Antarctica thereby sending huge icebergs into the Southern ocean. Further, it may lead to disintegration of other sections of ice shelves in the fringes of Antarctica's continental ice cover and can lead to melt down of grounded West Antarctic ice sheet in the longer term. It is assumed that these developments could cause the World's oceans to rise up to five meters, affecting marine life and lead to the deep ocean circulating system slowing down the production of smaller amounts of dense oxygen-rich sea water. [11] (IPCC, 2007)

Challenges to National Security and Policy Formulation

There is no doubt that environmental change could cause a redrawing of the physical map of the globe. As has occurred during past climatic shifts, there will be flooding of some areas while others will emerge from the melting of ice which might open up previously non-navigable sea lanes. This can open up potential conflict situations in an era of international law, in which political boundaries are closely and rigidly tied to physical ones especially when it comes to maritime borders which, legally, are often determined by coastlines. If so, a host of global political, economic and security issues would emerge. The ownership of strategic sea lanes might come into dispute. Remote island-based military installations and the right to locate them in those regions could be lost. Nations could find that their offshore resources are now in international waters. Debates between neighbours over tiny rocks anchoring vast maritime claims could intensify. Only around 160 of the potential 365 or so maritime boundaries worldwide have been agreed. [12] (UNFCCC, 1992)

The UN Convention on the Law of the Sea (UNCLOS), which came into force in 1994, attempts to create norms for determining boundaries [13] (UNCLOS, 1982) and the International Tribunal for the Law of the Sea (ITLOS) is designed to be a forum for resolving disputes. [14] (ITLOS). So it is unfortunate that many of the assumptions of geographical and hydrological stability on which UNCLOS is based might be compromised by climate change. UNCLOS freezes coastlines and borders at a specific point in time until challenged or revised. That leaves many grey areas when physical boundaries dramatically shift and change, for example, as a result of flooding. When such challenges are made, it could eventually result in foreign policy and security concerns.

It was only as recent as April 2007, that the United Nations Security Council (UNSC) debated 'climate change' for the first time. [15] (UNSC, 2007). Subsequently legislation was introduced in the United States asking for a National Intelligence Estimate on the security implications of 'global warming'. The Centre for Naval Analysis convened Military Advisory Board in a study entitled National Security and the

Threat of Climate Change noted, 'Projected climate change poses a serious threat to America's national security. Climate change acts as a threat multiplier for instability in some of the most volatile regions of the world...Projected climate change will add to tensions even in stable regions of the world.' [16] (CAN, 2007) Critically, by broadly labelling most environmental change-related security issues as being the result of 'global warming' or 'climate change', the international community is inadvertently limiting the range of possible responses, and potentially adding further confusion to an already complex problem.

Water Stress and Food Insecurity

In many regions, it will become increasingly difficult to guarantee the basic necessities of life, in particular water, food and shelter. This can lead to increased regional conflict, massive migration causing social and cultural disruptions and more opportunities for extremist ideologies and anti-social elements.

The glacier freshwater lakes in the Himalayas provide water directly to Bhutan, Nepal, Afghanistan, Bangladesh, Pakistan, China and India and are the sources for rivers including the Mekong, Ganga and Indus. Now, with all the glaciers showing alarming signs of melting, it puts close to half of the world's population under threat from flooding of their lands in the short run to droughts, water and power shortages in the long run. Sea level rise will accentuate this situation further by inundating the land near the coastlines and will contribute towards increasing salinization of the freshwater. All this, combining with other environmental change factors such as abuse of land and deforestation, could contribute to destabilizing the region by large-scale migration and through aggressive competition between countries for access to water resources.

India and China are two countries that depend heavily on agriculture making a significant contribution to their respective

GDPs. This sector also employs a huge workforce there by contributing to employment and poverty alleviation. Additionally, the agriculture sector also depends on the monsoons to a large extent. The stress over water resources and the rising sea levels when combined with increasingly erratic patterns of rainfall will have a direct impact on food security.

Scarcity of water will significantly affect irrigation, while rising sea levels will inundate fields near the coastlines. Additionally, the threat of flooding from swollen rivers due to the melting of glaciers in the short run and its drying up in the long run is ever present. The lingering social effect of increased poverty in the already suffering countryside, accompanied by increased migration to the urban areas, has been compounded by a failure of effective state response. The issue of farmers committing suicide because of heavy debts is now a constant feature in political debates in India. [17] (Paskal, 2010)

Other regions of the world are also getting affected by similar concerns. In 2006, climate conditions and beetles wrecked crops in Australia, Ukraine, Argentina and North America, driving wheat prices to a ten-year high. In the end, it is all likely to just make it even harder on poor people in rich countries and on poorer countries already suffering agricultural deficits. That could potentially lead to instability within and between nations, and formulation of policies with an objective to create preferential relationships with reliable agricultural producers. In 2005, a drought in Spain and Portugal destroyed nearly half of the cereal crop in Spain and led to a war of words between both countries over access to water resources. [18] (Ibid)

Melting of the Arctic Ice

The changes in temperature are expected to be relatively small over the oceans as compared to land, as the oceans can absorb a lot of heat. The Arctic ice, however, being light-coloured, reflects sunlight. As the ice starts to melt, less of this ultraviolet light will be reflected back into space and more solar radiation will remain trapped at the surface. Additionally, the warming of the surrounding waters can also contribute to faster melting at the ice edge, and this is further accentuated as the ice pack is at a lowered elevation. It has been noted that the sea ice is melting earlier in the spring and freezing later in the autumn, and its thickness is decreasing.

The Hadley Centre for Climate Prediction and Research in the United Kingdom, which is measuring the rate of melting in the Artic, predicts that the ice cap covering will disappear around September 2079. It has already noticed the shrinking of the area covered by the Arctic ice by twenty percent since the 1950 and the average winter thickness reduced by forty percent since 1970. [19] (Global Business Network, 2008)

Ros Hydro Met, Russia's hydro meteorological agency has projected a winter temperature increase of up to four degrees centigrade along Russia's Arctic coast by 2040. Base temperatures near minus forty degrees centigrade, however, mean that the winter ice of the coastal sea and rivers and temperatures will continue to be a challenge. Still, such a change in temperature would be significant, because it would lead to a shorter and less extreme winter in the North, with less time for ice to spread and thicken. Warming in the southern Arctic region of the watershed, estimated at two degrees centigrade, will gradually increase growing periods and lead to the melting of permafrost, slowly moving northward the accessibility of lands. [20] (Global Business Network, 2008)

The absence of ice covers can lead to the expansion of sea which in turn can increase evaporation thereby inducing more rainfall and with decreasing warm currents in the Gulf Stream around the British Isles potentially leading to freezing temperatures will pose a complicated challenge for Europe. Additionally, the warming of the climate will affect polar bears and seals and can increase the growth of plankton thereby enhancing the fish population in the region. [21] (Global

Business Network, 2007)

Interestingly, the melting of the Arctic ice is also opening up access to oceanic resources including the economic potential of offshore oil and gas deposits which were earlier trapped under the sea ice. The US Geological Survey estimates that the Arctic contains up to thirty percent of the world's undiscovered gas and thirteen percent of the world's undiscovered oil resources. It has also projected over sixty percent of the total resources (equivalent to about 412 billion barrels of oil) to be located in Russian territory, with all but a very small percentage on shore or inside the EEZ.

The area of greatest potential is in the Kara Sea basin, with smaller, yet still respectable, prospects in the Laptev and East Siberian seas. Advanced offshore techniques, including remote-exploration technology, directional drilling that allows a single well site to reach through the sea floor to tap deposits many kilometres away, and seabed-based production technologies, among others, are making development in the Arctic seas more attractive. [22] (Jakobson, 2010) Russia has long been a major producer of oil and gas from land-based resources. Now the resources of the Arctic continental shelf are drawing increasing attention. Deposits in the Barents Sea are already being developed, with other known deposits in both the Barents and the Kara seas being eyed for future exploitation. [23] (Antrim, 2010)

One of the many geopolitical results of this melting ice is that shipping routes through the Arctic will become more viable. It will open up the entire Northwest and Northeast Passage thereby shortening distance for ships between Europe and the Far East. Travelling between Asia and Europe through the Northwest Passage, which is mostly in Canada but might also include the waters of the United States, Denmark and other nations, is faster, and cheaper, than the current route through the Panama Canal. Russia is already making increasing use of its territorial Northeast Passage. It is using powerful ice-breakers to cut through thick layers of ice during summer and winter to escort ships.

Interestingly, while Canada claims that much of the Northwest Passage is part of its internal waters, a claim with a sound legal basis according to UNCLOS, the United States claims that the route is actually an international strait, open to free passage for all. Frequent flare ups between Canada and the United States over passage rights in the Bering Strait had resulted in the Arctic Cooperation Agreement in 1988 which stated that the US would ask permission before sending icebreakers through the passage but that, when so asked, Canada would give permission. The agreement however did not last and there have been various protests from Canada from time to time over passage of US and Russian submarines through the region. Although, Canada's claim is legally strong, the changing conditions caused by climate change create uncertainty and give an opening in which international politics can outflank international law. [24] (Backus and Strickland, 2008)

China is displaying a real interest in the Arctic, as attested by its applying for observer status at the Arctic Council in 2008. The Chinese Government has also allocated more resources for research in the arctic. Since China's economy is reliant on foreign trade, there are substantial commercial implications if shipping routes are shortened during the summer months each year. Nearly half of China's gross domestic product (GDP) is thought to be dependent on shipping.

The trip from Shanghai to Hamburg via the North-eastern Sea Route—which runs along the north coast of Russia from the Bering Strait in the east to Novaya Zemlya in the west—is 6400 kilometres shorter than the route via the Strait of Malacca and the Suez Canal. Moreover, due to piracy, the cost of insurance for ships travelling via the Gulf of Aden towards the Suez Canal has increased significantly. Hence, it is striving to position itself so that it will not be excluded from access to the Arctic. [25] (Lasserre, 2010) Up until now, China has adopted a wait-and-see approach to Arctic developments, wary that due to its size and status as a rising global power, any active overtures would cause alarm in other countries.

Chinese officials are therefore very cautious when formulating their views on the Arctic. They stress that China's Arctic research activities remain primarily focused on the climatic and environmental consequences of the ice melting in the Arctic. However, in recent years Chinese officials and researchers have started to also assess the commercial, political and security implications for China of a seasonally ice-free Arctic region. [26] (Sakhuja, 2010)

India also began its Arctic research programme in August 2007. The National Centre for Antarctic and Ocean Research, an autonomous institution under the Ministry of Earth Sciences, based in Goa, has been coordinating India's polar research. [27] (Ranjan, 2006) In July 2008, India established its own research station 'Himadri' at the Arctic at Ny-Alesund in Norway. [28] (Sunderarajan, 2008)

It was not until a comprehensive law of the sea was negotiated and implemented in the 1982 UNCLOS that rules applicable to the Arctic were agreed upon. Other laws and agreements, including the 1990 US-USSR Maritime Boundary Agreement, the 1995 Fish Stocks Agreement, and conventions and guidelines of the International Maritime Organization, have further extended the legal regime of the Arctic. The Arctic Council, established in 1996, provides a forum for collaborative study of issues of sustainable development in the Arctic. The Ilulissat Declaration of 2008 commits the five Arctic coastal states (Russia, the United States, Canada, Norway, and Denmark) to resolve issues through diplomatic channels.

However, it is already evident that the opportunities this new route opens up will increase tension between states. Several sovereignty issues have yet to be resolved: Russia and Norway have complex boundary and resource access issues to resolve, the United States may challenge some of Russia's claims of internal waters along the North-eastern Sea Routes, and the Commission on the Limits of the Continental Shelf has yet to decide whether to recommend recognition of Russia's expansive claim to much of the seabed on the Asian side of the Arctic. They are currently working to resolve their boundary in the Barents Sea and sovereignty issues around the Svalbard Archipelago. The increasing military importance of an ice-free Arctic is indeed reflected in decisions during recent years by all five littoral states to strengthen their military capabilities in the Arctic.

At present, the Arctic shipping season is of unpredictable length, dependent on changing climate patterns and sea and ice conditions that require ships designed specifically for passage through icy waters. The transport routes will not appeal to major shipping firms as a regular route until more experience is gained and the route is upgraded with modern aids to navigation, port facilities, and search-and-rescue capabilities. Over time, those developments, with or without further retreat of the polar ice, will make the Northeast Passage more attractive, particularly as the number of ice-capable vessels increases. By 2050, the sea route is likely to be a regular shipping route, beginning with seasonal service based on ice-class vessels and expanding as climate and ice conditions allow. As the Arctic becomes more accessible, the northern coast of Eurasia may take the place of Harold Mackinder's "geographical pivot", as both a route of passage and an area of exploitable resources. [29] (Global Business Network, 2008)

Altering Coastlines: Impact on State Sovereignty

One of the more significant long term physical impacts of climate change is the rise in sea levels. As sea levels rise, coastlines will alter and low lying islands may become uninhabitable. Inhabitants may have to be evacuated as salt water infiltrates groundwater, killing vegetation and animals and leaving those without desalination plants also without fresh water. There is a lot of uncertainty about how quickly this is happening, as protective barrier coral reefs seem to be trying to grow to keep pace with rising waters. Yet as water temperatures increase, the coral, which is temperature-sensitive, may die off. It is very likely that eventually at least one entire nation will have to be completely resettled.

It is worthwhile to note here that Article one of the Montevideo Convention on Rights and Duties of States details that a state to be recognised must have a permanent population, defined territory, a government and the capacity to enter into relations with other states. The last two qualifications are relatively easy to maintain, even in exile, assuming other states will continue to recognize the dislocated nation as a state. However, the first two, a defined territory and a permanent population, are complex issues that need to be address in a detailed manner. [30] (Seventh International Conference of American States, 1933)

Tuvalu, with a population of 11,000 people approximately, is made up of a string of atolls in the pacific with the highest point only 4.5m (15 feet) above sea level, making it extremely vulnerable to flooding. There is serious concern that rising tides and sea level will submerge the land and poison supplies of freshwater making the islands inhabitable. It is not just the shoreline that is at the mercy of high tides, reaching over three meters, but also water surging up from underground through the coral on which the islands are built. The IPCC has forecast the rise in tides by another half meter. In the space of an hour, all the lowest areas of the island, including the runway, which is a vital lifeline to the outside world, are flooded. [31] (BBC, 2009)

In October 2011, Tuvalu declared a state of emergency because of a severe shortage of fresh water. The nation, which normally expects to get 200mm to 400mm of rainfall every month, had not received rains for over six months. People were advised to not drink water from wells and neighbouring New Zealand was requested to provide water supplies and desalination units. Fearing that increasing emissions of harmful greenhouse gases into the atmosphere by nations could wipe it of the map, Tuvalu has aimed to depend on renewable sources, especially wind and solar power, to meet its energy requirements by 2020.

By going carbon neutral in an effort to reduce greenhouse gas emissions to zero, Tuvalu hopes to set an example for other nations to follow in the future. [32] (BBC, 2011) If Tuvalu does indeed go under water, the core question for external policy formulation will be—Can a nation exist without a physical state? Will it lose its seat in the United Nations (UN)? Will its current maritime exclusive economic zone revert to international waters? Will any nations assist in relocating its population? Can its people be shifted to another existing or artificial island nearby?

As with Tuvalu, the Indian Ocean nation of the Maldives is composed entirely of low-lying coral atolls. The IPCC has predicted that if the sea level rises over two meters, it will inundate nearly fifty percent of Maldives. Its president, Mohamed Nasheed, has been actively trying to secure a home for his citizens should evacuation prove necessary including land purchase. Another option is to use the value of national sovereignty to "pay" for relocation. In that model, neighbouring India, for example, might take in the Maldivian immigrants in exchange for India being able to extend its national waters to include Maldivian waters.

The proceeds from this extended EEZ (fisheries rights, seabed mining, etc.) could be used to resettle and set up a trust fund for Maldivian immigrants. Maldivians could also get preferential access to the waters for economic development and, should the islands ever re-emerge, resettlement could be possible. The advantage for India would be an orderly settlement of relatively wealthy immigrants, and an extension of its coastal security zone. [33] (Columbia Law School and Republic of Marshall Islands Co-sponsored Conference, 2011)

Another interesting case in point is the low-lying UK territory of Diego Garcia in the Indian Ocean Chagos archipelago that is used as a base by the US is at threat from rising seas. If Diego Garcia is lost to the sea, will the UK also lose exclusive access to that crucial tract of ocean and, in the process, lose a valuable bargaining chip with the United States? Will the US look to shift its base to another island nearby which could cause potential concerns for other rising powers in the region? Kiribati is another small island country that is also facing the threat of existence due to rising sea levels. Interestingly, because its islands are well scattered over a large section of the Pacific, it has a maritime exclusive economic zone approximately the size of India. If it does submerge in the future, it could lead to increased jostling among major powers including China, India and the US for seabed mining rights, shipping lanes and geo-strategic positioning. [34] (Paskal, 2010)

These dangers are not restricted to the small low lying islands. As around two-thirds of the world's population live near the coast, it is not surprising that sixteen of the world's nineteen largest cities including cities such as Shanghai, Mumbai, London, Washington and Paris are under threat from sea level rise. Additionally, sea-level rise compounds the effects of storm surges and other extreme weather events. India's naval bases situated around the Indian Ocean rim including Mumbai, Cochin, Karwar, Vishakhapatnam; the Joint Forces Command in the Andaman and Nicobar Islands and the Car Nicobar Air base will be adversely affected by tropical cyclones or tsunamis. China's investments in deep water ports and refuelling stations in Gwadar, Hambantota, Chittagong, Sittwe and Kyaukphyu along vulnerable coastlines will also be susceptible.

There are also long-term destabilizing consequences for internal security implications. For example, the on-going social disruption caused by the Katrina refugees is most obvious in neighbouring Houston. According to the National Hurricane Centre, New York City is the fifth most vulnerable place in the US. The risk area includes coastal New York, New

Jersey and Connecticut, an area with a combined population of around twenty million. Manhattan is only about three meters above sea level, with critical regional infrastructure, such as airports, even lower-lying. A major climate vulnerability study on the region for the US government's Global Change Research Program has warned that by the end of this century, flooding may occur at least once every decade for two-thirds of transportation infrastructure facilities with elevations at or below ten feet above sea level. This sort of vulnerability leaves nations open to international pressure, uncontrolled population movement and economic stress. [35] (Paskal, 2009)

Exclusive Economic Zones: Potential Conflict Areas

Under the law of the sea, an Exclusive Economic Zone (EEZ) is a sea zone over which a state has special rights over the exploration and use of marine resources, including production of energy from water and wind. It stretches from the seaward edge of the state's territorial sea out to 200 nautical miles (370 km.) from its natural coast. The exception to this rule is if a country's zone is adjacent and also overlaps against the zone of another country, in which case they usually split the difference equally and any point within an overlapping area defaults to the nearest state. States also have rights to the seabed of what is called the continental shelf up to 350 nautical miles (648 km.) from the coastal baseline, beyond the EEZ. [36] (UNCLOS)

The United Nations Environment Programme (UNEP), University of Dhaka, and the World Bank have published a map that shows the potential impact of a 1.5 metre sea-level rise that could affect fifteen to seventeen million people and twelve to fifteen percent of agricultural land, which is a loss of one percent of national rise production in Bangladesh. [37] (UNFCC, 1992). The Survey of India has been recording the sea level across twenty three ports in east and west coast of India. Tide Gauge records indicate a rise of the sea level in the Bay of Bengal by ten to twenty five centimetres over the last century.

More worryingly, the sea level is expected to further rise by another fifty centimetres at the turn of the twenty second century. However, drawing analysis from these data becomes complicated substantially as the region is also experiencing high subsidence due to the seismic activities of the Indian plate on the eastern boundary. Additionally, there is high sedimentation rate which means that particles in suspension will settle out of the water in which they are entrained, and come to rest against the coastline barrier. This would indicate that some of the areas along the coastline will also be expanding.

It is quite possible that rising sea levels may not flood Bangladesh, but, according to the IPCC, storm surges and cyclones in the Bay of Bengal are predicted to increase in intensity, causing flooding. Those two factors of environmental change alone have the potential further to exacerbate the two major international issues that climate change in Bangladesh might aggravate: increasingly desperate environmental refugees pushing towards India and tensions over maritime exclusive economic zones in the Bay of Bengal. [38] (IPCC, 2007)

One such hotly contested island in the Bay of Bengal was the New Moore Island or the Sheikh Mujib Island. Claimed by both India and Bangladesh amidst speculation over the existence of oil and natural gas, it was in a geo-strategic position, at the mouth of the Hariabhanga or Haribhanga River, the boundary between the two countries. Recently, it was discovered that New Moore Island had disappeared, probably due to a combination of rising sea levels, changes in monsoonal rain patterns which altered river flows and land subsidence. The problem of land loss, with other islands such as Lohachara and Ghoramara in the Sundarbans region eroding potentially leading to maritime zone loss, is likely to be a prominent feature in the near future.

Changes to maritime zones based on changing coastlines might also affect Bangladesh's ability to exploit offshore resources. The coastline of Bangladesh is extremely difficult to define as it is considered to be extremely fluid with liquid mud. Determining a maritime boundary becomes very complex especially as Bangladesh shares the arc of the Bay of Bengal with India to the west and Myanmar to the east. Its maritime claim is shaped like a triangle, squeezed on both sides by its neighbours as it extends further out to sea. The bay itself is suspected of containing considerable hydrocarbon deposits, making offshore maritime claims particularly valuable. Flooding is a serious yearly phenomenon in Bangladesh, with water levels rising by between thirteen centimetres and two meters. If its coastline were to retreat dramatically, in theory its maritime border would retreat commensurately, potentially completely squeezing it out of zones that are rich in hydrocarbons.

Similarly, it was reported in September 2009 that despite existing on maps for centuries, the tiny island of Bermeja, in the Gulf of Mexico, could no longer be found. The existence of Bermeja Island was crucial as Mexico was involved in a dispute with the United States to lay claim in the hydrocarbon-rich waters of the Gulf. It could by laying claim to the Island extend its maritime border by another eighty kilometres. The Mexican Government made numerous attempts by sending out expeditions to find the missing Island and even accused the United States of plotting its submergence. The US was quick to respond that since there was no island in sight, Mexico's claim over the extended area was invalid. [39]

Another case is the US-Cuba border which was agreed by a bilateral treaty in 1977 to be renewed every two years. The problem with the agreement reached is that the US shoreline that is used as a base measurement is down in the Florida Keys, an extremely low-lying region, while Cuba itself is relatively mountainous and not as likely to lose ground to rising sea levels. So, leaving the Bahamas aside, the hypothetical question is, if the Florida coastline retreats up towards the middle of the state, and Cuba stays more or less as it is, should the border be moved to reflect the new midpoint?

That would put the entrance to the Gulf of Mexico in Cuban waters and, while southern Florida would be submerged, it would still be an impediment to shipping, meaning traffic would have to loop down through Cuban waters. Given that the boundary is confirmed bilaterally every two years, there might be a case under international law for Cuba or the United States to seek a renegotiation on the grounds that reality has changed as a result of sea-level rise. But it is likely to be international politics and security concerns, rather than international law, that will determine whether the boundary changes or not. [40]

From a neorealist perspective, the modern state views sovereignty and territorial integrity as the focal ingredients of increasing power and maximizing national interest. However, it has been clearly established that the emerging environmental changes pose a significant challenge to these concepts in the twenty first century. If champions of environmental changes focus on highlighting the possibility of increasing conflicts over altering coastlines and maritime boundaries becoming a reality, states might be forced to eventually make an effort to cooperate and address these challenges in an effort to secure themselves from potential conflicts in the future. Instead merely expressing concerns over the sustainability of the environment for future generations will be dismissed by states, striving to compete furiously in a rapidly competitive world, as plain utopian or idealist pleas.

End Notes

1. Friedman, Thomas L. (2005), *The World is Flat–A Brief History of the Twenty First Century*, New York: Farrar, Straus and Giroux, April.
2. Vajpeyi, Dhirendra (2012), (ed.), *Water Resource Conflicts and International Security*, Lanham, Maryland: Lexington Books.
3. United Nations Framework Convention on Climate Change (1992), Article 1, Clause 2, fccc/informal/84 ge.05-62220 (E) 200705, p. 3, available at,

http://unfccc.int/resource/docs/convkp/conveng.pdf, accessed on 2nd November 2011.

4. IPCC Fourth Assessment Report (2007), Working Group I, Annex II, Glossary, p. 78, http://www.ipcc.ch/pdf/assessment-report/ar4/syr/ar4_syr_appendix.pdf, accessed on 25th September 2011.
5. Cleo Paskal (2007), "How climate change is pushing the boundaries of security and foreign policy", Energy, Environment and Development Programme EEDP CC BP 07/01, *Chatham House Briefing Paper*, June, pp. 2-3, available at, http://www.chathamhouse.org/publications/papers/view/108552, accessed on 18th September 2011.
6. Sushil Kumar Dash, *Climate Change: An Indian Perspective*, Centre for Environment Education, (India: Cambridge University Press, 2007), pp. 78-79.
7. IPCC Fourth Assessment Report (2007), Synthesis Report, Summary for Policy Makers, available at, http://www.ipcc.ch/publications_and_data/publications_ipcc_fourth_assessment_report_synthesis_report.htm Accessed on: 25th September 2011.
8. Ibid., pp. 80-81.
9. Ibid., pp. 82-83.
10. Suzanne Goldenberg, "Glacier lakes: Growing danger zones in the Himalayas", *The Guardian*, 10 October 2011, available at, http://www.guardian.co.uk/environment/2011/oct/10/glacier-lakes-melt-himalayas?newsfeed=true, accessed on 11 October 2011.
11. n. 4, pp. 83-85.
12. n. 3, pp. 3-4.
13. United Nations Convention on the Law of the Sea (1982), Preamble, available at, http://www.un.org/depts/los/convention_agreements/texts/unclos/preamble.htm, accessed on 13 October 2011.
14. International Tribunal for the Law of the Sea, available at, http://www.itlos.org/index.php?id=15, accessed on 13 October 2011.
15. United Nations Security General Debate (2007), "Secretary-General calls for unity against climate change, better access to resources", 17 April, available at,

http://www.un.org/Docs/sc/search2007.shtml, accessed on 8th October 2011.

16. Centre for Naval Analyses (2007), Military Advisory Board Briefing, "National Security and the Threat of Climate Change", April, http://www.cna.org/sites/default/files/Climate percent20Change percent20Briefing.pdf, accessed on 5th October 2011.
17. Cleo, Paskal, *Global Warring: How Environmental, Economic and Political Crises will Redraw the World Map*, (Canada: Key Porter Books Limited, 2010), pp. 144-148; 150-157.
18. Ibid., pp. 60-63.
19. Global Business Network, "The Future of Arctic Marine Navigation in Mid-Century", Scenario Narratives Report, May, 2008, available at, http://www.institutenorth.org/assets/images/uploads/articles/GBN-AMSA_Scenario_Narratives_Report_FINAL_May08_v1May.pdf, accessed on 30th September, 2011.
20. Ibid.
21. Arctic Marine Shipping Assessment, The Protection of the Arctic Marine Environment (PAME), "The Future of Arctic Marine Navigation in mid-21st Century", April 2007, available at, http://www.institutenorth.org/assets/images/uploads/articles/AMSA_Interview_Highlights.pdf, accessed on 30th September 2011.
22. Linda Jakobson, "China prepares for an Ice-free Arctic", *SIPRI Insights on Peace and Security*, n. 2010/2, March 2010, available at, http://books.sipri.org/files/insight/SIPRIInsight1002.pdf, accessed on 1st October 2011.
23. Caityln L. Antrim, "The Next Geographical Pivot–The Russian Arctic in the Twenty-first Century", *Naval War College Review*, Summer 2010, available at, http://www.usnwc.edu/getattachment/f8217b41-afd2-4649-8378-7b6c8a7e61d2/The-Next-Geographical-Pivot--The-Russian-Arctic-in, accessed on 3rd October 2011.
24. George A. Backus and James H. Strickland, "Climate derived tensions in Arctic Security", *Sandia Report*, n. SAND2008-6342, September 2008, available at,

http://est.sandia.gov/earth/docs/Tensions_in_Arctic_SecurityFinal.pdf, accessed on 25 September 2011.
25. Frederick Lasserre, "China and the Arctic-Threat or Co-operation Potential for Canada", *CIC China Papers*, n. 11, June 2010, available at, http://www.opencanada.org/wp-content/uploads/2011/05/China-and-the-Arctic-Frederic-Lasserre.pdf, accessed on 25th September 2011.
26. Vijay Sakhuja, "China-Breaking into the Arctic Ice", *ICWA Issue Brief*, available at, http://www.icwa.in/pdfs/ib percent20 percent20dr.pdf, accessed on 23rd September 2011.
27. Amitav Ranjan, "Next stop, next year: India in the Arctic", *The Indian Express*, 5th October 2006, available at, http://www.indianexpress.com/news/next-stop-next-year-india-in-the-arctic/14133/, accessed on 18th September 2011.
28. P. Sunderarajan, "New Indian research station at the Arctic", *The Hindu*, 2 July 2008, available at, http://www.hindu.com/2008/07/02/stories/2008070253572000.htm, accessed on: 18th September 2011.
29. n. 20.
30. Seventh International Conference of American States, Montevideo, Uruguay December 26, 1933, available at, http://untreaty.un.org/unts/60001_120000/18/31/00035536.pdf, accessed on 21st September 2011.
31. British Broadcasting Corporation, (2009)-"Tuvalu vows to go carbon neutral", 20 July, available at, http://news.bbc.co.uk/2/hi/asia-pacific/8158604.stm, accessed on 15th September 2011.
32. British Broadcasting Corporation, "Tuvalu declares emergency over water shortage", 3 October 2011, available at, http://news.bbc.co.uk/2/hi/asia-pacific/8158604.stm, accessed on 10th October 2011.
33. Columbia Law School and Republic of Marshall Islands Co sponsored Conference on "Threatened Island Nations: Legal Implications of a Changing Climate", available at, http://www.law.columbia.edu/centers/climatechange/resources/threatened-island-nations, May 23-25, 2011, accessed on 16th October 2011.
34. Cleo Paskal, "Strange case of the disappearing islands", April

2010, available at, http://www.nzherald.co.nz/world/news/article.cfm?c_id=2&objectid=10635956, accessed on: 7th October 2011.

35. Cleo Paskal, "From constants to variables: how environmental change alters the geopolitical and geo-economic equation" *International Affairs*, October 2009, available at, http://www.chathamhouse.org/publications/ia/archive/view/163045, accessed on: 10th September 2011.
36. United Nations Conventions on the Law of the Sea, Preamble, Exclusive Economic Zone, Part V, Article 55-75, available at, http://www.un.org/depts/los/convention_agreements/texts/unclos/part5.htm, accessed on 23rd November 2011.
37. n. 3, pp. 4-5.
38. n. 4, pp. 115-116.
39. n. 31.
40. n. 14, pp. 45-46.

Index

Index